DYNASTY

GLAMOUR, GREED & GLORY

DYNASTY

JUDITH A. MOOSE & PAUL D. KEYLOCK

Signing Stars
A Division of JM Media Group
701 Aspen Peak Loop, Suite 1712
Henderson, NV 89015

The authors have made every reasonable effort to contact all copyright holders. Any errors that may have occurred are inadvertent and anyone, who for any reason, has not been contacted is invited to write to the publishers so that a full acknowledgement may be made in subsequent editions of this work.

Authors have either paid licensing fees or have been granted permission for the use of all photos and other materials included in this book.

DYNASTY is the property of Aaron Spelling Productions, Shapiro Entertainment and The Oil Company. Distributed by the American Broadcasting Company (ABC), Metromedia Producers Corporation (MPC) and 20th Century Fox Television.

Library of Congress Cataloging – in – Publication Data

Judith A. Moose / Paul D. Keylock
Glamour, Greed & Glory: Dynasty – 1st Edition
ISBN 1-4196-0375-2
1. Television – Non-fiction
LCCN 2005908789

FIRST EDITION

For our families and friends

Thank you for sharing our yesterdays, today and tomorrows, and for always believing that we can do absolutely anything. It is your love and faith that always inspires us to keep reaching for our dreams.

'For Judy and Paul - Thank you for putting together this lovely tribute and asking me to be a part of it.'

Enter Alexis...

In July, 1981, while on vacation in Mirabella, Spain, I received a phone call from my then agent Tom Korman asking if I had ever heard of a series called *Dynasty*. It was old friend and producer Aaron Spelling's latest baby and after its first season wasn't performing up to the expectations of the network. After reviewing an earlier appearance on his show; *Fantasy Island* (in which I played Cleopatra), Aaron decided he wanted me to "spice things up a bit" and offered me the part of *Alexis Carrington*. At first I wasn't thrilled with the idea of doing a soap-opera styled show, but after reading the script I realized that Alexis wasn't just another part, she was the female version of *J.R. Ewing*. Despite being under contract to tour in the play *Murder in Mind*, I headed off to Hollywood thinking *Dynasty* was only going to run for another year. Who knew?

After hundreds of back and forth telephone calls, on a cloudless August day I returned to *Twentieth Century Fox* with the "Bitch-of-the-Year" role firmly in my hands. It had been twenty-seven years since I had first arrived on the lot as a young contract player and little did I know that my return would soon make Joan Collins a household name. The more *Dynasty* scripts I read, the more I saw Alexis' tremendous potential. She was conniving, brilliant, beautiful, completely bent on revenge with the nerve to say whatever she wanted to whomever she wanted and never look back. A strong-willed, powerful woman, Alexis was what women always wanted to be and what men had always feared.

It wasn't long before the ratings quickly rose and people became fascinated with, and often confused, *Alexis Carrington Colby* and her "alter-ego" Joan Collins. After all, there are certain similarities between us. Obviously we look the same, talk the same, basically dress the same and we both absolutely adore our children and grandchildren. Unlike Alexis, I don't focus my energy on getting even with anyone who crosses me. Don't get me wrong, I can be tough when I need to be but I prefer to simply take life one day at a time, fill the days with great joy and live each one to the fullest. That is, after all, what life is for…

The fans of this series were like none other and I would like to thank you for allowing me to enter your lives nearly every week for eight years. It was a wonderful run and with that in mind, it is my pleasure to invite you to join me as we revisit the glamour and glory that was *Dynasty*.

Joan Collins

A Dynasty of Our Own...

There were many things that came to mind as I sat down to write this book. I wanted it to reflect not only the show but also the feelings shared by fans of this classic series. *Dynasty*, its cast, creators and storylines gave millions of people and enormous amount of job and viewing pleasure for nearly a decade, and I for one feel that it is high time to say thank you for giving the world the gift of their talents and time.

Before I delve into the lives of the 'Carrington' and 'Colby' clans, I want to thank two people for allowing me to give vent to my writing ability and for helping to create my own miniature Dynasty along the way. Those two people are Paul Keylock and Joan Collins. Ten years ago, I was asked to help find a few videos to assist with research for Joan's new autobiography *Second Act*. I had previously written a small article about Joan that had been titled *A Star in My Eyes* and at the time I wrote it, I had no idea of how prophetic that title would be. There were five movies and a few television appearances that Joan wanted to see before adding anything to the manuscript for *Second Act* and I was asked to find them. I will never forget the day I called *Universal Studios* asking them to find the 1969 film *Can Hieronymus Merkin Ever Forget Mercy Humppe and Find True Happiness?* The person I was speaking with asked me what company I was working for and after scanning the room looking for anything that sounded official, my eyes caught the top of the article headline. In January 1995, *Stars In My Eyes* was born.

More research projects followed and I received my first national and international television and video credit for supplying much of the material for the *A&E Biography* on Joan. Ten years, and I can no longer remember how many books, movies and television shows later, *Stars In My Eyes* has branched out, changed its name to *JM Media Group*, and has become a full-service PR firm for the entertainment community. Although it isn't nearly as frequent, Paul still sends me the occasional odd project for Joan. He has become one of my best friends and she will always be that extraordinary star in my eyes.

So, I would like to thank Paul for his friendship and support for what will hopefully be many more years to come, and Joan for filling over two decades of my life with a strong-minded role model who isn't afraid to grasp life with both hands, and for inadvertently paving the way for my future. She is the reason I am in the position I am today and there are no words that will ever adequately thank her for the enormous impact she's had in my life.

To the fans of the *Dynasty*, I know this book has been a long time in coming but I hope you'll agree that it was worth the wait...

Judith A. Moose

Beginning as a star struck fan looking from the outside-in and finally from the inside-out, the road to and from Dynasty has been a wonderful journey and one that I have been very privileged to have been part of. I remember those days of coming home from college on a Friday night looking forward to the next enthralling episode to open up in the lives of 'The Carringtons'. To experience the glamour of its stars, the tangled lives they lead and the unhappiness that money can bring and loving every moment. How far would Alexis push Krystle? How far would Sammy Jo push Steven and to what ends would Blake go to destroy his competitors?

Now driving down Rodeo Drive in Beverly Hills, California, in a cream-colored Rolls Royce with Alexis, but really Joan Collins (a very real and down to earth Joan Collins) at the wheel may sound like more like a dream than a day at the office. However, for me, it is just part of the job as Joan's Personal Assistant. I often feel like pinching myself, I never take it forgranted. I still get that buzz every time I see Joan at home, in the office or at a celebrity function. The magic has never faded.

The path began when I was 15, writing several fan letters to this remarkable lady that eventually became the most famous face on the planet. For some time no reply was received, so I finally wrote "a sharp letter" and then I finally heard. I got a phone call a week later from one of Joan's then employees, saying "she has been distressed by the letter" and "would I like to join her for tea one afternoon?"

From these humble beginnings, a long standing professional and personal relationship developed, growing from year to year, to what it is today, becoming one of the biggest parts of my life. Meeting Joan has given me many experiences I may never have had. I feel lucky the way my life has developed.

To be part of this project has been a wonderful experience to give existing and new generations an insight into what was the world of 'The Carringtons' and their Dynasty.

Paul D. Keylock

DYNASTY

Chapter One

Let The Games Begin

In 1977, Aaron Spelling (unarguably the most successful television producer in history) split with longtime partner Leonard Goldberg. Together they had produced the hit series' *Hart To Hart, Starsky and Hutch, Fantasy Island* and *Charlie's Angels*. Soon after that split Spelling was teamed with E. Duke Vincent and together they shaped the 1980s decade with shows like *Vegas* with Robert Urich and ensemble shows such as *The Love Boat* and *Hotel*. Despite having a string of hits already on the air, ABC found it couldn't compete with the outrageously huge success of a CBS series called *Dallas*. At the bottom of the barrel in the ratings, ABC turned to Aaron Spelling and asked that he discover and produce a series to compete with *Dallas*. Aaron and Hollywood executive Douglas Cramer set out to do just that.

The former Chairman of ABC Entertainment, Ted Harbert explained the studio's point of view. "Television genres come and go and when *Dallas* became so popular the network decided that we'd like to do that too if we could find the right project. As it is well known in this industry, if you don't have the right project, it can fail big time."

The Spelling/Cramer duo was then presented with an idea by ABC called *Fort Worth*. After reading the script they decided the show was too close to *Dallas* and passed. Who would guessed that at about the same time a family on vacation was about to create the biggest hit of the 1980's?

Esther Shapiro and her husband Richard were known in the entertainment industry for writing social dramas such as *Intimate Strangers* and *Portrait of a Teenage Alcoholic*, among others. Theirs were scripts and films that challenged the search for self and control over destiny through themes that faced the era with issues people dealt with on a daily basis and could relate to. As time went by and the issues changed, so did Richard and Esther's view of the stereotypical *Leave It to Beaver* and *Brady Bunch* mentality where a family was perfect even when they weren't on their best behavior. They wanted to create a family with flaws and yet one that the public would still want to watch.

While the search for the new *Dallas* was getting underway, Richard and Esther took their two daughters Florie and Eden off to Hawaii for a family vacation. According to Florie, as they were sitting on the beach Esther and Richard "must have gotten bored or something. They started thinking and talking about their fantasies. A couple of hours later the premise for their new show idea *Oil* had been born. No one knew it would turn into one of the biggest shows of all time."

Oil would center on the Parkhurst family. Living in the oil-rich community of Denver, Blake Parkhurst was the head of his own company. Like *Dallas*, *Oil* followed the triumphs and tragedies of the rich and powerful. Ted Harbert remembers seeing *Oil* come in during the drama development season. "Those of us responsible for deciding what got made read it and decided that it would be done because it was filled with drama and conflict."

ABC ordered 13 episodes of Oil with one provision – the Shapiro's had to come up with a better last name for the family. The name was soon changed to Carrington. Esther, thinking back on the show's premise added, "The show was a fantasy about all of the things I would have loved to have lived. It had horse farms, oil companies, airplanes, football teams... With those kinds of trappings surrounding you we thought that we could do the problems of family and business and because of the elaborate backdrop, the audience would want to watch it."

"*Dynasty* was pure camp," says Aaron Spelling. "Women wore fashionable hats and designer gowns and fought with each other. There were long-lost sons and mothers, lost babies, kings and queens of foreign lands; illegitimate children, divorces, secret pasts, insatiable sex lives, sleek cars and beautiful mansions. *Dynasty* was responsible for showing that people over forty still fall in love and have sex."

The legendary producer with a platinum touch, Aaron Spelling worked his way through Hollywood from the ground up. Born in Dallas, Texas to David Spurling (changed to Spelling upon entering the United States) and Pearl Wald, Aaron was the youngest of five children. The family was incredibly poor and survived on day-old pastries, stale cookies and cake that Aaron would wait in line for hoping the bakery would take pity on him for being so frail because they couldn't afford to purchase the basic essentials.

Constantly teased in grade school for being Jewish, Aaron had a nervous breakdown and literally stayed home in bed for a year. During that year he accepted a challenge from his teacher that she would allow him to pass to the next grade if he completed six book reports. He completed 64 and became completely entranced with the art of storytelling. His tailor father had made a few suits for entertainers and introduced his son to vaudeville and the movies. One in particular *Tales of Manhattan* became the inspiration for what would later be two of Spelling's series trademarks: multiple storylines and glamour.

At 18, Aaron joined the Army and quickly began putting on plays and skits for his fellow soldiers. A true fan of actors and actresses he would often send messages to his favorites and after wishing them greetings for the holidays began receiving cards from Elizabeth Taylor, Fred Astaire and others. The brass thought he had major connections and put him in charge of the Special Service to entertain the troops.

After being discharged from the Army, Aaron Spelling enrolled at Southern Methodist University. He was made head cheerleader and became the first student to direct a senior class production. In 1947 Aaron won the Eugene O'Neill Award for writing the year's best one-act play titled *Is Everything Always Black and White?* A short time later he formed a comedy team named Slack and

Spelling (with friend Bill Slack) and was hired to direct plays for the Jewish community theater group as well as others.

Wanting to try getting that "big break" that so many people long for, Aaron packed up his little Plymouth and drove to New York and then to Los Angeles. Life still wasn't good for the would-be producer and he once went along picking up people's copies of the Los Angeles Times newspaper and sold them back to a newsstand to get enough money to eat breakfast. At a local coffee shop he met up with another actor who would share the Daily Variety and Hollywood Reporter want ads with him. The Oklahoman had just arrived in Hollywood and also wanted to be an actor. His name was James Garner.

After learning to format a television script and getting nothing but rejection for his efforts, Aaron received a phone call from George McCall asking if he would consider working as a band boy (which basically is referred to as a stagehand/errand person these days). While working at KTTV, Aaron directed a Los Angeles staged production of Garson Kanin's *Live Wire*. That would prove to be the biggest move of his life (so far). Writer/director Preston Sturges saw *Live Wire* and signed it immediately with Aaron Spelling as Director and his life was changed forever…

Two days before opening Live Wire the leading lady quit but was replaced with another young actress named Carolyn Jones (star of *The Addams Family* opposite John Astin). On opening night Carolyn was signed to a contract with Warner Brothers and the two began dating. Jack Webb of *Dragnet* fame had seen *Live Wire* and asked Aaron if he had ever acted. Not wanting to lose a chance at television he told Jack he'd been acting his entire life. A short time later, Aaron Spelling made his television debut playing a retarded young man in *Dragnet*. Two more episodes followed the same year and then it was on to two more classic appearances.

One of the most remembered and most aired guest appearances Aaron ever did was in a 1954 episode of *I Love Lucy* where he's opposite Lucille Ball and Tennessee Ernie Ford. In 1955, he appeared in an episode of *Gunsmoke* and credits that as his greatest acting ever. Of course, his acting career also ended in

1955 so it was pretty easy to understand why *Gunsmoke* made such an impression. Tired of waiting for him to get around to it, Carolyn Jones proposed to him in late 1955 and they married five days later.

Writer Aaron Spelling sold his first script in 1956 to Jane Wyman while she was co-producer of *Fireside Theatre* for $600 and that was the beginning. Later that year Dick Powell was rolling out his first production called *Dick Powell's Zane Grey Theater* featuring stories from the Western writer's vast selection and Spelling was hired to write three scripts for the show. It was also during 1956 that Carolyn appeared in the MGM film *The Opposite Sex* and Aaron would meet and become friends with an actress who would save his collective assets twenty-five years later: Joan Collins (who rather ironically played a character named Crystal).

In 1959, Carolyn introduced Aaron to Alan Ladd, who had him rewrite a script called *The Guns of the Timberland*. When Ladd called studio giant Jack Warner he told him, "Jack, I've had a rewrite on the script and now I like it. I'm going to do it. I'm working with the script right now. And Jack, my producer's name is Aaron Spelling. That's S-P-E-L-L-I-N-G."

Shortly before the demise of *Dick Powell's Zane Grey Theatre*, Dick introduced him to one of the acting industry's legends; Barbara Stanwyck. Missy (as she was called by her friends) introduced him to a friend, a virtual unknown by the name of Nolan Miller. Nolan was working as a florist and sometimes dress designer. As a favor to Barbara, Nolan was hired for Aaron's new show *Burke's Law* starring Gene Barry. The deal made to the actresses was $1000 for appearing on the show, a ride to the studio in a Rolls Royce and a free Nolan Miller gown. That would be a partnership to last a lifetime. In 1964, Aaron and Carolyn Jones were divorced and Aaron's career as a producer flourished.

Burke's Law was just the tip of the iceberg. Since 1964 Aaron Spelling has produced over 60 television series and 140 made-for-television movies including the mega-hits *Beverly Hills 90210*, *Melrose Place*, *Charmed*, *7th Heaven*, *Summerland* and last year's debut *Clubhouse*. With wife of 35 years, Candy and their two children (Tori and Randy) at his side, Aaron Spelling has gone from the sickly little boy who ate cookies for dinner to the Guinness Book of World Records as the most prolific television producer in history, logging in over 4300 hours of television and still going strong.

Esther Mayesh was born in New York City. Her Turkish-born father was a florist and her Greek-born mother a housewife. When Esther was an infant her family moved to Los Angeles where her father owned a flower shop. As a child, Esther was an avid reader and had received a certificate for reading 374 books in one year. Her imagination was peaked by everything from *The Bible* to *The Arabian Nights*. As a barter arrangement, her father would give a typewriter store fifty cents worth of flowers per week in exchange for a Remington typewriter so Esther could write. "When I was a kid, my great-aunts would congregate at the house and you'd look at the most staid, wonderful women who told stories that would put Jackie Collins to shame." At 15, she won a scholarship to the University of Southern California, where she earned a degree in comparative literature.

Richard Shapiro was born in Los Angeles, where his father was a men's clothier and his mother a housewife. He began writing short stories in high school but was unable to land a writing job after earning a bachelor's degree in English from UCLA in 1956. In 1959 he sold his first television script for the series *Manhunt*.

Richard and Esther met in a writing class at UCLA in 1956 and dated for four years before getting married. During their first year of marriage, they wrote one script, and they couldn't sell it. They did manage to get an agent and began churning out TV and B movie scripts but nothing ever got released. At that time, Esther was working as a substitute teacher and Richard was delivering lighting fixtures for his uncle's company for $70-a-week. Their first breakthrough was in 1964 when they were contracted by Warner Brothers for $700-a-week.

During the 1960s they wrote for shows like *Bonanza* and *Route 66*. Richard also wrote several episodes of *Ironside* starring Raymond Burr. In 1969, on the advice of a friend they took a $3000-a-week job writing for the popular daytime soap opera *Love of Life* but quit after seven months because they couldn't handle the unrelenting pressure and returned to prime time.

In 1976, Richard was completely devastated by the final product of his screenplay for *The Great Scout and Cathouse Thursday* that he and Esther packed up their daughters Florie and Eden and moved to Europe. They spent a short time in Turkey and Greece before settling in London. The climate of both the weather and the television industry got cold and ten months later the Shapiros returned to Hollywood with nothing but the determination to never write anything again that they didn't produce.

By 1977 Esther had become the Vice-President of Miniseries for ABC and had helped usher in rating winners such as *Masada* and *Inside the Third Reich*. She left the job two years later with a group of new skills such as cutting deals, casting and hiring and firing. Those skills would soon come in very handy after teaming with Spelling on *Dynasty*.

Aside from *Dynasty*, the Shapiros were also responsible for the creation of two other prime time soaps; *Emerald Point N.A.S.* premiered in 1984 and *The Colbys* in 1985. *Emerald Point* focused on a Navy Admiral and his lust-filled  daughters. Unfortunately neither series gained the momentum that *Dynasty* did and were cancelled within a few seasons.

With *Dynasty* behind them, Esther and Richard are still very involved with the entertainment industry and run their own company

Richard and Esther Shapiro Entertainment in Beverly Hills, California. The duo's most recent project is a feature film called *The Motel*. *The Motel* was the third project in which Esther and Richard's younger daughter Eden has shared the Executive Producer title. The film was released at the *Sundance Film Festival* on January 24, 2005 and won the Humanitas Award.

With the creating team in place, producers were faced with the task of assembling the finest team of professionals within the Entertainment Industry. Spelling, Douglas Cramer and E. Duke Vincent didn't have to look very far. As the series began to rise in the ranks of popularity the producers added more and more crew members to the mix. Those listed below are just a few of the thousands of people whose talents were utilized to produce each of the episodes.

THE CREW OF DYNASTY

PRODUCERS

Aaron Spelling – Executive Producer
Douglas S. Cramer – Executive Producer
Esther Shapiro – Executive Producer
Richard Shapiro – Executive Producer
Elaine Rich – Executive Producer
E. Duke Vincent – Supervising Producer
Eileen Pollock – Supervising Producer
Robert Mason Pollock – Supervising Producer
Philip Parslow – Supervising Producer
David Paulsen – Supervising Producer
Edward De Blasio – Supervising Producer

Ed Ledding – Associate Producer
John B. Moranville – Associate Producer

DIRECTORS

Dwight Adair
Gwen Arner
Gabrielle Beaumont
Bruce Bilson
Jeff Bleckner
Burt Brinckerhoff
George Sanford Brown
Jerome Courtland
Mart Crowley
Ray Danton
Lawrence Dobkin
Harry Falk
Kim Friedman
Scott M. Hammer
Curtis Harrington
Michael Hugo
Jerry Jameson
James W. Kearns
Richard Kinon
Alf Kjellin
Michael Lange
Philip Leacock
Harold Livingston
Nancy Malone
Don Medford
Irving J. Moore
John B. Moranville
Alan Myerson
David Paulsen
Ron Satlof
Robert Scheerer
Ralph Senensky
Lorraine Senna
Harold Stone

Bob Sweeney
Robert C. Thompson
Kate Swofford Tilley
Glynn Turman

ASSISTANT DIRECTORS

Ernest Johnson – First Assistant Director
Robert Jones – First Assistant Director
Les Landau – First Assistant Director
John M. Poer – First Assistant Director
Richard T. Schor – First Assistant Director
Alice Blanchard – Second Assistant Director
Connie Garcia-Singer – Second Assistant Director
Pamela Grant – Second Assistant Director
Wally Crowder – Second Unit Director
James M. Halty – Second Unit Director
Bea Ellen Cameron – Assistant Director Intern

WRITERS

Esther Shapiro - Creator
Richard Shapiro – Creator
Edward De Blasio
Tita Bell
Daniel Benton
Stephen Black
Donald R. Boyle
James H. Brown
Katherine Coker
Loraine Despres
Jonna Emerson
Priscilla English
Barbara Esensten
Frank V. Furino
Diana Gould
Don Heckman
Stephen Kandel

Stephen Karpf
Elinor Karpf
Chester Krumholz
Rita Lakin
Jeffrey Lane
Philip Leacock
Roberto Loiderman
Will Lorin
Leah Markus
Susan Miller
Dick Nelson
David Paulsen
Samuel J. Pelovitz
John Pleshette
Ron Renauld
Mann Rubin
A.J. Russell
Michael Russnow
Jeff Ryder
Frank Salisbury
Paul Savage
Robert Seidenberg
Harry Stern
Noreen Stone
Millee Taggart
Dennis Turner
Elizabeth Wilson
Richard Wilson
Shimon Wincelberg
Robert Wolfe

MUSIC

Bill Conti – Theme
John David
Gerald Fried
Ken Harrison
Marvin Laird
Ben Lanzarone
Dennis Mc Carthy

Greig Mc Ritchie
Angela Morley
Peter T. Myers
Lance Rubin
Mark Snow
Duane Tatro
Richard Warren

CINEMATOGRAPHERS

Michael Hugo
Richard L. Rawlings

EDITORS

Joanna Bush
Dick Darling
Jim Faris
Kenneth Miller
John Woodcock
Jeff Bradley – Assistant Editor
Jason Freeman – Assistant Editor
Scott Hamner – Story Editor
Ken Morrisey – Assistant Editor

CASTING DIRECTOR

Gary Shaffer

ART DIRECTORS

John E. Chilberg II
Frank Swig
Paul Sylos

SET DECORATOR

Brock Broughton

ART DEPARTMENT

Jeffrey Bellamy – Prop Master
Anthony Thorpe – Prop Master
Michael Douglas Middleton – Still Photographer

SOUND DEPARTMENT

Tom Gerard – Sound Re-Recording Mixer

Joseph Holsen – Sound Editor
Richard LeGrand Jr. – Sound Editor
Robert Rouge – Utility Sound Technician
Frank Sacco – ADR Editor
Jules Strasser – Boom Operator

STUNT DEPARTMENT

Wally Crowder – Stunts
James M. Halty – Stunts
Roy E. Harrison – Stunt Coordinator
Larry Holt – Stunt Person
John Meier – Stunt Coordinator
Jim Nickerson – Stunt Person
Ronnie Rondell Jr. – Stunt Coordinator
Janet Brady – Stunt Person
Jeannie Eppers – Linda Evans Stunt Double
Debbie Evans – Stunt Person
Dorothy Ford – Stunt Person
Mags Kavanaugh – Stunt Double
Lane Leavitt – Stunts
Jimmy Nickerson – Stunts
Melodee Spevack – Stephanie Beacham Stunt Double

ADDITIONAL CREW MEMBERS

Neil Argo – Orchestrator
Nancy E. Barr – Production Coordinator
Cynthia Clark – Medical Technical Advisor
Robert Gary – Script Supervisor
Paul Jacobsen – Electrician
Owen Marsh – Camera Operator
Serge Poupis – First Camera Assistant
Randall Robinson – First Camera Assistant
Michael J. Schwartz – Best Boy
Richard Ostlund – Dialogue Director

THE CREW OF DYNASTY - 1986

Chapter Two

Denver's First Family

The characters brilliantly portrayed by an ensemble of gifted actors and actresses are featured in this chapter. Please note that only those cast members who appeared in the series' opening credits feature biographies.

BLAKE ALEXANDER CARRINGTON
Portrayed by John Forsythe

Blake Carrington is a debonair family man who scraped his way to the top. He is the elder son of Thomas and Ellen Carrington and has a brother Benjamin. Blake worked throughout his youth on oil rigs and went to the School of Mines at night. In 1954, his then best friend Cecil Colby's girlfriend introduced him to a lovely young lady named Alexis Morrell. Blake was immediately smitten and after only three days, he proposed marriage. They were engaged for all of three weeks before getting married. Cecil Colby served as the best man and the new Mr. and Mrs. Blake Carrington set out on their adventurous life together.

In 1955, Alexis gave birth to their first child. Blake was ecstatic with the birth of their son Adam Alexander Carrington and vowed that he would eventually become one of the wealthiest men in the world. The young couple's life was turned completely upside-down when Adam was kidnapped. They waited for a ransom note but nothing ever came. As the months dragged on Blake became distant and cold. Instead of sharing his feelings about their missing son, Blake poured all of his energy into building Denver Carrington into a small powerhouse in the oil industry. When Alexis gave birth to their daughter Fallon, Blake showered his baby girl with attention and was once again pleased with the arrival of their third child Steven. Three years had passed with no word about their firstborn child so Blake ordered the search for Adam called off and continued his quest for wealth.

The early 60s were wonderful years for Blake Carrington. Denver Carrington One had come in and made him extremely wealthy. His business was slowly making its way up the financial ladder and his children were wonderfully happy. Unfortunately his wife wasn't... In 1965, Blake came back from another of his endless business trips and discovered Alexis in bed with Roger Grimes. He beat Grimes with a candlestick and then paid him off if he agreed not to press charges. Turning his anger on Alexis he ordered her to leave their home and to sign over full custody of the children. Blake sent Andrew Laird to force Alexis to agree to Blake's demands and told her that she was never to see or contact the children again. In exchange, Blake set up a trust fund of $250,000 per year to keep her away. Faced with raising the children on his own, Blake sent them to boarding schools and let them run wild.

In 1980 Blake fell in love with and married his secretary Krystle Grant Jennings. Despite the protests from Fallon and Steven's announcement that he is gay, Blake struggled to maintain peace in the family. After he accidentally killed Steven's former lover Ted Dinard, Blake was put on trial for murder. The trial brought out sorted details of the Carrington family's past but no one could have prepared Blake and his family for what was still to come: the return of Alexis Morrell Carrington.

On the stand Alexis explained nearly every detail of their "enforced" divorce. In what was perceived to be a foolish move on his part, Blake refused to allow Andrew to cross-examine Alexis. Blake was convicted of Manslaughter and sentenced to probation.

Blake was furious when Alexis moved into the studio in the backyard of the Carrington mansion. He threatened to burn the studio down with her in it when he learned of her involvement in Krystle's miscarriage. He was even less pleased when Alexis announced that she and Cecil Colby were getting married and the reception would be on the Carrington mansion's lawn.

Cecil's death both complicated Blake's life and did him a favor at the same time. It complicated it because Alexis was now at the helm of ColbyCo with the instructions to ruin him financially. It did him a favor because since she was now one of the wealthiest women in the country, she moved out of the backyard studio. Not getting a break at all, Blake's first fight was to retain control of Denver Carrington when Alexis had controlling interest in the company and announced a merger. The merger was called off because of Adam's deception. Alexis continued to be a thorn in his side every chance she got.

There were however, a few moments when they saw eye to eye and behaved as responsible parents. When Steven was presumed dead, Blake was so guilt-ridden that he went into denial and searched the world for his missing son. He was absolutely jubilant when Steven was found alive and well. When Fallon supposedly died in a plane crash, he went into a deep depression and was mournful every time he heard her name but was overjoyed when he learned she was living in California at the Colby mansion.

There were only two bright spots during that time. Krystle became pregnant and delivered a little girl they named Krystina and Blake learned that Alexis had given birth to a girl after she had been banished from Denver. Amanda Bedford was also his child.

When Alexis made a pass at him and he rebuffed her advances, she declared war again. This time bringing Blake's brother Ben back to Denver to sue for part of his father's estate. Blake was furious when he saw his brother. He blamed Ben for their mother's death and completely disowned him decades before. Blake was horrified when Ben and Alexis won the case and more so when Alexis announced she owned the Carrington mansion and Denver

Carrington.   Courtesy of a letter from Emily Fallmont, Blake managed to regain possession of both the mansion and company.

He went through hell when Krystina suddenly became ill and was diagnosed with congestive heart failure.   He felt incredibly weak when all he could do was stand by and pray that a donor could be found in time to save his three-year-old angel.   Blake was relieved when Krystina pulled through and his love for Krystle was stronger than ever.

Always having political ambitions, Blake entered the race to become Colorado's Governor.   He appeared to be doing well in the polls but Alexis decided to throw her hat into the ring and became a spoiler.   Although Blake was dead set against her being in the race at all, he was grateful when she took a bullet meant for him.

A few years later, his love for Krystle would be tested again when she formed a brain tumor and underwent surgery in Switzerland. Blake came back in mourning because he had been told that there was nothing he could do for his comatose wife.   After his return, Blake was the number one suspect in the murder of Roger Grimes. Grimes' body was found floating in the lake on the Carrington property.   While Blake, Dex and Jeff were trying to clear him of any suspicion they discovered that their fathers had been involved in war crimes and had plundered millions in treasures from the Nazi's. The material was all stored in tunnels under the mansion.

Blake was being threatened by Captain Handler to turn over the collection and was informed that Fallon and Krystina were being held captive.   A fight ensued in the foyer of the mansion and Blake as well as Captain Handler was shot.   Handler died and Blake was put in prison.   He was released after two years and spent his time clearing his name and getting Denver Carrington and all of his holdings back from a consortium that had taken over with a little help from Adam.   Krystle had made a complete recovery and the two were back in each others arms.

ALEXIS MARISSA MORRELL CARRINGTON COLBY DEXTER ROWAN
Portrayed by Joan Collins

In 1954, 17-year-old Alexis Morrell glanced up from a table and saw Blake Carrington across the room talking with Cecil Colby. As she watched them she took a deep breath and by the time she exhaled, she was completely in love. Blake asked her dance and as the band played Bewitched, Bothered and Bewildered, Blake fell for the English beauty. When they finished dancing Blake went to get them drinks. Alexis looked at her cousins and sister and said, "I have just danced with the father of my children." Three days later Blake proposed. Within a month Alexis Morrell was Mrs. Blake Carrington.

In the beginning Alexis wanted nothing more than to be Blake's adoring wife and mother to their first child Adam Alexander Carrington. Alexis reveled in motherhood and was very protective of her darling baby. On the morning of September 29, 1957 her happy existence was shattered when Adam was kidnapped. She reached out for Blake for support but was met with coolness. When she couldn't lean on him she turned to others. Cecil Colby was willing to lend an ear and before they knew it, they were having an affair. Feeling incredibly guilty about the fling with Cecil, Alexis devoted herself to being the doting wife Blake wanted her to be. She became pregnant again and gave birth to a baby girl. When Fallon was born she became jealous of the attention that Blake showered on his daughter. That jealousy remained even after giving birth to Steven because in the back of her mind, Alexis was upset with Blake for calling off the search for Adam and he was now trying to replace their first son with this one.

During their marriage Blake went on several business trips often leaving Alexis alone for weeks on end. She became lonely and looked for attention outside of their marriage. She had a few more affairs with Jimmy Decker and Sam Dexter among others. The final blow to Blake and Alexis' troubled marriage came when Blake found her in bed with Roger Grimes. After beating Grimes senseless, he threw Alexis out of the house. They attempted a reconciliation but it only lasted three months. Blake discovered that Alexis had seen Grimes again and exiled her from Denver for good. Giving in to his threats, Alexis left Blake and her children in 1965 with a $250,000 a year trust fund and the secret that she was pregnant with their fourth child.

Upon her return to Denver, Alexis had mixed feelings about Blake. On one hand she absolutely hated him for banishing her from her children. On the other hand she wanted nothing more than to hear him say that he loved her and wanted her back. Alexis married Cecil Colby and after his death a few minutes later, found herself one of the richest women in the world. She used the money and position to lash back at Blake as revenge for everything he had done to her throughout the years and God help anyone who tried to stand in her way.

Alexis was overjoyed when a young man named Michael Torrance presented her with a silver rattle and announced that he was Adam. Fallon and she haven't always seen eye to eye but they have forged a loving relationship. Steven was and still is his mother's favorite child. Although horrified when Amanda arrived in Denver and publicly announced that she was Alexis' youngest child, Alexis reluctantly gave in and adjusted to the fact that Blake had learned the truth.

Alexis has had more than her fair share of men in her life. After luring Mark Jennings to Denver to break up Blake and Krystle's marriage, she ended up sleeping with him instead then hired him to be her bodyguard. She dallied with Rashid Ahmed whenever they were in the same city. She met and married Farnsworth "Dex" Dexter. When she found Dex in bed with Amanda, she immediately divorced him. She was being wooed by the King of Moldavia but got rid of him when she discovered he was using her for her money. Then there was an innocent flirtation with Blake's brother Ben and finally the unfortunate marriage to Sean Rowan. Even with the array of men there was always something holding her back. Although she did truly love Dex and later Sean, Alexis' heart and soul would always belong to Blake.

KRYSTLE GRANT JENNINGS CARRINGTON
Portrayed by Linda Evans

Krystle Grant was raised in a small town just outside of Dayton, Ohio. Along with her sister Iris, Krystle used to spend time helping her grandparents on their farm. Krystle was very naïve when she fell in love and married tennis star Samuel Mark Howard Jennings. The "love match" was doomed from the start because of Mark's constant travel with the tennis tour circuit. Krystle left Mark and moved to Denver. She got a job as a secretary at Denver Carrington and it wasn't long before she captured the attention of owner Blake Carrington. Blake ardently began pursuing Krystle not knowing that she was already involved with geologist Matthew Blaisdel (while his wife Claudia was in a sanitarium). Krystle called it quits with Matthew and despite being tremendously overwhelmed by Blake's wealth, married him on May 24, 1980.

In the beginning, life in the Carrington mansion was anything but tranquil as Krystle was subjected to the ridicule of the staff and the insults routinely slung at her by Fallon. It appeared the only bright spot in the house was the friendship she had developed with Steven. Krystle also discovered that Blake wasn't always the gallant man she had fallen for. Blake was insistent that Krystle produce a child and when he discovered that she had been taking birth control pills, he raped her while in a rage which resulted in Krystle becoming pregnant. Their happiness was short-lived courtesy of Alexis. Not at all pleased at the thought that Krystle was going to give Blake a child, she fired a gun and watched her be dragged across a field and caused her to suffer a miscarriage. Krystle then contemplated having an affair with Dr. Nicholas Toscanni after seeing compromising photos of Blake and Alexis together in Italy but neither affair was ever to be.

Life was turned upside down again when Mark appeared claiming that they were never divorced thus making Blake and Krystle's marriage invalid. After definitely divorcing Mark, Krystle tried life on her own again but soon realized that she still wanted Blake so they married again in 1983. Krystle's dream of motherhood came true the following year when she gave birth to daughter Krystina.

Krystle's life seemed to be moving along beautifully until niece Sammy Jo and friends arranged to kidnap Krystle and held her captive in an attic at Delta Rho. A few years later, Krystina developed congestive heart failure and had to be subjected to a heart transplant. With her daughter's life hanging in the balance Krystle emotionally fell apart. When Krystina was pulled through Krystle appeared to have a new lease on life at least temporarily...

In 1988, Krystle began experiencing moments of what could be termed as temporary insanity. She would be fine one minute but completely someone else the next and suffering from blackouts. She left Denver and her family for Switzerland, where she would undergo brain surgery and remain in a coma for years.

Finally recovering from her coma, Krystle returned to Blake and Krystina. She was programmed to kill Blake but could never go through with it. Eventually she learned what had been triggering the suggestion to murder him and was able to control her mind against the instructions. Blake got the mansion and Denver Carrington back and Krystle melted into his arms.

ADAM ALEXANDER CARRINGTON
Portrayed by Gordon Thomson

Adam Alexander Carrington is most definitely his mother's son. The first child of Blake and Alexis Carrington, Adam was kidnapped shortly before his first birthday on September 29, 1957 and raised by Kate Torrance. Distraught over the loss of their son, Blake and Alexis spent three years searching for their firstborn but eventually called off the search and tried to move on the best they could. Adam was renamed Michael Torrance and led to believe that Kate was his grandmother and he was the sole survivor of an auto accident that killed both of his parents.

A lonely young man, Adam never quite fit in with his peers and turned to drugs as a way of escape. His drug use led to a nervous breakdown and a residual affect of sometimes distorted thinking. Putting his mental and dependency behind him, Adam went to Yale and graduated with a law degree. He returned to Billings, Montana and went to work as an attorney. It was on her deathbed that Kate finally told Adam who he was and supplied him with the proof needed to stake his claim to his birthright. Armed with a silver rattle Adam arrived in Denver and after being thrown out of Blake's office, he approached Alexis who (after seeing the rattle) immediately welcomed her baby back with open arms.

Adam has a very jealous streak, particularly when it comes to Jeff and in his distorted frame of mind, poisoned him in retaliation for coming to work at ColbyCo. He raped Kirby Anders and proceeded to pursue her even after she married Jeff. When Adam discovered Kirby was carrying his child, he did a complete turnaround and became a responsible adult (at least for a little while). He was mixed with hurt and rage when Kirby left Denver on Alexis' orders and proceeded to turn into a bit of a playboy with a sinister edge by making passes at Sammy Jo and eventually marrying Claudia.

After Claudia's death, Adam returned to his playboy ways and seduced Dana Waring as a ploy to get information for Alexis as Dana was Blake's personal assistant at the time. What Adam didn't count on was falling in love with and marrying the girl who had followed him from Billings, Montana with a secret that she'd been pregnant with his child but had aborted it many years before.

Desperate for a child, Adam fathered a son with surrogate Karen Atkinson. Fate again dealt a bad blow when Karen decided she wanted to keep the child and Adam was denied any type of custody or visitation. His marriage to Dana was over and the entire experience left Adam even more bitter. Like his mother, Adam has knows that there's a very thin line between love and hate, but it seems he's always ending up on the wrong side of the line.

FALLON MARISSA CARRINGTON COLBY
Portrayed by Pamela Sue Martin and Emma Samms

Fallon is the epitome of the spoiled little rich girl. The second child of Blake and Alexis's children, Fallon is willful, impulsive and fiercely protective of Blake. She is without a doubt "Daddy's little girl." Fallon hated Krystle when she married Blake. As part of a deal to bail Blake out of financial trouble, Fallon married Cecil Colby's nephew Jeff. Fallon was also having an affair with her father's chauffeur Michael Culhane at the time. The affair came to an end when Blake found out about it and fired Michael.

The hatred Fallon felt for Krystle grew when she found out that Krystle was pregnant. Feeling threatened, Fallon seduced Jeff and became pregnant as well, but after Krystle's miscarriage, Fallon wanted an abortion but failed to go through with it. With her sham marriage practically over, Fallon became involved with psychiatrist Nicholas Toscanni. Unfortunately she didn't realize that he was using her to get back at her father.

Blake Jeffrey Carrington Colby was born by cesarean section following a car accident in which Alexis confessed to Fallon that Blake may not be her father. Fallon lost control of her car when Alexis said her father may be Cecil Colby. She went into a severe depression and remained in it until blood tests proved that she is indeed Blake's daughter. Jeff and Fallon's marriage was strained even more when their son was put through heart surgery at a few days old. Nick soon realized that Fallon was going back to Jeff and took further steps to hurt the Carrington family by arranging for the baby to be kidnapped.

During the search for her baby, Fallon and the rest of the world discovered the secret of Adam's kidnapping. After the safe return of the baby, Fallon took over one of Blake's properties (La Mirada Hotel) and transformed it into an extravagant resort and changed the name to La Mirage. After nearly being seduced by Adam (not knowing they were related), Fallon unsuccessfully tried to discredit him.

With her divorce from Jeff final, Fallon moved on to her next two conquests. The first was tennis pro Mark Jennings. Mark was Krystle's ex-husband that had been tracked down and lured to Denver by Alexis. Alexis and Fallon had intended for Mark to break up Blake and Krystle but instead he fell for Fallon. Alexis didn't like what she was seeing and broke them up.

A short time later, Fallon met and fell madly in love with playboy Peter DeVilbis. Despite everyone's warnings, Fallon planned to marry Peter but he was only after her father's money. When she realized he had used her, she ran from the hotel and was struck by a car. The trauma of the situation left her temporarily paralyzed and caused her to have tremendously painful headaches. While having Jeff caring for her, Fallon realized just how much she truly loved Jeff. On Little Blake's second birthday, Jeff proposed and Fallon happily accepted.

On their second wedding night, Fallon had yet another massive headache. This time it was so horrible that she ran out of the house and drove away in the pouring rain. She was in a serious accident and several weeks later was said to have died in a plane crash with Peter DeVilbis. As her family mourned, Fallon was actually in Los Angeles, California suffering from amnesia.

She was unknowingly drawn to Miles Colby (not realizing who she is) and joins him on a trip to Colorado to attend a party at the Carrington mansion. When she arrives at the house, she is unable to go inside and she and Miles drive away without having made an appearance. Jeff is looking out the window when Miles pulls up and sees Fallon with him. Jeff moves to Los Angeles and arrives shortly before Miles comes home with his new wife "Randall." Jeff makes her realize that she's actually his fiancé and the mother of their child.

Fallon regains her memory and returns to Jeff, leaving Miles hurt and angry. Her marriage to Miles is annulled and she decides to marry Jeff again. Miles rapes Fallon and she becomes pregnant, causing her to not know if the child belongs to Miles or Jeff. Still living in Los Angeles at the Colby mansion, Fallon falls down a staircase and goes into premature labor. She delivers daughter Lauren Constance Colby and is relieved to discover that Jeff is her daughter's father.

On an unusually warm night, Fallon is stunned to be trapped in the desert and sees a very strange light. She walks slowly towards a spacecraft and boards the craft. Several hours later, she is found by the side of the road. Desperate to regain her senses, Fallon begs Jeff to take her back to Denver.

Once there, Fallon sends for the children and the Colby family moves back into the Carrington mansion. She tells Jeff of her experience and he thinks she's lost her mind. They continue to have problems and divorce again. She begins dating John Zorelli, a police detective investigating the death of Roger Grimes. It is later discovered that Fallon had killed Grimes as a child when she saw him beating Alexis. Fallon eventually moved back to California where she shared a home with her children and Krystina.

STEVEN DANIEL CARRINGTON
Portrayed by Al Corley and Jack Coleman

Steven is sensitive, caring person who his father has accused him of not being a real man. Steven is a homosexual, (although since he was married twice would actually be bi-sexual) and Blake completely blames Alexis for having coddled him too much as a child. He was always her favorite and she lavished him with the hugs and kisses she wished she could have given to Adam. They nearly lost him when he came down with pneumonia when he was five. Steven was completely crushed when (three days before his seventh birthday) Alexis left Denver. Blake never gave his son the amount of attention that his mother did. As he grew, Steven resented his father more and more. He was sent away to school in New York and attended college at Princeton. It was there that he had his first homosexual experience. After graduation he moved in with partner Ted Dinard. When Blake married Krystle and insisted that Steven attend, he broke up with Ted and returned to Denver.

Back in Denver, Steven told his father of his lifestyle choice and was met with severe resistance and anger. No son of Blake Carrington's was going to be a gay man. To annoy his father, Steven went to work for competitors Matthew Blaisdel and Walter Lankershim. Matthew befriended Steven but Steven ended up having an affair with Matthew's wife Claudia. Months later, Ted came to Denver to convince Steven to give their relationship another chance. Steven refused and as they were saying goodbye, Blake came in and became outraged over seeing the two men embracing. He shoved Ted to get him away from Steven and Ted lost his balance. Steven watched as his former lover fell backwards and hit his head on the fireplace. To their horror, Ted died and Blake was arrested for murder.

While his father was on trial, Steven was forced to tell the world about his sexual preference and his father's intolerance. Claudia was also forced to reveal their affair to the courtroom. With Fallon taking their father's side, Steven found himself fighting the battle alone but no one could have prepared any of them for what was coming next. When his mother entered the courtroom and revealed the circumstances of her "enforced" divorce from Blake, Steven resented his father even more. He welcomed his mother back into his life and listened as the jury found Blake guilty of Manslaughter.

Claudia was despondent over the destruction of her marriage and went into a deep depression. On the rebound and getting pressure from his parents to consider finding someone to love, Steven meets and falls for Krystle's niece Sammy Jo. Much to his surprise, both of his parents object to his newfound relationship. Sammy Jo introduced Steven to her racing friends and convinced him to participate in auto racing. Steven proposed and he and Sammy Jo eloped.

Blake and Alexis were furious and Krystle wasn't exactly pleased for the couple either. Sammy Jo began charging heavily on the Carrington credit and ended up having Steven continuously angry with her. The final straw came when Sammy Jo told Fallon that Blake wasn't her father. Unbeknownst to Steven, Alexis paid Sammy Jo to leave Denver and to stay out of her son's life. Steven found Sammy Jo in Hollywood and she told him what happened. He returned to Denver absolutely furious and told his family that he couldn't bear to be around any of them and made his family finally accept the fact that he's gay. Steven left Denver and joined a crew on an oil rig in the ocean off the island of Bali.

An explosion on the rig left Steven suffering from serious burns over part of his body. His face had to be completely restructured and his recovery was slow. When Dan Cassidy figured out that this stranger wasn't Ben Reynolds, as he had claimed to be, but was actually Steven, he called Blake and told him that his missing son wasn't dead after all. Blake rushed to Singapore to reunite with his son and to tell Steven that Sammy Jo had given birth to a son, then left him at the mansion while she continued her modeling career. Although Steven didn't want to return to Denver, he went with his father for the sake of his infant son.

When he arrived, Steven met his older brother Adam for the first time and disliked him almost from the start. He tracked down Sammy Jo in New York and tried to convince her to give their marriage another chance. Sammy Jo dismissed him so Steven returned to Denver to raise his son on his own. When Blake sued him for custody of Danny, Steven countered by marrying Claudia Blaisdel. Steven retained custody of his son, went to work for Alexis at Colbyco and eventually reconciled with his father.

His marriage to Claudia didn't last long. Steven became involved with Luke Fuller. Blake was less than enthusiastic about Steven and Luke's relationship but didn't argue when Steven invited Luke to Moldavia for his youngest sister Amanda's wedding. The wedding was interrupted by gunmen and when everything was over, Luke died of a gunshot wound to the head.

Sammy Jo returned to Denver and bonded with Danny. After Matthew's return and being held hostage, Steven killed Matthew in self-defense and wasn't charged. Steven tried to pull himself together after losing Luke and briefly reconciled with Sammy Jo for Danny's benefit. Blake appointed him his successor at Denver Carrington while he ran for Governor. Steven found himself in the middle of a virtual war zone with his siblings. He finally gave up trying to deny his true feelings about his life and moved to Washington D.C. where he lives with lobbyist Bart Fallmont.

AMANDA KIMBERLY CARRINGTON
Portrayed by Catherine Oxenberg and Karen Cellini

Amanda was raised to believe that she was the daughter of Hugh and Rosalind Bedford, two members of Alexis Carrington's household staff. She didn't realize that Alexis and Rosalind are cousins or that Alexis was her natural mother. Alexis was pregnant when she left Denver and in an attempt to keep Amanda's existence a secret from Blake, Alexis asked Rosalind to raise her daughter. Amanda never wanted for anything and thought that Alexis just showed love more easily than Rosalind.

When she was attending school in Paris, Amanda had to obtain a copy of her birth certificate and discovered the truth. She went to Denver to confront her real mother. Alexis was stunned and tried to make her understand her reasoning for giving her to Hugh and Rosalind. Backed into a corner, Alexis tried to convince Amanda that her father was an unknown ski instructor she had a fling with in Switzerland. Amanda didn't believe the story, nor did Blake when he heard it. Blake convinced her to take a blood test but it wasn't needed because Rosalind told her that Blake is her father.

Amanda was attracted to Dex and slept with him before he married Alexis. Alexis, sensing her daughter's attraction to her husband, tried her best to find a "suitable" man for her daughter to marry. She found that person in Acapulco when she, Blake, Dex and Amanda were on a business trip. Amanda fell for Prince Michael of Moldavia. Her fantasy is dashed when Michael tells her that he's already engaged to be married. It turns out Alexis knows Michael's father quite well; they were childhood loves. Wanting her daughter to be happy and away from Dex, Alexis strikes a deal with Moldavia's king. Let the children be married and she'll set up oil production in the small country.

Michael and Amanda were married in Moldavia. Unfortunately, their wedding turned into a bloodbath and Michael was told that his father was dead, thus making he and Amanda the exiled King and Queen of Moldavia. Returning to Denver, Amanda tries to make her marriage work but can't forget her feelings for Dex. After Alexis and Dex have an argument, Amanda takes advantage of his intoxication and begins having an affair with him. Alexis finds them in bed together. Amanda is immediately disowned and Dex finds himself with a divorce decree. Amanda tries to make piece with her mother but Alexis wants nothing to do with her.

When her relationship with Dex ends and her marriage from Michael is over, Amanda turns to other family members for support. Everyone is too busy to be bothered and after several cries for help go ignored, Amanda swallowed a bottle of sleeping pills. Alexis finds her daughter unconscious and rushes her to the hospital. Blake blames Alexis for turning against their daughter. Amanda reconciles with her mother but remains with Blake and Krystle.

Amanda becomes attracted to Clay Fallmont but he's involved with Sammy Jo. Sammy Jo senses Amanda's attraction to Clay and the two end up in a fight at La Mirage. When Claudia sets the hotel on fire, Amanda suffers from severe smoke inhalation and is rescued by an unlikely source. Michael Culhane is back in Denver and with a new life as a millionaire. He doesn't mention it to Amanda or anyone else but instead asked Blake for his job back. Blake reluctantly agreed but warned Amanda not to become involved with Michael. He pursued her relentlessly and she finally gave in to his advances.

Blake discovered the two of them kissing and immediately fired Michael. Amanda accused Blake of holding Michael's affair with Fallon against him and that his judgment is clouded because he won't let go of the past. Blake orders Amanda to stop seeing Michael. She retaliates by moving in with Michael. After she discovers that Michael has been conducting shady business dealings and that he was trying to set up Blake in a bad deal, Amanda left Denver for good.

JEFFREY BRODERICK COLBY
Portrayed by John James

Jeff is a wonderful man who wants nothing more than to make Fallon happy and provide for his children. He is the son of Jason Colby and Francesca Scott. Frankie was married to Jason's youngest brother Philip, but had an affair with Jason. When she gave birth to Jeff, Philip was fighting in the Vietnam War and was presumed dead. Frankie raised Jeff to believe that Philip was his father. When he was three-years-old, Frankie gave him to Cecil Colby and allowed Cecil to raise his nephew.

Living next door to the Carringtons, Jeff grew up with Fallon and Steven and from an early age loved Fallon. She never really gave him the time of day but he knew there was something special between them. He was thrilled when she asked him out on a date. Jeff had no idea that the date was set up by his Uncle Cecil. He also had no clue that his marriage had been a business transaction between Cecil and Fallon as a way to keep Cecil from calling in Blake's loan.

Jeff and Fallon tried to make their marriage work and when she said she wanted to try having a baby, he was ecstatic. What he didn't know was that Fallon only wanted to have a baby because Krystle was already pregnant. After Krystle's miscarriage, Jeff found out that Fallon was pregnant after he took a message from an abortion clinic confirming Fallon's appointment. He desperately tried to find out if there was any way to stop her from having the abortion, but was told that he basically had very few rights. Thinking that Fallon had killed their child, Jeff moved out of their bedroom and started divorce proceedings.

Drowning in his sorrows, Jeff was discouraged by Fallon's affair with Nick Toscanni and turned to Claudia for comfort. While he was sleeping with Claudia, Fallon gave birth to their son; Blake Jeffrey Carrington Colby prematurely. He later learns that Claudia was using him to spy for his Uncle Cecil. Cecil had blackmailed her by telling her that he would find Matthew and Lindsay in exchange for copies of Denver Carrington business transaction details. When he discovers what his uncle has done to him and to Claudia, Jeff tells Cecil that he never wants to see him again.

Jeff's world is turned completely upside down when his son is kidnapped. He is also faced with life and death when Cecil suffers a massive heart attack. While visiting his uncle in the hospital, he speaks of his son as if nothing was wrong and reconciles with Cecil. Jeff suddenly realizes that the cemetery caretaker took an unusual interest in the baby. Along with Blake, Jeff tracks down the caretaker and learns that he is the father of Alexis' former lover

Roger Grimes, and more importantly, that Nick Toscanni arranged his child's kidnapping to avenge his brother's suicide.

When Cecil died, Jeff inherited half of Colbyco with Alexis getting the other half. Although he was working with Blake at Denver Carrington, Jeff moved over to Colbyco after Adam took it upon himself to make executive decisions without consulting anyone. Adam retaliated by having mercuric-oxide mixed with paint and used it to paint Jeff's office. Jeff was slowly poisoned and collapsed. On the rebound from Fallon, he impetuously runs away and marries Joseph's daughter Kirby. The marriage is doomed from the beginning because of Jeff's feelings for Fallon.

Kirby and Jeff divorced after she lost the baby she was carrying. The child was Adam's and she insisted that her marriage to Jeff was a mistake. Jeff was immediately jealous of Fallon's relationship with Peter DeVilbis and warned her not to marry him. He picked up the pieces of her broken heart and was pleased when Fallon accepted his second wedding proposal. Everything was going along quite well until Fallon suffered a debilitating headache and left on their wedding night, leaving Jeff desperate to find her. He was inconsolable when he thought Fallon had been killed in a plane crash with Peter DeVilbis.

Still in mourning but receiving tremendous pressure from everyone to move on with his life, Jeff became involved with Lady Ashley Mitchell. She was a bit resistant at first but Jeff swore he was in love with her and proposed shortly before they left for Amanda's wedding in Moldavia. He was heartbroken again when he found out that Ashley was one of the people killed in the massacre.

Jeff was beside himself and reluctantly agreed to help Blake with the pipeline deal with Jason Colby. Neither Jeff nor Jason had any idea that he is Jason's son. While he is in California, his Aunt Constance presents him with her half of the family business. Jeff is stunned that he is now a partner in Colby Enterprises. He returns to Denver to tell Blake that he and his son are moving to Los Angeles to keep an eye on Jason's business practices. He receives further incentive when Miles shows up at the Carrington mansion with Fallon. Jeff leaves for California that night.

When Miles arrives back at the Colby mansion in Los Angeles, he shocks the family when he introduces them to his new wife Randall. Jeff delivers the larger shock, Randall is his missing Fallon. Jeff tries to help Fallon regain her memory by telling her about the times they shared and their son Little Blake (now going by L.B.). She eventually regained her memory, had her marriage to Miles annulled and remarried Jeff.

Jeff helped Fallon through her second pregnancy and tried to keep her calm about the thought that the baby may not be his. He was thrilled when she delivered a little girl and tests proved that Lauren was indeed his child. By now Frankie had confessed that Jeff was Jason's son and the two men were trying to forge a relationship.

After Fallon was kidnapped by aliens and they returned to Denver, their marriage went downhill. Jeff had an affair with Ben's daughter Leslie. Fallon again filed for divorce and Jeff became involved with Sammy Jo. As with every other relationship they've had, Jeff and Fallon found their way back to each other.

SAMANTHA JOSEPHINE "SAMMY JO DEAN" REECE CARRINGTON FALLMONT
Portrayed by Heather Locklear

Sammy Jo is a piece of work. She arrived in Denver when her assumed father Frank Dean asked Krystle if he could leave Sammy Jo with Krystle for a few days. That few days turned into months and eventually became forever. Sammy Jo is the daughter of Krystle's sister Iris and was led to believe that Frank Dean was her father. Iris died when Sammy Jo was a child and she spent the majority of her life traveling with Frank on the auto racing circuit.

Sammy Jo cozied up to Steven and despite the knowledge that he's gay, she encouraged their relationship to move from friendship to lovers. Steven proposed and Sammy Jo willingly agreed to elope. As soon as they returned to the Carrington mansion and announced their marriage, she began spending money. Alexis caught her buying herself a mink coat and had more information regarding the excessive spending her new daughter-in-law was doing. When Steven confronted her about her spending and the way she was behaving she threw Fallon's paternity in his face. It was something that she also tried to use against Alexis. She didn't realize that Alexis wasn't someone to play games with.

After Sammy Jo told Fallon that Blake isn't her father, Alexis decided she was finished tolerating Steven's mistake. Alexis paid $15,000 to get Sammy Jo out of Denver. Steven was furious and tracked her down in Hollywood. She was working as a model and told Steven that she no longer wanted anything to do with him.

When Steven was presumed dead, Sammy Jo returned to the Carrington mansion with a surprise for Blake. She handed him a baby and introduced him to his grandson; Steven Daniel Carrington Jr. but she just calls him Danny. After a few days Sammy Jo offers to sell Danny to Blake and Krystle. They are stunned and appalled by her demands. Blake gives her $100,000 so she can establish herself as a model on the condition that she take the baby with her. Sammy Jo then agrees to take the money but instead offers to allow Blake and Krystle to adopt the baby. When Steven turned out to be alive and back in Denver, she testified for Blake in his trial for custody.

Resentful of Steven's happiness with new wife Claudia, Sammy Jo returns to Denver again and threatens to take custody of Danny herself. When she found out that Frank Dean wasn't her father, but instead was Daniel Reece, she concocted a plan with Rita Lesley and Joel Abrigore to extort her inheritance out of Krystle. Things didn't go as planned and the three kidnapped Krystle and held her hostage. Rita moved in with Blake and the family and proceeded to poison Blake. They nearly succeed in killing him. Sammy Jo begged Krystle and Blake for forgiveness and they cautiously agree to give her another chance.

Once again, Sammy Jo decides she wants Danny and threatens to sue for custody after she marries Clay Fallmont. Sammy Jo thought she was pregnant and forced Clay to marry her. When it turned out that she wasn't pregnant after all she and Clay had the marriage annulled. Steven saw the fact that she was suffering emotionally and reached out as a friend.

As time progressed the two of them formed a caring friendship and after the family was held hostage by Matthew, Steven and Danny moved in with Sammy Jo. She was happy for a while but seduced Steven and assumed that they were back together and would have a future again as a couple. Steven broke her heart by telling her that their relationship was a mistake. Sammy Jo had a brief affair with football star Josh Harris and was devastated when he died of a cocaine overdose.

With Steven gone and Jeff filling her emotional needs, Sammy Jo finally had a chance to be happy. Then she met Tanner McBride. She immediately was attracted to him and was torn between him and Jeff. That is until Tanner revealed his true identity. He is a priest now wrestling with the feelings stirred up by Sammy Jo.

FARNSWORTH "DEX" DEXTER
Portrayed by Michael Nader

Having been "saddled" with his grandfather's first name and wanting something a little more hip, Farnsworth Dexter immediately took on the nickname Dex. He's tall, dark and drop-dead-gorgeous and from the moment he laid eyes on Alexis, he was in love with her. Dex is the son of Blake's longtime friend and board member Sam Dexter. Sam had suffered a massive heart attack and sent Dex to Denver to take care of business for his ailing father.

The first order of business was a board meeting in which Alexis calls off her intended merger between Denver Carrington and Colbyco. He is instantly attracted to her. Following the meeting, Dex arrives at Alexis' office and tries to temp her into a new business venture. She turns him down flat. Dex says he'll leave as soon as he does one more thing: he pulls her body next to his and passionately kisses her.

Te kiss and deal intrigued Alexis so she pursued the deal and tried to cheat him out of it. Dex got wind of what she was planning and beat her to it. She was less than pleased when she got there and found Dex waiting. He tried to seduce her and she brushed him off. The following morning, he apologized for his behavior and then carried her to bed.

They formed the Lex-Dex Corporation and went to work finding as many projects as they could that would infuriate Blake. Oscar Stone's oil wells were the final straw and Blake threw Dex off Denver Carrington's board. As the relationship progressed, Dex and Alexis had many, many arguments but managed to make up after a few hours, days or weeks. Dex realized they had a love that he found hard to live with and even harder to live without.

He spilt up with her in Hong Kong when he found her sharing her suite with Rashid Ahmed. He then went to bed with Tracy Kendall as a way to get back at her. Still wanting to keep track of her every move, Dex convinces the now unemployed Tracy to go to work for Colbyco and report Alexis' business dealings back to him. Tracy told Alexis of the arrangement when she quit Colbyco. Dex apologized to Alexis for creating a double standard and they reconciled.

The next hurdle to go over was Alexis being arrested for murdering Mark Jennings. Dex did everything possible to get her out of jail but aside from Fallon's funeral, he was unable to do anything. He and Adam re-enacted the evening of Mark's death and with the assistance of photos from a neighbor of Alexis', they discovered that Neal McVane had killed Mark. Dex and Alexis prepared to have a celebration to welcome her home and were surprised by the appearance of Amanda.

Dex doesn't get along well with Alexis and Blake's youngest child. He considered Amanda to be a spoiled brat who only wants to cause trouble between him and Alexis. Things get even more complicated when she constantly makes passes at him. While Alexis was desperate to get Amanda away from Blake, she asked Dex to take Amanda to New Mexico without her. They got trapped together in a blizzard and one thing led to another. The two had sex and then swore never to discuss the event. Matters were made worse when Alexis arrived and told Dex that they were flying to London to get married. Despite the feelings he's forming for Amanda, Dex goes through with the marriage.

He becomes seriously ill and is hospitalized with Malaria. While delirious he begs for forgiveness. The only problem is that instead of asking for Alexis' forgiveness, he asks for Amanda's. Alexis' suspicions of Dex's feelings for Amanda are made even clearer when he becomes defensive and objects to Amanda marrying Prince Michael. He grudgingly agrees to go to Moldavia but once there becomes jealous of the relationship between Alexis and King Galen. Alexis and Dex have another major argument and he leaves the palace. He's captured by revolutionaries and held hostage. Being a mercenary came in handy because he is able to escape and bursts into the chapel in the middle of the massacre.

After quite a few tense days, Dex and Blake rescue Alexis and Krystle from the new Moldavian leaders. Once back in Denver, he tries to make Alexis forget about what happened but the only thing he can do is agree to return to Moldavia to rescue King Galen. He agrees to do so on the condition that Alexis choose between them. Alexis tells him that there was never a choice. He pushes one time too many and gets thrown out of the penthouse. At La Mirage he runs into Amanda. They do quite a bit of drinking and end up in bed together. Alexis became worried about him and went to the hotel. They were completely surprised when the suite's door opened and Alexis walked in on them in bed. Feeling incredibly guilty, Dex begged her forgiveness. Alexis informed him that it was too late for apologies, she had just divorced him.

Knowing that his relationship with Amanda was wrong, Dex broke up with her. He was intent on getting Alexis back but she wanted nothing to do with him. Dominique provided a friendly shoulder and the two listened to each other's problems and made a pact to always be there for the other to lean on. Dex found himself of plenty of trouble with Alexis when he agreed to help Blake with the pipeline and his new company Carrington Ventures. While she confronted him about his involvement, a rainstorm keeps her at the site's trailer. Dex forces her to confront her feelings, which leads them to another reconciliation (in bed).

Ben Carrington was the next stumbling block to get over. He was blackmailing Alexis and Dex absolutely hated the man. Luckily, Alexis got rid of him on her own. Since they had an open divorce, Dex still had a few more men to contend with. The next on the list was Gavin Maurier. Gavin was a sexy, smooth talking man who had put the moves on Alexis. Dex punched him in the jaw and told him to leave her alone. When he told Alexis what he had done and she didn't react the way he wanted her to, Dex told her that she was a lonely lady who had no one in her life. She ran out the house and accidentally drove off a bridge.

Dex was still at the Carrington mansion when Matthew and his gang took the family hostage. He was shot trying to help the family escape. While he recovered, he had an affair with Ben's daughter Leslie. That relationship didn't last long. Dex was determined that he wanted to have Alexis but there was yet another stumbling block. His name was Sean Rowan.

Sean saved Alexis from drowning and she became infatuated with him. Paying no attention to anyone, Alexis married Sean. Dex wished them well but always had suspicions in the back of his mind. His suspicions proved to be correct again when Sean tried to kill him and Blake as part of his revenge against Alexis and Blake. Once again Alexis and Dex reconciled. Sean returned from the dead and tried to kill Alexis. Dex burst through the door and fought

Sean to the death. After the coroner removed Sean's body from her apartment, Dex took her to Los Angeles where another woman captured his attention.

Sable Colby is Alexis' cousin. She had only one goal in mind; to ruin Alexis. Dex spent quite a while in Los Angeles avoiding Sable but wasn't so lucky when she bought The Carlton Hotel out from under Alexis and moved to Denver. While Alexis was away trying to save her assets, Sable moved in on Dex. They eventually ended up in bed together. Alexis found out about the affair and told Dex that this time they were truly finished. Sable also decided that her affair with Dex was impossible because of his feelings for Alexis.

There's only one major problem; Sable is pregnant with Dex's child. After several arguments with both Alexis and Sable, Dex got into a fight with Adam. Adam swore Dex would never push him around again and shoved him. Dex lost his balance and fell into Alexis, who was leaning against a banister. The railing broke and both of them fell from the balcony to the floor below. Dex's fate remains unknown.

DOMINIQUE DEVEREAUX LLOYD
(MILLIE COX CARRINGTON)
Portrayed by Diahann Carroll

Dominique is a beautiful woman. A world-renowned singer, she owns nightclubs all over the world. She came to Denver with one thing in mind; to make Blake Carrington acknowledge the fact that she is his half-sister. Apparently his father Tom had an affair with her mother Laura. Blake refused to believe her and threw her out. She then came to his rescue while he was in financial trouble, bailing him out of debt with a check for fifty million dollars.

Doing so cost Dominique her marriage to record producer Brady Lloyd.

Blake made her work for the respect she eventually earned. When Tom Carrington had a massive heart attack and was on his deathbed, he finally confessed to the affair and admitted that she is indeed his daughter. Dominique was rather surprised when Tom's attorney split his fortune between her, Blake and Alexis and she was to be the executor of the estate. This unsettling news was taken in stride by Blake and made Alexis even more of an enemy than she already was.

While Blake was working on the pipeline with Colby Enterprises, Dominique met Jason's daughter Monica and offered to let her run a newly acquired company, Titania Records. It was then that she rekindled a romance with Jason's attorney Garrett Boydston. She and Garrett had been in love with each other years before but didn't pursue their love because told her that he was already married. Garrett pursued Dominique, telling her that his wife Jessica had died. Dominique had a rather large secret that was finally revealed. She had given birth to a daughter named Jackie. Although she told Jackie that her father was killed before she was born, Jackie's father was actually Garrett Boydston. Alexis delivered a bombshell to Dominique, Garrett was never married and his "wife" Jessica never existed. Dominique immediately called off their engagement and sent Garrett packing.

Dominique sold Titania Records to Zach Powers when Ben conspired with Alexis to bring Blake to his knees by suing for part of his father's estate. Eventually she got her money back after Ben was exposed as a liar. Her love life improved tremendously when she met Nick Kimball. Nick was a wildcatter in the oil industry who gained a fortune when an oil well he owned came in. Dominique was resistant to become involved but he was extremely persistent. Swept away by her feelings while attending Adam and Dana's wedding, Dominique accepted Nick's marriage proposal. The two left the wedding and took off to unknown whereabouts to be married.

BENJAMIN "BEN" CARRINGTON
Portrayed by Christopher Cazenove

Ben is younger brother of Blake Carrington. He left home at an early age after being responsible for his mother's death. Father Tom Carrington was away on business and his brother Blake was called out to an oil field because of a fire on a rig. Ben had been told to stay at home and take care of his mother. Ellen Carrington had broken her leg and was bedridden. Ben didn't pay attention to his brother's orders and left to spend the afternoon in bed with Senator Buck Fallmont's wife Emily. While they were having their affair, a fire broke out in the house and Ellen Lucy Carrington died in her bed. Blake and Tom blamed Ben for her death and exiled him from the family.

Decades later, Alexis decided she needed another tool to use in her quest for Blake so she tracked down his little brother. Traveling to Australia, Alexis persuaded Ben to come back to Denver with her to wreak havoc on Blake's life. Ben made his presence known at a masquerade ball and was met with an extremely cold reception from his brother. Ben filed suit against Blake, Alexis and Dominique for his share of Tom Carrington's estate and wins after he convinces everyone that Blake was the one having an affair. His claim was backed up by Alexis, who claimed that Blake was in bed with her at the time of the fire.

Alexis' sister Cassandra (Caress) tried to blackmail Ben so he had her kidnapped and sent back to a prison in Venezuela. When Emily Fallmont was struck by a car following an argument with her husband Buck and died, Blake discovered a letter she left for him. The letter exposed Ben's lie and confessed that she was the person with Ben on the day his mother died. Blake regained control of Denver Carrington and the mansion after threatening to have Alexis and Ben arrested for perjury and extortion. Alexis gave back the

property and Ben was forced to return the money he had won
Blake insisted that the three of them go to Hong Kong to straighten
things out with the government over the South China Seas leases.

While on their trip, Ben tried to rape Alexis, who had already sen
Adam to Australia to find anything out of Ben's past that she can
use against him. Adam learned that Ben was wanted by casino
bosses for theft and fraud. Ben agreed to free Alexis from the
threatening hold he had over her in exchange for her not turning
him over to the casino bosses. The following day, while the three
of them are on an oil rig in the sea, there is a massive explosion
Ben and Blake are caught under a collapsed ramp. Ben gets free
and then carries Blake to safety. The rig explodes again and they
are separated.

Ben is taken to a hospital in Hong Kong while Blake and Alexis are
sent to Singapore. Ben tries to convince Krystle and Dex that he
doesn't know where Blake or Alexis are. Once they are found
Blake goes back to Hong Kong and invites Ben to come home with
Krystle and him. He returns with them and the two brothers try to
put together a new relationship.

A short time later, Ben receives a surprise visit from his daughter
Leslie is the daughter Ben had while married to Melissa Saunders
He and Melissa had divorced and he lost touch with his daughter
At first, Leslie was furious with him but soon forgave her father
Ben became very protective of Leslie. He objected to her
involvement with Clay Fallmont. Clay's father Buck disapproved
even more and went as far as to accuse Ben of being Clay's father
The news ruined the budding romance between Leslie and Clay
and also ruined the relationship between Ben and his daughter
Ben left Denver after Adam and Dana's wedding.

CASSANDRA "CARESS" MORRELL
Portrayed by Kate O'Mara

Caress is Alexis' little sister. A writer, Cassie spent five years in a Venezuelan prison for murder on Zach Powers' yacht. While in prison she wrote a book about Alexis, which she titled; "Sister Dearest: The True Story of Alexis Morrell Carrington Colby as told by her sister Caress." Caress was convinced that Zach and Alexis had conspired to send her to prison for the murder of Zach's wife so they could be together.

Released from jail early for good behavior, Caress had already contracted her book with an American publishing house. Going to Denver, she confronted her sister and then moved into Alexis' apartment while Alexis was in Australia. She blackmailed Ben and Alexis with the knowledge that Ben was with Emily Fallmont when Ellen Carrington died. Ben had her kidnapped and sent back to prison. She managed to get a letter to Blake, who sent Dex and Clay to break her out and bring her back to Denver.

Caress decided she couldn't live on the money Alexis was paying her for the column she wrote for The Denver Mirror newspaper. She proceeded to blackmail Emily Fallmont. Emily beat Caress to the punch and told her husband Buck the truth about her affair with Ben. Blake paid Caress the money she was asking Emily for and told her to leave town. Before she left, Ben also tried to have her killed. Caress left Denver but not before warning Alexis to be careful and never to turn her back on Ben.

CLAYBURN "CLAY" FALLMONT
Portrayed by Ted McGinley

Clay Fallmont is the son of Senator Buck Fallmont and his wife Emily. Clay is a daredevil explosives expert who gets a job working with Dexter International. The Fallmonts and the Carringtons have been rivals for years and Buck has no intention of letting go of his grudge against Blake. While attending a party celebrating the pipeline deal, Clay meets Sammy Jo. They are instantly attracted to each other.

Sammy Jo and Clay begin dating and Sammy Jo threatens Steven with another lawsuit for custody of Danny. Clay wanted to remain footloose but Sammy Jo had something else in mind. She told Clay that she's pregnant and after quite a bit of pressure, he proposed. The two eloped to Las Vegas on the same night that his mother was struck by a car and died. They heard the news of Emily's death the next morning on the radio.

When they went back to Denver and told Buck of their marriage, he accused Clay of betraying the family. Mourning his mother's death made Clay appreciate the fact that Sammy Jo was going to give him a child. He was incredibly disappointed when he discovered that Sammy Jo wasn't pregnant and that she had withheld the information from him. After blowing up at Sammy Jo, Clay brutes for a while and then asked her to take him back. Sammy Jo refused and had their marriage annulled.

Clay then became involved Ben's daughter Leslie. Although completely opposed by both Ben and Buck, Leslie and Clay ignore their fathers and begin sleeping together. As things start getting serious, Buck tells Blake that he has to step in and stop the affair. Buck swears that Ben is Clay's father, thus making Clay and Leslie brother and sister. Both men take blood tests to determine paternity. The tests come back inconclusive so Clay decides to leave town in order to avoid his feelings for Leslie.

DANA BETHANY WARING CARRINGTON
Portrayed by Leann Hunley

Dana Waring was born and raised in Billings, Montana and grew up worshipping a young man named Michael Torrance. While they were in high school Dana and Michael both attended a party after which a very drunk Michael seduced Dana. Michael had no clue of anything happening and Dana thought he would think she was lying if she told him about the evening. She became pregnant that night and instead of telling Michael the truth, she had an abortion.

Several years later, Dana Waring became a secretary at Denver Carrington. When Ben fired her, Adam made sure that she remained in her position. He took her to lunch and as he was leaving Dana read an old newspaper clipping. It talked about how Michael Torrance was in fact Adam Carrington.

Adam originally only wanted Dana for the sake of obtaining the contents of Blake's personal files. As time went on Dana and Adam grew closer. Within months they announced their engagement and married a short time later.

During their honeymoon in Hawaii Adam began pressuring Dana to start a family immediately. Dana was reluctant to discuss the idea and tried to put Adam off each time he brought the topic up. After they returned to Denver she went to the doctor. The news she had gotten years earlier was confirmed once again, complications from the abortion made it impossible for her to have a child. Adam was crushed so Dana began searching for any way to make his dream a reality.

She thought she found it when she watched a television show that talked about surrogates who carry babies for others who can't have their own. Adam and Dana met with an attorney who introduced them to his choice for a surrogate; Karen Atkinson. Karen was a divorced woman who needed the extra money to care for her two daughters.

Karen became pregnant almost immediately and despite the attention Adam was lavishing on her, Dana felt threatened by Karen carrying Adam's child. Karen tried her best to reassure Dana but nothing seemed to work. The situation became even more complicated when Karen's husband Jesse showed up claiming they were never divorced. He also begged her to take him back, which she did. No one knew that Alexis' new husband Sean had hired him to show up.

As Adam did battle with Jesse to get him out of Karen's life, Dana became increasingly nervous. Karen went into labor and delivered a healthy baby boy. Adam and Dana prepared to bring their son home when Karen changed her mind and refused to give the baby up. Adam immediately filed suit for custody and although she desperately wanted the baby, she couldn't take him away from his mother. Dana asked the judge to award custody to Karen. Adam was livid but that anger soon turned to hurt after Dana told him about their deceased baby and how it was conceived.

When the judge did award custody to Karen and Jesse, Adam went off the deep end and blamed Dana for the loss of his son. Dana knew their marriage was over and would never be able to be saved so after letting him make love to her for the last time, she packed her bags and permanently left the Carrington family.

CECIL BALDWIN COLBY
Portrayed by Lloyd Bochner

At one time Cecil and Blake were the best of friends. They had always been business rivals but took pride in the fact that they were able to separate their business dealing and personal feelings. In 1954, Cecil Colby was dating a woman but became enamored by a stunningly beautiful English girl. At her 17th birthday party, and at his girlfriend's insistence, Cecil invited Blake to join them. Before the night was over, Cecil had lost every chance he may have had with the young woman. A few weeks later he served as Best Man at Blake's wedding to Alexis.

Following Adam's tragic kidnapping, Blake poured himself into Denver Carrington and basically ignored his devastated young wife. Cecil was there to lend a shoulder for her to cry on and the two had a brief affair. Alexis felt tremendous guilt and tried to become the saintly wife Blake wanted. Cecil, on the other hand, wanted Alexis even more. His fantasy would have to wait an additional sixteen years before Alexis came back into his life. In the meantime, he built Colbyco into a giant conglomerate and raised his nephew Jeffrey.

Blake owed Cecil nine million dollars and didn't have it so Cecil (being the kind friend he was) negotiated a deal with Fallon. He would give Blake an extension on the loan if she agreed to marry Jeff. Fallon agreed and Cecil delighted in seeing his nephew happy. Blake is less than thrilled about it when his chauffeur Michael tells him what Cecil had done. That and several other business dealings over the years put yet another wedge into their friendship.

A few days after Alexis testified against Blake in his murder trial,

Cecil returned from a business trip. She requested Cecil come to her studio to discuss Steven. When Cecil refused to help her with Steven, Alexis dropped the bombshell that Fallon is his daughter. He was floored especially when he remembered that he and Fallon had almost ended up in bed one night. When Alexis threatened to tell Blake, Cecil called her bluff but gave in and agreed to talk to Steven as a favor to her.

Cecil took advantage of Claudia Blaisdel's fragile sanity after her husband Matthew took her daughter Lindsay and left. He convinced her to spy at Denver Carrington in exchange for information about her loved ones. When word came in that Matthew and Lindsay were dead, Jeff found out about his uncle's treachery and banished him from his life.

Cecil was furious because of the influence Blake had over Jeff and put together a diabolical plan to bring Blake to his knees. Cecil's first item on his list of things to do was to propose to Alexis. She had been verbally assaulted by Blake one too many times and was tempted by the Colby fortune. She agreed to marry him.

Next on the list was to purchase a tremendous amount of Denver Carrington stock. He assumes a fake identity and conducts business under the name Logan Rhinewood. When it appears Blake may stand a chance of remaining on his feet, he arranges for a meeting in Las Vegas. Blake threatens to destroy Rhinewood, not having a clue that he's being videotaped. Unfortunately for Cecil, before he has a chance to enjoy the fruits of his labor, he suffers a massive heart attack while in bed with Alexis.

Although in critical condition, he married Alexis anyway. Immediately following the ceremony Cecil began drilling Alexis about what she and Blake had talked about on their wedding night. Alexis tried to avoid the questions but he kept pushing until he upset himself. That upset proved to be more than his heart could handle. He had another heart attack and died. During the reading of his will Colbyco and all of his holdings was split between Jeff and Alexis. Cecil got the last laugh from the grave. Blake was furious when Cecil was revealed as Logan Rhinewood and made his final wish that Alexis bring Blake to his knees.

MATTHEW BLAISDEL
Portrayed by Bo Hopkins

In 1967, nineteen-year-old Matthew Blaisdel met a sixteen-year-old girl named Claudia. They had a secret romance that was made complicated by Claudia becoming pregnant. Matthew married Claudia two days after he was informed of her pregnancy. Trying to supply his wife and daughter with a good life, Matthew worked his way through the Colorado School of Mines. In 1978 Claudia had a nervous breakdown that required her to be committed, leaving him to care for their ten-year-old daughter.

Matthew became a geologist and started working for Blake Carrington. Continuously lonely and missing the feel of a woman, Matthew fell in love with a secretary who also worked for Blake. Her name was Krystle Grant Jennings and she was everything he had ever dreamed of. The two had a passionate affair but Matthew felt compelled to remain married to Claudia while she was ill.

Matthew and Blake parted ways and he teamed up with wildcatter Walter Lankershim. The two were nearly ruined when an explosion ripped through their oil rig but they recovered when another rig came in. Matthew also befriended Blake's homosexual son Steven. When Claudia was released from the sanitarium she vowed to be a good wife to Matthew. He ended his relationship with Krystle and she married Blake Carrington.

Matthew was furious when he heard Claudia disclose the details of her affair with Steven during Blake's murder trial. He took their daughter and left Denver. Supposedly dying along with Lindsay in an auto accident in the Peruvian jungle, Matthew pulled a fast one.

Seven years after his supposed death, Matthew and a group of followers ambushed the Carrington mansion after Adam and Dana's wedding. Matthew said he had come back to get the only love of his life; Krystle. He held the family hostage for two days before Blake and the police tracked him down to the site of Lankershim-Blaisdel One (the oil rig that came in). He released the family but kept Krystle in the small cottage so Blake ran in to save his wife. When an explosives salesman told the police that he had sold Matthew explosives, Steven rushed back into the cottage and without realizing what he was doing, stabbed Matthew to death.

CLAUDIA MARY (BARROWS/JOHNSON) BLAISDEL CARRINGTON
Portrayed by Pamela Bellwood

Claudia was sixteen when she met Matthew Blaisdel and became pregnant. Her daughter was born in 1968 and the three began life as a happy family. Ten years later, Claudia suffered a complete mental breakdown that required her to be institutionalized for two years. Upon her release, Matthew stood by her despite his love for another woman.

It was while Matthew and Walter Lankershim were working as wildcatters that Claudia met Steven Carrington. Matthew felt sorry for Steven because he was being ostracized for being gay, so he invited Steven home to dinner. Claudia found him to be sweet and charming. They became quick friends and the friendship soon turned into a loving affair. She was forced to disclose the affair during the Ted Dinard trial and was horrified when Matthew entered the courtroom and listened to her confess to sleeping with his friend.

While trying to avoid him after her confession, Claudia took Lindsay and tried to leave Denver. Emotionally unstable, Claudia lost control of her car and had a serious accident. Claudia was hospitalized with a concussion and other injuries. Lindsay was uninjured and released to her father. Still furious over Claudia's affair, Matthew packed up his daughter and left Denver for good.

When Claudia was faced with live alone she attempted suicide. Blake hired Nicholas Toscanni to care for Claudia and moved her into the Carrington mansion. Blake also gave her a job at Denver Carrington to help her get her mind off of her problems. It was while she was working at Denver Carrington that Cecil Colby bribed her with information about Matthew and Lindsay in exchange for spying on Blake's business dealings. When news came that Matthew and Lindsay were presumed dead after an accident in Peru as well as learning about Matthew's affair with Krystle, Claudia shot herself in the head.

Claudia survived the shooting but once again fell into a state of insanity. She was one of the suspects when Little Blake was kidnapped after being seen with what appeared to be a baby. The police, Carringtons and Colbys confronted her on a roof causing her to drop the "baby", which turned out to be a porcelain doll. Claudia is taken into custody and sent back to High Grove Sanitarium.

A year later, Claudia was doing much better and was released. Steven was the first person to welcome her back to the "real" world and the two ended up in bed together. When Blake sued Steven for custody of his son, Claudia had quite a few run-ins with Sammy Jo. Finally having had enough, Claudia suggests a plan to Steven that works perfectly; they took Danny, flew to Reno and got married. The judge dismissed Blake's suit the following day and Claudia returned to the mansion as Mrs. Steven Carrington.

Life was going beautifully for Steven and Claudia until flowers began mysteriously arriving with a note attached reading "Remember... Lancelot." Claudia was spooked because that was her nickname for Matthew. Phone calls also began coming in. It was always Matthew's voice and seemed to be a loop. She discovered that Matthew's mother had sold the tape to Morgan Hess, who had been hired to torture Claudia by Sammy Jo.

When Steven began to show interest in Luke Fuller, Claudia had an affair. Steven refused to forgive her for her indiscretion. They separated and eventually divorced. Being the "concerned" brother-in-law that he is, Adam gives her the attention that Steven no longer does. They wind up becoming involved and despite Blake's objections, get married in San Francisco. Adam and his new wife remain in the Carrington mansion, making life at home very strained until they too split.

Claudia eventually learns how calculating Adam is when she discovers paperwork proving he tricked his ill father into giving him power of attorney over Denver Carrington. She blackmails her estranged husband into giving her back Lankershim-Blaisdel One by threatening to go to Blake with what she knows. Adam signed the worthless well back over to her. Claudia goes on a massive shopping spree before discovering that the well is totally worthless. Distraught over the way her life has turned out, she lights candles in a suite at La Mirage. One of the candles fell out of its holder and lit the draperies on fire. Claudia was trapped inside the burning inferno and died.

DR. NICHOLAS "NICK" TOSCANNI
Portrayed by James Farentino

Nicholas Toscanni used to be a highly sought-after neurosurgeon that began practicing psychiatry after one of his patients died during surgery. He felt the death was his fault and then refused to perform any others. Nick was brought in to treat Claudia after her two suicide attempts and at the same time, he treated Krystle for depression after her miscarriage.

Nick came to Denver bent on seeking revenge for his brother's suicide. He feels Blake is responsible because his brother was fired for drug use while working for Denver Carrington. As a way of getting back at him, Nick seduces Krystle. He nearly succeeds and would if Blake hadn't been blinded and begged her to come home. Nick does succeed with Fallon, until she gives birth to Little Blake and decides to give her marriage to Jeff one more chance.

Nick's final attempt at revenge was arranging the kidnapping of Little Blake. Nick paid Alfred Grimes to take the baby from the Carrington mansion. Alfred was the father of Alexis' former lover Roger Grimes. Jeff and Blake tracked Grimes down and recovered the baby. Nick was never seen or heard from again.

SAMUEL "MARK" HOWARD JENNINGS
Portrayed by Geoffrey Scott

Mark Jennings was a player on the pro tennis circuit until an injury sidelined his promising career. While touring on the circuit he was married to Krystle Grant but they split because of the amount of time he spent on the road. Krystle packed up and moved to Denver. Wanting a way to drive Krystle out of Blake's life, Alexis tracked Mark down and convinced him to come to Denver under the pretense that Krystle was in trouble and needed him.

Mark thought it over and arrived in Denver. When he got there he checked into La Mirage and applied for the job as the tennis pro. Fallon hired him after finding out that he's Krystle's ex-husband. When he saw Krystle he knew that he had been used and she had no clue of his existence in Denver. Mark had important news for Krystle. He never filed for divorce in Mexico and their marriage is still valid. Krystle was devastated as she told Blake that she was still married to Mark.

Following their quick divorce, Mark turned back into a playboy. He seduced Fallon at the same time as he was sleeping with Alexis. Alexis tricked him into a compromising situation and arranged for Fallon to see them together as a way to break them up. It worked.

When Steven's cabin was lit on fire with Alexis and Krystle inside, Mark had gone to the cabin to talk to Krystle and ended up pulling the two injured women out of the burning building. Alexis showed her gratitude by telling the police that Mark had motive to kill her so he was arrested. He was released and the charges dropped when Joseph confessed to setting the fire in a letter. Alexis was still afraid for her safety and hired Mark to be her personal bodyguard.

Mark moved into Alexis' penthouse and turned it into a party place whenever she wasn't around. Mark was also privy to Alexis' business dealings and was convinced to spy on her for Congressman Neal McVane. One of the items he had knowledge of was the trip to Hong Kong in which Alexis paid Rashid Ahmed five million dollars to ruin Blake's deal with the Chinese government over the South China Sea leases. He blackmailed Alexis with the information and was given a check for $100,000.00 to keep quiet.

With his money in the bank, Mark decided he was leaving Denver and went to Krystle to say goodbye. He made a cryptic comment about being on top of the world but knowing someone who wanted to knock him off of that world. Later that evening, Neal McVane broke into the penthouse, dressed up as Alexis and pushed a drunken Mark Jennings over the balcony to his death.

DANIEL REECE
Portrayed by Rock Hudson

Daniel Reece is many things. He's a multi-millionaire, a horse breeder, a mercenary, and Sammy Jo's biological father. Daniel had a fling with Krystle's sister Iris but Daniel wasn't in love with her and left Ohio. After moving to Denver and setting up house at Delta Rho, Daniel was considering donating a wing to Cheney Hospital. It was there that he saw a woman from his past; Krystle. She was there visiting her newborn daughter. Daniel immediately wanted more information about her and as a Christmas gift, sent a photo of the two of them in a very expensive frame. Krystle angrily went to confront Daniel as well as return the gift but she realized he had no idea of anything she was talking about. When one of his horses was having trouble giving birth, Daniel allowed Krystle to lend a hand. He then encouraged her to start her own business, a business that Blake wholeheartedly disapproved of.

Daniel and Dex were old friends, at least as mercenaries anyway. He approached Dex with a mission that he immediately turned down but after a fight with Alexis decided to go on after all. Daniel hadn't returned from their mission and Dex went back to save him. He did so and the two swore that was their last mission as partners.

Blake was increasingly jealous of Krystle's infatuation with Daniel so he confronted him while Daniel was flying across country. The pilot passed out and the plane fell from the sky, crashing in the mountains, trapping the three men in a blizzard. Dex, Steven and Jeff searched for them and eventually found all three. Krystle knew at that moment that Daniel had to know the truth. Krystle broke her promise to her sister and told Daniel the truth about his daughter.

Daniel and Krystle immediately flew to New York. When they arrived at Sammy Jo's apartment they were stunned to see a woman who looked exactly like Krystle leaving. Waiting inside the apartment they saw the type of sexy modeling Sammy Jo had been doing. Sammy Jo arrived and made several rude comments to Krystle. Daniel grabbed her and forced her into a chair. After he told her that she would treat her aunt with respect he introduced himself to a very surprised Sammy Jo.

The following day, Daniel and Sammy Jo had lunch together and made an attempt to get to know each other. It wasn't long before another mission came up and Daniel asked Krystle to keep an eye on his daughter. Several days later a newspaper had the story on the front page; Daniel Reece was dead. When his will was read it was revealed that he would leave everything to his newfound daughter but with one condition; Krystle would control the entire estate.

LADY ASHLEY MITCHELL
Portrayed by Ali MacGraw

Lady Ashley Mitchell is a photographer who would like nothing more than to seduce Blake Carrington. The widow of Lord Maynard Mitchell, Ashley has traveled in the best social circles for decades. She met both Dominique Devereaux and Alexis Carrington in Europe and became friends with both. Following her husband's death, Ashley returned her attention to her photography career and set out to do a feature for World Finance Magazine. Her subject would be the infamous oil tycoon Blake Carrington and his deal of the century.

The two would meet for the first time in Paris. Ashley was immediately taken with Blake's dazzling looks and charm. She proved to be a valuable asset when she turned up in Acapulco to assist Blake in securing his leases from the Chinese officials. Blake showed his appreciation with dinner and a dance. Ashley took that as a sign to try to become more involved with him. She convinced Blake to allow her to photograph him in Denver at the office and at home. Her ardent attention to Blake didn't go over very well with Krystle. It wasn't long after the photo shoots that photographs began arriving for both Blake and Krystle. The ones going to Blake were of Krystle with Daniel and those coming to Krystle were of Blake and Ashley.

Alexis and Dominique both warned Krystle about Ashley's thirst for men but Krystle could never prove that Ashley was sending her the photos. When Dominique was rushed into emergency open heart surgery, Ashley tried to warm up to Blake and comfort him in his hour of need. Finally having seen through her act, Blake told her that he appreciated her friendship but that there would never be more than that.

Ashley then turned her attention to the younger crowd and became involved with Jeff. Although she put up a struggle in the beginning days of the relationship, she soon allowed herself to be seduced by the young Colby heir. She showed him photos that she had taken over the years and one in particular caught his attention. Taken in Los Angeles the year before was a photo with a woman who was an identical match to Fallon. Not wanting to allow himself to become caught up in memories and false hope again, Jeff proposed to Ashley. She resisted giving him an answer and unfortunately never could. While shooting the photographs of Amanda's wedding, Ashley was shot several times and died. Her body was removed before Jeff could say goodbye and flown back to England for burial next to Lord Mitchell.

JOEL ABRIGORE
Portrayed by George Hamilton

Rita Lesley was an actress Sammy Jo met in a New York bar. She was trying to avoid her producer boyfriend who had given her a black eye. Sammy Jo offered to let her stay with her if she would agree to help her with a plot to get even with Krystle. Rita looked quite a bit like Mrs. Carrington and Sammy Jo was anxious to lash out at her aunt.

Enter Joel Abrigore, Rita's half-sane/half-evil producer boyfriend. Joel listened to what Sammy Jo had in mind and they devised a plan to have Rita impersonate Krystle as a way to gain access to Sammy Jo's money. After plastic surgery is completed on Rita, the three make their way to Denver. Sammy Jo pretends to want a copy of Krystle's dress for a charity ball and Krystle unwittingly shows up at Delta Rho while Rita is there. Joel knocks Krystle unconscious and Rita is forced to go to the Carrington mansion as Krystle.

Rita begins faking headaches and starting arguments to keep from having to get close to Blake. Joel, on the other hand, is doing everything he can to get close to Krystle. When Rita tells Joel about Blake's advances, he encourages her to go ahead and sleep with him but to drug him at the same time. He gives her heart medication that slowly makes him ill. Rita stands at the bottom of the staircase and watches Blake collapse. Sammy Jo finds the vial of medication and tells Steven that his father is going to die. The two of them arrive at the mansion and find Blake not breathing.

At the hospital Blake fights for his life and Rita barely escapes with hers when Alexis arrives and rips her head off. Sammy Jo tells Steven the truth and goes to Delta Rho to let Krystle out of the attic. Rita has also gotten there and she and Krystle fight until Rita is knocked out. Krystle changes clothes and sneaks downstairs with Sammy Jo but is caught by Joel. She convinces him that she's Rita and leaves. After Sammy Jo confesses and Blake recovers, Rita and Joel flee Denver for South America.

LESLIE SAUNDERS CARRINGTON
Portrayed by Terri Garber

Leslie is the daughter of Ben Carrington and his wife Melissa Saunders. Leslie's mother had died and she decided that she wanted to confront her father for leaving them so many years before. She went to Australia to search for him but instead ran into Adam. When she went to Denver she met with Adam again and questioned him about her father. She also ran into two people she knew; Dex and Michael Culhane. She had been treated rather badly in the past by Michael and decided to get a little revenge by seducing Michael and then stealing his clothing.

After a few days Leslie worked up enough courage to confront her father. Ben is stunned to see her and is upset to hear of Melissa's death. He tries to apologize for leaving but Leslie doesn't want to listen to anything he has to say. Blake visits her at The Carlton Hotel and tells her to give her father a chance. She agrees to have dinner at the mansion and the two grow closer after Krystina is hospitalized with congestive heart failure.

After convincing Dex to give her a job at the pipeline site, Leslie and Clay Fallmont begin seeing each other. They become serious but the relationship doesn't last long. His father Buck Fallmont lies to Blake and convinces him that Ben is Clay's father. When Leslie hears the news and confronts her father with the news he is forced to admit to the affair with Emily Fallmont. When the paternity tests come back Clay says they're inconclusive and breaks off their relationship completely. Ben also leaves Denver immediately following Adam and Dana's wedding because he doesn't want to hurt his daughter any more than he already has.

While the family being held hostage by Matthew and his group, Leslie tries to seduce one of the men in an attempt to allow Dex to escape. Dex is shot in the process and Leslie is roughed up a little. When the situation is over, she spends quite a bit of time at the hospital with Dex. She helps him when he gets home and ends up in bed with him on more than one occasion. When they split up, Leslie goes to work for Alexis.

Alexis makes Leslie her personal assistant and Leslie makes herself an Alexis clone. She emulates every move all the way down to her fashion sense and taste for men. Leslie's first prey is Jeff. He and Fallon are having problems and she offers him a shoulder to cry on. They end up spending the night together in New York after Leslie insisted on flying out with him. After Fallon found out about the affair, she filed for divorce. Jeff told Leslie that he didn't love her and that their one-night stand was exactly that.

Leslie's next conquest was Alexis' new husband Sean Rowan. Sean decided he wanted Leslie and she was overly ambitious so he promoted her into an executive position in exchange for sexual favors. When Leslie started asking questions about Sean's business dealings and past he threatened to kill her. She confessed the affair and threats to Dex shortly after Alexis was shot. Alexis fired her and called her more than one unsavory name not limited to "company whore".

When Sean returned to Denver after the explosion in which he supposedly died, he kidnapped Leslie. They went to his cabin in the woods where he had stashed Adam's son. Leslie managed to call the Carrington mansion and tell Steven where she was. Sean stopped the conversation and proceeded to beat her before leaving with Adam's son. Adam and Steven called for an ambulance and went after Sean. Leslie was never heard from again.

MICHAEL CULHANE
Portrayed by Wayne Northrup

Michael Culhane started out as Blake Carrington's chauffeur. Quite the ladies man, Michael seduced Cecil Colby's secretary to gain information for Blake and seduced Fallon for his own personal fun. When Fallon agreed to marry Jeff, Michael was less than pleased and managed to get the truth from Jennifer (Cecil's secretary) that the marriage was an arrangement. Michael ran straight to Blake with the information. Blake was furious with Fallon but grateful to Michael for telling him. That gratitude turned to anger when Blake found out about Michael's  affair with Fallon. He accused Michael of using his daughter for financial gain and fired him immediately.

Fast forward five years. Michael Culhane is now a multi-millionaire (courtesy of a shady property deal) and works with Zach Powers. Zach isn't terribly thrilled with Blake's new deal with Jason Colby and feels he should be part of it. Michael wants to get back at Blake for humiliating him so many years before and he's come up with the perfect way to do it.

When La Mirage burns to the ground, Michael saves Amanda by carrying her out of the burning structure. Blake is grateful and Amanda convinces him to give Michael his job back. Blake reluctantly agrees but also warns him about using Amanda the way he did Fallon. Michael takes his job back and plots with Zach to purchase half of Blake's new crater project. Zach pretends to be the front man when in actuality Michael's money being used for the deal.

Michael also goes after Alexis to create a business partnership. Alexis agrees to go in on a deal and then decides to also cut him out of her other ones. Michael isn't happy with her and warns her not to think about double-crossing him. The final piece of his plan comes together when Amanda agrees to move in with him. The relationship infuriates Blake and Alexis both but Amanda tells both of them to stay out of her personal life. When Amanda learns the truth about Michael's plan, she leaves two notes and heads back to London for good. Michael tries to pick up his business dealings with Alexis and she too cuts him off at the knees. Blake discovers Michael's involvement in the crater and immediately shuts it down. Michael is hit with a huge financial loss and leaves Denver.

PETER DE VILBIS
Portrayed by Helmut Berger

If you open a dictionary and look up the word playboy, a picture of Peter DeVilbis is probably sitting next to the definition. Spending most of his time in South America, Peter went to Los Angeles to watch his race horse Allegree run at Santa Anita. While there, he meets Blake, Krystle and Fallon. Immediately sensing Blake's bank account Peter decides to make a move on Fallon. She was very vulnerable from her divorce from Jeff and ruined relationship with Mark. Peter tried to play himself off as fabulously wealthy but is looking for a partner in his racehorse. Fallon suggests Blake be that partner.

Blake is slightly suspicious of why Peter would want a partner but Fallon's enthusiasm is enough to convince him to go ahead, so he purchases the horse as Krystle's wedding present. Peter's problems aren't confined to money. He's heavily into using cocaine and mixes the drugs with alcohol. According to Alexis, he sleeps around with assorted women and even left one of his ladies when she became pregnant and refused an abortion.

Peter arranges for Allegree to be kidnapped and then has a ransom note delivered saying that the horse will be killed if two million dollars in diamonds aren't delivered in Los Angeles. Blake puts up his million and while he's out of town, Peter takes the money and supposedly purchases the diamonds for delivery. A few days later the horse is returned to the Carrington stable safe and sound.

Peter proposes to Fallon in the middle of the lobby of La Mirage. He takes her by complete surprise but she accepts the proposal anyway. Jeff and Alexis constantly warn Fallon not to go through with the marriage. Jeff also discovers that Peter never bought diamonds and that he may have arranged the kidnapping to get Blake's money. When Fallon tries to confront Peter, his attorney Dirk Maurier tells her that Peter's gone and never wants to see her again.

Fallon ran out of the hotel and was hit by a car. While she laid in the hospital unconscious, Blake called the police and headed for the airport. Peter was caught with cocaine in his briefcase and tried to escape when Blake and the police arrived. Blake had the pleasure of slugging Peter in the face a few times before the police broke them up and arrested Peter. Months later, Peter was released and was chasing Fallon in Seattle. His plane went down shortly after take-off and Peter was killed.

PRINCE MICHAEL OF MOLDAVIA
Portrayed by Michael Praed

 Michael is the crown prince of the small European country Moldavia. The son of King Galen, Michael was in Acapulco at the same time Blake, Alexis, Dex and Amanda were. Amanda originally mistook him for a waiter but Blake quickly set her straight. Michael was very attracted to Amanda and the feeling was mutual. While still in Acapulco, Michael and Amanda spent nearly every moment together and ended up in bed. The next morning Michael told her that they would never have a future. He was already engaged to be married.

Alexis, wanting to get Amanda away from Dex, called one of her first loves; King Galen of Moldavia. She arranged a meeting with him where she offered to give Moldavia huge financial gains in exchange for Michael and Amanda's marriage. Michael was told nothing about the arrangement. Alexis told Michael how much Amanda cares for him and wants to see him. Michael flew back to Denver with Alexis and was less than pleased at Amanda's lack of enthusiasm to see him.

He proposed marriage and Amanda accepted but made the condition that the marriage would be in name only. Michael surprised her by accepting her conditions and arrangements for the royal wedding were underway. Amanda and Alexis went to Moldavia much earlier than expected after Amanda was kidnapped. Dex managed to catch the car and rescued Amanda. Upon their arrival in Moldavia, Michael introduced his intended bride to King Galen. Galen in turn presented Michael's original fiancée Elena.

Elena went to Michael and tried to get him to change his mind. When he wouldn't she went to Amanda and told her that Michael is still sleeping with her. Amanda confronts Michael. He immediately denies any wrongdoing but she doesn't want to hear it and calls off the wedding. It isn't until Dex practically beats him up that Amanda changes her mind and says the wedding is back on.

As the ceremony is coming to an end revolutionaries burst into the chapel and opened fire. Michael is hit in the shoulder and King Galen is struck in the chest. Michael is told that his father has died and ascends the throne of his now overthrown country. He moves back to Denver with the Carrington family and takes over running La Mirage. When news comes that his father is still living, Michael and Elena team up to try to overthrow the revolutionaries holding Moldavia hostage.

Alexis and Dex rescue Galen and bring him back to Denver. Michael is pleased his father is living and thanks Alexis and Dex for saving his life. Michael also tells Dex to stay away from Amanda. Amanda resents Michael's possessive behavior and their marriage quickly goes downhill. Galen tells Michael that he is using Alexis. Michael doesn't think highly of his father's plan to regain the throne at Colbyco's expense but reluctantly goes along with it. Alexis throws Galen out and cuts him off when she overhears his plans.

The final straw comes when Amanda winds up in bed with Dex. Michael is heartbroken when he finds out about the affair and takes a few swings at Dex. He tries to appeal to Amanda to end the affair and give their marriage another chance. She refuses and a crushed Michael leaves Denver.

KIRBY ALICIA ANDERS COLBY
Portrayed by Kathleen Beller

Kirby has a case of "upstairs, downstairs" syndrome. She is the daughter of the Carrington's majordomo Joseph Anders and his wife Alicia. Kirby grew up with Fallon, Steven and Jeff and often was included in the children's' parties. Alicia left when Kirby was two and she was raised by her father. Joseph provided his daughter with the best life he could. She attended school at the Sorbonne in Paris and obtained a degree in Humanities.

While living in Paris, she had an affair with a married French Count. Upon her return to Denver, Kirby's childhood crush on Jeff returned in full force. As a way to stay close to him she accepted a job as a nanny for Little Blake.

Adam was attracted to Kirby and even more so when he realized that she wanted Jeff. He offered Kirby a job with Colbyco as a translator and although she didn't take the job on a full time basis, she did agree to translate a few documents for him. As a thank you, he invites her to dinner. She accepts the invitation and comes to dine at Alexis' penthouse. Adam gets aggressive and although she tries to get away from him, he rapes her.

Afraid to be alone with him, Kirby objects to going to a conference with Adam but he swears he'll be on his best behavior. While she's sleeping he stops at a motel and tries to seduce her again. Jeff bursts through the door and rescues Kirby from Adam's clutches. Jeff and Kirby grew closer and made love. A few weeks later Jeff proposed marriage. She immediately accepted and they ran off to Reno to elope. At long last Kirby had achieved her dream of being Mrs. Jeffrey Colby. The fairy tale didn't go as planned.

Within a month of getting married, Kirby discovered she was pregnant. She and Jeff were overjoyed about the news until her obstetrician told her that she was over three months pregnant instead of the month she thought she was. Kirby was horrified to realize that her unborn child was Adam's. She tried to induce a miscarriage by falling off a horse but it didn't work. Her world was turned upside down after Joseph confessed to trying to kill Alexis and Krystle then shot himself to death. Faced with the truth coming out about the baby, Kirby told Jeff about the rape and the fact that the baby isn't his. Jeff beat Adam to a pulp for raping Kirby and told him she was carrying his child.

Adam did a complete about-face and begged Kirby to give him a chance to be a good husband and father. Kirby agreed to marry Adam as soon as her divorce from Jeff was final. Things took another turn for the worse when she developed preclampsia. She paid no attention to the doctor's warnings and ended up being hospitalized with hypertension. Her condition got substantially worse and became life threatening. Doctors delivered a baby girl but the child died shortly after birth.

Distraught over her loss of her child, her marriage and her father, Kirby snapped when Alexis decided she wanted Kirby out of Adam's life. She offered her a job in Paris that Kirby declined to take. As a last-ditch effort Alexis showed Kirby newspaper clippings that proved that her mother was still living and being held in a prison for the criminally insane after she killed her lover in a jealous rage. Kirby realized that Joseph killed himself to keep Alexis quiet and decided to kill her. She confronted Alexis with a gun. Alexis watched as a very shaky Kirby put the gun down and accepted Alexis' offer to go to Paris. She packed up and left without a word to Adam or anyone else.

Years later, Adam and Kirby met again in Switzerland. While she tried to help Adam rescue Jeff, she discovered that she really was in love with Adam. They made peace with each other and when he proposed to her, she willingly accepted.

SEAN ROWAN ANDERS
Portrayed by James Healey

Sean is the up-to-now unknown son of Joseph and Alicia Anders. While Joseph was living and Kirby was in Denver there was never any mention of two other children. Sean came to Denver to avenge his father's suicide and his sister Kirby's humiliation at the hands of the Carrington family. Sean was driving when he looked in his rear view mirror and saw a car plummet off a bridge. He stopped the car and dove into the lake to get the driver out of the car. The driver of the car was Alexis Carrington Colby. Sean took her to the hospital and left without giving anyone his name.

Alexis tracked him down to a cabin in the woods. She walked up behind him while he was chopping wood and thanked him for saving her before he brushed her off. His coolness only served to peak Alexis' desire so she asked Morgan Hess to find out everything he could about Sean Rowan. While attending a party at the mansion, Alexis received a call from Hess telling her exactly where she could find Mr. Rowan.

Sean was watching video clips of Alexis' testimony at the Ted Dinard murder trial at a private screening room. He was surprised when Alexis sashayed through the door complete with a catered dinner. She came on aggressively and was promptly turned down. She offered Sean a room at The Carlton and left. Later that evening he took her up on her offer. The next morning he took her to bed.

His plan moving along beautifully, he moved on to phase two. Taking Alexis to a little island off the Mexican coast, he left her alone in a raging storm. Returning the next morning to a very frightened Alexis, Sean was in the perfect position to propose. Although she had tremendous reservations about the idea, Alexis agreed and they were married that afternoon.

Everyone was stunned when Alexis and Sean returned married. Adam didn't trust Sean at all but didn't let on about it and Dex was rather disappointed that she was no longer available. Sean was put off by Alexis' decision to run for Governor but saw an opportunity for a little more destruction when she asked him to run Colbyco for her.

Wanting to advance in the company, Leslie propositions Sean for a new executive position. He agrees to consider the promotion if Leslie agrees to an affair. She doesn't want to hurt Alexis but Sean is of the attitude that what Alexis doesn't know won't hurt him. Silly boy... Alexis finds the bracelet she gave Leslie under their bed and immediately knows Sean is cheating on her. Alexis devises a little plan of her own and confronts Sean about his infidelity. He denies her accusations and counters with the ludicrous idea that she and Blake had a fling while they were snowed in on a campaign junket. They call a truce but Alexis is determined to teach Sean a lesson.

In the meantime, Denver Carrington and Colbyco have both entered into an oil deal in Natumbe'. Steven is the only one who thinks participating in the deal wasn't a good idea but Dex is also suspicious. Dex begins investigating Vitron and Harry Thresher's connection to Sean. What he discovers is that Sean isn't what he claims to be. Dex tries to warn Alexis but she protects her husband.

Leslie follows Sean one day as he goes to a cemetery. She watches as he stands in front of his father's grave vowing revenge. During their trip to Natumbe' Sean threatens to kill Leslie when she says she's going to tell Alexis his true identity.

When they get back to Denver Leslie tells Dex about his threats and who Sean Rowan really is. Dex went to Alexis, who then went to Blake. Blake and Dex left for Natumbe to get to the bottom of things. Sean found out that they had gone and immediately took a flight to Natumbe. Sean locked Blake and Dex in the hold of a tanker and rigged the tanker with explosives. He berated Blake for the way his father lived but apologized to Dex for having to kill him too. As Sean put it, his only sin was his affiliation with Alexis. Blake and Dex managed to get out of the tanker shortly before it exploded. Port Authority officials found a body in the water with the watch Alexis had given Sean on it so they assumed Sean was dead.

A few weeks later Alexis received a phone call. The caller didn't speak but the breathing was something Alexis recognized immediately. It was Sean. He returned to Denver to wreak havoc on the Carrington clan once more. He had already arranged for Jesse Atkinson to return to ruin Adam's chances of getting custody of his son but then he kidnapped the baby as well. To complete his plan he kidnapped Leslie but when she called Steven and told him where to find Sean and the baby, Sean beat her and ran away.

Adam and Steven caught up with Sean and fought but Sean got away. He went straight to Alexis' suite and shot at her. Dex burst through the door and fought Sean. The gun went off causing the two men to fall to the ground. Alexis was horrified at the site but was relieved when the dead person turned out to be Sean.

BRADY LLOYD
Portrayed by Billy Dee Williams

Record Producer Brady Lloyd was married to entertainer Dominique Devereaux. Heavily involved in his own company, Brady often went weeks without seeing his wife. When she unexpectedly moved to Denver Brady couldn't understand what Dominique could possibly be thinking. He was equally confused and angry when she turned down a headlining engagement in Las Vegas to perform at La Mirage instead.

His wife was up to something but he had no idea what.

Brady was livid when Dominique sold part of her holdings to go into business with Blake Carrington. Since his recording company had been failing, Brady had been taking money from their joint accounts. When he finally demanded that she tell him what she's doing in Denver he's stunned to hear her tell him that she is the illegitimate half-sister of Blake Carrington.

As Dominique's obsession grew, Brady's patience was stretched thin. Finally deciding he could no longer deal with Dominique and her quest to make Blake acknowledge her true identity, Brady filed for divorce and went to Los Angeles.

JOSEPH ARLINGTON ANDERS
Portrayed by Lee Bergere

Starting out as a butler for Blake and Alexis Carrington in 1956, Joseph had an instant dislike for the lady of the house. Alexis had a habit of speaking down to her servants and Joseph was at the top of her list. His wife Alicia had left him for another man in 1960 and Joseph moved his daughter into the Carrington mansion so he could care for her at the same time as his employers. When Alexis was banished from the mansion in 1965 Joseph was ecstatic because he no longer had to put up with her insulting demeanor.

Joseph ingratiated himself to Blake and was rewarded with a permanent position as the Carrington majordomo. It was a role that fit him perfectly. As Kirby grew he tried to give her the best life possible and had told her that her mother was dead. Alicia was actually serving a lifetime sentence in a facility for the criminally insane for killing her lover in a jealous rage. Joseph was extremely proud when Kirby graduated from the Sorbonne with a humanities degree. When Kirby returned to Denver he encouraged her to return to Paris and further her studies. What he didn't want was Kirby to become involved with Jeff Colby.

With Alexis' return to Denver, Joseph took pleasure in reminding her that she is no longer the lady of the house and that there is a new mistress of the manor. Alexis grew tired of Joseph's attitude and threatened to tell Kirby the truth about her "dead" mother. Joseph became distraught at the thought of Kirby learning the truth so he decided he had to stop her.

Krystle and Alexis were meeting at Steven's cabin under the pretense of talking about Danny's upbringing. Joseph followed the women to the cabin and while they were inside he padlocked the door and doused the wooden cabin with gasoline. Tossing a match onto the gasoline Joseph watched as the cabin went up in flames. He escaped when Mark Jennings arrived. When Mark rescued the women Joseph knew he had to try again so he donned a surgical mask and scrubs and tried to suffocate Alexis with a pillow. She woke up in the middle of the attack and he managed to run out of the room unseen by the hospital staff. Finally realizing he would eventually be caught, Joseph left a note for Blake and placed a final phone call to his employer. Blake and Jeff raced to Joseph's old home and walked in just in time to witness Joseph's suicide.

TRACY KENDALL
Portrayed by Deborah Adair

Beautiful, ambitious and with the drive to bring down anyone who gets in her way, Tracy Kendall is a mixture of a man's fantasy and their worst nightmare all in one. Tracy wanted to be an executive at Denver Carrington and didn't think twice about sleeping her way to the top. She almost made it to her goal but Blake Carrington decided to put Krystle in the position instead. Feeling burned by her employer, Tracy put together a plan to make herself indispensable to Blake while kissing up to Krystle at the same time.

Soon Tracy decided that being the head of PR for Denver Carrington wasn't what she wanted after all. She aimed higher and set her sights on none other than Blake Carrington. While Krystle was in the early stages of her pregnancy she was told not to travel so Tracy had to join Blake in Hong Kong. While there she put her plan in motion and made a rather clumsy pass at Blake. He fired her on the spot and told her that he'd be returning to Denver alone.

While still in Hong Kong Tracy ran into Dex in a hotel bar. He had just discovered Alexis with Rashid Ahmed and was feeling pretty bad himself. Tracy took full advantage of Dex's mood and convinced him to spend the night with her. In bed they hatched a plan for Tracy to get a job at Colbyco. She would work for Alexis and report back to Dex. After a few weeks of performing her duties Tracy told Alexis about the plan, quit her job and stormed out of Alexis' office. She was never heard from again.

SARAH CURTIS
Portrayed by Cassie Yates

Sarah Curtis and her husband Boyd were two of Dex's oldest friends. Dex used to joke that Sarah was the one that got away when she married Boyd. Boyd, Sarah and their three-year-old daughter Cathy were involved in a car accident. Hit by a drunk driver, Boyd was killed, Sarah wasn't seriously injured but Cathy had been declared brain dead.

Dex knew that in San Francisco Blake and Alexis were desperately searching for a donor heart for Krystina. Dex called Blake and arranged a meeting with Sarah. After several hours Sarah agreed to allow Cathy to be the donor and they flew to California. The following day Krystina had still not been taken to surgery because Sarah changed her mind. Sarah felt that if Cathy's heart was still beating that she was still alive. Dex finally convinced her to let go of her daughter and let Cathy's heart save Krystina. The transplant was performed and was a success.

Sarah returned to Wyoming where she tried to commit suicide. Krystle found her and brought her back to Denver. Blake wasn't sure having her there would be the best idea but Krystle insisted. Sarah developed an unhealthy attachment to Krystina and went so far as to dress her like her dead daughter. When Blake decided it was time for Sarah to leave, Sarah kidnapped Krystina. She moved into an apartment with Krystina and panicked when Krystina developed a fever and refused to take her medication. Krystle eventually figured out where Sarah had gone and went to get her daughter back.

Sarah lapsed into a catatonic state and was brought out of her silence with the aid of medication. Refusing to believe her daughter was dead she dared Krystle to prove her story. Krystle and a doctor flew Sarah to Wyoming and showed her Cathy's grave. Sarah was committed to a mental institution to receive treatment.

LINDSAY BLAISDEL
Portrayed by Katy Kurtzman

Lindsay was born to 19-year-old Matthew and 16-year-old Claudia Blaisdel. Her life was one filled with trouble from the beginning. She always thought that she was the reasons for her parents' problems. When she was ten her mother suffered a nervous breakdown and was placed in a sanitarium for several years.  While her father was working in the Middle East, Lindsay was left with his mother. Matthew's mother had always felt Claudia ruined her son's life and shared her views with Lindsay.

After Claudia's release from the sanitarium Lindsay and Matthew welcome her home. Everything seems to be going well until Steven Carrington befriends Claudia. Lindsay discovers her mother's budding romance and runs away. She's found and returned home but refuses to talk about why she left. When Claudia is forced to talk about her affair with Steven in court, she tries to take Lindsay away from Matthew. Lindsay and Claudia are in an auto accident and while Claudia is injured, Lindsay is okay and leaves Denver with Matthew. A few months later it was reported that Matthew and Lindsay were killed in a Jeep accident in the jungles of Peru.

WALTER LANKERSHIM
Portrayed by Dale Robertson

Walter Lankershim is a good-hearted man with quite a few loves. Primary among them were women, alcohol and playing the piano. Walter had been a wildcatter for decades and always had the dream that one day a well of his would come in and he would be a millionaire.

In the meantime Walter is desperate for Matthew Blaisdel's help after borrowing money from Blake Carrington and finding himself unable to pay back the loan because none of the wells hit. Worried about taking care of his family, Matthew declines to assist Walter. Shortly before Blake marries Krystle Walter's rig explodes. Blake is immediately made prime suspect number one. A very drunk Walter crashes Blake and Krystle's reception and levels his accusations at Blake. Walter is escorted from the premises and is nearly beaten to death before being rescued by Matthew.

Walter is still trying to recover from his wounds and the shock of his rig explosion. He gets into an argument with his crew and also gets the support of two new people; Matthew and Steven Carrington. Steven is out to prove to Blake that he can make it on his own and Walter is more than happy to let him work on his project. Partially as a joke, Walter took Steven to a bordello and paid for him to have an "experience" with a woman. No one told Walter that all Steven did was talk to the hooker.

Unbeknownst to Walter or Matthew, Blake had a plan to trick them into losing their Lankershim-Blaisdel One rig and both of them fell into the trap. Finding out what Blake had planned, Krystle pawned her jewelry and gave Matthew the money to get out of harms way.

Walter fired Steven when someone sabotaged part of the rigging equipment. Eventually the oil well hit and made Walter and Matthew a small fortune. Four years later Walter died. He left Claudia the deed to Lankershim Blaisdel One but failed to mention that it had been absorbed into Denver Carrington's holdings.

ADDITIONAL SUPPORTING CAST MEMBERS

Ray Abruzzo - Sergeant John Zorelli
Christopher Allport - Jesse Atkinson
Richard Anderson - Senator Buck Fallmont
Kerry Armstrong - Elena, Duchess of Branagh
Lou Beatty, Jr. - Rudy Richards
William Beckley - Gerard
Kevin Bernhardt - Father Tanner McBride
Troy Beyer - Jacqueline "Jackie" Devereaux
Brandon Bluhm - Blake Jeffrey Carrington Colby (1987-1989)
Hank Brandt - Morgan Hess
Janet Brandt - Mrs. Gordon
Paul Burke - Neal McVane
Justin Burnette - Steven Daniel Carrington Jr. (1988-1989)
William Campbell - Luke Fuller
Kevin Conroy - Bart Fallmont
Pat Crowley - Emily Fallmont
Jon Cypher - Dirk Maurier
George DiCenzo - Charles Dalton
Shay Duffin - Joseph the Butler (1981)
Stephanie Dunnam - Karen Atkinson
Joel Fabiani - King Galen of Moldavia
Cheyenne Fitch - Fallon Carrington (as a child)
Grant Goodeve - Chris Deegan
Betty Harford - Hilda Nealsen Gunnerson
Virginia Hawkins - Jeanette Robbins
Jim Ishida - Lin
Paul Kennan - Tony Driscoll
Matthew Lawrence - Steven Daniel Carrington, Jr. (1984-1985)
Richard Lawson - Nick Kimball
Timothy McNutt - Blake Jeffrey Carrington Colby (1984-1985)

Liza Morrow - Virginia Metheny
Ashley Mutrux - Blake Jeffrey Carrington Colby (1985)
J. Eddie Peck - Roger Grimes
Ben Piazza - Charles Hampton
Jessica Player - Krystina Carrington
Peter Mark Richman - Andrew Laird
Jameson Sampley - Steven Daniel Carrington, Jr. (1985-1988)
John Saxon - Rashid Ahmed
Susan Scannell - Nicole "Nikki" Simpson DeVilbis
Tom Schanley - Josh Harris
James Sutorius - Gordon Wales
Kim Terry-Costin - Joanna Clauss Sills
Kenneth Tigar - Fritz Heath

Chapter Three

History In The Making

Casting for *Oil* began in the spring of 1980. The first role to be cast would be Blake Carrington. Blake would need to be both strikingly handsome and sophisticated with the ability to reign over his little kingdom with an iron fist. Although Aaron Spelling had originally asked for his longtime friend John Forsythe, ABC wanted someone younger with "movie-star" appeal. They settled on George Peppard, who had appeared in quite a few movies including *Breakfast at Tiffany's* with Audrey Hepburn.

To play opposite Peppard, Linda Evans was chosen to play his secretary turned wife Krystle. "I hadn't seen Linda since the *Big Valley* days." Aaron fondly remembers. "When Linda came into my office to read for the part, we instantly knew she was Krystle Carrington." Producer Elaine Rich adds, "We were looking for an actress who was beautiful and yet vulnerable, which is exactly what Linda is." "Linda Evans has a look that's good and everything that women want to be and men want to love and she's strong. She was the moral core of the series," says creator Esther Shapiro.

Linda agreed to take the part but with a little trepidation. "When I first accepted the role, I was told that Krystle would go through many changes. I really dislike being unhappy, so the last thing I wanted to do was cry and be depressed at work. I had to decide if I wanted to spend five or ten years going in a direction I was unwilling to follow before. But Krystle was idealistic and believed love would cure all things. That's what drew me to the part."

After casting the two leads producers turned their attention to casting the roles of Blake's two children. Al Corley was cast as Blake's homosexual son Steven. "The only reason I actually took the role was because it was a homosexual character and that was

something new in television and would be a challenge."

The part of Blake's spoiled, indulgent, sharp-tongued daughter Fallon went to Pamela Sue Martin. "I remember that my manager at the time was saying something that this part was going to be very powerful and yet you're going to be playing the exact kind of person you don't like very much."

Character actor Lloyd Bochner was added to the cast as Blake's business rival Cecil Colby and his nephew would be played by John James. "I originally read for the part of Steven," says James. "The casting people seemed pretty impressed with me but not for that role. My agent called one day and said that they were writing in a new character named Jeff Colby and it would be mine. Jeff was intelligent, headstrong and was coming out of his cocoon. He was

raised on silk sheets and was always told that what was right was wrong. He started making his own choices and finally came into his own."

The cast was completed with Bo Hopkins and Pamela Bellwood as oil geologist Matthew Blaisdel and his mentally unstable wife Claudia along with Dale Robertson as Walter Lankershim, Katy Kurtzman as Matthew and Claudia's daughter Lindsay and Lee Bergere as the faithful Carrington majordomo Joseph Anders.

Originally wanting to shoot the series in Denver, producers discovered that it was far too expensive so they set out to find the most magnificently lavish estate in all of California. They found it just outside of San Francisco in a town called Woodside. The 48-room Filoli Mansion had been used in the 1978 movie *Heaven Can Wait* with Warren Beatty.

"I saw the mansion and actually started to cry," says Esther Shapiro. "This was my fantasy coming to life. I became so attached to the rooms that I said we have to shoot this here and we did."

The cast and crew assembled at Filoli in the summer of 1980 to begin production on the pilot for *Oil.* Less than three weeks into the production, producers discovered that they had quite the problem with their star. George Peppard was increasingly difficult and would constantly tell producers what he was and wasn't going to do. He also didn't like the fact that Blake was so heavy-handed with his children and business.

As good an actor as George Peppard was he wasn't working out as the father figure and again insisted to the producers that things were to be done his way. A few days later, Esther and Richard Shapiro joined Aaron Spelling, Douglas Cramer and the ABC brass in a meeting in which they threatened to walk away from the show unless Peppard was let out of his contract. It wasn't long before the meeting had been wrapped and Peppard's fate sealed. He would no longer be Blake Carrington.

Now faced with having no leading man, Aaron Spelling got his wish. "I called my friend John Forsythe, who had been the voice of Charlie for me on *Charlie's Angels* and was also known as Bentley Gregg in the sitcom *Bachelor Father.*"

A past President of the *Screen Actors Guild*, John wasn't exactly thrilled with the prospect of replacing another actor. The studio had to seriously push to sell Forsythe on the role and eventually he agreed to take the part. "Getting John Forsythe was the beginning of everything," says Aaron. "I can't imagine anyone playing Blake Carrington but John." Douglas Cramer agreed saying "John just seemed like the perfect television father."

Although John agreed to play Blake he did place a stipulation on the producers. He would only take the role if they allowed him to make Blake a little softer. This was the same complaint that George Peppard brought up but this time the producers caved in a bit and Blake was made into the family man that millions of people loved.

With John firmly in the fold, the producers, cast and crew returned for another three weeks at the Filoli estate to reshoot the pilot. On January 12, 1981 as a midseason replacement, the series (now named *Dynasty*) premiered to bland reviews. John Forsythe was rather distressed by some of the things said about the show. "One of the terrible things that happened in the beginning of the show was that we were considered a clone of *Dallas* by the critics. We were assailed on every side by people who said "why it's nothing more than a rip-off of *Dallas*." I found that very offensive because we were not trying to do that. We were trying to be something vastly different than *Dallas* ever was."

In the beginning *Dynasty* looked nothing like the series it would become. The first season's storylines surrounded life in the trenches and focused on characters like Krystle's former lover Matthew Blaisdel and Walter Lankershim. The first 13 weeks were extremely hard because the audiences just didn't seem to be taking an interest in the Carrington clan.

ABC and Aaron Spelling took a hint from the audience reaction and realized that they needed to shift gears and become a glossy soap opera about the rich and focus more on the women instead of what oil well was going to come in tomorrow. *Dynasty* needed a villain and not just any villain. This one had to be as devious as J.R. and someone that not only men would want to emulate but women as well.

Eileen and Robert Mason Pollock came to the rescue without the standard villain but instead came up with the ultimate villainess. Originally named Madeline but soon changed to Alexis, the exiled first wife of Blake Carrington was about to create havoc in Denver when she returned to testify for the prosecution as Blake Carrington stood trial for murder. Not having an actress to portray Alexis, the powers that be got one of Esther's friends to simply walk into the courtroom toward the witness stand.

Embarking on a search that for television could have rivaled that for Scarlett O'Hara in *Gone With The Wind*, ABC wasn't enthusiastic about the choices the Shapiro's and Spelling were suggesting and ordered them to find someone along the lines of Elizabeth Taylor's fame. Liz turned the role down as did Sophia Loren and Raquel Welch.

It was Candy Spelling who came up with the brass ring so to speak when she reminded Aaron of an old friend of theirs. Her name: Joan Collins. That suggestion was frowned upon by the studio who referred to Joan as a "washed up B-movie actress" but Aaron showed them a scene from an episode Joan had done of *Fantasy Island*. "She was dressed as Cleopatra." Spelling remembers, "Joan camped up the role so beautifully that I was blown away." Eventually the ABC programming executives agreed and the second season of *Dynasty* opened with Joan Collins as the very glamorous and vengeful Alexis Morrell Carrington.

Douglas Cramer has a theory about the topic of putting people in various roles. "In television," he observes, "there is nothing more important than the casting. It's at least 60 percent of the formula. One strong actor can make a show. *Dynasty* was a bomb during its first season. Only when Joan Collins joined the cast in the second season did the show turn around." John James agreed, "People have asked what made the show successful. I think it's a special blend of cast and crew and it's just a magical thing when it happens."

This point was made more evident to the network through their revenue dollars. In 1981 BC (Before Collins) ABC was getting $80,000 per thirty second commercial. Shortly after Joan joined the show, the network started getting $135,000 per commercial.

The audience immediately fell in love and hate with Alexis. The tabloids began their crusade of publicity with headlines like "Alexis set to dethrone J.R." This turned out to be the popular opinion of most people but Joan always believed that J.R. was infinitely more evil than Alexis. She just had more tact and style. "I don't consider her to be totally bad. Because she's a woman, a lot of people have said that she is an evil, bitchy villainess. If the character were a man people wouldn't have said that. Blake Carrington is a far more ruthless and manipulative person than Alexis. Blake is a murderer, J.R. is a murderer but Alexis is pure as the driven slush. Granted, Alexis had the sharp tongue and she hated Krystle but most women do hate their ex-husband's new wife. As for playing the "bad girl" Lady Macbeth is a lot more fun to play than Juliet. All of the great classic roles that have been written are women who were either neurotic or strong or a little bit wicked or in Alexis' case all three."

When the series writers tried having Alexis seduce Blake at a villa in Rome, John Forsythe had one of several moments when he put his foot down about the thought of Blake being unfaithful to Krystle. It was soon written in that under no circumstances would Blake ever do anything that would hint at adultery even later in the series when he has amnesia, thinks he's still married to Alexis and is supposed to fall into bed with her.

While *Dynasty* etched its way through the second season, Al Corley became very unhappy with the way his character was being portrayed. The television censors were so opposed to any showing of gay relationships that Steven was suddenly married off to Krystle's young niece Sammy Jo (played by newcomer Heather Locklear). Thanks to Alexis,  Sammy Jo left Steven and completely disillusioned, Al Corley antagonized ABC by appearing on talk shows saying, in essence, "*Dynasty's* just a load of crap and only fools watch it." After several heated discussions with the producers and network executives, Steven Carrington was temporarily written out of the show as was Sammy Jo.

Alexis was proving to be living up to the bitchy reputation people had given her. One of the most dastardly deeds she ever went through with was to cause the ever-so-saintly Krystle to lose her unborn child by firing a shotgun in the air while Krystle was taking a gentle ride on a horse. Fans of the series never forgave Alexis for that horrible act but filming the scene was almost as bad as the storyline. On a freezing November morning, Al Corley and Joan Collins were filming a skeet shooting scene. Not terribly familiar with guns, Joan delivered her lines and promptly let off a round of ammunition that ended with the bullet going straight through the surrounding of an arch lamp, which promptly exploded. Nine takes later, having finally made it through the lines with Al, Joan again started to aim the rifle but the butt of the gun got stuck in her scarf and when she inadvertently pulled the trigger, promptly shot herself in the foot.

One of the scenes that really put *Dynasty* ratings through the roof was the one in which Alexis, using every ounce of her feminine wiles, lures her fiancé Cecil Colby, to her boudoir where, in the throws of passionate lovemaking, Cecil suffers a major heart attack. Horrified, Alexis in her usual charming and delightful way starts slapping Cecil across the face in a frenzy shouting "Don't you dare die on me, Cecil! We're getting married tomorrow..."

That scene was considered to be so daring and sexy for network television that many precautions had to be taken to satisfy the ever vigilant censors. Not one but two censors were on the set the day that scene was filmed. One of them insisted on sitting on the side of the bed while the scene was shot to be sure that the satin sheets covered the purple strapless body suit Joan was wearing. Every one of the producers with the exception of Aaron Spelling and Douglas Cramer were also on the set looking very anxious.

Joan Collins shares a wonderfully amusing story about the filming of the scene. "I asked Lloyd Bochner if Cecil was going to die and he said he thought so because his agents were informed that he wouldn't be back next season. As we rolled around in the bed the directors yelled "Cut" because they could see my Lurex suit. After seven takes from a variety of angles, my voice was hoarse from screaming "Don't you dare die on me, Cecil." When it was time for Lloyd's close-up I sat next to our cinematographer Richard Rawlings but was in Lloyd's eyeline and gave him the appropriate noises. Lloyd's only dialogue was an assortment of passionate moans that were to turn to the pain of the heart attack. When the director finally yelled "Cut" he quietly added "Did you come yet, Lloyd?" The crew and censors broke up and Lloyd, being the good sport that he was, did too." The scene turned out to be exactly what Spelling and the network had hoped for and *Dynasty* zoomed to number one the following season.

As a way to garnish higher ratings, *Dynasty* executives put their leading ladies at odds every chance they got. Catfights were the new order of the day and Linda Evans loved them because it gave her the chance to do the stunt work that she learned during Big Valley with Barbara Stanwyck. Joan, on the other hand, took the advice of longtime friend Gene Kelly who told her to use a stunt person whenever the opportunity presented itself.

Since *Dynasty* has long ended, Douglas Cramer has the freedom to engage in a little Hollywood dishing. "Those mud-fights between Alexis and Krystle? Linda Evans and Joan Collins weren't just acting. Their feelings for each other were similar to their characters'.'" Cramer himself came up with the idea of the catfights. "It was one of my greatest creations," he says. "There was so much tension between them in terms of press, clothes, scenes and lines. After one of the fights, things were noticeably easier on the set for weeks, because they were able to relieve the tension." But, Cramer adds, "Once Linda got going, she got going. We were always worried, because Joan was not as strong as Linda. Joan always came out of those black and blue."

In response to questions about the most famous of the fights (commonly known as the lily pond) Linda stated, "I have to admit I enjoyed the mud-fight with Joan in the pond. That was great fun. It was outrageous and something really not done much on television. It shocked people, but we had a lot of laughs doing it." Joan has a bit of a different slant on that story. "At the beginning of the fight Linda was supposed to haul off and pull back her arm as if to sock me in the jaw, but before her fist connected with my face, Irving Moore would yell, 'FREEZE", which she was supposed to do. Then there would be the word "CUT" at which time our doubles would take our places. But on the first take Linda let it rip on me and ever a jock, her fist connected with my chin. 'Freeze my ass!' I fell into the lily pond wondering if my jaw had just been broken. The woman has a right hook like Mike Tyson."

Introducing new characters to suit whatever direction the writers wanted the storylines to go was pretty easy for the *Dynasty* staff. In the beginning of the third season it was revealed that Blake and Alexis had a child that was kidnapped before Fallon and Steven were born. It was a convenient little wrench to throw into an  already bizarre new season. With Fallon's baby stolen by Nick Toscanni (played by James Farentino) and Claudia walking around with a doll thinking that it was her deceased daughter Lindsay, it seemed like the perfect moment for Alexis to beg for her son's return at the same as the family pleaded for Little Blake's safety. Gordon Thomson joined the cast as the well-meaning but diabolical Adam Alexander Carrington.

Lloyd Bochner's prediction about no longer being on the show was brought to reality leaving Alexis a very, very wealthy woman. Along with the arrival of Gordon Thomson, Geoffrey Scott was also signed on to play Mark Jennings. Mark was the first and as in soap opera fashion, the never-divorced and therefore current husband of Krystle Carrington.

Heather Locklear reprised her role as the nymphet Sammy Jo and returned with the child of Blake and Alexis' technically bi-sexual son Steven. A few episodes later the presumed dead Steven is discovered alive but because of an oil rig explosion has had reconstructive plastic surgery and what do you know – there's a new Steven! Jack Coleman was hired to replace Al Corley. Lest we leave out another character brought in at the same time, Kathleen Beller was introduced as Kirby Anders, the daughter of majordomo Joseph, who had her sights set on Jeff and ended up with Adam briefly. Being stuck in a dead-end role, character actor Lee Bergere grew tired with the monotony and opted to leave thus setting up the cliffhanger for the third season in which Krystle and Alexis are left to die in a cabin fire set by Joseph who then commits suicide to satisfy Alexis' need for hatred.

1983 proved to be a year that several cast members will never forget. John Forsythe flipped his wig when he discovered that 50-year-old Joan Collins would be gracing the cover of Playboy Magazine's December issue. Telling the producers that Joan's layout was "a disgrace to our fine show" and that they should never allow her to "bring down the reputation of this series", he was adamant that it would be nothing but dirty filth. That issue is to date the highest selling single copy of Playboy ever published and the world embraced Joan for showing that life didn't end at 40.

The 1983-1984 Season started looking up as producers decided that Fallon and Alexis needed new mates. Helmut Berger had been brought in to play a new love interest for Fallon named Peter DeVilbis. Helmut made no secret of his love for nightclubs and unfortunately for him, his clubbing affected his performance and he was continuously having trouble learning his lines. So much so that an additional character (Dirk Maurier) had to be written in so Helmut's lines could be cut back to a minimum. Needless to say, his departure from the series was imminent.

The casting call to play opposite Joan brought out hundreds of willing men including the late Jon-Erik Hexum (who was engaged to Emma Samms and appeared in *The Making of a Male Model* with Joan). After weeks of auditions, Michael Nader joined the cast as Farnsworth "Dex" Dexter. He and Joan

Collins hit it off immediately and the audiences loved every minute they were together. "Michael was sexy, fun and a terrific kisser," said Joan in several interviews. Michael remembers, "There was one scene where Dex gave Alexis a passionate kiss and I really planted a ferocious one on Joan. It was a great kiss but I hurt her bottom lip and she walked around with an ice pack for the rest of the day." Laughingly, he adds, "You know, sometimes I really miss those bubble baths..."

One departure that no one saw coming was that of Pamela Sue Martin. Pamela had grown tired of playing the spoiled little rich girl and found that the notoriety of being on the number one television series in the world wasn't where she wanted to be anymore. Asking the producers to let her out of her contract, Aaron Spelling obliged and Fallon mysteriously disappeared shortly before she and Jeff were to be remarried.

During the same season Geoffrey Scott had outlived his usefulness. He had always had trouble delivering his lines and had consistently held up shooting so Mark Jennings was tossed off of Alexis' balcony by a former congressman bent on revenge and the season finale featured Alexis clad in a scarlet red dress being tossed behind bars for murder.

Moving into Season Five, the writers decided that Blake was a bit more fertile than he was aware. Krystle became pregnant and later delivered daughter Krystina and at the same time Alexis had mysteriously given birth to a 20-year-old daughter whom Blake knew absolutely nothing about. Needless to say, Amanda (Catherine Oxenberg) turned out to be Blake's child too so now he had a replacement for Fallon, at least temporarily.

Cashing in on the huge success of the series, *Dynasty* producers pulled out all the stops and hired not one but five huge names to be on the show. Out of the five, only one survived for more than one season.

Diahann Carroll was known to the world as a singer, stage performer and as the first African-American woman to star in a television series (*Julia*). "In 1983 while watching an episode of *Dynasty*, I thought 'that's where I want to be and that's where I'm going to be.'" On a fateful night in early 1984 she had arranged to sing at a party being hosted by Aaron Spelling. As the two began

talking about miscellaneous items Diahann made the comment, "So when are you going to introduce the first black bitch to television?" The answer was the end of the 1983-1984 Season and Diahann would play Blake Carrington's illegitimate half-sister Dominique Devereaux. Diahann relished in her new character's personality. "Dominique was strong, demanding and giving as good as she gets."

Dominique would hang on for three seasons, which is far more than could be said for the other four actors. Billy Dee Williams was hired to play Dominique's husband Brady Lloyd. He appeared in just a handful of episodes before being written out.

Love Story heroine Ali MacGraw and screen legend Rock Hudson were brought in to cause havoc in Blake and Krystle's fairy tale existence. Ali was to play Lady Ashley Mitchell a love interest for Blake as Rock was to play Daniel Reece, a mystery man with past ties to Krystle. As he stated early in the series, John Forsythe flatly refused to allow Blake to pursue a relationship with anyone but Krystle so that idea went out the window.

Daniel Reece on the other hand, did make a play for Krystle and turned out to be Sammy Jo's real father. When Rock was hired for eight episodes, no one had seen him in several months. When he arrived on the set the cast and crew members were stunned to discover that his stunning good looks were virtually gone. He seemed exhausted, gaunt and hollow-eyed. He chained-smoked  through his make-over each day and some of the crew members began speculating that he had AIDS but no one had any type of confirmation. Aaron Spelling recalls, "Rock was a great name for us, and we thought having him on *Dynasty* would be good for the ratings and make for truly good publicity. None of us ever imagined that this would be his final role or that he would be dead shortly after his episodes aired." During the course of the shooting of his final scenes, Rock (who was suffering from the disease) faced one of his most agonizing moments: he had to kiss Linda Evans. Not wanting to have to admit to the producers, actors or world that he has the deadly AIDS virus, Rock set out to do what the script called for but when the kiss took place he placed his mouth close enough to hers to make it appear that they had actually kissed but didn't perform a "full stage kiss". He had done so through three different takes because he wanted to protect Linda. When Rock died later that year, *Dynasty* received a ton of publicity but unfortunately it was geared towards whether or not Linda Evans had been infected with the HIV virus.

Ali MacGraw stayed around a little longer but not much. Understandably nervous on her first day, Ali went to lunch with old friend Joan Collins. Joan explained to Ali that the set of a television series was a far cry from that of a movie. ABC wanted to let Blake have a fling and since Alexis was already involved with Dex (not that it would have mattered if Blake had approached her) the powers that be opted for Lady Ashley. After John demanded upon script changes Ali's scenes were cut to shreds and she was kept around for the sake of decoration.

In the infamous finale of 1985, Amanda is to marry Prince Michael of Moldavia (Michael Praed) in an elaborate royal wedding arranged by Alexis (of course). Since it was the end of the season and contracts were up for renewal the producers gaily walked around either sprinkling or practically pouring "blood" on the actors. The main producer who went from character to character was Elaine Rich. She and her assistant Richard Osltund spent quite a while making sure everyone looked the part of either holding on by a thread or completely dead on the floor. After the episode was shot, a season wrap party was held at the Beverly Wilshire Hotel where everyone gathered to eat, drink and watch gag reels from the season. At the end of the evening, Aaron Spelling went to the dais and introduced John Forsythe. John then introduced all of the other actors. One by one each took a bow then with one quick line, "A lovely lady who, unfortunately, will not be back with us next season" Ali MacGraw was unceremoniously dumped from the series.

Creator Esther Shapiro conceded that a few of the storylines were way over the top but delighted in the reviews the series was getting. "One of the secrets of the show was the element of unpredictability and excitement of seeing something that you don't expect. Sometimes I have to admit that the storylines were so outrageous but I remember a critic once said, 'People on *Dynasty* aren't afraid to tie two people to a railroad track and have the train run right over them!' The less formula there was the better it seemed to work. If anything, what you did was come up with what you thought the character would do, then step back and say no then do the exact opposite."

During the spring of 1985, the powers that be decided that since they were now holding the number one spot in the ratings that perhaps they should spice things up little more and miraculously return Fallon from the dead. Tori Spelling (Aaron and Candy's daughter)

told her father that Emma Samms from *General Hospital* would be a great replacement and since the producers had managed to replace Steven, why not Fallon too? Only problem with this bright idea was that Emma Samms is most definitely British and that she was still under contract to *General Hospital*. They weren't exactly thrilled with the idea of Emma leaving and because of contractual problems she spent the entire summer shuttling between the two studios. In the end, Holly Sutton Scorpio (Emma's G.H. character) was killed and Fallon Carrington Colby was resurrected on the season finale complete with a new height, different colored eyes and a British accent.

The "Moldavian Massacre" was the highest rated episode in *Dynasty's* history and the fans waited with baited breath to see who would survive the carnage. The cast members who were left each received an "I Survived Moldavia" T-Shirt as a souvenir of the cliffhanger. When the dust cleared, Ali was gone as was Billy Campbell (later on the hit series *Once and Again*) leaving the audience with their cast fully intact; almost. Alexis was very obviously missing from the season premiere and the show explained it as "let's just say Mrs. Colby is beyond talking."

Joan Collins had been in France shooting the miniseries *Sins* for the entire summer and renegotiating her contract at the same time. As rumor had it, she wasn't coming back to the show unless she received a pretty hefty raise and used the fact that she was one of the main reasons people watched the series to get precisely what she wanted. Then there was talk about Joan being exhausted from the extensive work on the miniseries and had simply gotten the time off. Either way, as it was put by one of the crew members, "It cost producers a small fortune to shoot around her." The producers had also come up with a back-up plan in case the absence wasn't resolved quickly: kill Alexis and have a closed casket at her funeral. Whichever story is true depends on who you talk to but Alexis was front and center, alive and kicking on the second episode of the season.

With Alexis safe and the family back to normal (or as close as the Carrington and Colby clans could get), fans of the series began to revolt as they watched Emma Samms week after week. They didn't find her to be a suitable replacement for Pamela and bombarded the studio with complaints. Emma had known she would have trouble filling her predecessor's shoes but the backlash was unrelenting. To make matters worse, she was thrown from a horse while filming a scene and was carried off the set on a stretcher. The fall had ruptured a disc, caused nerve damage in the lower part of her body and affected her reflexes in her knees and ankles. "It was tremendously painful," Emma recalls. "Nothing from the waist down functioned properly and my work situation became a nightmare. My scenes had to be rescheduled because I couldn't work for almost a month." The rumor mill was circulating with the gossip that Emma was being fired and that *Dynasty* was already searching for her replacement. In a show of sincerity and solidarity, Esther Shapiro released a statement to the media that criticized *Dallas* for not standing by Donna Reed when Barbara Bel Geddes left and Reed stepped in as Miss Ellie. That one statement could be read many ways but in the minds of those who read between the lines it was clear – Emma's job was safe.

Just when it appeared that *Dynasty* could stay in the number one spot for a while, Diana Gould and Dennis Hammer concocted a storyline that even for *Dynasty* was a stretch and featured the biggest waste of good talent when they cast George Hamilton in the role of Joel Abrigore.

George Hamilton has always been known for that flashy smile and year-round tan not to mention quite a few movies and television appearances. The storyline would feature George as a sinister yet sometimes bumbling film director who helps Sammy Jo gain access to her late father Daniel Reece's fortune by kidnapping Krystle and putting a new Krystle in her place. Linda Evans took on double duty as Krystle and would-be actress Rita Lesley. For at least a quarter of the season fans were "treated" to Krystle being locked in the attic and Rita avoiding then poisoning Blake while Alexis was dressing like a nun and hell-bent on rescuing King Galen from his imprisonment in Moldavia. As the old saying goes, it's all downhill from here…

Joel Fabiani joined the cast briefly as King Galen of Moldavia.

Supposedly one of Alexis' loves before she and Blake met, Galen has decided that he wants Alexis as his queen. Thankfully the fans of the series put an end to that plot by flooding the studio with mail swearing that they'll stop watching if the writers pair the two. So despite filming the scenes of the second "royal wedding", Alexis would have to survive without becoming Queen.

ABC was feeling the need to be greedy and approached Spelling Entertainment to come up with a spin-off of *Dynasty*. The Spelling/Shapiro production team put their heads together and came up with the concept of sending Jeff Colby to California to run the Colby family business. The series would be set in Los Angeles and had more star power than any other show at that time. Silver Screen legends Charlton Heston and Barbara Stanwyck had been signed as Jason Colby and Constance Colby Patterson, Katharine Ross as Francesca, Stephanie Beacham as Sable,

Maxwell Caulfield as Miles, Tracy Scoggins as Monica, Claire Yarlett as Bliss and let's not leave out Ricardo Montalban as villain Zach Powers. *The Colbys* was anything but a tranquil show. During the first week of production, two million dollars worth of furniture and sets were torn to shreds because the surroundings didn't appear to have the same opulence as *Dynasty*. John Forsythe, Diahann Carroll and Gordon Thomson were the only cast members who would make the leap from show to show. Joan Collins and Linda Evans refused to guest star on the series because they had (rightly) become convinced that it would steal ratings from *Dynasty*.

Behind the scenes, Charlton Heston bellowed commands as only Moses could, Katharine Ross raged about the storylines she was presented with and Barbara Stanwyck basically turned the set into a living hell. Bitterly unhappy from the first day of filming, she constantly fought with the producers over the scripts. Add to that publicly embarrassing her younger co-stars by berating them for not knowing their lines or coming in late, Barbara turned what should have been a warm working environment into a freezer. Her tirades reminded producers of another actor they had worked with by the name of George Peppard. Conveniently, Constance Colby Patterson disappeared after one season

and at end of the second season in perhaps the most bizarre cliffhanger on television (Fallon being abducted by aliens) *The Colbys* was also gone forever.

The Colbys proved to be far more expensive than the producers could have ever imagined. As a result of their spin-off, *Dynasty* lost a good share of its viewers, lost its number one rating and also its time slot. The precious hour on Wednesday night was gone and the show was left to fend for itself on Thursday opposite huge hits on both of the other networks.   Not even the additions of Christopher Cazenove as Blake's baby brother Ben and Kate O'Mara as Alexis' writer sister Caress (a character who bore a striking resemblance to Joan's sister Jackie Collins) would be enough to pull *Dynasty* out of what was becoming storyline oblivion.

Catherine Oxenberg also learned a thing or two about the inner-workings of Hollywood.   There are two things you never do when dealing with an Aaron Spelling production: Ask for more money without having the clout to back up your demands and never have a baby while you're on a series. This was once again definitely the case on *Dynasty*. When Kathleen Beller became pregnant Kirby was banished from Denver and went to Paris.   When Pamela Bellwood became pregnant Claudia was whisked away to a mental institution. When Catherine Oxenberg decided that she wanted more money to play the spoiled Princess of Moldavia, Spelling execs dumped her on the spot and replaced her with American actress Karen Cellini (as if no one would notice again). The producers had agreed not to speak about the dismissal but the following morning there was a headline in the Hollywood Reporter reading *"Dynasty's Oxenberg Fired."* The article quoted the ABC press release stating that "the termination was due to failing to reach a suitable financial arrangement."

Despite the fact that Blake was in the process of strangling Alexis for taking the mansion away from him when *Dynasty* entered its seventh season, the ratings continued their downward slide. The days of having huge names for guest stars was over, the sets were scaled back to a minimum and the bitchery of the old days seemed to be missing. Even Alexis was revealed to have a truly loving side when Blake is struck with amnesia. In the two best episodes of the season, she's trying to trick him into signing over oil leases by allowing him to believe they're still married. Despite this fact, John

Forsythe still refuses to let Blake be unfaithful to Krystle so a story is created of him knowing that something isn't right between him and Alexis. She gets the leases she wants but tears them up after Blake tells her that he loves her and instead confesses her undying love for him.

As if the audience hadn't been tortured enough by then the writers reached into their bag of tricks and came up with another one. Krystina (now three and played by Jessica Player) had been struck with congestive heart failure and was in dire need of a transplant. At the same time, Adam was courting his new bride to be Dana (Leann Hunley of *Days of Our Lives* fame) and Ben's long lost daughter Leslie (Terri Garber) appeared from out of nowhere. Cassie Yates is introduced to the storyline as Sarah Curtis just in time to donate her child's heart to save Krystina. Another elaborate wedding is planned for the Carringtons and the season seven finale is truly filled

with surprises. Bo Hopkins rejoined the cast as Matthew Blaisdel and is back to take Krystle away with him forever and Alexis drives a car off of a bridge and into a lake. Diahann Carroll, Christopher Cazenove, Karen Cellini, Wayne Northrup and Kate O'Mara had all left by the end of the season.

By the opening of Season Eight, the cast of *Dynasty* was truly growing tired of the farfetched storylines and revolving door of guest stars but unfortunately for most of them, the show wasn't over just yet. In a move that angered quite a few loyal viewers Dex and Alexis were split up again. James Healy was signed to portray Sean Rowan. Sean would be the person responsible for saving Alexis from her watery grave and eventually her fourth husband.

Always wanting to keep a bit of bizarre intact, the writers made Sean Rowan and another sister (Victoria) the older children of Joseph and Alicia Anders. Who knew Kirby had siblings? James was a mediocre actor with an ego the size of a small country and was constantly bragging to his fellow actors that he was close friends with Sir Laurence Olivier. The cast and crew tried their best to get along with him but were thankful when he was released from the series at the end of the season as was Terri Garber.

It was quite clear that ABC wanted the series off the air in 1988 because the network brass felt the show was out of date. One of the network executives even went so far as to say "This show is like the Wicked Witch of the West. It just refuses to die. We'll have to drive a stake through its heart." The final swing was taken at the series when the head writer was replaced (again) with David Paulsen. David had been a line producer on *Dallas* and was hired to bring *Dynasty* into the 90s. ABC wanted the show to meld with the other series of the time such as *Roseanne, Cheers* and *Murphy Brown.* Unfortunately no one bothered mentioning that *Dynasty* wasn't supposed to be a comedy series. Joan Collins summed up the situation quite beautifully, "David Paulsen was desperately trying to fulfill his brief to bring the show into the same milieu as *Roseanne* and *The Golden Girls.* But although these shows were sardines on toast and *Dynasty* was caviar, we were losing our style, our mettle and our remaining viewers at an alarming rate."

The ninth season opened with a very different feel around the studio. With the exception of the Carrington mansion, the opulent sets were gone and had been replaced by hotel interiors that Spelling had purchased years before. The storylines were geared toward the younger characters and Linda Evans stunned the world with the announcement that she was leaving. "I was at a place in my life where I wanted to relax. I wanted to be out of the limelight so I moved away from Hollywood and bought a house in Washington. I don't regret that decision for a minute."

Faced with having no heroine producers brought Stephanie Beacham from *The Colbys* back to life to be the "sometimes saint/sometimes sinner" Sable to befriend Blake and ruin Alexis at the same time. Although able to keep the same per episode salary, as a way to save money Joan had been regulated to appear in only half of the season's episodes and then was only in two or three scenes per show. It was very clear that *Dynasty* had become a sinking ship so Joan as well as co-star Michael Nader announced that this too would be their last season. ABC was ecstatic because the series was finally in a position to have the life-support plug pulled and that's exactly what they did.

Blake Carrington was left lying in a pool of blood at the foot of the mansion's staircase while his beloved Krystle was in a coma in Switzerland. Fallon and Krystina were trapped in a cave with the son of Alexis' former lover Roger Grimes. Sable, Monica and Adam watched in horror as Alexis and Dex fell from a balcony at The Carlton Hotel. The fans that remained were outraged. The cast and crew were outraged. The network didn't care. As far as they were concerned the Wicked Witch was finally dead and there would be no looking back. They were wrong. Fans bombarded ABC with angry mail and thousands threatened to boycott all of the network's shows if *Dynasty* wasn't properly ended. The network later announced that *Dynasty: The Reunion* would begin filming that summer.

"To say that *Dynasty: The Reunion* was a massive disappointment would be like saying Hitler was a naughty boy." – Joan Collins

How correct she was! *Dynasty: The Reunion* was even more far-fetched than the series ever dreamed of being. John, Linda, Joan, John James, Emma Samms, Kathleen Beller and Heather Locklear reprised their roles without problem. Gordon Thomson was on the soap opera *Santa Barbara* and because his agent never relayed the shoot dates was unable to get time off so he was replaced by British actor Robin Sachs (who looks and sounds NOTHING like Gordon). Gordon also sued *Spelling Entertainment* for mismanagement in coordinating the shooting schedule with the powers that be on *Santa Barbara*. Jack Coleman wasn't interested in coming back to the show at the time so the producers replaced him with the ORIGINAL Steven, Al Corley (as if no one would notice). Michael Nader was on *All My Children* and couldn't get time off so perhaps Dex was the lucky one because no one bothered to do anything with his character except to say that "he didn't fare too well", whatever that was supposed to mean. There was no mention of Sable or Monica, even though Miles was in The Reunion and you would have thought that at one person might have made a comment about the baby she and Dex were expecting. Unfortunately, the inconsistencies didn't stop there.

The interior sets had been completely dismantled and destroyed when the series ended so a new interior of the Carrington mansion was constructed. The fates of Blake, Krystle, Alexis, Dex, Fallon and Krystina were covered in less than two minutes and the miniseries continued with a completely  unbelievable plot about Denver Carrington being taken over by a consortium out to rule the world and helped along by Adam. Alexis no longer ran a company called ColbyCo but instead was running one called Colby Enterprises (which was the name of Jason Colby's company, not Cecil's) and it no longer dealt with the oil business but with the fashion trade instead. In fact, at no time during the entire miniseries did anyone conduct any type of business that concerned oil. The writing staff had completely forgotten where *Dynasty* left off because all of the characters were running around arguing about things that had been worked out in seasons six, seven and eight. While the cast enjoyed seeing each other again and felt as if it had only been two months break instead of two years, the script left quite a bit to be desired. The first night of the miniseries drew in a respectable 35 share in the ratings. The second night was considerably less because viewers were disappointed that the characters they loved were so completely different. At the end of *The Reunion* the truth was unmistakably obvious – *Dynasty* was officially dead.

Adding insult to injury, the cast of the series should be sitting pretty with residual checks pouring in every month. They aren't and they never will be. When *Viacom* was in the process of obtaining *Spelling Entertainment*, *Dynasty* cast members were presented with buy-out offers that gave each one of them a lump sum instead of residuals. They had been told that *Dynasty* would probably never run more than two or three times in syndication so each one of them accepted the offer.

Over twenty years since the first episode aired, *Dynasty* has been seen in the United States on FX and Soapnet and continues to air in syndication in nearly 60 countries worldwide. Joining the popular craze of releasing television shows to DVD, on April 19th Twentieth Century Fox released Season One. Season Two is currently being formatted for release and commentary negotiations are underway.

There has been a great deal of speculation throughout the years of what Season Ten would have consisted of. Heather Locklear was rumored to have stated on *Larry King Live* that several episodes of the new season were already in production. Unfortunately for the fans of the series that is not the case. According to four different sources, including *Spelling Entertainment*, there were no episodes taped nor to knowledge are there any scripts calling for the funerals of Dex and Alexis, Adam being arrested for two counts of murder or Blake receiving organs from a dead Dex in order to remain alive after the shooting. As pitiful as it was, the fans of the series will have to go on with only the tidbits shared during those two minutes during *Dynasty: The Reunion,* and the knowledge that the series, the cast and everyone else involved deserved better.

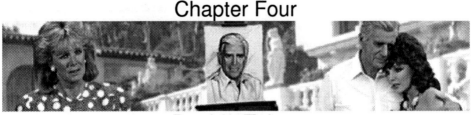

Chapter Four

Double Takes

Ah, the Continuity Department... Was there no one in that room? There are so many blunders and outright mistakes roaming through this series that it's surprising that the cast knew what characters they were actually playing from week to week! While this section could fill an entire book on its own if it weren't condensed, here are just a few of the little nagging items and we're starting with the one that is the most bothersome.

How long were Blake and Alexis married? It started as nine years then later in the series moved to seven. Now by chronological statistics neither one of those statements is correct. They were married in 1954 and Alexis was banished in 1965 so they were actually married for eleven years. Granted they weren't terribly happy for some of them but was it really so bad that they each forgot a different number of them along the way?

The story of the mansion is also up for debate. Alexis says Blake bought the house as a showplace for her after Adam was kidnapped. Blake says he bought the house after Adam was kidnapped while building Denver-Carrington into the powerhouse it is. So far so good right? Wrong. When Amanda and Alexis are talking about the possibility of Blake being dead (during the episode in which he and Daniel Reece are in the plane crash), Alexis tells Amanda a story about when she and Blake were first married a fire broke out in the mansion and after she and Adam were safely out of the house Blake risked his life to run back in and save their butler Joseph. Now if Denver Carrington wasn't yet a fully operational company and Blake was a wildcatter at the time they got married, how could they afford the mansion, a butler and a really bad nanny for Adam?

Which brings us to Adam. He spends most of his life thinking he's Michael Torrance then discovers he's Adam Carrington and then gets blackmailed by Neal McVane with the news that he's not Adam after all. A few months later he finds out that he is indeed Adam Alexander Carrington. Now for someone who is so completely anal about the idea that he's never been treated like a "true" Carrington, you would think he would be shouting the news of his lineage from the rooftops but no. He'd rather sulk and say nothing. Then again, why should he considering Blake and Alexis adopted him? Now, not only is he their biological child but their adopted son too. He could have at least told them…

Fallon is a true piece of work. She was so completely spoiled that she would throw a tantrum and vow to destroy anyone that Blake paid attention to (she got that from her mother). Isn't is a little odd that she tried to sabotage Krystle for years, came completely unglued when Adam was introduced as her big brother and yet didn't blink an eye when she discovered that she has a sister who her father spent a great deal of time talking about while they were together?

How quickly we forget… In the episode *The Honeymoon* while Cecil is trying to convince Fallon to marry Jeff in exchange for his helping Blake, Fallon asks him if he has any other nephews that she could choose from to which he says no. Was Cecil thrown out of the Colby clan so long ago that he had forgotten that Jason and Sable had Miles? Not that it mattered because it turns out that Fallon managed to find him all by herself in Season Six! But that doesn't count either because in Season Nine we learn that Miles isn't really Jason's son but Jeff is so technically

Cecil was right after all… But then again, Jeff and Miles make several comments about being brothers in *The Reunion* so your guess is as good as mine!

Somebody needs to teach Dex how to count. In Season Nine while he tries to explain why he slept with Sable, he told Alexis that he had spent the past eight years loving her. Unless he (like so many others) developed amnesia three years prior to meeting her and forgot everything, Dex had only been in Denver for five years. Maybe the relationship was so drawn out it just felt like eight.

Dynasty's version of Denver must be considerably smaller than the real one is because you would think the Carrington, Colby and Dexter clans could find other people to sleep with. Poor Blake was the only one who didn't seem to have a very good time bed hopping… The "keeping it in the family prize" goes to Jason Colby with Dex Dexter coming in a close second with only Tracy knocking him out of the top spot. Jason slept with two sisters and a cousin while Dex went with the two cousins, a daughter and his ex-wife's niece approach. Forget about the fact that Jeff and Fallon are second cousins or that Jeff's aunt (Sable) is also his ex-stepmother or that his mother-in-law (Alexis) is also his aunt and cousin. It's just another example of being one big, happy, dysfunctional family. Perhaps this is a topic for comedian Jeff Foxworthy to study as this family tree may be missing a few forks…

Speaking of a love life, can anyone disagree with the fact that love is apparently blind, deaf, dumb, stupid and every other euphemism known to man to describe Alexis handing over full control of everything she had to Sean Rowan? The woman spent the vast majority of her time back in Denver making everyone feel like they were always on the verge of entering the gates of hell and in one thoroughly ludicrous moment she opts to run for Governor. Instead of getting one of her fairly well-trained sons or hundreds of other ColbyCo executives to take care of things, she places the entire conglomerate into the hands of a complete unknown. Heck, at the time the only real thing she knew about him was that he was good in bed, and heaven knows if that's the biggest credential he could offer then Dex would have had controlling interest a long time ago...

The governor story in itself was a little more than odd. In case the writing staff had missed the end of the first season and the beginning of the second, Blake Carrington was convicted of manslaughter for killing his son's lover, which obviously was forgotten along the way because as I recall the law states that a convicted felon can't vote much less hold public office. While we're still on this topic, what the heck was Alexis thinking by throwing her hat into the ring? The first thing political campaigns do is reach for the jugular and dig up every negative thing out of the candidate's past. Were we really supposed to believe that none of her well-publicized affairs, dysfunctional children and their past weren't going to be brought up somewhere along the way? The two of them couldn't even keep their companies or family managed well, how were they going to run the state of Colorado?

Another odd part would be the reading of Cecil Colby's will. In the document he leaves everything to Alexis with the provision that she has provided an heir and if not then it gets split between her and Jeff. Here's the problem: Alexis was 17 when she and Blake married in 1954 but she and Cecil didn't marry until 1983. Fertility treatments weren't even remotely as far as advanced as they are now so how could Cecil expect Alexis to deliver a child at the age of 46?

Age is a huge factor when it comes into play especially for Fallon. During the second season opening episode when Alexis has returned to testify against Blake she makes the comment that she had left three days before Steven's seventh birthday. Fallon is two years older than Steven, making her nine when her mother left Denver. Fallon adds that she hasn't had a mother in 16 years, which makes her 25 when Alexis returned in 1982. When Lauren was born in 1987 Fallon's hospital chart reads that she is 25 instead of the 30 that she actually was. This same item happens again in the ninth season when Fallon and Alexis are talking about her mother's affair with Roger Grimes. Alexis comments that Fallon was only five when that was taking place but since it was Fallon that shot Roger (supposedly now at five) when Blake had banished Alexis from Denver, how could Alexis have left three days before Steven's seventh birthday because if we follow this time frame Steven is only three!

Now that we've decreased Fallon's age, what's up with Amanda's? When she joined the family in 1984 she commented to Blake that she would be 21 in April. If we go back to our friendly mathematics problem above we know that Alexis left Denver in 1965 and Amanda was born in April of 1966. If Amanda were going to be 21 in 1985, she would have to have been born while Alexis was not only still in Denver but nearly two years before Blake's enforced divorce.

Let's talk about the affair Cecil had with Alexis and how he was a contender for Fallon's father. This is yet another little item that doesn't add up. Adam and Fallon are a year apart in age and Adam was kidnapped shortly before his first birthday. If that's the case, Alexis was already pregnant with Fallon before Adam was kidnapped. Since Blake and Alexis both admitted that they didn't start having problems with their marriage until after Adam was taken and that he didn't start going off on those endless trips until after the kidnapping, then when and why would Alexis have been be sleeping with Cecil?

The extended family isn't any exception to oddities either. Take Kirby's for example. She was continuously around Fallon, Steven and Jeff while they were growing up, as was Joseph, but isn't it a little more than convenient that at no time during the first eight seasons was there ever a brother and sister mentioned? Considering how long Joseph worked for Blake you would think he would have said something about his other two children.

Although when you think about it, Blake and Alexis aren't any better in that department. With as much media coverage as Alexis said there was when Adam was kidnapped (remember she always blamed Blake for Adam not being returned because of the police and media involvement), you would think someone would have brought that up long before Little Blake's kidnapping. Surely if there were gossip columnists that were keeping tabs on the adventures of the Carrington clan, one of them would have stumbled on something to do with the missing firstborn child. Fallon even made the comment to Steven that their parents' fights were legendary and that she and Steven had been the laughing stock of the club circuit for years. Did the whole of Denver decide to block out Adam's existence the same way his parents did for all those years?

Blake's mother; Ellen Lucy Carrington, must have had one hell of an afterlife. Since she died when Blake was four-years-old and since Ben was at least five years younger than his big brother and couldn't have been born at the time of her first death, the writers of the series conveniently decided to bring her back to life only to kill her in a fire in 1954 when Ben was old enough to be sleeping with Emily Fallmont. They also changed her name because in the second season her name was Fallon; as was mentioned during a not-so-pleasant exchange of words between Alexis and her daughter, in which Fallon says she was named after Blake's mother. Then again, what's in a name?

Did you ever notice that the babies born on the show all looked exactly alike? At least they did in photographs. Fallon has a lovely shot of Little Blake sitting on her desk at La Mirage. The same photo gets used as Blake and Alexis beg for the return of their grandson. So far so good, but then it's used again when Sean takes Adam's son. You can't tell me that Adam didn't take a couple dozen film rolls worth of pictures of his new son. Not to mention, he had a different one of the baby the following season while showing it to Virginia, so why didn't they use that one while looking for his son instead of using a shot of L.B.?

We also don't want to leave out the fact that the one of the above mentioned photos was also supposedly Krystina. Krystle told Krystina that the photo was taken at the hospital on the night that she was born. Considering that Krystina was nearly two months premature, was in pretty bad shape when she was born in the master bedroom at the mansion and then spent weeks hooked up to monitors and tubes at the hospital, who took the picture of the perfectly healthy baby with the uncanny resemblance to the photo of Adam's new son?

In the Moldavia storyline King Galen often spoke of the love he and Alexis shared and how they used to spend days on end making love until his father forbid them to marry and split them apart. In court and other places Alexis said she was very young and virginal when she and Blake married. So now the question becomes how did Alexis spend days on end making love with Galen before she was the virginal bride of Blake Carrington? I could really use a copy of "Sister Dearest" right now…

Were Blake and Alexis so completely caught up in destroying each other that they managed to miss the incredible transformations that their children made throughout their adult lives? First Fallon starts out as a pure-blooded American girl-next-door type but she gets amnesia, and when she finally remembers who she is not only has her life changed but so has  the color of her hair and eyes, she's shrunk about two inches and she suddenly speaks with a British accent. On the flip side of that coin, Amanda is definitely British, (having been raised in England) and has her mother's accent down pat. Then one fateful night she and Sammy Jo get into a fistfight and fall into the pool at La Mirage. Sammy Jo must pack one hell of a punch because she not only rearranged Amanda's face but her body's build and amazingly completely erases her British accent! Adam used to be drop-dead-gorgeous or at least he was until *The Reunion* but there again, no one notices a thing. The winner for the "most changed" is without a  doubt Steven. Did he decide he didn't like the new face anymore so he took a photo of his original self and was transformed back? Since Alexis had studied his new face so closely when Blake brought him back to Denver after the oilrig explosion, you would have thought she would see the difference.

Are we actually supposed to believe that no one in the Colby family (at least those in California) recognized Fallon when Miles brought her home? Sable and Alexis were still close when Fallon, Miles and Monica were children so wouldn't you think she would have had a clue…

Amnesia wasn't only left to Blake and Fallon, it also spread to the rest of the family and the people they're acquainted with. Case and point, Dex and Alexis spent the night together in his trailer at the pipeline site. During their lovemaking session, Alexis asked Dex what tore them apart to which he answered that he "made a mistake with Amanda". It was fresh enough in her memory to fly to the Caribbean for an immediate divorce and drive her daughter to the point of attempting suicide, but Alexis couldn't remember it a few months later while she and Dex were between the sheets? Sorry, but sleeping with my daughter wouldn't be something to slip the mind no matter how good he is in bed!

Kirby suffered from the same kind of "selective" memory loss. In *The Reunion* she picks up her relationship with Adam again but obviously forgets her grudge about the fact that he had raped her once and tried again, impregnated her, lied to her, and tried to force her to marry him. But all that aside, she willingly comes back to Denver on his arm forgetting that "Mommy Dearest" Alexis had threatened to press charges against her several years before for holding her at gun point. Did she even remember the time frame that she was married and lying to Jeff because she never even acknowledged him during *The Reunion* even after saving his life? Oh well, what's done is done, over and yes; forgotten.

Let us not leave out the ever-so-sterling Krystle. There are quite a few things that don't add up but for the moment let's focus on her first pregnancy and her love for horses. When Alexis shot the rifle that threw Krystle off of the horse and caused her miscarriage, everyone (including Krystle) commented about how inexperienced she was with horses. Two years later she's helping Daniel Reece out at Delta Rho with the delivery of a foal and made the comment about how much she had missed being with horses. Then after Krystina's surgery she and Sarah Curtis are out riding and Krystle makes the comment that she had grown up helping out on her Grandparents' farm and how much she had always loved to ride horses. So unless Krystle's grandparents bought that farm after she had her miscarriage, how could Krystle be a novice on horseback?

Sean shooting Alexis at the Governor's debate had its moments even if at least one of them was rather odd. When Alexis gets out of the chair and walks over to Blake she's facing him with her back to the camera, audience and Sean's aimed gun. So could anyone explain how she got hit in the right temple and how, despite the fact that she falls into Blake and hits the right side of her head on his face and suit, he doesn't have a drop of blood on him? We'll have to worry about figuring out how she  was hit from the back and have the bullet end up grazing her forehead and being lodged in her skull instead of going straight through later.

Why is it that people could get to Natumbe' so quickly? Blake and Dex left at 10:00 PM one night and were there the next morning. Sean got wind of the fact that they were gone sometime before noon and managed to get there and blow up Blake's tanker on the same day. Another thing; how was it that Blake could take the plane to Africa but it couldn't be taken to Singapore or other foreign destinations?

Another nagging issue about memory problems is Kirby and Adam. As we know, Kirby left Denver on Alexis' orders. Before she left she visited her mother's grave and was told that she had died only the year before. So how is it that in *The Reunion*, she tells Adam that her mother has been dead for 15 years? Did she not remember the fact that Adam was with her when she saw her mother's grave? Then she talks about Joseph and the circumstances of his death must have changed along the way too because suddenly Adam claims that he hadn't ever known him. Considering that he was living in the mansion at the time of her father's death, I find that a little hard to believe.

Was the renovation at Delta Rho the fastest thing you've ever seen in your life? When Sammy Jo and Clay are in the process of having their marriage annulled the house looks like it has since Sammy Jo moved in and yet three shows later when Steven moves in, the entire floor plan and all of the décor has changed!

What did they mean in *The Reunion* when they said Dex didn't fair so well? Is he dead or just massively injured? They said Alexis managed to flip in mid-air and land on him. If that were true then Dex would have had to turn her because at the speed they were moving, she would have landed on her face and considering how vain Alexis was, I don't think she would have gone with that approach. Not to mention, if Dex had died do you really think Alexis wouldn't be carrying at least a little grudge against Adam?

I realize that Krystina's congestive heart failure was weighing heavily on everyone's hearts and minds but does anyone else find it a bit odd that the only one who acknowledged the fact that Fallon had given birth to her second child was Alexis?

Someone should have reminded themselves of the season eight cliffhanger before starting season nine's episode. Season Eight ended with Sean and Dex fighting over a gun in Alexis' suite with her backed into a corner looking frightened. That fight and the subsequent shooting of Sean must have scared her more than anyone thought because when they opened Season Nine her hair was suddenly about three and a half inches longer than it was when the show went off the air the season before.

In the seventh season, Blake has to give Ben 1/3 of his inheritance from their father Tom. When Alexis brings Blake to his knees and takes everything away from him, she leaves him practically broke. Suddenly he remembers the hundreds of acres his mother left to him that contains an abundance of natural gas. Forgive me, but didn't Blake tell Fallon that his family was "dirt poor" during the years he was growing up? So where did the hundreds of acres come from?

The musical wardrobe... No I don't mean that literally but how many of *Dynasty's* outfits were used on other shows? Nolan Miller made several copies of a few outfits. The most obvious one I can remember is the white dress that Alexis wears on the night she takes the mansion away from Blake. Nolan actually made three different versions of the same dress. Joan's was short and came to just  below her knees. Linda had one that she wore in the miniseries *Bare Essence* that was done as a full-length and Connie Sellecca had a full-length version with a small train that she wore in a 1986 episode of the series *Hotel*. Several of the outfits that Leslie wore were also from *Hotel*, as was the black and white number that Alexis wore in Season Seven at Dana's apartment when she and Blake told Adam that they didn't care if he was their natural son, was also worn by Connie Sellecca and even a few of Krystle's outfits managed to be used by Stefanie Powers during the run of *Hart To Hart*. The women weren't the only ones who had shared wardrobe. John Forsythe's jacket and several of his sweaters also found their way to the *Hart To Hart* set as *Jonathan Hart's* clothing. The most obvious one is the red and black skirt suit that Leslie wears in Season Eight that comes back to life in Season Nine in Sable's wardrobe.

Now for a few of the more obvious mistakes –

In the Season Six episode *The Triple-Cross*, Alexis and Ben have a fight after Ben double-crosses Alexis and has the Chinese minister give him sole custody of Blake's South China Seas oil leases. Alexis is standing with a cigarette in her right hand. Despite the fact that she never puts the cigarette down, when she lunges at Ben the cigarette is gone. When Ben leaves she clutches her wrist with still no cigarette. By this time shouldn't the couch or some other piece of furniture have been on fire?

In the second season opener when Fallon and Steven are getting ready to go into the courtroom to hear more of the testimony in Blake's murder trial, Fallon is wearing a lovely lilac suit with matching scarf. Do my eyes deceive me or is she wearing a white shirt with a red jacket when she sits down inside the courtroom and wasn't her hair a different style? Talk about a quick change!

While Blake and Fallon are standing in front of the nursery window looking at her newborn son, Blake comments that his grandson is three weeks old. In the next scene with Fallon, Jeff makes the comment that their two-month old son could really use a name. Boy time really flies in Denver doesn't it?

The first glimpse Adam has of his mother is as she's escorted from the hospital where Cecil has died. Did someone bring her clothing because she was wearing her white wedding attire when he died so how could she have left dressed for mourning in solid black?

When Rita is in the process of poisoning Blake, Joel (as Dr. Travers) takes the vial that the heart medication was in away from Sammy Jo after she found it outside Rita's bedroom door. So how is it that she produced the same medication vial at the hospital when the doctors needed to begin treating Blake?

Bodies were always fun. Did you ever notice that when someone had died and an outline was needed, that the outline never matched how the person was actually lying on the ground? If you need examples, watch the episodes when Steven kills Matthew and Dex kills Sean.

Did anyone else happen to notice that the Swiss headquarters of the "Consortium" in *Dynasty: The Reunion* is the palace where Amanda and Michael were married in Moldavia?

While we're talking about *The Reunion* would it be safe to assume that all of the writers missed the last three seasons of the series? What's with Steven being so angry at Blake over his gay lifestyle again? Why are Steven and Sammy Jo fighting over Danny spending time with either parent again? How long does it take to get a divorce, especially since Fallon served Jeff with papers before the series went off the air and he was engaged to Sammy Jo? The biggest question  of all – were the fans of this classic series actually supposed to believe that even with Blake in prison, Alexis would have let anyone not only buy the mansion but gut the interior and completely remodel it? Considering that (aside from Blake) it was the one thing she always wanted back, it's pretty hard to believe that she would let it go without putting up one hell of a fight. Not to mention while her driver is putting her auction purchases in the limo, Alexis comments to "be careful, that's 18th Century, but knowing Blake it's probably fake." If they are fakes then technically wouldn't that be her fault, as she walked around at the beginning of the second season pointing out to Krystle that she sees Blake didn't change the decor much and how she had decorated the entire mansion all by herself?

Did the Carrington, Colby and Dexter clans have a permanent private room reserved at Cheney Hospital? It didn't matter which person it was that was in the hospital, every time you saw the place the camera always aimed at the same window on the third floor.

When did Alexis merge ColbyCo with Jason's company? When *The Reunion* rolls around to the first shot of Alexis' office, the sign out front reads Colby Enterprises and isn't it a little odd that the shape of the building changed too…

Was it just me or did anyone else notice that Joseph's replacement Gerard also was the Maitre D' at the St. Dennis Club in the second season? Did Blake pay so badly that his staff had to moonlight at other Denver establishments?

Another one of those moments of Alexis conveniently forgetting little things – Shouldn't someone have reminded her that Dirk Maurier was Peter DeVilbis's shady lawyer during the time that he was sleeping with Fallon? Perhaps if someone had, she wouldn't have lost a fortune trying to take over Trouville Industries!

Has anyone noticed the little plug that Joan got for her line of jeans in the second season? In the episode *The Miscarriage* Alexis sits down with to Claudia have a conversation about Krystle and being outsiders. Alexis is wearing blue jeans and a pink shirt with a sweater tossed over her shoulders. When she gets up to leave the camera follows her from behind. If you look closely you will see that across her right pocket is an embroidered signature. The signature reads Joan Collins.

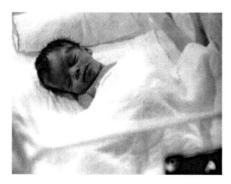

The Colbys wasn't immune to little oops moments either. If you watch the episode in which Fallon gives birth to Lauren, they show Lauren in her hospital basinet. Anyone else happen to notice that the footage used for that particular scene was actually from Dynasty and the baby is Little Blake?

Chapter Five

You Too Can Dress Like Alexis

"The writers started acting like I was the enemy... The clothes were becoming more important than the scripts!"

"Dynasty" provided a weekly cocktail of wealth, sexual intrigue and fantastic accessories, and completely dominated the Eighties. It didn't just illustrate a way of life; it dictated a way of dressing.

Nolan Miller has enjoyed a career as a top fashion designer catering to the needs of some of the most glamorous women in the entertainment industry. Miller, (during his Dynasty days) was the highest paid costume designer in Hollywood and continues to enjoy designing clothing for some stars, licenses his designs to a New York, NY-based apparel manufacturer and regularly appears on the QVC shopping channel to promote the Nolan Miller Glamour Collection. Even 16 years after Dynasty came to an end he has no plans to retire but will be the first to tell you that his glory days are behind him.

But what days they were, Miller used to fit some of the entertainment industry's most glamorous women – Barbara Stanwyck, Lana Turner, Joan Crawford, Bette Davis, and Jane Wyman. While the 70-year-old Miller still designs clothing for some stars – Joan Collins chief among them – most of today's movie and television stars do not wear the kind of clothes for which he is famous.

"I'm kind of a dinosaur," Miller says, noting that actresses today are more likely to wear casual clothing than the couture-style gowns in which he specializes. "There's no real excitement in dressing somebody who wears blue jeans and a sweatshirt throughout the movie."

At one point in the 80's, Nolan had 40 people working for him at his shop on South Robertson Boulevard in Beverly Hills. He was designing costumes for six television shows, including "Fantasy Island", "The Love Boat", and the show that made him famous, "Dynasty" – all produced by Aaron Spelling. At the time, Miller was making $35,000 a week, making him Hollywood's highest-paid designer.

The time was a bit surreal. "We thought we were living in 'Dynasty," We didn't know the party was ever going to end," he says, "The '80s, the glorious '80s. The '80s were wonderful."

Wonderful, but also tiring. Workdays often started at 5 a.m., when Nolan would do a fitting with Joan or Linda. Sometimes the day wouldn't end until 3 a.m., when he was putting the finishing touches on a gown needed on "Dynasty" or "Hotel" the next day. "When I'm 90, my name will still be synonymous with shoulder pads."

"With "Dynasty" I was in heaven. There was nothing holding me back. This show was all about the lifestyles of the ultimately wealthy. I could be as extravagant as I wanted. The first episode had a wardrobe budget of $10,000.00 but that was soon raised to $30,000.00 a week. But I was always over budget. I remember for one episode with a wedding scene, I spent $125,000.00. The most expensive piece I ever designed was an evening dress for Linda Evans. It was nude chiffon, completely encrusted with diamante, and the labor alone cost $12,000.00."

But it wasn't only eveningwear that Nolan Miller created. Every time Alexis sat down with her grapefruit and glass of champagne for breakfast, she had to be wearing a different silk negligee. Every time she wore a power suit, another pair of matching gauntlet gloves had to be specially made.

Nolan found a fellow devotee of high glamour in Joan Collins. The egged each other on to extremes. "Joan would tear every picture out of every magazine. Once Princess Diana was photographed wearing a Russian-inspired outfit that Joan loved. The following week, Alexis wore this glamorous grey coat, trimmed with Russian broadtail and a huge Cossack hat and muff." Their bond has endured to this day. "Whenever she is in town (Los Angeles), Joan will storm into my shop shouting, 'Darling, I have just seen something wonderful!'"

As the Eighties ended, so did the audience's appetite for gravity-defying hair and earrings so big you had to take them off to answer the phone. "I didn't mind. In a way, it's understandable. Towards the end, Dynasty got quite extreme. The hats, the hairstyles, the shoulder pads – everything just got bigger and bigger, until by the end of the series Linda's shoulders were bigger than John Forsythe's."

Content to be in the one town where there are still some women who know how to carry off a couture gown, Nolan Miller is rarely tempted back into film and television. However, one project he couldn't turn down was the 2001 film "These Old Broads" starring Joan Collins, Elizabeth Taylor, Debbie Reynolds and Shirley MacLaine. In an amusing case of life imitating art, MacLaine, he says, became incensed at what she saw as favoritism – Joan was getting all the best outfits. "I kept telling Shirley to read the script. Joan is supposed to look glamorous. She is married to the head of the Mafia. Shirley and Debbie's characters don't have a cent."

Now in 2005, Nolan Miller continues designing couture and has a thriving business with his jewelry line. One long-term project is still a possibility. There's talk that there may be a book someday featuring some of his best work. "I have a warehouse full of stuff from Dynasty – dresses, shoes, gloves, bags, hats, everything…"

Of course, Nolan's clothing isn't the only merchandise available from 'Dynasty'. In 1987 A.J. Scheierson, a Kayser-Roth division of the Wickes Company announced plans to launch a Dynasty lingerie collection exclusively for J.C. Penney stores. According to Marvin Sabesan, executive vice president of Schneierson, the first line includes items for day and night wear. The daywear includes petticoats and teddies with the thrust of the line is charmeuse colored.

Esther Shapiro said she had always wanted to find a lingerie license "since a great deal of the show was shot in the bedroom. Since the show's characters, Alexis Colby and Krystle Carrington, were frequently seen in beautiful lingerie it was important to find a company that could combine elegance and a look at an affordable price.

Another Dynasty merchandising license was given to Alfred Angelo, Inc. based in Willow Grove, Pennsylvania. The line of gowns ranged in price from $500 to $5,000 each. The first collection included two bridal gowns, a gown for remarriage and a bridesmaid's gown. Marilyn Spiegel of Alfred Angelo said the advertising campaign was shot on the Dynasty set.

One of the most popular launches of Dynasty material was the product line introduced by Gorham. Esther Shapiro noted that the license for china, crystal and tableware is one of her personal favorites. "We created heirlooms. Dynasty represented tradition and a family who cared about each other. The gifts reflect an emotional appeal and permanence."

Collector dolls of celebrities became the rage in the 70s and 80s and Dynasty dolls were in high demand. World Doll was enlisted to create two dolls of Linda Evans and two of Joan Collins. The lower priced dolls were made of vinyl and featured Linda in a black and gold gown and Joan in red. They were issued as limited editions and put out in 1985.

The higher priced versions were crafted in porcelain and featured Linda wearing the gown from Blake and Krystle's second wedding and Joan in the pink gown from the episode in which she sings *See What the Boys in the Back Room Will Have.*

For the poor little rich girl who has absolutely everything one dozen porcelain dolls were handcrafted with original Nolan Miller clothes, real furs and jewelry. Linda is wearing the gown from the Carousel Ball and Joan is wearing the dress from Fallon's engagement party. The twenty four dolls (12 per woman) were priced at $10,000.00 each.

When Krystle gave birth to Krystina, Dynasty producers were given another opportunity to commercialize on the show's success and the new Krystina Carrington doll was introduced. Esther Shapiro originally hated the look of the doll and told designers to get with Linda Evans and model Krystina from Linda's baby pictures.

Chuck Ashman (President of Merchandising at 20th Century Fox) used to field hundreds of requests from fans as well as photos from fans that went as far as to recreate rooms from the mansion. "The mail that came in was often directed to a dress as much as it was to a star." Fans of the series had been asked what drew them to the show. "As many people mentioned the clothes as the characters. We used to send out sketches of the outfits (sometimes as many as 200 per week) to viewers who asked for them." Sensing that they had another prime opportunity McCall's was granted the rights to license the Dynasty Collection patterns.

Collectors were wild for anything Dynasty. Among other selections of the merchandise released on the series included three books. They are Dynasty: The Authorized Biography of the Carringtons, Dynasty by Eileen Lottman and Alexis Returns also by Eileen Lottman.

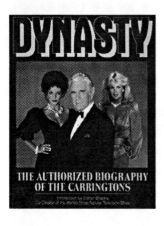  

Plates were the next hot item on the list. Royal Orleans was commissioned to do two collectors plates. The first of the two features Blake, Krystle and Alexis. The second features Krystle with Baby Krystina.

The 1986 Dynasty Calendar was a huge success. Featuring great shots of all of the stars, this was a must-have item for all Dynasty fans.

1984 saw the introduction of the Dynasty puzzle. Three puzzles were issued featuring Blake and Krystle as The Happy Couple, Linda Evans as Krystle and Joan Collins as Alexis.

Moving into the personal care department, Dynasty toiletry items were created and sold in the European markets.

Perhaps the most successful piece of Dynasty merchandise is the perfume Forever Krystle. Released in October 1984 it quickly became one of the most popular scents on the market. Produced by Charles of the Ritz, Forever Krystle commercials featured Linda Evans standing in the bedroom of the Carrington mansion reading a note from Blake that came with a gift of her own fragrance aptly named Forever, Krystle.

On April 12, 1985 Charles of the Ritz again announced a new fragrance but this time it would be for men. Carrington was introduced in 2,500 department stores and was then distributed to over 8,000 drug stores that carried Forever Krystle. Like its counterpart, Carrington features John Forsythe in all of the marketing material.

Forever Krystle and Carrington also had joint advertising campaigns and promotional items. Carrington didn't last very long although you can still find a stray bottle here and there. Forever Krystle is still available at select stores throughout the United States.

Chapter Six

Media Madness

Tucked into the next 72 pages are just a few of the publications *Dynasty* and/or its cast was featured in. They range from magazine covers from the United States to other countries around the world. There's the artwork from TV Guide, the *Daily Variety* artwork for Joan Collins' thank you after her *Golden Globe* win, the hysterically funny *Mad Magazine* comic version called *'DIE-NASTY'* and more.

Another little bit of trivia; did you know that the first two magazines to run a cover of *Dynasty* was *TV Guide* and *Soap Opera Digest*? It wasn't until the second season that the show suddenly got hundreds of requests every day for interviews and photo opportunities.

Although one thing everyone could have lived without were the articles constantly in the tabloids. There was a production staff member who routinely would leak information and always managed to stretch the story completely out of proportion. For example, while there were costume discussions from time to time, there was never a case of any of the cast members throwing clothes at Nolan while swearing, yet somehow all of the women had supposedly done so at some point during the series' run.

Joan Collins' divorce from 'The Swede' was splashed on every tabloid and tabloid news show in the world. The media followed every move Linda Evans and Yanni ever made. Catherine Oxenberg was scrutinized when she was pregnant with daughter India because she refused to publicly name the father. Michael Nader was dragged through the mud after being sent to rehab for drug use. Joan was accused of robbing the cradle when she married Percy Gibson. Personally speaking, I only hope that when I'm 72, I'll have a man who adores me as much as he does her.

TV GUIDE

Local, Network and Cable Pay Listings

DALLAS VS. DYNASTY
WHICH SHOW IS BETTER?
By Stephen Birmingham

TV GUIDE

Local, Network and Cable Pay Listings

Reviewing the Past Season

THE BEST AND WORST WE SAW

TV GUIDE

Local, Network and Cable Pay Listings

THEY'RE STARS— BUT CAN THEY ACT?

Casting Director Judge TV's Top Performers

Valerie Bertinelli: Must avoid being 'too cutesy.' 'Can break into movies'

Alan Alda: A consummate actor. Will be around forever'

Erik Estrada: 'Lucky to have a series'

Linda Evans: 'Good actress with a limited range. Dynasty is beginning to help her'

TV GUIDE

Local, Cable Network and Pay Listings

A Social Climber's Guide to TV
By Stephen Birmingham

'Rich people never say goodbye; they just hang up'

'Rich people don't really use their eggs. They just play with them, which is how they stay thin'

'It is now acceptable for rich women to exchange pecks on the cheek with headwaiters'

TV GUIDE

42000 Americans Tell...
What's Right—and
Wrong—with TV

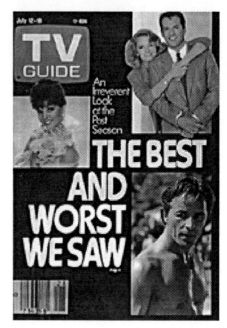

July 12–18

TV GUIDE

An Irreverent Look at the Past Season

THE BEST AND WORST WE SAW

TV GUIDE

Hollywood Love Scenes: The Scares, Laughs, Romance

TV GUIDE

For Distinguished Foolishness
TV Guide's Sixth Annual J. Fred Muggs Awards

On Dynasty
Why Heather Locklear Can Now Stand Up to Joan Collins

March 23–29 • $1.00

TV GUIDE

How Movies Get Oscar
Behind the Oscar Night Glitter
Page 34

A New Life on Dynasty
The Rise and Fall—and Rise Again—of Diahann Carroll Page 28

TV GUIDE

Is TV Keeping America Too Well-Informed?
How All the Bad News Affects Us

Dynasty's Emma Samms
I'm No Delicate Flower, I Am Definitely the Boss

TV GUIDE

Nov. 30–Dec. 6

Is Knots Landing Now Better Than
Dallas and
Dynasty?

TV GUIDE

March 5–3 19

A Government Official's Critique
What I Knew vs. What TV Reported
By John Hughes, former State Department spokesman

Conquering Personal Problems
Playing Krystle Helped Linda Evans

Linda Evans • *Dynasty*

April 18-21 75¢

TV GUIDE

TV Evangelists—
The Scandals May
Not Be Over Page 6

'I'm No Angel:'
Joan Collins'
Parting Shots
at Dynasty Page 8

Joan Collins Leaves
Dynasty and
John Forsythe

May 16-22 75¢

TV GUIDE

Dynasty Star
The Truth About
Tracy Scoggins—
Why She's So
Hard to Figure Page 12

Problems, Jokes, Deals, Fears
Family Ties:
The Inside
Story of Our
Last Season
By Michael Gross Page 6

Is TV News
Getting Better
—or Worse?
By Ed Joyce, former
president of CBS News Page 30

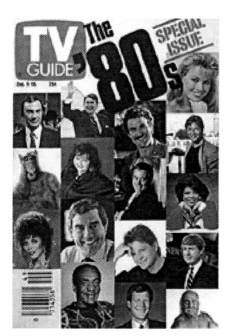

TV GUIDE The '80s SPECIAL ISSUE

Dec. 9-15 75¢

A SPECIAL CABLE EDITION
Nov. 24-30 75¢

TV GUIDE

Linda Evans:
Her life
after
Dynasty—
on and off
the screen

America's
biggest
beefs
about TV

Julio Iglesias:
Why he
drives
women
wild

Linda Evans stars
in a new TV movie
this week

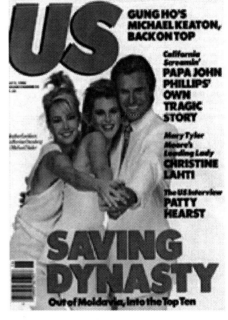

COSMOPOLITAN

Why
Catherine O
took
Joan
Collins'
man

How to
stay single
though
married

See
Fascinating
Aida
at our
cabaret

Never
tinker
with
a fairy

Rare men
Bob
Geldof
Ken
Livingstone

Two 2CVs
to win

Fiction
Tom Wolfe's
shattering
forecast

Baseball's Wackiest Outpost–The Bullpen

TV GUIDE

PLUS

DYNASTY'S
SEDUCTIVE JACK COLEMAN

Terry Lester's Life Is
Just Like A Soap

VERONICA

PAMELA BELLWOOD ZIE JE
NIET MEER HUILEN!

JON VOIGHT: A SINGLE DAD'S STRUGGLE

People
weekly

Debbie Harry vs.
Andy Kaufman

Six stars
face life after
baseball

SEXY
FOREVER

How Linda Evans,
Dan Travanti,
Linda Gray and
Stefanie Powers
make older
look better

Michael Jackson,
Diana Ross &
Stevie Wonder
toast Motown's
25th year

MAD MAGAZINE SALUTES DYNASTY

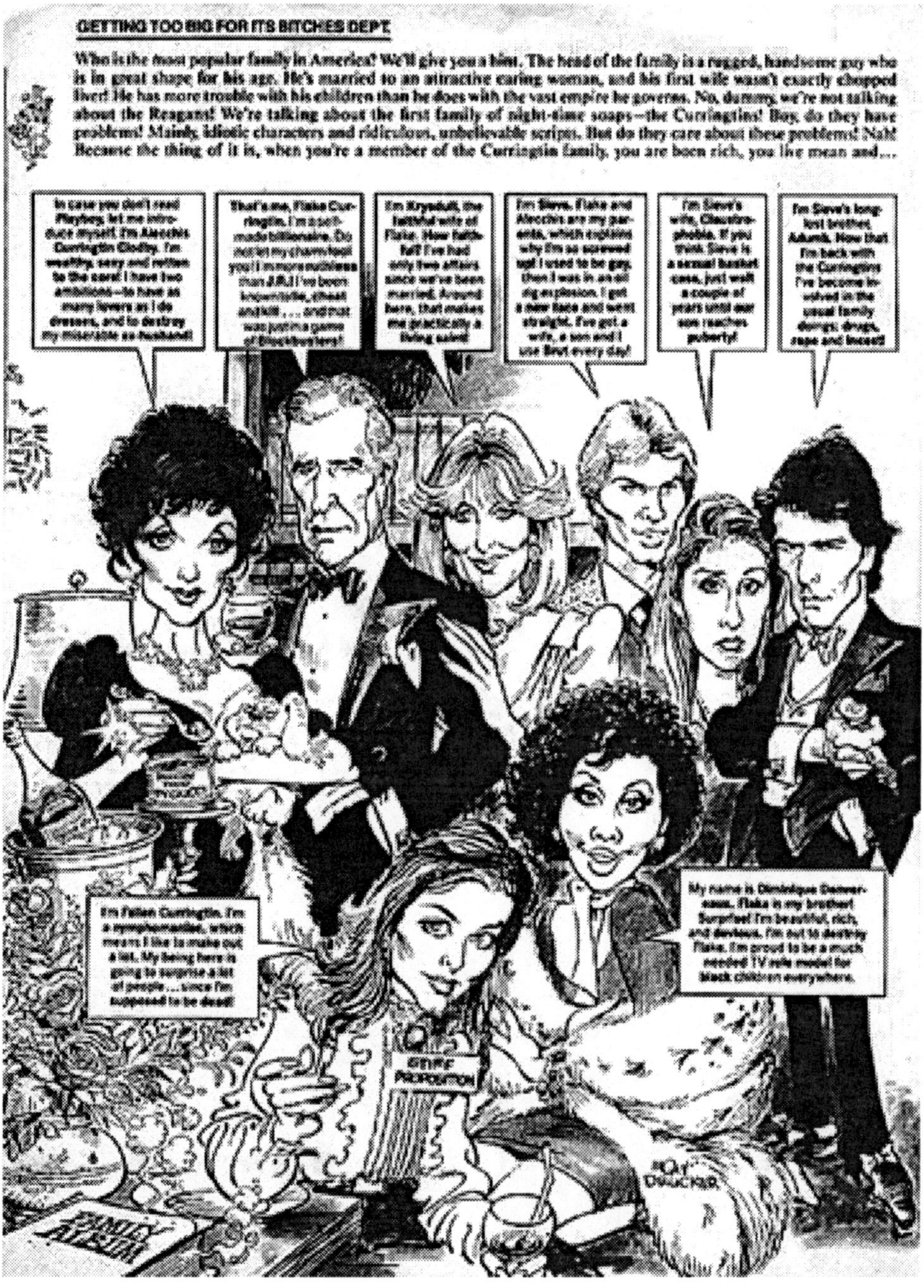

DIE-NASTY

ARTIST: MORT DRUCKER   WRITER: LOU SILVERSTONE

THE ART OF TV GUIDE

January 12, 1981

January 19, 1981

New conflict hits the proud Carrington family.

BLAKE CARRINGTON
Desperate for his new wife's love. Struggling to hold his empire together.

KRYSTLE CARRINGTON
Trying to be faithful to Blake and forget her love for Matthew.

CLAUDIA BLAISDEL
Fighting to overcome her illness and save her marriage to Matthew.

MATTHEW BLAISDEL
Battling the Carrington Empire and his longing for Krystle!

starring JOHN FORSYTHE   LINDA EVANS
PAMELA BELLWOOD   BO HOPKINS

January 26, 1981

The compelling new drama of America today!

INVOLVING!
A story of intrigue, love and greed.

ACTION PACKED!
With passionate people fighting for their beliefs.

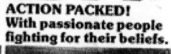

starring
PAMELA BELLWOOD   LINDA EVANS
JOHN FORSYTHE   BO HOPKINS
PAMELA SUE MARTIN   DALE ROBERTSON

February 02, 1981

**Secret deals threaten
to topple the
Carrington Empire!**

**Blake's cruelty
drives Krystle into her
old lover's arms!**

JOHN FORSYTHE   LINDA EVANS   BO HOPKINS
PAMELA SUE MARTIN   PAMELA BELLWOOD
DALE ROBERTSON   AL CORLEY

February 23, 1981

SPECIAL TWO-HOUR DRAMA!
An evening of conflict, passion and triumph.

Pressures
drive
Blake to
assault
his own
wife!

Matthew
and
Walter
strike it
rich.

Fallon tries to save Steven
from his own desires!

JOHN FORSYTHE   LINDA EVANS   BO HOPKINS
PAMELA SUE MARTIN   PAMELA BELLWOOD
DALE ROBERTSON   AL CORLEY

March 03, 1981

November 04, 1981

IS BLAKE CARRINGTON GUILTY OR INNOCENT?

SEASON
PREMIERE

DYNASTY

November 11, 1981

February 03, 1982

February 10, 1982

April 28, 1982

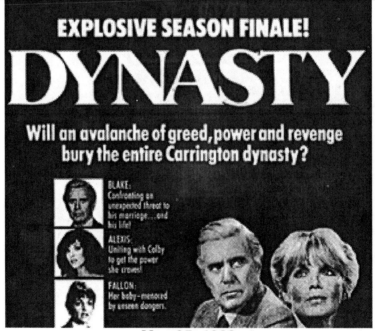

May 05, 1982

DYNASTY

Tonight, you're in for some shocking surprises when these mysteries are unraveled:

Who stole Fallon's baby?

Will Colby's heart attack kill Alexis' plan?

Is this the end for Blake?

October 27, 1982

CLIFF-HANGER!

CORNERED ON A ROOFTOP— WILL THE KIDNAPPER TAKE THE LIFE OF AN INNOCENT BABY?

Fallon's afraid she's lost her baby to a maniac!

DYNASTY

November 03, 1982

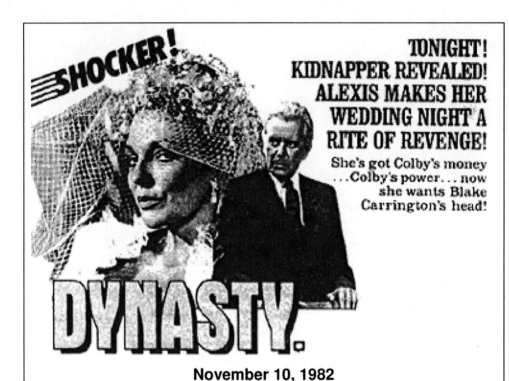

SHOCKER!

**TONIGHT!
KIDNAPPER REVEALED!
ALEXIS MAKES HER
WEDDING NIGHT A
RITE OF REVENGE!**

She's got Colby's money
...Colby's power... now
she wants Blake
Carrington's head!

DYNASTY.

November 10, 1982

WICKED!

Colby's voice speaks from
the grave...and makes
a shocking request of
Alexis! Plus: A tragedy
from Blake's past
returns to haunt him!

DYNASTY

November 17, 1982

HIGH DRAMA!

One of these men is Krystle's lawfully wedded husband! But which one?

DYNASTY.

December 01, 1982

POWERFUL!

Will this beautiful woman destroy Fallon's marriage?

Kirby Anders, Joseph's daughter, returns to the mansion! And a diabolical murder plot takes shape!

DYNASTY.

December 08, 1982

PASSION PACKED!

Alexis' scheming turns Fallon's dream party into a nightmare for Krystle and Blake!

DYNASTY.

December 15, 1982

SAVAGE!

Adam attacks Kirby and plots to destroy Jeff!

DYNASTY. 10:00PM

January 05, 1983

SAMMY JO RETURNS!

A LOVE TRIANGLE?

January 19, 1983

TREACHERY!

IS FALLON'S DIVORCE MARK'S OPPORTUNITY? Will Alexis gain control of Blake's company?

February 02, 1983

THE FURY EXPLODES!

POWER PLAY!

Alexis makes her move to crush Blake. And destroy the dynasty!

DYNASTY.

February 23, 1983

CAN JEFF SAVE KIRBY?

DYNASTY.

BLAKE AND STEVEN REUNITED!

DYNASTY.

March 02, 1983

September 28, 1983

October 05, 1983

EXPLOSIVE CUSTODY BATTLE DIVIDES THE CARRINGTONS!

DYNASTY

November 02, 1983

A BEAUTIFUL BUT DANGEROUS STRANGER INTRUDES ON THE CARRINGTONS!

DYNASTY

November 16, 1983

November 23, 1983

December 21, 1983

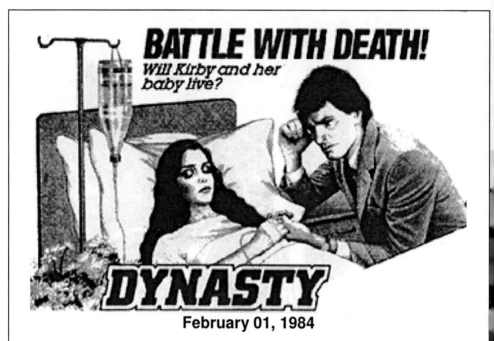

February 01, 1984

February 22, 1984

February 29, 1984

May 02, 1984

September 26, 1984

October 10, 1984

October 10, 1984

October 24, 1984

October 31, 1984

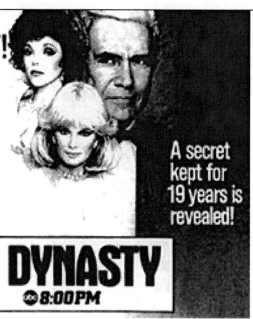

November 14, 1984

CHILD OF SCANDAL!

IS SHE BLAKE'S DAUGHTER?

DYNASTY

⊛**8PM**

November 21, 1984

KRYSTLE IS SHOCKED TO LEARN THE "TRUTH" ABOUT BLAKE'S REVENGE!

DYNASTY

ALL NEW!
8:00PM

November 28, 1984

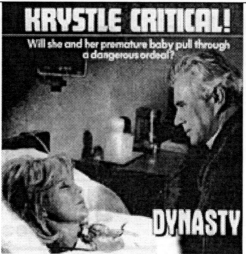

December 05, 1984

December 19, 1984

January 23, 1985

January 30, 1985

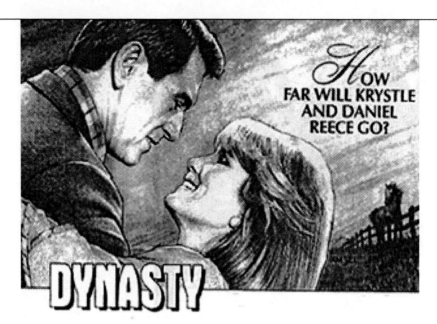

February 06, 1985

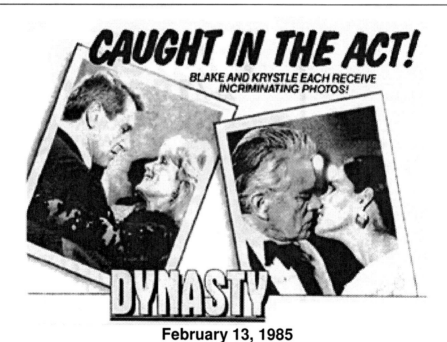

February 13, 1985

February 20, 1985

May 08, 1985

May 15, 1985

September 25, 1985

October 09, 1985

October 16, 1985

November 20, 1985

November 27, 1985

November 28, 1985

December 05, 1985

February 05, 1986

February 12, 1986

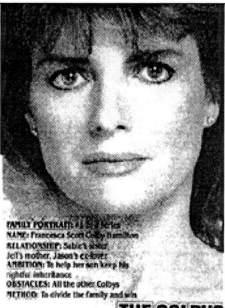

FAMILY PORTRAITS #1
NAME: Francesca Scott Colby Hamilton
RELATIONSHIP: Sable's sister
Jeff's mother, Jason's co-lover.
AMBITION: To help her son keep his
rightful inheritance.
OBSTACLES: All the other Colbys
METHOD: To divide the family and win

THE COLBYS

February 13, 1986

Blake.
It's always been you.
Never anyone else.

It's not just drama, it's
DYNASTY

February 19, 1986

February 20, 1986

February 26, 1986

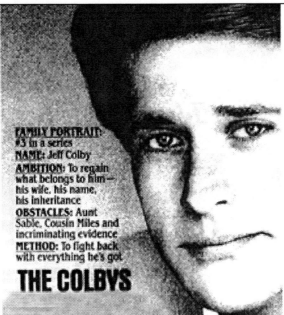

FAMILY PORTRAIT:
#3 in a series
NAME: Jeff Colby
AMBITION: To regain what belongs to him—his wife, his name, his inheritance
OBSTACLES: Aunt Sable, Cousin Miles and incriminating evidence
METHOD: To fight back with everything he's got.

THE COLBYS

February 27, 1986

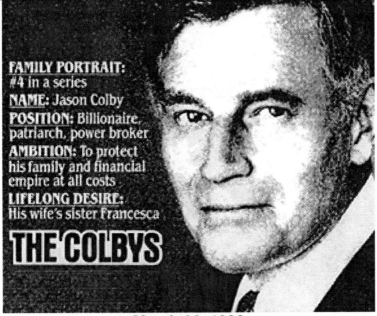

FAMILY PORTRAIT:
#4 in a series
NAME: Jason Colby
POSITION: Billionaire, patriarch, power broker
AMBITION: To protect his family and financial empire at all costs
LIFELONG DESIRE: His wife's sister Francesca

THE COLBYS

March 06, 1986

March 20, 1986

May 21, 1986

May 22, 1986

September 17, 1986

...THIS IS **THE COLBYS**   PREMIERE

September 24, 1986

THE COLBYS   8:00PM

THE COLBYS   8:00PM

September 25, 1986

MERCILESS?

PENNILESS?

DYNASTY

October 01,1986

MRS.

MISTRESS

THE COLBYS   8:00PM

October 02, 1986

October 23, 1986

November 06, 1986

Nothing is private
when you live
in my house.
The Colbys

November 13, 1986

It's time to teach
someone a lesson.
Dynasty

November 19, 1986

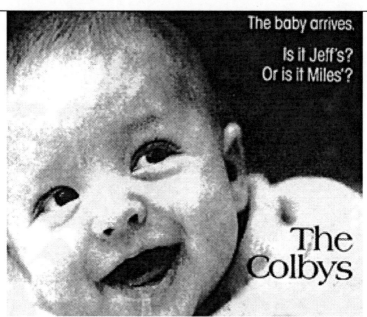

The baby arrives.

Is it Jeff's?
Or is it Miles'?

The Colbys

February 05, 1987

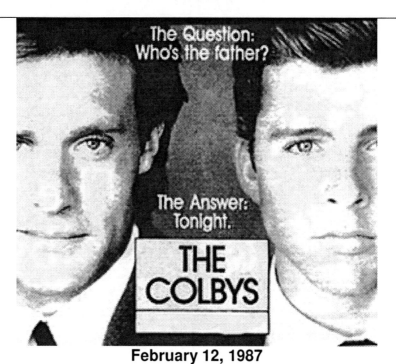

The Question:
Who's the father?

The Answer:
Tonight.

THE COLBYS

February 12, 1987

February 26, 1987

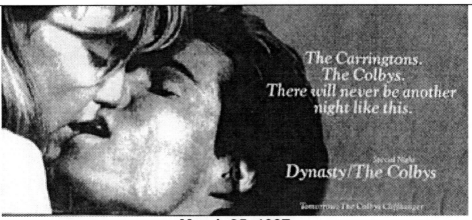

March 25, 1987

The cliffhanger that will amaze you.

The Colbys

March 26, 1987

 The Season Finale.
Dynasty

May 06, 1987

DYNASTY *Season Premiere.*

September 23, 1987

He saved her from a watery grave. Now, he's in over his head.

Dynasty

October 14, 1987

"'Dynasty' is sexy again." —USA Today

Dynasty

November 18, 1987

Steven. Fallon. Adam.
Tonight—
who will assume
control of the
family empire?

Dynasty

November 25, 1987

No Fallon.
No Steven.
Tonight Jeff and Sammy Jo
stop living their lives for others.

Dynasty

February 10, 1988

Dynasty Season Finale

Tonight. All hell breaks loose.

March 30, 1988

SEASON PREMIERE

A gun shot. A proposal.
A disappearance. A court decision.
A mysterious note. Questions answered.
and a touch of Sable, tonight.

DYNASTY

November 03. 1988

**"Sorry about Sean, Alexis...but with you,
death has always been a simpler solution
than divorce, hasn't it?"**

Sable Colby's
putting the nasty
back in Dynasty.
DYNASTY

November 10, 1988

"The only joy greater than marrying you
is marrying you again."

Tonight,
a candlelight wedding.
DYNASTY

January 12, 1989

"The game is hearts,
Alexis. The object is
Dex. May the best
woman win."

DYNASTY

February 16, 1989

Tonight, The Grand Finale.

May 11, 1989

Thank You All So Much — Joan Collins

Best Television Actress in a Drama Series
"Dynasty"

Joan Collins Thank You Ad – Daily Variety

DYNASTY ANNIVERSARIES

THE HOLLYWOOD REPORTER

HAPPY ANNIVERSARY
Dynasty

Thanks for nine great years
Love,
Linda & John

Congratulations
and love to everybody on
Dynasty.
Joan Collins

CONGRATULATIONS "DYNASTY"

THANK YOU FOR SURROUNDING
ME WITH BEAUTY FOR EIGHT YEARS.
NOLAN MILLER

Anna
Continued success
with our appreciation.

Michael Nader
& John James

WITH
THANKS
& LOVE
TO
EVERYONE
I'VE
WORKED
WITH
ON
"DYNASTY"
FOR THE
LAST 7 YEARS

To my new family

Congratulations
and a big thankyou

Stephanie Beacham.

DYNASTY'S 150TH EPISODE

DYNASTY'S 150TH EPISODE

DYNASTY'S 150TH EPISODE

DYNASTY'S 200TH EPISODE

DYNASTY'S 200TH EPISODE

DYNASTY'S 200TH EPISODE

DYNASTY'S 200TH EPISODE

Chapter Seven

And The Winner Is…

Like several other shows on television, Dynasty was showered with its share of criticism as well as tremendous praise. This was quickly made apparent as the series and its stars began being nominated for and winning many, many awards for their efforts. In this chapter you will find all of the awards Dynasty and The Colbys were nominated for and/or won.

First we'll start with the one achievement that most television and movie actors strive for: a star on the Hollywood Walk of Fame!

John Forsythe received his star on the Walk of Fame for his participation in film before his triumphant role as Blake Carrington. John's star is located at 6549 Hollywood Boulevard between Whitley and Schrader.

Screen Legend Charlton Heston received his star long before The Colbys. His is located at 1628 Hollywood Boulevard.

Barbara Stanwyck also received a star back in the days of Big Valley. Hers is located at 1751 Vine Street near the famed intersection of Hollywood and Vine.

On December 14, 1983, Joan Collins received her star on the Walk of Fame. Aaron Spelling was on hand to speak at the presentation and reminded people, "For those of you who frequent Hollywood Boulevard, keep in mind that Alexis Colby doesn't like to get stepped on." Joan's star is located at 6901 Hollywood Boulevard in between Mann's Chinese Theatre and the Kodak Theatre.

With John Forsythe and friend Bunky Jones by her side, Linda Evans was presented with her star in the mid 80's. Linda's star is located at 6834 Hollywood Boulevard. It is placed at the now famous corner of Hollywood and Highland near the Kodak Theatre.

Diahann Carroll was presented a star on the Walk of Fame for her musical contribution to the industry instead of one for television. Diahann's star is located at 7005 Hollywood Boulevard near the corner of Hollywood and Orange Drive.

DYNASTY

1981 – Emmy Award Nomination – Outstanding Art Direction for a Series for the premiere episode "Oil" - John E. Chilberg II (art director), Paul Sylos (art director), Frank Swig (art director) and Brock Broughton (set decorator)

1981 – Emmy Award Nomination – Outstanding Achievement in Film Editing for a Series for episode number three "The Dinner Party" – Dick Darling (editor)

1982 – Emmy Award Nomination – Outstanding Lead Actor in a Drama Series – John Forsythe

1982 – Emmy Award Nomination – Outstanding Drama Series – Aaron Spelling (executive producer), Douglas S. Cramer (executive producer), E. Duke Vincent (supervising producer), Edward Ledding (producer), and Elaine Rich (producer)

1982 – Golden Globe Award Nomination – Best Performance by an Actor in a TV Series – Drama – John Forsythe

1982 – Golden Globe Award Nomination – Best Performance by an Actress in a TV Series – Drama – Joan Collins

1982 – Golden Globe Award Nomination – Best TV-Series – Drama

1982 – Golden Globe Award Winner – Best Performance by an Actress in a TV Series – Drama – Linda Evans (tied with Barbara Bel Geddes of Dallas)

1982 – Young Artist Award Nomination – Best Young Actress in a Television Series – Katy Kurtzman

1983 – Emmy Award Nomination – Outstanding Lead Actress in a Drama Series – Linda Evans

1983 – Emmy Award Nomination – Outstanding Lead Actor in a Drama Series – John Forsythe

1983 – Golden Globe Nomination – Best Performance by an Actress in a TV Series – Drama – Linda Evans

1983 – Golden Globe Nomination - Best TV-Series – Drama

1983 - Golden Globe Award Winner – Best Performance by an Actor in a TV Series – Drama – John Forsythe

1983 - Golden Globe Award Winner – Best Performance by an Actress in a TV Series – Drama – Joan Collins

1983 – TP de Oro Winner – Best Foreign Series (originates in Spain)

1984 – Emmy Award Nomination – Outstanding Lead Actress in a Drama Series – Joan Collins

1984 – Emmy Award Nomination – Outstanding Lead Actor in a Drama Series – John Forsythe

1984 – Emmy Award Nomination – Outstanding Costume Design for a Series - Nolan Miller (costume designer) for the episode "The Wedding"

1984 – Emmy Award Nomination – Outstanding Cinematography for a Series – Richard Rawlings for the episode "New Lady in Town"

1984 – Emmy Award Nomination – Outstanding Art Direction for a Series – Tom Trimble and Brock Broughton for the episode "The Voice: Part Two"

1984 – Golden Globe Nomination – Best Performance by an Actress in a TV Series – Drama – Joan Collins

1984 - Golden Globe Nomination – Best Performance by an Actress in a TV Series – Drama – Linda Evans

1984 - Golden Globe Award Winner – Best Performance by an Actor in a TV Series – Drama – John Forsythe

1984 – Golden Globe Award Winner – Best TV Series – Drama

1984 – Soap Opera Digest Award Winner – Outstanding Prime Time Soap Opera

1984 – Soap Opera Digest Award Winner – Outstanding Villainess in a Prime Time Soap Opera – Joan Collins

1984 – Soap Opera Digest Award Winner – Outstanding Actress in a Prime Time Soap Opera – Linda Evans

1984 – Soap Opera Digest Award Winner – Outstanding Actor in a Mature Role in a Prime Time Soap Opera – John Forsythe

1984 – Soap Opera Digest Award Winner – Outstanding Actor in a Prime Time Soap Opera – John Forsythe

1985 – Casting Society of America Artios Award Nomination – Best Casting for TV, Dramatic Episode – Gary Shaffer and Marc Schwartz

1985 – Emmy Award Nomination - Outstanding Costume Design for a Series - Nolan Miller (costume designer) for the episode "Royal Wedding"

1985 – Emmy Award Nomination – Outstanding Achievement in Music Composition for a Series (Dramatic Underscore) – Angela Morley for the episode "Triangles"

1985 - Emmy Award Nomination – Outstanding Art Direction for a Series – Tom Trimble and Brock Broughton for the episode "Royal Wedding"

1985 - Golden Globe Nomination – Best Performance by an Actress in a TV Series – Drama – Joan Collins

1985 - Golden Globe Nomination – Best Performance by an Actress in a TV Series – Drama – Linda Evans

1985 - Golden Globe Nomination – Best Performance by an Actor in a TV Series – Drama – John Forsythe

1985 – Golden Globe Nomination – Best TV Series – Drama

1985 – People's Choice Award Winners – Outstanding Actress in a Drama Series – Joan Collins and Linda Evans (they tied)

1985 – Soap Opera Digest Award Winner – Outstanding Villainess in a Prime Time Serial – Joan Collins

1985 - Soap Opera Digest Award Winner – Outstanding Actress in a Prime Time Serial – Linda Evans

1985 – Soap Opera Digest Award Winner – Outstanding Actress in a Supporting Role in a Prime Time Serial – Catherine Oxenberg

1985 – Soap Opera Digest Award Winner – Outstanding New Actress in a Prime Time Serial – Catherine Oxenberg

1986 - Emmy Award Nomination - Outstanding Costume Design for a Series - Nolan Miller (costume designer) for the episode "The Vendetta"

1986 - Emmy Award Nomination – Outstanding Achievement in Music Composition for a Series (Dramatic Underscore) – Angela Morley for the episode "The Subpoenas"

1986 – Emmy Award Nomination – Outstanding Achievement in Makeup for a Series – Jack Freeman, Robert Sidell and Bruce Hutchinson for the episode "Masquerade"

1986 – Emmy Award Nomination – Outstanding Achievement in Hairstyling for a Series – Gerald Solomon, Cherie and Linda Leiter Sharp for the episode "Masquerade"

1986 - Golden Globe Nomination – Best Performance by an Actress in a TV Series – Drama – Joan Collins

1986 - Golden Globe Nomination – Best Performance by an Actress in a TV Series – Drama – Linda Evans

1986 - Golden Globe Nomination – Best Performance by an Actor in a TV Series – Drama – John Forsythe

1986 - Golden Globe Nomination – Best TV Series – Drama

1986 – Golden Globe Nomination – Best Performance by an Actor in a Supporting Role in a Series, Mini-Series or Motion Picture Made for TV – John James

1986 – People's Choice Award Winner – Outstanding Drama Series

1986 – People's Choice Award Winner – Outstanding Actress in a Drama Series – Joan Collins

1986 – Soap Opera Digest Award Nomination – Outstanding Actor/Actress in a Comic Relief Role on a Prime Time Serial – Joan Collins

1986 – Soap Opera Digest Award Nomination – Outstanding Actor/Actress in a Comic Relief Role on a Prime Time Serial – Heather Locklear

1986 - Soap Opera Digest Award Nomination – Outstanding Villainess in a Prime Time Serial – Joan Collins

1986 – Soap Opera Digest Award Nomination – Outstanding Actor in a Prime Time Soap Opera – John Forsythe

1986 - Soap Opera Digest Award Nomination – Outstanding Villain in a Prime Time Serial – Gordon Thomson

1986 - Soap Opera Digest Award Nomination – Favorite Super Couple on a Prime Time Serial – Linda Evans and John Forsythe

1987 - Emmy Award Nomination – Outstanding Achievement in Hairstyling for a Series – Gerald Solomon and Cherie for the episode "The Ball"

1987 - Emmy Award Nomination – Outstanding Art Direction for a Series – Tom Trimble and Brock Broughton for the episode "A Love Remembered - Part Two"

1987 - Golden Globe Nomination – Best Performance by an Actress in a TV Series – Drama – Joan Collins

1987 - Golden Globe Nomination – Best Performance by an Actor in a TV Series – Drama – John Forsythe

1987 - Golden Globe Nomination – Best TV Series – Drama

1988 - Emmy Award Nomination – Outstanding Achievement in Hairstyling for a Series – Gerald Solomon, Cherie and Monica Hart Helpman for the episode "The Fair"

1988 - Golden Globe Nomination – Best Performance by an Actor in a Supporting Role in a Series, Mini-Series or Motion Picture Made for TV – Gordon Thomson

1988 - Soap Opera Digest Award Nomination – Outstanding Villainess in a Prime Time Serial – Joan Collins

1988 - Soap Opera Digest Award Nomination – Outstanding Villain in a Prime Time Serial – Gordon Thomson

1988 - Soap Opera Digest Award Nomination – Favorite Super Couple on a Prime Time Serial – Linda Evans and John Forsythe

1988 – Soap Opera Digest Award Nomination – Outstanding Actor in a Supporting Role: Prime Time – Christopher Cazenove

1988 – Soap Opera Digest Award Nomination – Outstanding Prime Time Serial

1989 - Soap Opera Digest Award Nomination – Outstanding Actor in a Supporting Role: Prime Time – Gordon Thomson

1989 - Soap Opera Digest Award Nomination – Outstanding Actress in a Supporting Role: Prime Time – Leann Hunley

1989 - Soap Opera Digest Award Nomination – Outstanding Prime Time Serial

1989 – Young Artist Award Winner – Best Young Actor Under Nine Years of Age – Justin Burnette

1990 – Soap Opera Digest Award Nomination – Outstanding Prime Time Serial

1990 - Soap Opera Digest Award Nomination – Outstanding Storyline: Prime Time – The "Sable/Alexis" Rivalry

1990 - Soap Opera Digest Award Nomination – Outstanding Lead Actress: Prime Time – Stephanie Beacham

1990 - Soap Opera Digest Award Nomination – Outstanding Supporting Actress: Prime Time – Heather Locklear

1990 - Soap Opera Digest Award Nomination – Outstanding Lead Actor: Prime Time – Michael Nader

THE COLBYS

1986 – Emmy Award Nomination – Outstanding Cinematography for a Series – Richard L. Rawlings

1986 – Soap Opera Digest Award Nomination – Outstanding Villainess on a Prime Time Serial – Stephanie Beacham

1986 – Soap Opera Digest Award Nomination – Outstanding Actor in a Leading Role on a Prime Time Serial – Charlton Heston

1986 – Soap Opera Digest Award Nomination – Outstanding Villain on a Prime Time Serial – Ricardo Montalban

1986 – Soap Opera Digest Award Nomination – Favorite Super Couple on a Prime Time Serial – Emma Samms and John James

1987 – People's Choice Award Winner – Outstanding Drama Series

1987 – People's Choice Award Nomination – Outstanding Actress in a Drama Series – Stephanie Beacham

1988 – Soap Opera Digest Award Nomination – Outstanding Lead Actor in a Leading Role – Charlton Heston

1988 – Soap Opera Digest Award Nomination - Outstanding Villainess: Prime Time – Stephanie Beacham

1988 - Soap Opera Digest Award Nomination – Outstanding Villain: Prime Time – Ricardo Montalban

1988 - Soap Opera Digest Award Nomination – Outstanding Actress in a Supporting Role: Prime Time – Shanna Reed

1988 - Soap Opera Digest Award Nomination – Favorite Super Couple – Emma Samms and John James

1988 – Young Artist Award – Best Young Actor – Guest Starring in a Television Drama – Coleby Lombardo

Chapter Eight

After All These Years

During the process of writing this book, we received many messages from fans of Dynasty and the cast. They shared their favorite memories and crushes along the way. After reading them, we decided to add a section dedicated to the fans of Dynasty. Two of the fans expressed their thoughts through examination of the storylines and characters as they would relate to others in history or psychology. It is an eclectic mix of thoughts and opinions that grace the next twenty pages. Paul and I hope you'll enjoy sharing these memories with fellow fans as much as we enjoyed including them.

GORAN MARKOVIC - SERBIA

In 1984, when the news of broadcasting Dynasty in Serbia was announced, there was a lot of commotion because the communist government thought the show would have a negative influence on the nation by spreading capitalistic ideas with the story about wealth and luxury and this way destabilize the communist regime. It only made the nation more intriguing when Dynasty began airing. I remember sitting with my family at our home when the first episode was on. No one said a word until its end. It was a beginning of a fairy tale in the lives of my family but also, the beginning of incredible euphoria in all of the country. It was the most popular show for years, and I couldn't face missing an episode. Years went by and my country and the surrounding area was struck by war, bombarding and terror, communism fell and now my country lives in freedom with hope of a better life ahead. All the time Dynasty was a refuge from problems and the difficulties of everyday life. The show especially marks the period when I went to school to another city. Season 4 was on, I was in the dorm. We stayed awake even after our bedtime because the show aired in late hours and my roomies and I watched it in secrecy so that our teachers wouldn't catch us. We stayed awake 'till morning, talking about events and characters. My imagination went wild. I pretended to be one of the characters. I imagined I was in the Filoli mansion, checking its every corner. The world of Carrington's was my world. It is still my great wish to visit America, meet some of the actors and visit the Filoli mansion. I spent years collecting pictures and episodes of the show. I almost have all Dynasty and the Colbys episodes taped, and thought it was time to create and present a site from which my all time wish comes through. The memories today are still very much vivid and alive. I share them with my family, friends and fans. Dynasty is my dream and my reality.

ROBIN WILDSCHUT – THE NETHERLANDS

I am 28 years old, so when Dynasty was on the air, I was still a kid. I can't remember when I started watching the show, but my memory goes back to the day Amanda and Prince Michael got married in 1985. It was written in every Dutch magazine that was available and I think my passion for Dynasty began at that time. It was a 4-episode 'movie' and I watched it with my mother. And I was shocked. All those people who got killed! I wanted to see what had happened the next year and since then I was crazy about Dynasty. I wanted to see what happened in the beginning and I started to collect pictures and stuff from the magazines. I started to collect the synopsis for each episode. At the time I started to watch I met the 'new' Fallon (Emma Samms), although I never saw the old Fallon, so I was very curious. Why wasn't I born a few years earlier, so I could have seen all the episodes! A few years after Dynasty was of the air, THANK GOD, they had reruns of the show. But they stopped in the year that Adam was blackmailed by Neal McVane about his identity and little Krystina got her heart-transplant. But hey, I did see that episodes anyway. Still, I am still not over the Carrington-saga, which I will love till the day I die. What I liked the most? I really don't know. It is just a feeling you get, which no one can understand, unless you are a fan yourself. I think it is the glamour, the beauty and the excitement. It is a mix of everything, I guess. As I said, it is a feeling and I feel it right now while I am writing to you. Strange, don't you think? Blake, Krystle, Alexis... I will never forget them. They are part of my youth, my life AND my future. And thanks to you and all our DYNASTY-fans in the world, I don't have to worry about that future.

DENIS KELLY CAPWELL - CROATIA

Dynasty: such a magical word. To me, boy of seven that I was, Dynasty opened many doors and learned me so much. With Dynasty my love of acting was shaped and I knew then what was my life's calling. I was a kid who was very ill and visiting hospitals, always being the look out, was so much easier with Dynasty there. Pretending to be a Carrington, building my dream world from which I never stepped out. And I'm grateful for that. There are so many things I relate to Dynasty, periods of my life. Aaron Spelling became my role model and my teacher. To a scared little boy he showed it is all right to be gay. There is nothing wrong with that. And the little boy wasn't so lonely any more. Aaron Spelling; through out my life, has thought me so much. I could talk about Dynasty memories for days I think. Bu the most important thing I learned watching this magnificent soap, is how to dream.

YANIV SHLAMBERG - ISRAEL

I actually grew up with The Carringtons. I remember when Dynasty came to air in Israel I was only 8 years old and my parents didn't agreed that I'll see the show, so when they weren't watching I used to go out of my room, hide behind the closet in the living room and watch the show... My first fresh big memory is the last episode of season 3, when Krystle and Alexis got stuck in the burning cabin. Few moments before the episode was over - the power went down and I was so upset that I couldn't find out what exactly happened in the end of the episode, then I didn't know yet "they" left us 'hanging in the air'. When I heard Dynasty going to be cancel in the US at 1989 I was so down, I couldn't believe it. The 219th episode was very popular here and I plan the VCR to tape it two days earlier. Two years later when the Reunion aired, I was mostly disappointed. Sable and Monica was gone and nobody talked about them, so many mistakes and stories was still hanging in the air and left us with so many questions marks. At that day I thought and wrote not only a miniseries to continue the saga, I also started to write an original super-soap of my own, about an Israeli family, in the holy land. My inspiration was of course, Dynasty, and the series I wrote is in negotiations today with an Israeli TV networks - and I owe this to my first love to the Carringtons, especially to Alexis, Blake and Krystle who was for me, the responsible to this success of the show. Today I have two dreams come true: I'm writing Dynasty myself, as a fan fiction though, but for me it's like the real thing. The other of course, it my show, that called by the way on the name of the greatest home I ever saw in my whole life: The Mansion. You know of course, which home I'm talking about...

INNA MISHINA - ESTONIA

I did not watch Dynasty from the beginning, just by accident I switched on our local channel at 11.30 pm (the time when Dynasty was on the air here) and saw there Gordon Thomson. So I guess I missed whole first episode. I had to watch this opera not in my native language but in English with subtitles in Estonian, so I had to learn languages. Not many people watched Dynasty here because of not convenient time and languages, so that never was popular here. I liked Dynasty because that was very different from other soap operas. Even Santa-Barbara had too many stupid story lines but in Dynasty I liked everything expect the case when Fallon have a contact with UFO. In the time when I watched Dynasty I decided that someday I will go to USA but it's only part of my dream. I liked Jack Coleman as Steven Carrington very much. He was very nice and caring person. And of course Joan Collins was marvelous. I will not talk about Gordon Thomson because I am his biggest fan.

TIMOTHY PASKALJEVIC - CROATIA

There aren't so many nice things in my life that I remember, but one part of my childhood will always carry some dazzling moments - mostly because I have grown up watching one beautiful TV-show called "Dynasty". Perhaps some people would say that "Dynasty" is nowadays a rusty phenomenon, but it's understandable that every decade contains some special charm which is the sign of that respective period, so therefore "Dynasty" nowadays can't "buy" for itself such a percentage of popularity like twenty years ago. Nothing is the same any more. Nevertheless, this soap-opera is (un)fortunately much better than many other TV-shows of the 80's and it must not be forgotten. Why was "Dynasty" so important to me? Perhaps the word "importance" is an inappropriate one - let's say that "Dynasty" became a refreshing part of my life. I didn't feel myself obliged to watch it, only that I want to watch it. It wasn't an obligation, it was a love. Love can perform miracles - and it did. Watching "Dynasty" during the 80's, my life didn't become simpler (or much more enjoyable) but it has offered me since than so many useful hints how to defeat habitual life-obstacles that I have encountered. Briefly told, I became a part of something that I could make a grab at whenever I felt sequestered or depressed. After some time I finally realized that "Dynasty" episode is not just an episode, actually, each episode is a reflection of one miserable (sometimes even sarcastic) drama with a wise point - wealthy people are also doomed to misery, perhaps even more than the others. But, frequently, that's their weapon for hurting their beloved ones even stronger. Is that a nasty habit of theirs or just a mournful irony?

MARI KUOSMANEN - FINLAND

I was born 1985, so I can't remember anything of Dynasty when it was on air first time. Year ago in June I turned on my TV at about 5 pm and a beautiful tune came out of the Telly. I wondered "what is this fabulous program?" I watched the whole show in that day and then ran to newspaper and read the name: Dynasty. I tried to watch every show. Then I loved Krystle and her kindness. I thought that this fun wouldn't last forever so I taped my first episode, which was that when Fallon opened La Mirage. From Michael and Amanda's wedding I have seen all the episodes. When Krystle was kidnapped I got bored of her. Alexis knew how to work and she was so bitchy! Ah! I loved her tricks. I noticed when she was with Dex, she and Blake were even friends. I can watch Dynasty episodes again and again and never get bored with it!

ALEXANDER YOUNG - CANADA

Hello, my name is Alex and I loved Dynasty! I watched right from the premiere of Episode one, right from the first season. I have to admit I was at first unsure whether Dynasty was going to be a success until the cliffhanger, and the alluring introduction of Alexis Carrington. Right from that moment I was hooked and anxiously awaited for season two. The introduction and the arrival of Alexis to Denver was a high-ratings success!!! This bold move by Richard and Esther Shapiro, and Aaron Spelling to introduce a conniving and evil villainess to Primetime was a success. It helped to draw millions of viewers to sit on the edge of their seats also awaiting the return of "super-bitch", Alexis. The introduction of a powerful and ruthless woman in an oftentimes dominated male industry in the oil business was enticing and intriguing! On Dallas, men were the main focal point in the arena of power and money but on Dynasty it was the woman who shared this highlight. Powerful woman like Alexis, Dominique Devereaux, and Sabella Scott Colby proved that women would not take a backseat to men. Another particular interest in the creation of Dynasty was the catfights between the women which in the end also lured millions to Primetime to witness the scraps between archenemies and foes alike. Alexis and Krystle would duke it out in lily ponds, cabins, and yet again in Dynasty: The Reunion. Sammy-Jo and Fallon would also duke it out in a mud fight on the Carrington Estate within the proximity of the Horse stables. Dominique also retaliated with a slap to Alexis that was heard round the World. Archenemy and cousin, Sable Colby also scrapped with Alexis within the lobby of the Carlton Hotel.

On Dallas the men fought but on Dynasty the women duked it out! Dynasty was a success airing for nine seasons. The cliffhanger during season nine left the fate of such characters as Alexis, Blake, Fallon and other such interests up in the air with the cancellation of Dynasty. This was to be resolved in the two part special, Dynasty: The Reunion!!! As I continue to muse and remain fascinated with Dynasty I am amazed that despite the passing of a decade, Dynasty continues to live on!!! The many articles, pictures, websites, and VHS tapes that exist to this day are a fact that Dynasty was a powerful tool that gripped the World. Almost everyone I know is aware I am a Dynasty fan. So much so, that they refer to me as Alexis, even though I later switched my favorite character from Alexis to Sable.

With the birth and spin off of Dynasty II: The Colbys, I became fascinated with Sable, who was married to Jason Colby (Charlton Heston). Sable was much more powerful in that Jason was an L. A. based billionaire. Sable was also ruthless and in my opinion gained the victory in her ongoing battle with Alexis. Remember it was Sable who confronted Alexis, by arriving in Denver to come to the aid of Blake Carrington. Sable was provoked and also scrapped it out with Alexis and was a crucial witness to Alexis' downfall. (Quite literally) On the second floor of The Carlton, Adam hurled Dex towards the balcony where he crashed into Alexis, with Sable and Monica being present to witness this downfall! The balcony railing gave way and Alexis and Dex plummeted to uncertain doom in what was the season cliffhanger and the eminent cancellation of what was one of the all time greatest primetime serials next to Dallas to air during the eighties. Dynasty was very much a success and will continue to live on thanks primarily to such fans and the various websites devoted to Dynasty. My synopsis and detailed explanation of this Primetime serial like the rest of these detailed explanations by other fans are indeed proof that Dynasty was wonderful beyond what words can describe!!!! Together we can take Dynasty into another decade and continue to remain united in our love of this wonderful primetime serial by Aaron Spelling, who continues to bless us with other successful shows.

MARC SMEYERS - BELGIUM

DYNASTY / THE COLBYS: FREUDIAN, HISTORICAL AND MYTHOLOGICAL

I have always loved 'Dynasty' and 'The Colbys', and even now, when both series are off the air in Belgium, I think back of them every day. I will not argue about who the strongest, most powerful or weakest characters were, nor shall I give my comments on the most romantic or most violent scenes. Yet, I have never forgotten the scene in which Alexis fires her shot gun into the air, causing Krystle to fall off her horse by which she has a miscarriage. To this very day, I've always felt that the writers acted unworthily when they did this, especially, since I am convinced that Alexis was not an evil woman at all, but merely a victim of the harsh vicissitudes that had taken place in her life. In 'Past Imperfect', Joan Collins also says, that the people never forgave Alexis for hurting Krystle in that way. I don't think Alexis deserved that, besides, in the end, she at least always cared for her children. In season 7 she even offered her moral support to Krystle, at the same time consoling Blake, encouraging him not to give up hope, when Krystina was in hospital, desperately waiting for a heart transplant. I quote: 'She is a Carrington, Blake!' What I actually mean is that when Alexis has to take the blame for many nasty schemes, she also deserves to be given the credit for some noble actions, for example, accepting and adopting Adam, after he has been blackmailed by frustrated Congressman Neal McVane. At the time 'Dynasty' and 'The Colbys' were on the air in Western Europe, I was reading a lot about Sigmund Freud, the Austrian neurologist who lived from 1856 until 1939. I noticed that some of his theories were implemented into the series, as it were. For example, the fact that a girl tends to love her father more than her mother, by which a sort of rivalry develops between mother and daughter (this is what Freud called the 'Electra-complex'), and that a boy tends to love his mother more than his father, by which the same rivalry develops, but this time between father and son (this is what Freud called the 'Oedipus complex'). Although, Freud claimed, that these particular stages in life occur in one's childhood, they were used by the writers in Fallon and Steven's lives, at least, in my opinion, when they were much older; when Alexis returns to Denver, Fallon rejects her mother, being daddy's little girl, but Steven welcomes her with open arms, still being very resentful and hostile against Blake, for accidentally having killed Ted Dinard.

Yet, it should be noted, that Freud's theory concerning homosexuality states that a boy, for example, will most certainly turn out to be gay, when there is an absence of the Oedipus complex, whereas modern psychology claims the reverse of his theory causes homosexuality, thus when the Oedipus complex is present very intensely. The other Freudian theory I detected was the one by which Freud tried to prove that all people are born bisexual and may develop a sexual preference later in life; Steven is gay, however, after his affair with Ted Dinard, he marries Sammy

Jo and later on he takes Claudia Blaisdel as his second wife. Thereafter, he returns to his gay lifestyle having an affair with Luke Fuller, who gets killed during the Moldavia massacre, ending up with Bart Fallmont, with whom he leaves Denver to live in Washington DC. Admittedly, it is also undeniably true that some people have sexual experiences with both genders before their final sexual preference becomes clear, a fact, which Freud did not include in his theory, but which is illustrated to the fullest by Steven's life. Perhaps I go too far with this, but I think it is an interesting fact about the series, besides many Freudian similarities occur in 'The Colbys'; Miles has the same mother-son relationship with Sable, however he is not gay, on the contrary, and Monica is Jason's little girl. Yet, you see, we mustn't take our Sigmund Freud too seriously either, for in my opinion, his theories are pleasant to read and talk about, however, I do believe that the good old doctor, may his soul rest in peace, wasn't so much of a doctor, but merely a very good judge of character.

Although 'Dynasty' and 'The Colbys' both had a strong influence on society, thus on people, I always considered them as just a form of entertainment. When they were on I sat back, tried to forget reality, and live in a fantasy world for three quarters of an hour. However, some people among my immediate entourage, who also watched the series, sometimes tried to impersonate some of the characters; during those moments they really represented everything I hated and made me want to commit arson of some sort, I mean, to have a real Alexis, or Blake, or Krystle, or whatever character in the series in your living room. Just imagine! I sometimes had to remind them of reality after all, every Dynasty-Colbys character was a fictional one! Both 'Dynasty' and 'The Colbys' also shared enormous similarities with some real American or European dynasties, royal or presidential, particularly, The Tudors and the Stuarts in 16th-century England. Alexis and Sable, their rivalry, their hatred for each other, could, in many ways, be compared with Elizabeth I and Mary Stuart and their relationship with each other. Claudia marrying Steven, and after that his brother, Adam, could easily be compared with Catherine of Aragon, who first married Arthur, first son of Henry VII, and then Henry VIII, second son of Henry VII. Some of my closest friends also claim, that 'Dynasty' had some Greek mythological tinges, in that sense, that minor incestuous relationships also occurred occasionally during the series' run; they then refer, for example, to the story line, in which Amanda and Dex fall in love; at that time Dex is actually Amada's stepfather, since he is married to Alexis, Amanda's mother. Let's take a good look at Lesley and Clay's love affair; how desperate and hopeless they become, when Clay turns out to be Ben Carrington's son, actually being Leslie's half-brother and sharing the same bloodline unknowingly. Greek mythology is full of incestuous relationships after all, Oedipus kills his own father, marries his own mother and has children with her, also unknowingly. Perhaps, it is a little exaggerated, but they do have a point there, I think. However, be all that as it may! 'Dynasty' and 'The Colbys' were my favorites during the eighties, no matter what! Compared with 'Dallas' and 'Falcon Crest', they were the crème de la crème of television's greatest moments!

HEATHER LAURIN – TEXAS, USA

I was 12 years old when Dynasty premiered, and I have been a fan since the very beginning. I started watching the show because I wanted to see the face behind the voice of Charlie Townsend, the character portrayed by John Forsythe on "Charlie's Angels". I was also a major fan of Linda Evans, having become hooked on the "Big Valley" reruns. Linda is still my very favorite actress today. I wrote her a fan letter when I was sick with the flu, and she sent me a beautiful get well card and an autographed picture, both of which I still cherish today. This show had everything that a viewer wanted: action, romance, and glamour. This along with the talented cast of actors made Dynasty the best television show ever.

JENNIFER ELLIS – AUSTRALIA

During the 1980's Dynasty was very popular here in Australia. We girls and women admired Alexis's character of the feminine, sexy, feisty yet vulnerable female business tycoon. I think she was one of the first female characters to match the dominating powerful male roles in soap operas of the day.

Dynasty's popularity was increased even further when the Aussie actress Kerry Armstrong joined the cast to play the jealous and beautiful Elena, The Duchess of Branagh. Kerry was a familiar face already on our screens playing Lyn Warner in Prisoner. At the time it was a big deal for us in Australia when Australian actors made it into overseas shows, as there were not many then. I remember talking about the episode we watched the night before with girls at school the next day or to the neighbors at the fence in the backyard. I can't remember the exact year when Dynasty first aired here but I watched the show right through the first episode throughout the 1980s and also the Reunion in the early 1990s. Seeing English is our first language we had the American version of Dynasty. In 2000/01, the series was shown again on Austar's Arena channel. This was so great, like seeing an old friend again.

Dynasty influenced Australian fashions too. Most of my friends started wearing shoulder pads, sparkled tops and skirts, metallic dresses with peplums and big bold belts and jewelry. I loved Krystle's hair and I remember a lot of ladies tried to imitate her big fringe.

Being a young teenager, I really had a big crush on sweet Jeff and the dark, brooding Adam. I also liked Pamela Sue Martin's version of the spunky Fallon and I wanted to be beautiful, delicate Kirby with her long ebony hair. I loved the glamour of the clothes and the richness of the sets. Also, I loved the catfights that none of the other prime time soaps seemed to have. I used to look forward to every week to watch an episode.

Dynasty still gives me pleasure today as I enjoy reading other fans' comments on the various websites. I have even written some Dynasty fan fiction stories that have had positive comments from lovely Dynasty fans from all over the world. It is lovely to think that so many fans from around the world still love this fun, entertaining show.

E. JULIAN – BARCELONA, SPAIN

I remember my first contact with Dynasty in 1982. Spanish TV cancelled Dallas at the end of the second season and it never returned. I loved the series and I was very angry, but then came Dynasty on the same channel and same time... and sadly, the same fate: it was cancelled in the middle of season two. Unlike Dallas, Dynasty came back in 1984 and then we enjoyed the complete run of the series. The Pilot was great and the Carringtons were really rich people making the Ewings look like "new riches." Not only the settings but the characters were good and complex in the first season. There were not full heroes or villains, they were grey... Even beautiful and sweet Krystle had feelings for another man and lied to her new husband to help her former lover. My favorite Carrington was Fallon (Pamela Sue Martin). She was so wild, this spoiled little rich girl so close to Dad, making life miserable for Krystle and so hungry for sex... I loved Alexis too, like everybody, she was such a bitch! I think the series lost quality season by season, giving all the attention to the settings and outrageous plots, forgetting characterization, but I followed it to the end and it has a special place in my memory.

DOUGLAS RICKARD – LONDON, ENGLAND

My imagination was caught up most during the time "Dynasty II: The Colbys" was birthed. It was such an exciting promise of more Dynasties in the future. The bigger, richer, "The Colbys" had modern art in their mansion, was sunnier and captured the romance of California with such a sense of noble family heritage. I felt like I was being taken out West on a pioneering adventure!

However, I've realized without Season Nine, I wouldn't feel the same way about Dynasty. The characters seemed to let loose and be freer and yet everything was deadly real now. Murky Carrington back-stories planted in my subconscious over the years were being brought to life with a tangible effect on me! Now, Krystle's headaches were serious and when Alexis arrived back after an episode or two absent I sat up. This wasn't just because the actors might leave! Dynasty went full throttle in ahead in Season Nine, yet respecting the past and me at the same time. Blake was the hero again and Sable a catalyst for empathy and suspicion all at once. The balance was just right – in a world of escapism for the view, actions brought consequences.

DANNY ROUSSEL – VACHERIE, LOUSIANA, USA

I have loved Dynasty since it started. The second season was my best, with Alexis living in the art studio, her and Fallon plotting to get rid of Krystle, Sammy Jo, Nicholas Toscanni, etc… The show was what I would get punished from when I did bad in school, but when I would fill my teachers in on their missed episodes I suddenly started getting better grades because of our shared love of Dynasty. It elevated me to teacher's pet!

BRIAN ROSE

My favorite aspect of the show might sound unusual, but the thing I love about Dynasty the most is, by far, the theme song and the opening titles. I love the theme that composer Bill Conti came up with. I am constantly whistling it everywhere I go. I think it is one of the best TV theme songs EVER! As for the opening titles, I cannot even begin to describe how much I am fascinated by the title design. I love the motif of the ascending and descending bars that reveal shots as the move up and down the screen. Whoever came up with that is a genius! I think those are the best titles in the history of television. If I had my way, they would be used for more than just the opening credits, but also within each episode itself, maybe to transition from one scene to the next. Some might say that's overkill but not me!

JASON

I don't know if I would classify her as my favorite but if I have to pick the character I've enjoyed watching the most on Dynasty, I'd nominate Fallon. I don't think I have a particular favorite episode but I guess the one that stands out the most is Pamela Sue Martin's last episode. I've sort of lost interest in the show after that. It's so hard to pick a favorite scene but I'd go for the opening of La Mirage.

STEFFI – GERMANY

I have been a very big fan of Dynasty since I started watching it last year. It didn't take much time to me a big fan. I love it, the characters, the story, the music and everything else. My favorite characters are Krystle, Blake, Alexis, Fallon (Emma Samms), Dex and Amanda (Catherine Oxenberg). My favorite couple is Blake and Krystle. Without this everlasting love Dynasty wouldn't be so great. I like the catfights between Krystle and Alexis. Then I like the business aspect: Blake and Alexis fighting each other for years and not getting tired of it.

JAMES HOLMES

I have enclosed some thoughts about the show's first three seasons.

Seasons One and Two: The Alexis Effect

I think that Dynasty had the best first season of any of the primetime soaps. I loved how all the storylines was inter-dependent, like a house of cards, and the way that every plot twist led up to the events of Blake's court trial. Even Michael the chauffeur's seemingly pointless flirtation with Cecil Colby's secretary resulted in pillow talk revealing the pawning of Krystle's necklace, and Steven's relationship with Claudia Blaisdel. Both pieces of information were passed on to Blake, with tragic consequences.

I loved the juxtaposition between the Carrington and Blaisdel lifestyles in Season One. Having a relatively "normal" family like the Blaisdels served to ground the show in some sort of reality, and by extension gave the Carringtons more credibility than they would have in later years. The characters of Krystle and Claudia seemed to mirror each other as well – each was struggling to find their way forward in a new family situation, while at the same time haunted by their (partly shared) past. Claudia draws this comparison is Season Two: "You and me, we did the same thing... we had an affair. You've still got everything. I've got nothing, I've got me."

The reason Krystle still has everything is because, when push came to shove, she was willing to perjure herself under oath when asked about Blake's violent tendencies, while Claudia could not bring herself to lie about her relationship with Steven in court. In fact, almost all of the characters in the first season are morally compromised. Krystle, Fallon, Steven, Claudia and Matthew all betray people who love them, while Blake is completely ruthless in business and violent in his personal affairs. In Season Two, the moral balance of the show shifts, with the original Carringtons being depicted as innocent victims of Alexis, Nick Toscanni and Sammy Jo.

Blake, who begins the season as "convicted killer," is transformed into "unjustly accused victim" as a result of Nick's misplaced vendetta over his brother's suicide. As in Season One, Krystle comes close to an extramarital affair but, instead of acting on her own impulses and desires as she did with Matthew, she is portrayed as blameless and whiter than white – cruelly manipulated by Alexis and Nick.

Most significant, in terms of the show's shifting relationship to its main characters, is Fallon's change of attitude towards "what it means to be a Carrington." In the first season, she is clear-eyed and cynical, educating Krystle – and the viewer – in some non-sugarcoated, hard facts about Carrington life. No one else on Dynasty, or Dallas for that matter would dared to have come out with lines like these, though doubtless they would apply equally to the Ewings as to the Carringtons: "At the upper management level (of Denver Carrington), there are no blacks, no Jews, no Eskimos and no women." This is equally good: "Steven comes from a world where culls, cripples and homosexuals are taken out behind a barn and slaughtered before they get a chance to breed."

At the Carrington party in the first season, Fallon casts herself as the family rebel – she gets stoned, goes skinny dipping and mocks

Jeff's belief that, having been born into money, they both have responsibility towards those less fortunate. ("You wanna join the Junior League and knit booties for orphans, Jeff? Go ahead!") By the time of the party to celebrate Steven and Sammy Jo's marriage in Season Two, Fallon's function has changed. The role of Carrington rebel is now taken by Sammy Jo, whom Fallon reprimands (just as Krystle did her a year earlier) for getting drunk and – gasp! – dancing sexily. Like the show itself, Fallon is now unquestionably pro-Carrington. She tells Steven earnestly how lucky she feels to have been born into that family, and is virtually suicidal when Sammy Jo tells her she might not be Blake's daughter. As with Krystle and Blake, "Fallon the troublemaker" has been replaced by "Fallon the victim". In this case, she is a victim of Alexis and Sammy Jo.

That said, I think Season Two is great. Alexis is like an evil troll living at the bottom of the garden, and her lurking presence in the mansion, spying from behind pillars and hiding behind doors, gives the place a campy yet sinister atmosphere. This season has an energy that the show lacked in later years. The second half of Season Two has a strangely fevered, delirious quality, detectable in both the storylines (Blake going blind, then recovering his sight, then pretending to still be blind; Nick exchanging psychiatry for brain surgery just in time to dislodge a bullet from Claudia's brain; Blake offering to adopt Jeff; Cecil turning out to be Logan Rhinewood, etc), and the musical score which seems to grow more insane by the episode! There are time when the orchestra seems so out of control, I swear my television set is about to split itself in two from the sheer hysteria of it all!

Season Three

Even though this is when the campiness and ridiculous hats began in earnest, there is an almost operatic life-and-death BIGNESS to the storylines in Season Three, which matches the show's campy excesses. First, we learn that Blake and Alexis have a long lost son whom they have given up for dead (the after-effects of his disappearance slotting very neatly into the back story of Blake and Alexis's marriage), then up springs Adam, alive and well. Just as the family is adjusting to his arrival, they must deal with the apparent death the resurrection of their other son, Steven.

There are many changes in Season Three, not all of them for the better. Paradoxically, Alexis's newly acquired wealth and power (courtesy of dead hubby Cecil) actually serves to weaken the status of her character within the Carrington dynasty, and subsequently the series itself. When she still lived in the shed at the bottom of the garden, she was regarded as a quasi-member of the family and granted virtually free reign of the Carrington mansion. In Season Three, however, the widow Colby, now living in her deluxe penthouse, is more physically removed from the object of her obsession (i.e. Blake), and her intrusions into the family home are barely tolerated. Far from the "feminist icon of the 80s" she was hyped as at the time, Alexis now seems less the role model, more the unwelcome aunt at a family function wearing a silly hat, or the crazy neighbor in the sitcom who bursts in halfway through an episode, paranoid that she is last to know what's going on.

Speaking of comedy, Alexis and Adam, who talks in a sort of Esther Shapiro-meets-Shakespeare way (rather than "us Carringtons", he will proclaim "Carringtons we!" like Henry V with hair gel), do make a very funny, if quite bizarre, mother and son double act in their penthouse in the sky. While Adam rants on, quoting Benjamin Disraeli over breakfast, an unimpressed Alexis, breasts oozing out of some ridiculous negligee, sits nibbling on a chocolate covered strawberry. There is an unmistakable whiff of incest following Adam around following his arrival in Denver: As well as his innocent flirtation with sister Fallon, there is an element of perversity in his relationship with his mother who teases, flirts and withholds her affection from him as if he were her prison bitch. He also makes at least one jealous double entndre about Alexis's desires towards Jeff, at which mummy is suitably offended (although one gets the distinct impression that she wouldn't have been at all disappointed had Jeff accepted her invitation to move into the apartment), and, in a particularly surreal moment, Adam even makes an envious comment about the beauty of Jeff's skin to an understandably confused Blake.

When Kirby appeared I thought her the most irritating character to date: the bambi eyes, the cloying sweetness, that ridiculously enormous pigtail that hangs down to her waist – I found myself imagining that if one were to yank on it hard enough, one would hear bells ringing inside her otherwise empty head. After a few episodes, however, an interesting duality in Kirby's identity begins to emerge. On one hand (as far as her father is concerned), she is an innocent virgin who has broken off her engagement, still holds a torch for young Master Jeffrey, and is happy to play nanny to the Carrington heir; on the other, she is the former mistress of a married man, has a reputation as a European "party girl," and is determined to escape the "life of servitude" she was born into. (I'm pretty sure the Shapiros must have watched a LOT of Upstairs, Downstairs before sitting down to write Dynasty!) It is the second Kirby that Adam (himself a "downstairs" boy made good) seems intuitively to recognize. When he takes her back to Alexis's apartment to rape her, she starts off by protesting and resisting his advances. There comes a point, however, where she SUBMITS and arguably ALLOWS Adam to rape her. That is not to suggest that she WANTS to be raped or that she ENJOYS it, but perhaps something in Kirby feels she DESERVES to be raped – as though, now that Adam has seen through her virginal charade to the part of her life she is ashamed of, it is just that she be punished for her deception. It is my understanding that Dynasty was criticized at the time for trivializing the rape story, but Kirby's immediate reaction – to make light of the ordeal (it is not even referred to as rape until Season Four), to blame herself rather than Adam, to attempt to carry on as though nothing has happened – makes complete sense, psychologically speaking.

Kirby then attempts to purify herself by readopting the "innocent virgin" persona, and "losing her virginity" by making love to Jeff. Like a virgin touched for the very first time, Kirby then hopes that her life with Jeff will be enough to erase her "sordid" past, both in Europe and with Adam. She even recreates the rape scene with Adam by allowing herself to be alone in a motel room with him. This time, however, she is able to rewrite history to include a happy ending by calling Prince Charming (a.k.a. Jeff), who arrives at the last moment to rescue her. They are married, but if Kirby thinks she can escape her past "non-virgin" identity simply by becoming "Mrs. Jeff Colby", she is mistaken. She realizes as much in the cliffhanger, when she discovers that the baby she is carrying is actually the product of her rape by Adam. Jeff thinks that he is the father, and so the duality continues.

Let us not forget Kirby's hilarious father Joseph, who delivers his lines like a malfunctioning robot. And, if we are meant to believe that this is really him we are seeing from behind setting fire to Steven's cabin in the season's closing moments, then all I can say is that the old majordomo has a tighter ass than any of us had a right to expect.

Mark Jennings is a decidedly less complex character than Kirby. While Bo Hopkins (Matthew Blaisdel) and James Farentino (Nick Toscanni) each brought a palpable sense of history to their roles of Krystle's previous love interests (we sensed that these characters had existed prior to popping up in Dynasty), Mark does not seem to have any purpose or existence outside of his love scenes with Fallon and Alexis. Despite copious flashbacks on Krystle's part (if you ask me, THIS is how the brain tumor gets started), one never gets a real sense of Mark and Krystle as a couple, or of Mark as a three dimensional human being.

With Claudia dispatched to the sanitarium (after descending the Carrington staircase wearing a fur stole in a cheesy Sunset Boulevard parody that really felt as though the producers were mocking both her character and the sense of humanity she brought to the series), Krystle remains the audience's main point of identification during this season. Her conflicted feelings of joy and loss upon learning Steven is alive (believing him to be dead, she and Blake had planned to adopt his son) are movingly conveyed by Linda Evans, still managing to give a heartfelt and believable performance in the midst of the increasing artifice surrounding her.

Steven's disappearance finally brings the feud between Krystle and Fallon to a close, thus heralding the end of "Fallon the Bitch". With her character's acid wit and fierce intelligence a thing of the past, Pamela Sue Martin opts to walk through her scenes in a kind of zonked out, slightly stoned fashion, which belies her character's new identity as a hugely driven career woman – so driven, in fact, that Fallon begins working at La Mirage LESS THAN TWENTY-FOUR HOURS after her kidnapped newborn is returned to her!!

Following this trauma, she spends roughly an hour a day with her son, yet the audience is meant to applaud her both as a woman who is "finding herself" (i.e. making money) AND as a mother! Truly, the 80's were a strange time!

The one character who seems completely out of place is Jack Coleman's Steven. When Al Corley played the role, he did so in a way that was full of emotional life. He was confident, hesitant, uncertain, sweating, stammering, tormented – and alive! In comparison, Jack Coleman is like something out of Thunderbirds – save for the odd frown, his face is expressionless, a blank. There is no emotion, no inner conflict. Instead of torment, he gives up petulance. It is as though Steven has been injected with some sort of emotional botox during his plastic surgery. (Steven's surgeon, by the way, was played by James Wong, fresh from Falcon Crest where he memorably fingered Julia Cumson – not literally – in that she's Season Two cliffhanger.) Frankly, if I were Blake Carrington, I'd sue this Zombie Steven for custody of Danny too!

Chapter Nine

I Remember It Well

Now here's a little fun for all of you Dynasty buffs! Think you can remember everything about the series? Well let's find out!

1. In what year did Blake and Alexis marry and how old was Alexis?

2. What was the name of Cecil Colby's secretary in the first season and third season?

3. How many times did Roger Grimes die and what were the circumstances of his death each time?

4. What is the name of the song playing the first time Blake and Alexis danced together?

5. What was Dex Dexter's real name?

6. What was the name Blake and Krystle were originally going to name Krystina?

7. What was the year Alexis left Denver after Blake exiled her from the children?

8. What is Dominique Devereaux's real name?

9. What was the title of Caress Morrell's book?

10. Who were Sammy Jo's parents?

11. Where did Alexis work as an artist's model?

12. What couple raised Amanda for Alexis?

13. What was Mrs. Gunnerson's first name?

14. What kind of car did Fallon drive in the first three seasons?

15. What was the name of Sable's company?

16. What was the name of Krystle's racehorse?

17. What song did Alexis sing while trying to buy oil wells from Oscar Stone?

18. How much did Blake pay Alexis to stay away from the children?

19. What was the original name of Fallon's hotel?

20. Who was Peter DeVilbis's lawyer and what was his connection to Alexis?

21. What are the names of the couple that have custody of Adam's son?

22. Where did Blake and Alexis spend their honeymoon?

23. What was the name of the sanitarium that Claudia was committed to?

24. What meal did Alexis make for Blake while they were in Singapore?

25. What were the names of Blake and Alexis's fathers?

26. Who replaces Joseph after his tragic death?

27. Steven is forced to kill one of his best friends. Who is this friend?

28. What is the name of Krystle's first husband and how does he eventually die?

29. How does Adam prove he is Blake and Alexis' son?

30. How much does Alexis offer Sammy Jo to leave Denver?

31. How many women is homosexual Steven married to during the series?

32. Why did Joseph, the butler, commit suicide?

33. Blake struggles to accept the loss of Steven after the oil rig accident in which he disappears. Why does he finally accept his son's presumed death?

34. How does Krystle manage to get away from Joel Abrigore after being imprisoned for weeks?

35. What pair of siblings has been romantically involved with Steven and Sammy Jo?

36. Which sibling pair almost commits adultery by nearly engaging in an incestuous relationship?

37. What is "Lancelot"?

38. How does Adam arrange for Jeff to nearly go insane?

39. How is the first Fallon replaced with the second?

40. Who was Nicole Simpson?

41. Who was Luke Fuller and how did he die?

42. Why did Fallon marry Jeff in the first place?

43. How does Krystle lose her first baby?

44. Who lights the fire when Krystle and Alexis are locked inside a burning cabin?

45. Steven and Adam are both named after someone - who?

46. How does Blake react to discovering the Krystle didn't want to have a child with him?

47. What was Blake and Alexis's "master plan"?

48. What was the name of the tabloid that put Blake and Alexis on the cover when they were cozy in Rome?

49. What was the name of Daniel Reece's pilot?

50. What was the name of the jewelers Blake, Krystle and Alexis always used?

51. Who painted the picture that Roger gave to Alexis?

52. What nickname did Alexis have for Blake when they were married?

53. Where did the elder Carrington children attend school?

54. What color was Morgan Hess' tacky suit jacket?

55. Who verified that Adam was really the missing Carrington baby?

56. What nickname did Monica have for Dex?

57. How did Fallon get the name Randall?

58. What was the name of the nun who told Alexis that Galen was still alive?

59. Where did Fallon always go when she was upset and needed to be alone?

60. How many children were invited to Krystina's third birthday party?

Chapter Ten

Tune In Next Week…

Where did Fallon always go when she wanted to be alone? What did Daniel Reece give Krystle for Christmas? In what episode did Sarah run away with Krystina? All of the answers to those questions and many more can be found in Dynasty's episode guide. Each episode has been covered on its own page complete with guest star listings as well as the Writers and Directors credits. A fabulous photo accompanies each synopsis.

Quite a few people have asked for the Nielsen ratings for the show's run. Here it is folks. Dynasty finished its first season at number 45, Season Two at number 19, Season Three at number five, Season Four at number three, Season Five at number one, Season Six at number seven, Season Seven at number 24, Season Eight at number 33 and Season Nine at number 57. The Reunion produced dismal results and spelled the end for any future attempts at another miniseries.

Now that we've gotten the statistics out of the way, now would be the time to grab a drink, get comfy and remember all of the moments of Dynasty. To start things off, Jennifer Ellis has written a piece of fiction surrounding the events leading up to Dynasty as we saw it. Her piece is titled The Courtship of Blake and Krystle. After her story you can enjoy the synopsis' for all 219 episodes plus Dynasty The Reunion and end your reading with a fictional piece I had written ten years ago. (Fair warning, if you're a major Krystle fan, you probably aren't going to like it…)

Ready for that walk down memory lane?

The Courtship of Blake and Krystle
By Jennifer Ellis

The tall tower building of Denver Carrington Co. loomed up before Blake Carrington as he ran towards its entrance. He was late for a meeting with his Board of Directors of which he was the chairman. Not only that but he was the founder and owner of Denver Carrington Co., an oil company that was one of the elite companies dominating the oil business in America. He had spent many years working hard for this company to be at the top.

As he ran past the gray marbled walls of the foyer all eyes turned towards him. He was a tall, distinguished gray haired man in his expensive blue suit. His muscles rippled beneath it as a silver watch chain glinted across the gray of his formal waistcoat.

About the same time Krystle Grant Jennings stepped into one of the lifts, holding a pile of files. She had been working at Denver Carrington Co. for a month now and had settled in well. In that short time she had gained a reputation of being a helpful co-worker. She was in a good mood because she had gone over the files last night in her cheerful smart apartment and was ready to type them up today.

"Hold those doors!!!", came a deep authoritative voice from across the foyer. Krystle's eyes widened as she gazed at this legendary man which until now she had only seen his picture in the society section of the Denver Gazette. She swallowed nervously and pressed the open button of the lift, pausing the doors. "I don't believe it's him!!! So this is the famous Blake Carrington.", she thought as he strode into the lift as if he owned it, "Which he does." , she smiled wryly. From under her long lashes she watched him in admiration, for he had such compelling warm eyes, tough and firm mouth and mature, dramatic facial bone structure. He smiled at her,

"Thank you Miss.....?", he lifted an inquiring eyebrow. Krystle cleared her throat, "Krystle Grant.", she said in her sweet husky voice. She had recently divorced her husband Mark Jennings and didn't like to use his name. She looked up at him with big blue eyes, "I suppose you want the boardroom's floor, sir?" He slowly appraised her thoughtfully, his eyes lit with frank pleasure over her statuesque, graceful frame, "Yes please." and she pressed the top floor button and the lift doors closed, shutting them in. They were the only ones in the lift suddenly making the atmosphere more intimate.

Blake gazed narrowed at her, he liked the look of this beautiful woman standing before him. She looked elegant in her pale pink two-piece jacket and knee-length skirt. The pearl blouse underneath her jacket outlined her curvy breasts nicely. Her silvery blonde hair was neatly styled into a flattering bun on top of her lovely pert head. She pressed the button for the fourteenth floor.

Before he could stop himself Blake blurted, "You work at Denver Carrington Co? For me?" She gave a little start, "Well sir you could say that. I started at Denver Carrington Co. about a month ago." He looked at the lit up button marked four, "On the fourteenth floor?", he persisted, "Isn't that Paul Deck's Department?" He couldn't help but stare down at her petal soft pink lips that had an enchanting grin now. She laughed, its delicate sound sent a delicious tingle all throughout Blake's body. "Yes Mr. Carrington, I'm his secretary."

Paul Deck was one of the directors that would be at the meeting this morning. Blake thought to himself, "I'll have to ask Paul about this Krystle Grant." He surprised himself in his interest in her. Over the years he had had little dalliances with women since his divorce from his wife Alexis but nothing serious. Alexis had left him to rear his two children Steven and Fallon alone. It had been a bitter split where he had found Alexis had been unfaithful so he had banished her from the house and hadn't heard from her since. But this lovely face in front of him intrigued him. There was a genuine quality about her, "A true lady." , thought Blake in wonder. He just knew inside of him that she would be impressed by a person's character and not power and wealth.

Suddenly they came to a stop at the fourth floor and the lifts silently slid open. "I'm sure we will meet again, Miss Grant." ,Blake smiled down at her. She nodded, "I'm glad I've met you at last, Mr. Carrington, I hope the rest of your day is pleasant." With that she stepped out and Blake watched her curvy figure walk away with glittering eyes. He felt a stupid sense of loss now that she had gone as the lift doors closed again. But then he felt comforted by the scent of her perfume that still lingered with him all the way to the top floor. He had a burning yearning to get to know her better.

As Krystle walked away from the lift she could feel Blake still staring at her back before the doors of the lift closed again. She shook her head, still un-nerved by his intense study of her. "No!! He couldn't be interested in me, he is way out of my league. He is a multi-millionaire for goodness sake." Herself and the other secretaries had fun times looking at his pictures in the society magazines in which he was usually holding hands with some pretty model, celebrity or rich socialite. The office grapevine said he still hadn't got over his bitter split with his ex-wife Alexis and that he would never settle down. Although many women tried to tame him.

Reaching her office, she went inside and sat at her desk. She knew that Mr. Deck was waiting in the boardroom for Blake Carrington. Sighing, she put a sheet of paper into her typewriter and started to hit the keys with her fingertips but she couldn't get Blake Carrington's handsome face out of her mind. She had a feeling that their fateful meeting in the lift wouldn't be the last time she would be in his company.

After the successful boardroom meeting that morning the directors went back to work in their own offices. Blake invited Paul Deck for a drink in his office. They were seated in the comfortable plush leather lounge chairs there, drinking glasses of brandy. For 15 minutes or so they talked business then Blake tried to sound casual as he said, "So I hear you have a new secretary?" Red haired Paul grinned and pushed up his glasses along his thin nose as they had a tendency to slide down, "Yes Blake, a Miss Krystle Grant, she has been a very diligent worker and I'm rather pleased she is working for me. Kate, my last secretary that I had for some years had to leave to help nurse her sick mother. Miss Grant seems to work well with my other staff. She even takes work home and sometimes works overtime too." Blake quirked his eyebrows and a calculating light came into his bright eyes, "Oh that must be hard on her family then, being so dedicated." Paul shook his head, "No I think she is able to take work home because she doesn't have any family commitments. It seems she had just moved here from Ohio

running from a nasty divorce and she has no children either. Good for me though, ha!" Blake had a sense of relief to know that Krystle was single. Blake leaned over and patted Paul on his arm, "Yes, you are a lucky fellow to have the perfect secretary." At that moment Blake knew he wanted Miss Grant to be his own personal secretary where she would be only a few feet away and he could see her face everyday.

All that following week every morning when Krystle approached the lifts she would get flutters of anticipation expecting to see Blake Carrington's face. However she always felt a little disappointed that he didn't show. She didn't realize that Blake usually came in earlier than everyone else as he felt lonely in the mansion without Steven or Fallon there. That particular day she had encountered him he had been in a traffic jam and therefore he had came in the same time as his workers.

At the end of that week on the Friday as she went to her desk she noticed sitting on it a lovely crystal vase. In it was a single dark red gerbera. "How exquisite.", she thought, "Mr. Deck must have placed it there as a reward for me working so hard, what a sweet boss." Just then Paul Deck walked in and greeted her, "Nice Flower Miss Grant, it's nice of you to bring it to brighten up the office for us." Krystle looked puzzled, "Oh but I........yes flowers are nice and cheerful I think." He smiled and went to his office door and paused, "After you get your breath back could you come in here and take some dictation for me? You are doing a swell job my dear, even the big boss was asking about you the other day." Krystle blushed, "You mean Mr. Carrington?" Paul's smile widened, "Yep, nothing around here gets past his attention, but don't worry, I only told him the truth about you - the dedicated secretary." Paul mused, "I guess that's why he is the top dog here, he takes an interest in all the employees of Denver Carrington Co." He winked, "Come in when you are ready Miss Grant, we have a full day ahead." and with that he went into his office and shut the door.

Krystle picked up the beautiful vase and gazed at the delicate flower. "I wonder if it was Blake Carrington who put this here for me.......Oh dear, what am I thinking, a tough ruthless tycoon like him wouldn't do such a sweet thing - get a grip girl." She placed it back on the desk and sat in her chair. She absently picked up her gold pen and rested the end of it on her lips, "Although, he did ask Mr. Deck about me." She laughed at herself and shook her head at her fanciful thoughts. She then got up and reached for her notepad and went into Paul Deck's office.

Every morning for the next week, Krystle came into her office to discover there was a fresh gerbera of a different color standing in

the little slender crystal vase. It had become the amusing topic of office gossip. All the other secretaries teased Krystle that she had a secret admirer. Krystle thought one of them was playing a joke on her but she looked forward everyday to see another bright flower on her desk.

That night Blake was sitting by the glowing fire in the library at his grand mansion listening to some classical piano music on his record stereo player. His devoted Butler and old friend Joseph Anders came into the room bringing him a nice hot cup of coffee. "Thank you Joseph. Just put it on the table, that's all for tonight, goodnight." Joseph looked at his old friend in a perplexing way when he saw the tender, dreamy expression on Blake's face. He had that look now every night this week when he had come home. Joseph rarely saw that expression over the past years and only when Fallon hugged her father or did something to amuse him but she was away at the moment. The tall lean butler was curious as to what was making Blake so happy lately but was glad for him. Joseph went out leaving Blake alone staring into the flames. This time of night was the time Blake's mind strongly dwelt upon Krystle Grant. He had been thinking of her more over the last week. He kept having visions of her not just being at his workplace but sitting here with him near the fire or walking with him in his large garden. "She would fit just right here in my home with me. This place needs a warm gentle lady and Steven and Fallon would benefit from a kind heart like Krystle's. I've been lonely for too long now." He knew he had fallen in love with her.

He picked up the coffee cup and took a sip, "Ah I hope she likes the flowers I put on her desk, she should always have flowers around her, she is like one herself - beautiful and special." He laughed at his crazy impulse to give her a flower each day. He was secretly thrilled to have this anonymous contact with her and wondered if she guessed the flowers came from him. A few times that week he even purposely walked past her office just to take a peek at her sitting there so efficiently typing but looking so enchanting at the same time. She was so absorbed in her work that she didn't even notice him. It was almost becoming an addiction for Blake to want to see her serene face. He sat back, put his feet up on a stool and closed his eyes, "Yes, there must be a way to persuade Paul to get her to work for me." Blake was determined that before the next month was over he would make it happen. "That will be the first step in my plan and then let her get to know me over time as employer and then friend. After that I will have to go slowly with her to woo her. Hopefully she will grow to love me over time."

Two weeks later, around the office grapevine it was soon known that Blake's secretary was taking her sixth month holiday leave and then was being transferred to a Dallas Oil company to be close to her daughter who was due soon with her first baby. The Denver Carrington secretaries were all very excited as her position was up for grabs. Everyone wanted this prestigious job as being Blake's secretary meant the best salary with the boss of all bosses.

Being new to Denver Carrington Krystle didn't want to apply for it as she had only been with Mr. Deck for a month or so and didn't want to hurt his feelings. Also on a subconscious level she secretly felt a connection with Mr. Blake Carrington and she didn't want to be in a relationship with any man just yet, let alone her boss! However fate seemed to play its hand for during the weeks Krystle had worked for Mr. Deck, he had gained a lot of respect for her as worthy person and worker. He knew she had been through a very rough time with her husband and she had the brains and talent to go up in the Denver Carrington Company. He also had hopes of developing a romantic relationship with the lovely lady, "That would be easier if she didn't work directly for me anymore.", he thought with a shy smile.

At the end of the week Krystle was tidying up her desk and gathering her handbag ready to go home. Paul Deck came to stand beside her, "Err Miss Grant, I know you didn't apply for the secretary position for Blake Carrington. You didn't do it because you wanted to spare my feelings but you deserve that position. I put an application in for you." Krystle's blue eyes went even wider and bluer as she looked up into Mr. Deck's fair freckled face, "Mr. Deck,

there was no need and it was very kind of you but I'm happy here with you." He patted her blue silk shoulder padded shoulder, "No my dear, I insist. I will be sorry to let you go though. I'm sure he will choose you, your qualifications are excellent.", and he winked. Krystle felt slightly faint at the thought of working for the top boss that she had to lean back against the table.

"It's just not my day today," ,poor Krystle sighed as she pulled over her small white Holden car to the side of the road. She had only driven a few blocks from the Denver Carrington Building on her way home from work when she felt the car shuddering and knew the car had a flat tire. She got out to survey the damage and then to top it all off it had started to rain in heavy droplets. She shivered as she felt the cold raindrops wetting her hair and face. Krystle wrapped her arms around her waist and decided to get back into the car and wait for the rain to stop. Her hand was just touching the car door handle when the purring sound of a much powerful vehicle caused her to look up. She turned and her eyes peered through the rain and she saw a sleek black stretch limousine pull up behind her little Holden car.

It's chauffeur Michael Culhane, a tall young man with dark curly hair stepped out holding a big umbrella and strolled over to her. He stood close so that the umbrella was covering them both, "Miss Grant? Mr. Carrington said he will take you home if you will follow me please." Krystle blinked some of the raindrops from her lashes, "That's very kind of him but what about my poor car?" He smiled, "Now don't you worry about it miss, after I drop you home I will come back and fix the tire and deliver the car to you tomorrow morning." She got her handbag out of her car, locked it and gave him her car keys. He then took her arm and led her to the shiny limo, "In you go miss, don't want to stand out here too long." He opened the back door for her and  she got in and looked straight into the laughing, gleaming eyes of Mr. Blake Carrington who sat opposite her.

"So we meet again Miss Grant." His warm low timbered voice caressed Krystle's senses. Krystle's cheeks turned a becoming rosy hue as Blake took in her wet, embarrassed appearance. "Great," , thought Krystle, "I must look a mess, " and she could feel some raindrops trickling down her cheek. Blake's smile widened, she looked like a cute wet kitten all soaked and vulnerable, and he loved how her blue silk dress now dampened was molding to her delectable curves. He couldn't believe his luck when his chauffeur told him on the intercom that he recognized Krystle Grant standing with her car on the side of the road. Krystle heard a buzzing sound from behind her and slightly turned her head to see the tinted glass partition smoothly sliding down to reveal Michael Culhane sitting in the driver's seat in the front. "Miss Grant's car seems only to have a flat tire sir, so I will take her to her apartment now and drop you off at the mansion and come back to fix it." "Right Culhane, good man." Blake then to Krystle's astonishment told the chauffeur her address. Seeing her look, Blake smiled, "Yes Miss Grant I have read your personal dossier and that's why I know your address." The buzzing sound came again as the glass partition closed leaving Blake and Krystle alone together in the warm luxurious interior. The engine purred as Culhane drove it back onto the highway.

Krystle said, "It was good of you to stop and help me, Thank you Mr. Carrington." Blake took out of his pocket a large gray handkerchief that had an embroidered silver letter B in its corner. "It's no trouble Miss Grant. I like saving damsels in distress especially blue eyed water nymphs." With that he proceeded to lightly and gently dry her face with his handkerchief, "There, that's better." ,he laughed and put the hanky back in his pocket. She smiled gratefully, "Oh dear, I'm sorry I think I'm going to ruin your velvet car seat." Her gaze took in the plush surroundings, the quilted velvet ceiling, the gold fixtures, the television screen, the telephone and the mini-bar. The sound of classical music wafted sweetly in their ears. It seemed to Krystle that Blake and she were in their own cozy world cocooned from the cold rainy day outside. Blake bent down and took a small fluffy towel from a cupboard hidden under his seat, "Here, this will help you to dry off. Don't worry about the seat, it doesn't matter." He seemed to take great pleasure and amusement watching her pat herself dry with the towel. Then he took a flask from the mini-bar and two brown pottery mugs.

While he poured the steaming hot liquid into the mugs he said, "This is my housekeeper Jeanette's home made hot toddy. This should warm you up." , he passed her a mug. She took a tentative sip and it tasted delicious, melting all the coldness from her body and relaxing her. Blake put the flask back and took a sip of his own mug. "Ahhhhh heaven," , he sighed, "Oh one more thing to complete the picture." He took the red tartan woolen lap rug that was folded next to him and opened it, placing it firmly on her lap. He couldn't help feeling a shudder of pleasure on feeling her shapely thighs under the blanket as he tucked it around her. "Does that feel better?", he smiled at warmly at her. Krystle couldn't speak as she was in shock that Blake Carrington - ruthless business tycoon was tenderly administering to her needs like she was a small child. She swallowed a lump in her throat and just nodded. He sat back, "God dam it!!! She brings out all the protective instincts in a man.", he thought with wonder. It had been a long time since he had tender feelings for a woman.

He took another sip of the warm brew and said, "I'm glad you are here because it will save me from telling you later. But I have gone through the applications for my secretary position and I've decided your qualifications make you the one I want." Krystle almost choked on her drink, "I'm flattered that you picked me Mr. Carrington and I'm looking forward to working with you." Blake held up his mug, "Shall we toast to it then? To our working relationship, may it benefit us both." They tapped their mugs together, "Please since we will be together on every working day, call me Blake and may I call you Krystle?" Krystle smiled, "Yes if you like Mr..... I mean Blake." He loved the sweet breathy, husky way she said his name and his heartbeat accelerated. They sat in companionable silence while they finished their drinks and listened to the soothing music. While Blake put the empty mugs away Krystle  pondered over this charismatic man, "Oh when he turns on his charm and tenderness it's hard not to get caught up in his spell. Working with him would never be dull."

When they arrived at Krystle's apartment building Blake insisted on walking her to the entrance and luckily it had stopped raining. As they were walking it seemed to Krystle that they had just come back from a date, she grimaced at her fanciful thoughts. Blake took Krystle's soft pale hand and firmly held it between his two large hands, "I'm sure we will be a great team Krystle." She felt a warm tingle all the way to her toes at his touch. She smiled at him and nodded and went into the building.

All the way back to the mansion Blake gently held his handkerchief that had touched Krystle's angelic face. It had dried now and there was a pale pink smudge left by Krystle's lipstick. Blake touched it reverently to his own lips, "Ahhhh sweet Krystle we will be perfect together in the office and eventually at the mansion where you belong." Deep in Blake's heart he knew he would do his best for it to be so.

In her apartment Krystle was curled up in a comfy lounge chair watching the television dressed in her warm nightgown. She was glad now that she worked for the famous Mr. Blake Carrington and couldn't believe how swiftly these last few weeks with him had flown. She smiled as she remembered her first day as she walked to her new desk. On it was a huge crystal vase that held lots of multicolored gerberas and tied to it with curly blue ribbons were a bunch of big pink heart shape balloons. Resting at the bottom of the vase was a little card and on it in bold sweeping black handwriting were the words "Welcome to the first day of your new job, May you find the many days ahead working with me very rewarding!! Blake." She had trembled with delight at the knowledge that Blake was responsible for her daily dose of gerberas in Mr. Deck's department.

The following month and a half proved Blake right that he and Krystle made a good professional working team. Their personalities seemed to click and it was as if they had worked together for many years instead of only weeks. Blake looked forward to going to work everyday to enjoy Krystle's gentle company and between them they were able to get through heaps of correspondence. Krystle found Blake to be a very kind, friendly and considerate boss to work for and the days seemed to flow in happy harmony. Blake did his all to become friends with her and it seemed they had created a good friendship with each other.

The next week Blake was called away to China to review some oil leasing deals there with his Chinese staff. He was tempted to take Krystle with him but she had a lot of paperwork to do for him and her workload would be too much if she went on the trip. So it was with great regret that Blake left on his private jet at the end of the week. Sitting on the long soft cream leather lounge in his spacious plane Blake gazed out of one of the many windows. He took a sip of his brandy and looked out at the cotton wool like clouds floating below him. He felt a pang of guilt that he had arranged for one of his men to watch over Krystle, "Someone has to make sure she is alright while I'm gone," he tried to convince himself that his actions were justified. But deep down he knew for his own peace of mind that he wanted a weekly report on her to know if she was seeing other men while he was away.

He suddenly felt like a heal and frowned, ground his teeth together anxiously because he knew if Krystle ever found out she would be very angry and may even leave Denver Carrington but he was prepared to risk that. His fingers tightened around his glass, "She must never know. But least I'll be able to sleep nights knowing what she is up to and that she is ok." Blake didn't want Krystle to know this possessive and ruthless side of him. During the month and a half Krystle had worked with him Blake was enchanted by Krystle's kind and generous nature. Krystle had persuaded Blake many times to give large donations to various local and world charities. She, also under his approval set up a crèche for the working mothers at Denver Carrington. She even made cakes for the other workers for their coffee breaks. When Blake was sick with the flu Krystle made him up a hot honey and lemon drink and massaged his shoulders, then made him go home for the day much to his delight. Her thoughtfulness towards others inspired Blake to want to be a better humanitarian himself. Her gentleness made him aware of his ruthless nature and she seemed to bring out a softer side to him that he hadn't shown for quite some time. However he couldn't help being possessive and determined in his pursuit to win her love. So he had weakened and had her watched.

Krystle missed seeing Blake's strong handsome face around the office during these past few days. He rang from time to time to check that everything at Denver Carrington was alright. Krystle was busily typing when Mr. Deck strolled up to her desk. She looked up, "It's nice to see you again Mr. Deck, and Mr. Carrington is still way in China." Paul Deck sat on top of her desk and smiled engagingly. To Krystle he always reminded her of a little schoolboy with his glasses sliding down his nose and his fire-red hair falling over his high forehead, "Um Miss Grant, it's you I wanted to see. You have been working very hard these past couple of months and contributed to Denver Carrington so I thought you deserve a treat. Would you have dinner with me and afterwards we could go to the theater to see a play?" Krystle thought to herself, "Why not, I can't remember the last time I went out to dinner with a man and Mr. Deck has been a lovely, nice boss." She nodded, "I'd be delighted, please call me Krystle." He smiled again, "Oh you must call me Paul then." Then they discussed when Paul would pick her up.

Krystle and Paul had a pleasant night out on the town together eating and going to a show. Krystle had an easy rapport with him and he didn't make her feel all the intense feelings or her pulses race like Blake did when they were together. Even when she was in Paul's company she couldn't help comparing him to the powerful and charismatic Blake Carrington. Paul dropped her off at her apartment around 1.00am and lightly kissed her cheek before he left her. His kiss felt like the kiss of a friend and didn't stir Krystle's senses at all. They didn't notice that across the road from them, a bald headed man in a dark sleek car was watching them intently.

Meanwhile on the other side of the world, Blake had just finished having a meeting with the Chinese staff and was relieved to get back to his expensive hotel suite. He had just kicked off his shoes and loosened his striped tie when the telephone rang. He sat back tiredly against the floral black lacquered headboard of the bed and answered it. "Hello Mr. Carrington, Bob King here. There is a new development concerning Miss Grant." Blake tensed, "Well spit it out man.", he said in a taut authoritative voice. King coughed nervously down the other end of the line, "Miss Grant has been seeing Paul Deck over this past week." Blake grimaced, "Thanks King, you have been very observant." he hung up the phone and felt a cold feeling of jealousy go through his body. He knew that the time for patient friendship with Krystle should now be turned into something more and the first thing he would do when he went back home was to ask her out. "Ah but maybe I can give her a hint to my feelings." ,and with that thought he straightened his clothes again and went out the door with the intention of looking at the exotic jewelry shops at the bottom floor of the hotel.

The next day Krystle received a package in express post, which was delivered to her apartment. She sat with it on her soft brass bed and opened it with excitement. Inside it was a black and gold jewelry box that had a beautiful red Chinese dragon on its lid. She opened the lid with trembling fingers and gasped to see a pair of lovely intricately carved jade earrings and the card placed with them said in Blake's sweeping bold handwriting in gold letters "I miss you Krystle, Love Blake" She went to her oval mirror and put them on. They looked beautiful and were a perfect setting against her silvery blonde hair. She touched them lightly with her fingertips and thought, "Could Blake really have feelings for me too?" She couldn't wait until he came back.

Blake was aching to be back in Krystle's company as soon as he could so he arranged to come back two days later. He gave orders for Michael Culhane to pick Krystle up to meet his jet at the airport. Krystle was excited when Culhane rang her to tell of this arrangement. She put on one of her smartest dresses, a sunflower yellow one with green edging. She decided it would match Blake's lovely earrings as she wanted to look her best for him.

She was sitting in the luxurious interior of the now familiar limousine when out of its window she could see Blake's jet gliding slowly down back to earth. Culhane with a knowing, sly look, told her to wait in the car while he met Blake and dealt with his luggage. Krystle sat nervously, and touched her jade earrings then clasped her hands together on her lap to keep them from shaking.

About ten minutes later Culhane opened the limo door for Blake who gracefully sat down opposite Krystle. He was tired from the trip but his face lit up when he looked into her smiling face. His gaze lingered on the beautiful jade earrings contrasting nicely with

Krystle's lovely fair hair. She had left her hair down today in a softer feminine style. His eyes were frankly admiring now as he took in her rounded figure lovingly enfolded in the bright yellow dress. He

 warmly smiled at her, "Hello Krystle, ah I see you got my little gift. Jade looks lovely on you. It's wonderful to see your sweet face again." Krystle reached out and took his hand and gently held it, "It's good to see you too. Thank you for the earrings it was a nice surprise and I adore them. I hope the trip was successful for you." He placed his other hand over hers so that their hands were intimately entwined. He leaned forward slightly and stared intently into her blue eyes that were a deeper shade of blue now that they were filled with emotion, "I meant what I wrote on that card Krystle, I missed you so much. Will you have dinner with me tonight so we can talk?" Krystle blushed a becoming pink, she could feel her heart beat strongly with excitement, "Yes Blake, I would love that very much, I missed you too."

Krystle was walking on cloud nine after the limo had dropped her off at her apartment. Blake said he would pick her up himself in his blue Mercedes bends at 7.00pm and that she should dress up for the occasion. He had taken her hand and kissed the back of it in a very gentleman like fashion that had melted Krystle's heart. Krystle was certain now that Blake's serious intense manner towards her meant he wanted their close friendship to become something more. She was looking forward to tonight and went to some trouble selecting the right gown to wear.

She was just brushing her flowing long hair when she heard the knock on her door. She took one last look at herself in her oval mirror assessing her beautiful silver beaded gown with pleased eyes. She sprayed Midnight Mist perfume, gathered up her blue gauze wrap and little matching evening bag and answered the door. Blake stood there looking strikingly handsome in a black suit with a silk blue shirt and black tie. Krystle gasped in delight to see the beautiful bunch of dark yellow roses Blake held out to her, "For you dear lady.", he said with a wink. Krystle grinned, 'Why thank you kind sir." She took them from him and invited him to sit down while she looked for a vase to put them in. Blake sat down on one of the soft lounge chairs and slowly surveyed the apartment taking in the tasteful furnishings and cheerful light décor. "This apartment mirrors her essence of elegance and charm.", Blake thought.

He smiled as he watched her arrange the flowers on the kitchen bench. He loved her in the silver beaded gown, it had a plunging neckline and back, exposing her creamy white skin. It clung to her figure accentuating her lovely breasts, small waist, and flared hips to fall in floating folds around her ankles and above her silver sandals. Around her neck was a long silver necklace with a diamond heart shaped pendant. "Yes,", he thought, "She is very elegant and sexy tonight." Aloud he said, "You look enchanting my dear." He stood up, "Shall we go?" Krystle finished with the flowers she so loved and gathered her wrap and bag and took Blake's arm.

The restaurant was classy and intimate and had a French theme. The French waiter led them to an elegant table. It had an arrangement of red and yellow roses in the center grouped around slender lighted candles. In the background the sound of sweet romantic violins could be heard. Blake slid Krystle's chair out for her and then sat down himself. The waiter came back with a dark bottle of French wine. He poured it and said something in French to Blake who in turn smiled and replied in French. The waiter left them to their drinks and Krystle whispered, "What did he say Blake? You know I don't understand a word." Blake smiled indulgently at her, "He said I hope you and the beautiful elegant lady enjoy your time here." Krystle laughed and they both picked up their wine glasses. Krystle couldn't believe she was sitting across from her boss, the powerful yet tender Mr. Blake Carrington in such intimate and romantic surroundings. She was suddenly over awed by the whole idea. Her nervous hands were shaking so much that she was afraid of spilling her wine. Little did she realize that Blake was surprised at himself at how vulnerable she made him feel. He was finding it difficult to project the self-assured strong image that he displayed to world. Just looking into her misty blue eyes and soft petal pink lips always made him go weak at the knees. His hand was slightly shaking as he lifted his glass to his lips, "To us Krystle." They both sipped the rich red wine. To break the tension Blake said, "Do you like it? It's a little wine I discovered in France during the war." Krystle laughed again, "Ah how clever of you, it's perfect and tastes divine." The waiter came and placed two delicious dishes before them. Blake said, "I hope you don't mind but seeing I speak French, I ordered for you the Veal with lemon capers with sorrel for the entree, its my favorite and I thought you might like to try it." Krystle smelt the mouthwatering aroma and said she was glad he had ordered.

Over the main meal and desert they found that they were able to relax and talk about themselves to each other. Krystle talked about growing up in Ohio, her mother, her sister Iris who had passed away and her wayward niece Sammy Jo. She didn't mention her ex husband or her past involvement with Mathew Blaisdel. Blake talked about his boyhood and his children Fallon and Steven. Krystle said with real concern, "You really miss them don't you." Blake nodded.

It still niggled Blake that Krystle had gone out with Paul Deck and he wanted to know if she had any feelings for the pleasant red-haired chap. Casually he asked, "Did you do anything interesting while I was away?" Krystle knew that Blake would eventually find out on the office grapevine about her and Paul's growing friendship but she wanted to clear it up for him anyway. "Oh I went out a couple of times with Paul." Blake frowned and tried to keep the anger out of his voice, "You mean Paul Deck?", he felt conflicting emotions, he admired her honesty but he felt the same jealous feelings taking hold of him again. Krystle put her hand over his, "When you were away I missed you so much that I was miserable and Paul was nice enough to take me out. He was good company." Blake tensed, "Paul!!!! She called Deck by his first name." Krystle could feel Blake's arm muscle tighten under her hand, "I only see him as a good friend Blake, nothing more than that." Blake placed his other hand on hers and his eyes gleaming, "And how do you see me Krystle? Could we be more than friends?" Before she could answer him he placed his hands on her smooth warm shoulders and urgently said, "Don't you feel this connection between us? I felt it as soon as I first stood near you in the lift when we first laid eyes on each other." Krystle sighed, she could feel Blake's strong fingers digging into her shoulders, "Oh Blake I have strong feelings for you, you make me feel things I haven't felt with a man in a long time." Blake relaxed his hands and caressed her shoulders and smiled. He placed his lips to her soft cheek, inhaling her perfume and rasped against it, "I'm so very glad." , and tenderly gave her a butterfly kiss with his lips, causing Krystle to quiver with the wonder of such a sweet gesture. He stood up and took her hand in his, "Shall we dance my darling?" She nodded feeling very lightheaded and he led her onto the dance floor.

As they walked to the center of the dance floor the violins started to play the slow, haunting , romantic tune "You were meant for me" from Singing in the Rain. Blake smiled tenderly down into her upturned face as he gathered her to him. He lightly placed one of his hands on her small waist and held her hand in his other. She placed her other hand on his shoulder. Gazing up into his dark piercing eyes Krystle was overwhelmed how being in such close proximity to him made him seem stronger and taller than ever. Even though she was a tall woman he was one of the few men that made her feel small, dainty and very conscious of her femininity.

Krystle couldn't help but tremble in his powerful arms aware of the leashed male energy within him. He felt her trembling and was aware of her nervousness as they began to sway slowly to the music. He pulled her closer so that his two large hands were now spanning her small waist as she rested her two hands against his shoulders. He bent his head so that his lips were touching her ear. She could feel his intoxicating warm breath as he crooned, "Just relax Krystle, let yourself go with the music and enjoy being in my arms. You are safe with me."

Krystle sighed and rested her cheek on his chest and closed her eyes.

Blake could feel her body slowly melt into him and it felt right holding her, like coming home. He loved the feel of her soft curves against his upper body, the top of her soft blonde hair brushing the tip of his nose, "I could hold her all night like this." , thought Blake dreamily. Dancing with Blake was a pleasant sensation, Krystle could feel Blake's hard muscles beneath his suit and the brush of his long firm legs against hers. She loved the fresh clean smell of his aftershave too. She felt as if she was floating on air. They were hardly moving now, savoring this newfound closeness. They stayed in this intimate dreamy embrace for quite some time absorbed in their own private world.

Little did they know that a young blonde girl who was sitting at a table nearby with her partner was watching them with narrow, calculating green eyes. Valia Davis was one of Fallon's closest friends. They had grown up together and even went to the same private schools over the years. While Fallon was away studying in Switzerland doing hospitality she had asked Valia to keep an eye

on her famous powerful father for her and to let her know of any developments of his romantic conquests. Fallon had her father's possessive streak and was very protective of him and her brother Steven. She hero-worshiped Blake and didn't think there was any woman worthy of his company. It secretly suited Fallon just fine that he was unattached as he treated her as his little princess and indulged her every whim. She liked being the young mistress of the Carrington Mansion.

Valia's boyfriend Leo waved his hand in front of her eyes, causing her to look at his cute sunny face. "Hey, what are you staring so intently at? You are supposed to be looking only at me." Valia smiled and brushed her short blonde curls away from her eyes. She discreetly pointed to the dance floor, "Isn't that Blake

Carrington dancing so closely with a mystery woman? I haven't seen her in our social circle before." Leo shook an admonishing finger at her, "Now now Valia, I can see your little scheming mind turning. So what if he is with someone, its none of your business." Valia quirked one of her finely plucked eyebrows at him, "You know Fallon relies on me to keep her up to date with the Denver goings on and especially her father. I promised her." Leo put a hand through his wavy brown hair in a frustrated gesture, "Why can't females stop interfering in men's business. Leave the poor man alone.", Leo gazed at the striking tall silvery couple on the dance floor while he sipped his wine. He admired the lovely statuesque lady Blake was holding so lovingly to him, "I must say, any man wouldn't mind being in Blake's shoes tonight.", then he gave Valia a cheeky wink. Valia lightly tapped him over his knuckles with her silver desert spoon, "Just for that silly comment, my idiot, you now have to dance with me." She thought to herself, "I wonder who she is? I'm going to find out." With that she dragged the now laughing Leo onto the dance floor.

Valia purposely steered Leo near the entwined couple until they were dancing quiet close to them. Valia firmly tapped Blake's shoulder, breaking Blake and Krystle's loving spell, "Why, it is you Blake. How nice to see you again." Blake gently released his hold on Krystle who had now raised her head to look at them. Blake smiled politely, "Hello Valia, Leo. Nice evening for dancing isn't it. Oh this lovely lady is Krystle Grant, Krystle, Valia is Fallon's old friend. I've known her since she was a little tot and this is her

boyfriend Leo." Krystle went bright red under this girl's persistent enquiring eyes, "It's nice to meet you both." Valia's smile held a trace of scorn, "Are you new in town? I don't think I've seen you at any of our little gatherings?" Leo coughed uncomfortably and said, "Um come on Valia we should leave these two alone, pleasure to have met you Miss Grant." But before he could take Valia's arm Blake said with pride in his voice, "Well Krystle's only been with us for about three months from Ohio. She has become a very good

friend and I'm blessed that she is also my secretary, the best thing that's happened to Denver Carrington. She has set up so many productive projects to help the workers." Krystle turned pale with embarrassment as she could sense Valia's disapproval. Valia looked her up and down as if she found her sadly lacking, "Aren't you the lucky one Blake? Well it was good to see you again. Enjoy your night. Say hello to Fallon next time you talk with her." With that she took Leo and danced away from them. Looking up at Leo's disgruntled face Valia cattily purred, "Well well Blake is mixing with the hired help!! The old man must be getting senile. Fallon is just going to die when I tell her." Leo tightened his hold on her red satin figure, "Valia, it may just be a business dinner, not that it's any of our concern." She jeered up at him, "Huh!!! Nice work if you can get it then." Leo shook his head and sighed, "Women!!! Come on girl, just dance and think of nothing but me for a change, you little gossip monger." She giggled, "Okay big boy." and battered her eyelashes at him.

Blake continued to dance with Krystle but could feel her stiffen and their intimate mood had changed. He looked down at her, "What's wrong darling?" Krystle was trying not to cry, "Blake, I have a slight headache, maybe the wine. Could you take me home please?" Blake was all tender concern as he bundled her into his Mercedes bends. Their ride home was driven in silence. Krystle's confidence was shattered by that contemptuous look of Valia's. She rested her head wearily against the high back of her car seat, "Who am I kidding trying to play with the rich. I'm just a secretary from Ohio. Why couldn't Blake be just an ordinary man." When Blake stopped the car at the front of her apartment she plucked up the courage to tell him how she felt, "Blake, meeting Valia and Leo has put this thing between us into perspective." They unbuckled their seatbelts, turned to stare at each other's shadowy features in the dim light. She placed her hand on his cheek, "Blake, I don't belong in your rich and powerful world." Blake exhaled a harsh angry breath and growled, "Rubbish!!!!! That little chit of a girl is a snobby brat. You are worth a million rich, spoilt brats. You and I, being together feels so right." He suddenly held her to him as if he would never let her go, "I love you Krystle, do you hear me? I love YOU!!!" Krystle was crying now, "I love you too, Blake." He tenderly kissed her moist quivering lips, relishing their sweet softness, "Only what we feel and want for each other matters and damn everybody else." He breathed into her mouth the words, "We belong, we belong together." Krystle drew back and nodded while tracing his firm lips with her fingertips. She realized tonight that she loved this enigmatic beautiful man with all her heart. Next morning's sunlight warmed Krystle's cheek as she awoke from a pleasant deep sleep. A big satisfied smile played on her lips as she recalled the events of last night. She was still in shock from Blake's passionate declarations of his love for her. Her mind flashed back to Blake's tender good night. He had walked her to her door, his arm possessive and warm around her shoulders. She had tentatively asked him in for coffee and he ruefully grinned, "I think you have had enough for one night, my love." He had then reached out to stroke her long hair, his hands running through the fine silky strands. His eyes took on a serious hue, "Krystle, I want you to slowly get use to this change in our relationship. It's still very new and a lot for you to take in right now. Please believe me that I think you are very special and so is our relationship and I want to treat it as such.". Krystle had felt another wave of love for him at his thoughtfulness, he really was a true gentleman to her. She had held his hands and gently kissed him goodnight. She realized then that he was serious about her and didn't want to treat her like his past conquests that she had seen him with in the pages of the Denver Gazette.

Fallon Carrington was enjoying the sensuous play of a very masculine hand moving slowly along her naked sleek back under the silken sheets. It belonged to Karl Yurgen the Swiss Director of the luxurious hotel in which Fallon was staying. He was fun company and a very generous lover. She giggled as he slid his hand over her hip to lightly tickle her belly button. She was just about to roll over to give him a kiss when her telephone rang. Sighing she turned and reached over Karl's broad hard chest,. her small curvy breasts lightly brushed his nipples as she reluctantly answered it. Karl frowned, tugged playfully at Fallon's long feathered brown hair and looked at her through half closed heavy eyelids. She sleepily murmured in a low husky voice, "Fallon here." , and half rested on Karl with one hand holding the phone to her ear and the other resting on Karl's neck. "Fallon, it's Valia." , said the high-pitched girlish voice, "Hi darling, are you sitting down? Have I got news for you!!!!" Fallon laughed, "Hello Valia, well I'm not standing up, so fire away." Valia's Denver gossip always amused Fallon. "Well Leo and I bumped into your father and his er... 'lady friend'... at that intimate little French restaurant we always go to."

Fallon stiffened at Valia's disapproving tone, "I gather this lady friend of Daddy's is not to your taste then? Who is she?" Valia said with some relish, "Sweetie, I think Blake has gone a bit gaga over his hired help!!" Fallon creased her forehead trying to rack her brains over which of the staff it could be. At the same time Karl started to bite her other ear and his hands wandered down to curve over her pert behind. She pushed his head back onto the pillows, glared at him and shook her head. He smiled maddingly up at her, enjoying the soft feel of her. He loved it when her eyes flashed with anger or passion and loved to tease her in more ways than one. "Come on Valia, which one of the servants is Daddy so interested in then?" Valia said in hushed appalled tones, "His new little secretary a Krystle Grant, can you believe it? From Ohio of all places!!" Fallon relaxed against Karl's warm velvet skin, "Oh Valia, they were probably on a business dinner, good god you scared the dickens out of me."

Valia gave a delicate sniff, "Oh and does talking business over dinner involve being pressed up against your boss with your head resting on his chest while he is tightly holding you to him swaying on the dance floor? Wake up Fallon!!!" Fallon felt a heavy feeling of dread go through her, "I see.....thanks for letting me know. It maybe just an office dalliance. I'm sure he will soon tire of Miss Grant's 'charms'. Keep me posted on the situation, talk with you later." Fallon put the phone down and looked down into Karl's big enquiring hazel eyes, "Family trouble, Fallon?" Fallon sighed, "Nothing I can't handle. Karl, I'm not in the mood now, could you please go? We can resume our playtime later." Karl shrugged and knew not to argue with her when she was upset. He slowly got dressed and left her with a lingering kiss. Fallon rolled over onto her stomach, with her hands under her stubborn chin and thought, "No, no daddy!!! What are you doing? I'm not going to let some money grabbing conniving Ohio bitch get her claws into you. I'll give you a month to have your fun with her and if you don't tire of her then I'll have to do something about it. Someone has to look out for you."

Over the next two weeks Blake took Krystle out to various places where they enjoyed being together. Each time their outings with each other ended, the kisses and their caresses got longer and more intense. At the Denver Carrington office it was getting harder and harder for them to stay being a professional team. They had a fierce awareness of each other that kept interfering with their work. Blake would be in the middle of dictating a letter to her while staring, utterly fascinated with her long legs shapely or admiring how she held her pen. Sometimes he would stumble with his words or repeat a sentence over and over again. Krystle couldn't concentrate on writing either as she was contemplating what new adventure or place they would go to that night or being hypnotized by the rich low tones of his voice. They would suddenly become aware of each other's interest in the other which usually ended up with them hugging and laughing. Blake would then give up and say, "Hey let's escape and take an early lunch break." Even the Carrington workers noticed their infatuation with each other and the gossip grapevine was having a field day much to Paul Deck's disappointment.

During that time Blake showed Krystle his very impressive 48 room mansion set against Denver's blue-green mountains. When they had driven through the giant decorative iron gates Krystle could see in the distance behind the mansion a high charming clock tower with a graceful pale dome on the top supported by slender roman columns. She felt faint as the mansion's majestic form loomed up before her eyes as she stared at the brown brick walls with their multiple classic windows and chimneys from her seat in the limo. Over the front entrance was a massive cream-colored balcony for the second floor, supported by huge thick columns, with purple wisteria enchantingly hanging over it, "Oh Blake, it's sooo big! But it's very beautiful and grand." Blake chuckled, "It's just home to me Krystle. Yes, I suppose it does have a certain splendor to it but it's only bricks and mortar." He winked at her as Michael Culhane opened the limo door to let them out. Once they were standing near its entrance Krystle gazed about her in wonder. Surrounding the mansion were extensive manicured gardens, filled with all kinds of trees, multicolored flowers, fountains, ponds, hedges and brick paths. Blake smiled at Krystle's stunned expression, 'Come my darling, Jeanette has prepared us a lovely afternoon tea in the library. Afterwards I'll give you a tour around my humble abode." He took her arm gently and guided her towards the grand opened door where Joseph's austere face was there to greet them.

Krystle nervously held Blake's hand as she looked up into Joseph's cold expression. Blake had told her about devoted Joseph of whom he was very fond. Joseph had been in Blake's service for years ever since Blake had first bought the mansion. Joseph had helped Blake out with many family dramas and in turn Blake had helped him. They both had a strong bond being disillusioned husbands and single fathers who had been broken hearted by their wives. Blake's via adultery and Joseph's with his wife's violent mental state. Blake smiled warmly at him, "Good afternoon Joseph. Miss Grant has finally agreed to visit us at last. Krystle, this is my right hand man Joseph, friend and butler. I don't know how us or this house would function without him." Joseph forced himself to smile politely at Krystle. He nodded slightly, "Welcome, Miss Grant." , his tone was very formal and his tall, lean figure was very stiff in manner. Before

Krystle could reply to him he said in clipped tones, "Mr. Carrington, you are too kind sir. Jeanette has prepared tea in the library."

Blake patted Joseph on the back, "Thank you Joseph. There's no need to take us into the Library." With that Blake escorted Krystle further into the spacious foyer as Joseph closed the large oak door. Joseph stared at Krystle's elegant back and long silver hair. His eyes narrowed, "So that is Krystle Grant, the secretary who wants to be a rich Carrington." Joseph and the house staff knew Krystle had been Blake's secretary for a few months. They would hear Blake praise her up to his friends and business associates about how efficient she was in her job and all the positive things she had done for Denver Carrington workers. They were pleased that Mr. Carrington had another loyal worker. However, Michael Culhane started giving them all the juicy details of Blake and Krystle's new romantic relationship. They were horrified to learn that Blake was head over heels in love with his new secretary.

Joseph turned to go back into the kitchen to see if everything was running smoothly and sniffed in disapproval when he saw a group of some staff peeping at Krystle from one of the many doorways. He ushered them back to the kitchen. Michael Culhane was sitting at the kitchen table, he jeered at them, "Get a good look at her, hey? Wow, she's a looker I must say. Can you see what I've been talking about? She's got him by his short and curlies for sure." The gentle sweet housekeeper Jeanette always the romantic, winced at him and said, "Now Michael that's a bit crude. But it's no wonder that Mr. Carrington has been smiling a lot lately, Miss Grant seems to be a very beautiful woman." Mrs. Gunnerson, the round little cook nodded knowingly to her, "Yes, beauty as well as brains it seems if she is going for her boss. She's hit the jackpot hasn't she!! Fancy her wanting to be above herself. If she does become mistress, we will be taking orders from a secretary!! What experience has she to run a grand house such as this?" A young maid chimed in, "Miss Fallon will soon put a stop to it!" Joseph put up his hand to silence them all, "There will be no more gossip while you are in my company. We should all put our faith in Mr. Carrington's judgment. He has had lots of lady friends without one becoming Mrs. Carrington so I don't want to hear anymore about it." But he knew with a sense of dread that this woman had Mr. Carrington's heart as he never brought his women back to the mansion.

Joseph wouldn't dream of talking badly about his boss to the staff. "She has bewitched him," he thought and felt a little jealousy. Over the years he had been Blake's confidant and liked to think Blake depended on him emotionally and needed Joseph's friendship. Now he realized that if Blake took a new wife that he mightn't need his attention any more. Also he would have to take orders from the new mistress of the house. He wouldn't mind so much if Blake's future wife was a worthy proper lady from a rich and prominent background to match the Carrington family name. But one from the lower classes was incomprehensible to his feudal mind set.

Meanwhile Krystle, still tightly holding Blake's hand took in the spectacular decor of the foyer. The inside of the mansion seemed to her like a mini palace. There was a sweeping staircase that wound up to the second floor. Above her was a giant glittering chandelier that hung from its very high richly decorated ceiling. Down the hall were several doors on either side. On the walls were expensive paintings and golden mirrors. There were large vases filled with ferns and statues spread here and there against the walls. Blake took Krystle to the equally grand library. It was a surprisingly cozy room with whole walls shelved with books. A sumptuous leather lounge suite was situated near a big open fireplace. A table was laden with silver tea things. Blake beckoned her to sit while he poured them steaming cups of brewed coffee. Blake smiled, "Ahhhh, Mrs. Gunnerson, my best cook has made her famous apple slices." Krystle took one that he offered her. Blake sat down and leaned back in his chair. He had an air of contentment as he gazed at her, "At last, she is where she should be." To him, she looked sooo adorable in her elegant lavender floral blouse and plain dark purple slacks. Sitting so gracefully eating her cake and looking at him with soft misty sky- blue eyes, Blake thought she looked like the lady of his mansion.

He hoped all these signs of his wealth surrounding them wouldn't scare her off him. He so desperately wanted her to love his home. For he was determined more than ever to make her his wife. As if she was reading his mind Krystle said, "Mrs. Gunnerson's slice is very delicious, remind me to thank her. Your home is very beautiful, Blake. Thank you for bringing me here." They ate and talked for

about 20 minutes. Then Blake took her hand and showed her around the mansion and even introduced her to the kitchen and cleaning staff.

When they went into the massive drawing room Krystle's eyes were immediately drawn to a painted portrait of a lively, beautiful young girl in a shimmering red dress above the mantelpiece. Krystle knew it was Fallon's picture as she had seen pictures of the girl in the society pages of various magazines. "Oh Blake, she is very pretty." Blake smiled tenderly looking up at it, "Yes, my Fallon. She is lovely, she has my mother's magic eyes.

She is also very spirited. I've always regretted that she didn't have a mother's influence. I have tended to indulge her because of it. But she would do anything for me though and looks out for me." Krystle looked at the confident almost defiant expression in the beautiful face and knew this girl had her father's strong will, personality and drive. She wondered if Fallon would accept her but knew instinctively that Fallon was used to getting most of Blake's attention so it would be hard for her to adjust to a usurper.

On the mantelpiece was a large photo of a fair-haired sensitive looking young man, "Steve? He has very gentle, kind eyes and a very sweet face. Very handsome indeed too." Krystle could see a vulnerability to Steven that wasn't apparent in the portrait of Fallon. Blake looked down at his feet and shifted uncomfortably, "Yes my son Steven. Still away working on one of the oilrigs. His nature is more complex than Fallon's. He feels things more and needs to toughen up. I just don't understand the way his mind works. I think he was affected when Alexis left us. I don't think he has forgiven me that." Blake sighed and took her hand in his, "Come, lets go outside to the back gardens for some fresh air. I think you will like them." Krystle learned that Blake's relationship with his son was a complicated one indeed. The rest of the afternoon was spent happily strolling through the lush gardens. They kissed tenderly by the clock tower. Blake smiled to himself and felt a thrill of pleasure as he remembered his fantasy of them wandering the garden together had at last come true.

That night back at her apartment, Krystle lay in her bed trying to go to sleep. She tossed restlessly as her mind went over the things in Blake's world she would have to deal with if she eventually became a big part of it. Could she cope with all that power, wealth and status and all that it entailed? Would Blake's children and friends accept her as part of their privileged lifestyle? Would the servants accept her as the new mistress of the mansion? She sighed and punched her pillow,

"I would cope with anything if it means I can always be by Blake's side and have his love." She knew her love for Blake and his love for her would get them through anything that the future may bring. With that reassuring thought she snuggled back under the cozy covers and drifted off to sleep.

The following week, Fallon was staring intently at the Denver Mirror newspaper clipping that Valia had sent her. She felt slightly sick in the pit of her stomach to see the picture of her father and Krystle looking lovingly into each other's eyes while being in an intimate embrace. The headlines underneath it read, "Business tycoon Mr. Blake Carrington and his lovely secretary Miss Krystle Grant seem to have eyes only for each other while they were dining and dancing at the Carlton last night. Could this be serious folks? Maybe Cinderella will get her handsome prince!!! A Denver fairytale?" Fallon's lovely face screwed up with rage and she violently ripped the clipping into tiny pieces and threw them over her high balcony, "Damn that common trashy tramp!!! That's it! I'm going home to see daddy. This nonsense has got to stop now for his own good."

Krystle came into Blake's office holding up the Denver Mirror, "Blake, have you seen this? I didn't realize that while we were dancing last night, the nosey press were there too." She looked very embarrassed and felt that her privacy had been invaded, "Oh no," she thought anxiously, "now everyone knows about me and Blake. I wonder how he feels about it?" Krystle bent over his desk to where he was sitting behind it and handed him the paper. He looked at their picture and laughed, " A lovely one of us, don't you think? Give the gossips something to talk about. Don't look so devastated darling. I'm glad, because now the whole of Denver knows that I love you."

He put the paper down on his desk while staring at her intently. He got up to walk around his desk to hold her closely to him. He bent his head to whisper in her ear, "I want you to realize you have become the most important person in my life." He then rubbed his cheek lovingly on hers in a intimate gesture, reminding Krystle of a powerful jungle cat sensuously claiming its mate. "Only you make me burn up inside, lady. Come to me tonight at the mansion Krystle and I promise this will be a special night for us both. I'll have Culhane pick you up at eight." Krystle loved it when Blake spoke to her in seductive rasping tones and she could feel her pulses racing in answer to that tone. She buried her nose at the base of Blake's neck just above his green collar as if seeking affection like a small kitten. His unique masculine scent filled her with delight, "I'll be there Blake. I love you so much." She placed his hand over her breast where her heart was pounding underneath, "Feel what you do to me when you talk and hold me like this?" She felt his heavy warm hand gently squeeze her breast, they both trembled with the sexual heat that had suddenly intensified between them. Blake took his hand off her breast to press her lower half to his, "Feel what you do to me Krystle!" She could feel the coiled hardness against her, their hips were aching to have closer contact. Krystle reluctantly broke Blake's hold on her, "Till tonight, my love." She kissed him sweetly on his lips and walked gracefully out of his office door. Blake leaned back against his desk, trying to calm his heavy aroused breathing, "Yes until tonight my sweet Krystle."

Krystle dressed with care that night. Her heart bursting with heady anticipation and excitement. She wondered what things Blake had planned for them. What ever they were it would culminate in Blake making her his at last. She hoped he would find her alluring in her shimmering flowing blue and silver evening gown. Its blue shade matched the color of her eyes. She wore her fair hair half up in a loose elegant soft bun, the rest of her hair falling to her shoulders. She left some of the strands to curl enchantingly near her cheeks. Her diamond earrings and matching bracelet sparkled in the light. She had been waiting for this night for weeks.

She was ready when Michael Culhane picked her up in the limo at 8.00pm. He couldn't help but stare at her lovely appearance, "Yep Mr. Carrington sure is one lucky bastard." When they arrived at the mansion Culhane told her to let herself into the mansion. He said Mr. Carrington had given most of the staff the night off. He gave her a single red gerbera that had a card attached to it. Its words were, "My sweet flower, Follow the rose petals for your heart's delight as this will be the beginning to our magical night! Your Blake." Krystle smiled, "Ah curious and curiouser" as Michael drove the limo away. She gracefully walked to the door of the mansion and opened it. All was still and the massive foyer was dimly lit with hundreds of candles, their glow giving the mansion an almost dream like quality. Krystle felt like she was in a romantic fantasy as she looked down at her feet as sprinkled on the carpet was a trail of red and yellow rose petals leading down one of the long hallways. Suddenly she could hear the haunting song "You were meant for me" that they had danced to on their first date. "How sentimentally charming of him.", she thought. It seemed to come from the direction that the rose petals were leading. Their musky scent was heavy in the air as she walked on them. She slowly followed the floral trail thinking, "What is my sweet man up to?".

The lovely music got louder as she finally walked into the grand ballroom. She gasped as the room was like some fairyland, it seemed to be lit by hundreds of moving circles of light, which reflected off the giant mirror ball hanging off the high ceiling. There was also cute little rainbow colored soap bubbles floating in the air. In the middle of the room was a beautiful white lace table filled with sumptuous dinner for two. Around the room's walls were more flowers and groups of balloons that were pale pink and white decorated with colored curling ribbons. The song ended and the mirror ball stopped leaving the room in a romantic glow from the candles in silver and gold holders positioned here and there. Then Blake entered from one of the many French glass doors. Through the glass Krystle could see the gardens softly lit by the moon and stars. Blake looked gorgeous in a black smart dinner suit. He came up to her and smiled, "How do you like that start of our night together, darling?" Krystle reached up and kissed him, "All this is so magical Blake, you are the weaver of spells. There are no words to describe it." He placed his hands on her shoulders, "You are the magical one Krystle. Your magic has done it's work on my heart and my life. Will you be mine tonight?" and before she could answer him, he got down on one knee. He took from his pocket a small velvet box. He opened it to reveal an exquisite blue sapphire and multi-diamond engagement ring, he gazed seriously up into her wide eyes, "Krystle Grant, love of my life, would you do me the honor of becoming my wife? Will you make me feel complete and be my other half?" Krystle couldn't speak so just nodded in excited wonder with tears of happiness in her eyes. He stood up and placed the ring reverently on her engagement finger. He kissed her tenderly as the haunting melody "Our love is here to stay" wafted in the air and the mirror ball was turned on again. He silently took her into his arms and they danced slowly and intimately, their eyes and hearts only for each other. They both knew that this night's magic would only get better and the best was yet to come.

Krystle and Blake enjoyed dancing in one another's arms for a while. They then sat in the glow of the candlelight to enjoy Mrs. Gunnerson's special dinner. While they were eating a sudden thought struck Krystle, "Blake, I don't want to spoil this romantic mood but how will Steven and Fallon take this? They haven't even met me yet!!" Blake put his fork down and smiled at her, "So like you sweetheart to have concern for other's feelings. I did plan for you to meet them before I proposed to you but I couldn't wait somehow. You enchant me too much. Anyway we could fly to visit Fallon in Switzerland and Steven is coming home in a month's time so he can find out then as we can't contact him. I don't think Steven would worry so much. Fallon may be surprised as she worries

about her old father. But honey, when they see your sweet kind face, I know they will fall for you too. Besides I'm sure they would be pleased that you make me so happy." Krystle sipped her wine and said sincerely, "I'll do my utmost to assure them I love you and I really want to be their friend."

After their meal, Blake suggested that they take a moonlit stroll in the gardens. It was a beautiful clear night with the moon and stars twinkling high above them. The air was fragrant with the scent of the various flowers and the trees were tall large dark ethereal shapes, which seemed to make the gardens surreal and intimate in the moonlight. Blake guided Krystle down one of the garden paths and at its end was a swinging bench seat. On it sat a silver bucket of champagne and two fluted glasses. They sat down and Blake poured them champagne. Sitting side-by-side Blake put his arm around Krystle's shoulders. Krystle turned to him and raised her glass, "To our everlasting love and may our marriage be filled with happiness and fulfillment." They tapped their glasses together. Sipping from them they relaxed back to gaze at the stars while Blake gently rocked the seat back and fourth. They finished their drinks and just held each other marveling at the night sky.

Krystle was lulled to sleep by the swinging motion and the champagne. She also loved the feeling of being safe and warm in Blake's arms. Dimly she felt Blake's strong arms lift her so that her head was resting on his shoulder. When she next awoke she was laying on a big soft satin covered bed. She felt Blake's kisses on her throat and stirred, "Ah so my sleeping beauty awakes!!!.", Blake smiled tenderly

into her sleepy blue eyes. Krystle touched his cheek and said huskily, "How did we get here, Blake?" He laughed, "The next time we go star gazing, I'll remember not to give you too much champagne or rock you like a baby. I carried you here of course. I like the feel of you in my arms. It's a habit I'm going to enjoy for many years to come." Krystle half sat up and looked about her to find she was in the richly decorated master bedroom. It too was lit by candles and she was touched to see bunches of yellow and red roses here and there.

Blake slowly pulled the pins from her hair so it all tumbled down in soft waves about her shoulders. He threaded his fingers through the back of her hair cupping her nape and pulled gently so that her head was angled for his butterfly kisses on her eyelids and the tip of her pert nose. He then let her relax back down on the soft pillows with a sigh. He picked up a silky pale strand of her hair and rubbed it between his fingers and then brushed it with his lips as if the sight and texture of it fascinated him. He leaned over her and whispered, "Be part of my world forever and let me love you Krystle." Krystle's answer was to reach up and pull his head down so that their lips met and clung for a few passionate seconds. She breathed into his mouth, 'Yes Blake, so I can love you too. You are my world." She felt him quiver in excited anticipation. They slowly undressed each other in between gentle loving kisses. Each enjoying the sight, touch, feel and taste of the other. Blake drew her bottom lip into his mouth and sucked it sending shooting sensations of desire through her . Then he began a series of long intense kisses making her breathless, their tongues toying with each other. Their heartbeats increased as Blake caressed her soft breasts and smooth stomach. She moved her hands over his broad back, loving the feel of his taut whipcord muscles as he arched over her. His long heavy powerful legs gently rubbed against hers with restrained strength. Wherever Blake led her Krystle followed in heated desire and erotic passion until they came together in a blissful loving union. Floating back down to earth Blake held her tightly in his arms and said contentedly, "Now I'm yours and you are truly mine at last. That was heaven, thank you, my love." Krystle drained but happy, smiled and snuggled into him enjoying the heat and velvet hardness of his big naked body so entwined with her soft curvy one, "I love you Blake, I told you, you are the weaver of spells." They drifted off to sleep. Early in the morning they made love again, to both of them it felt so right like coming home.

They slept till noon the next day. Blake had bought Krystle a lovely cream lace blouse and green skirt to wear. It fitted perfectly and she was relieved and touched that he thought of it. She was slightly embarrassed about the servants and didn't want to confront them wearing last night's evening gown. Blake was amused that she cared what they thought, "Darling you will have to get use to them you know. Don't worry about them so." Jeanette had buzzed on the bedroom intercom that lunch would be served for them in the dinning room. They took a leisurely shower together reveling in this newfound intimate experience. Blake insisted on soaping Krystle and she felt very pampered and every now and again he would drop biting little kisses on her neck, shoulders or breasts making her tingle. She enjoyed the warm sliding of his slippery wet hands on her moist skin. He then wanted to dry her with a huge soft fluffy towel, she couldn't control her giggles as his hands tickled her. He even wanted to brush her hair and sitting at the dressing table Krystle found it to be a soothing experience. She looked at him in the mirror's reflection and was amused at how serious he was concentrating on slowly running the brush through her silver waves trying not to hurt her, afraid of knots. She still marveled that the ruthless tough business tycoon was gently brushing her hair. He also ran his hand down her hair loving the smoothness of it. She sensed he enjoyed this tactile experience and realized he had a sensualist side to him. This soft side of Blake, which he only displayed to a privileged few, was what she loved about him most and he never ceased to surprise her with it.

When they went down the stairs they reached the bottom to find that the staff had cleared all the candles and petals and put the mansion back to normal again. As they were enjoying their lunch Joseph came in and said, "Mr. Carrington, Miss Fallon is on the phone, you could take it in the hall." Blake stood up and excused himself and went to answer the phone. Joseph followed but not before glaring at Krystle, he thought, "Miss Fallon will soon see you out of here my fine lady, poor Mr. Carrington, how are we going to protect him. You may have wheedled your way to the master's bed but it won't be for long." Krystle flushed under his beady-eyed stare, she knew he didn't approve of her, ever polite he said, "Excuse me Miss Grant." and he walked out the room. Krystle sighed, "Yes, I'm going to find it tough coping with the servants."

Blake picked up the phone, "Fallon sweetheart, how's my little girl?" Fallon said, "Daddy? It's good to hear your voice again. Are you alright? I've missed you so much and I'm coming home for a while. I'll arrive tomorrow about eleven in the morning. Could you arrange for the limo to pick me up?" Blake smiled, "Wonderful Fallon, I couldn't be better actually. In fact, I have something very special to tell you and can't wait to see you too. I'll come home for lunch to chat to you." When they said their goodbyes Blake went to join Krystle. "Fallon's coming home tomorrow. I'm going to tell her about our engagement tomorrow. I'm going to tell her at lunchtime. Then you could come for dinner to see her. Would that be alright, darling?" Krystle felt anxious at the thought of meeting Blake's daughter but said, "Of course, Blake. I hope she likes me." Krystle wondered what sort of reception she would receive from Fallon Carrington tomorrow.

As her plane touched back down onto Denver soil Fallon was going over in her head what she was going to say to Blake. She swallowed nervously, "Am I too late? I should have come home a few weeks ago - poor deluded daddy." Ever since her phone call with Blake yesterday she was wishing with all her heart that 'daddy's' something special he had to tell her wasn't what she dreaded most. She wished she could contact Steven so he could have been here with her. They could have put up a united front and Fallon wouldn't feel so sick at the thought of confronting her father.

Michael Culhane greeted her as she walked down the plane's ramp. She thought he looked handsome and smart in his blue chauffeur's uniform. She liked the way his curls peeped from underneath the chauffeur cap. As she came towards him, he looked her up and down with narrowed eyes and drawled, "Good morning Miss Fallon. I hope your journey was pleasant. Switzerland suits you I see." She seemed to get more beautiful to him each time he saw her. She looked young, attractive and slender in her designer jeans and close fitting red velvet jacket. She flushed at his admiring stare, "Why thank you Michael. Switzerland did do me the world of good." , she smiled in remembrance of Carl's exciting love making, "But I'm glad to be back home again." He smiled mockingly at her. He knew she was aware of the sexual chemistry between them but she always tried her best to hide it, "Only a matter of time." ,he thought, "This little princess won't be getting daddy's attention now and I'm just the shoulder she will need to cry on."

Culhane collected her luggage and Fallon settled into the limo. During the drive to the mansion Culhane enjoyed watching Fallon via the rear view mirror as the partition was half way opened. He couldn't resist needling her, "There's been a lot of goings on at the mansion while you have been away, miss." She had been glancing out of the window, lost in her own thoughts but sharply looked up into his arrogant eyes that were now laughing at her in the mirror, "Oh really? And what would they be then?" ,she asked, aching to know from him if her suspicions were true. He glanced back to the road and said, "Ah Miss Fallon, I wouldn't want to spoil your daddy's surprise news now would I? Let's just say that Mr. Carrington is very pleased with Miss Grant's work. He became a very happy man last night at the mansion." Fallon felt angry now and pinched her cupid bow shape red lips and thought, "My god, even the servants are making fun of daddy and that woman." Aloud she huskily hissed at him, "I don't like your insolent tone or words Michael!! Kindly keep your opinions to yourself. I'm going to have to tell daddy about your attitude if you keep this up." He looked at her with mock meekness, "Will you now. I'm so sorry my lady, didn't mean to offend. I'm just preparing you for what may come. Just remember I'm always at your service." Fallon glared at him and pressed a button and slowly the partition slid shut, blocking his smug teasing features from her view. Just before it completely closed, she quipped at him, "Just concentrate on what you are being paid for - driving!!!" She heard him softly chuckle.

She clenched her hands on her lap in frustration, "Infuriating, arrogant man!! I don't know what it is about him that I find so attractive, a servant of all things." She knew that deep down he was an enigma as he was one of the few men that didn't fear her or suck up to her and maybe that's what she liked - a challenge, "Although if daddy can dally with the hired help, maybe I can too. It would serve daddy right if I did." She smiled spitefully. She could

 feel her temper rising at the thought of Krystle spending any time at the mansion or with Blake. When they arrived at the mansion Culhane opened her door and took her hand to help her out. What Fallon didn't realize was as she got out, Culhane purposely tripped her foot so that she landed into his arms. He held her tight for a few seconds while she got her breath back, savoring her sexy feminine shape. He felt triumphant as he could feel her tremble in delicious response to being held so close to his tall solid body, "Oh steady on there miss. You nearly fell. Must be a stone on the driveway." She violently pushed him away from her with a little grunt, tossed her head and stormed into the mansion.

Fallon was restless, she couldn't stand waiting for Blake and hated the tension she could sense in the servants. She decided to go for a ride on her horse. It was her favorite way to relax and calm her.

She rode for about half an hour enjoying the Denver wind rushing through her long brown hair. She loved the sense of freedom it horse riding gave her and it was a pleasure to see the beautiful scenery around her home. Fallon couldn't bear the thought that another woman might become the new mistress of all she held dear. She was enjoying herself so much that she was running late to see her father and decided to gallop up to the mansion's front entrance.

Blake was standing near the limo talking to Michael Culhane and was just about to go inside when he caught sight of Fallon galloping towards him. He laughed indulgently at her as she halted and gracefully jumped down off the chestnut thoroughbred to rush into his arms. "Daddy, I've missed you." He lifted her up and twirled her around and kissed her cheek. He still couldn't believe how she was blossoming into a beautiful young woman but she would always be his cute little girl, "Fallon, how well and pretty you look. Come on, let's go inside darling. You will have to tell me all about your adventures in Switzerland and I have so much to tell you too." Tony, the young dark handsome stable hand, walked towards the horse to take it back to the stables. But before he could Michael Culhane gave him a knowing wink, "The fur's about to fly now!!! Too bad we can't eavesdrop on them." Tony shook his head in disgust, "Sleazy creep! Why doesn't he mind his own business" , he thought, as he couldn't stand Culhane and he thought very highly of the Carrington's as they were very good to him. He ignored the smirking chauffeur and took the horse by the reigns and walked back to the stables.

Blake took Fallon into his study where Mrs. Gunnerson had placed their lunch. They were both seated when Fallon took a deep breath and went straight to the point, "Daddy, I'm worried about you. Isn't it about time this little affair between you and your little secretary stopped? Denver society is having a field day and even the staff are gossiping about you." Blake frowned at her, "I never brought you up to be a snob, Fallon. It's not just an affair, I've fallen in love with Krystle. I've asked her to marry me and she has accepted." Fallon gasped in horror. Blake continued, "I'm sorry my dear, I know I haven't given you or Steven much time to get use to this." Fallon choked on her coffee, "But daddy, little affairs are all well and good but marriage? Are you serious? What do you know of this woman? Obviously she is after your money, being a little nobody from a hick little town." She was working herself up now, her voice rising in angry panic, "How can you daddy, how can you do this to Steven and me? How can you..." Blake put up his hand and stood up, he said sternly, "Enough now, stop it Fallon!!!"

Then he softened when he saw the look of hurt in her face, which had tears there now, "I know you are concerned for my welfare, but I'm a grown man sweetheart. I've got to know Krystle really well since she has been working with me everyday for the last three months. She is the kindest, most gentlest and sweetest woman I know. If anything, I had to chase her. She rejected me because of my status and riches until I convinced her that our love was worth fighting for. She makes me feel happy and alive, Fallon. Can't you understand that?" He came over to her and pulled her from her chair and hugged her, "Just give her a chance. I've invited her over tonight to meet you and I want you to behave and be nice to her for my sake." It had been a long time since Fallon had seen her father feel passionate about anything other than business. She hiccupped, sniffed and wiped her tears, "Alright daddy, I don't want to anger you or upset you. I'll meet her tonight." Blake smiled and kissed her, "That's my special girl. I knew I could count on you." She nodded meekly and thought, "We will see daddy, we will see."

From behind the other side of the study's closed solid oak door Joseph's ear was pressed up against it. He had given all the servants errands and tasks to do. He couldn't help himself in wanting to hear personally what Fallon was saying to Blake. He knew if anyone could talk the boss out of making the biggest mistake of his life then it would be Fallon. His heart sank when he could hear their raised voices. He also knew that when Blake made up his mind to do something that he carried it through. He quickly walked away towards his own room and with a sad feeling and knew Fallon had failed to sway her father. He realized that soon he will be taking orders from Krystle Grant the future Mrs. Blake Carrington.

Later that night Fallon had just finished dressing for the dinner with Blake and Krystle. She looked at herself in the mirror and smiled for she knew she looked good. The linden green chiffon sheath dress clung in all the right places. This confidence with her appearance made her more ready to face Krystle. She narrowed her eyes at her reflection and murmured, "And let the games begin!!" Just then there was a tap on her bedroom door and Blake entered. Fallon smiled, "Daddy, I'm ready. Is she here yet?" Blake stood near her and held her hand, "You look beautiful. I'm glad you are making an effort for me. Krystle is waiting in the drawing room. I told her I would come and fetch you. Sit here with me for a minute darling."

He guided her to the pale pink couch. They sat down and he took her hands in his and looked earnestly into her eyes, "Fallon, I know this must be hard for you to deal with but I love Krystle and I intend to make her my wife. But sweetheart, I want you to know that no matter what, you will always be my special little girl. I love you very much. I'll always be here for you." Fallon's eyes misted over, "Oh daddy." Blake took out of his pocket a flat black velvet box, "This belonged to my mother and I want you to have it. You are so much like her." She took it from him and opened it. Inside was a necklace of deep red rubies surrounded by tiny emeralds. She gasped as Blake put the necklace around her slender throat, "There, you are a young woman now and I know mother would have wanted you to enjoy them. It looks exquisite on you." Fallon hugged him to her and was more determined then ever to protect her father from gold digging trollops. They then walked arm in arm down the sweeping staircase.

Krystle was standing nervously near the large fireplace gazing up at Fallon's portrait. The door opened and there, holding Blake's arm was Fallon looking more vibrant and beautiful than her picture could capture. They went over to Krystle and Blake put his hand on Krystle's arm, "Darling, this is Fallon." Krystle smiled warmly at her and sincerely said, "Hello Fallon. You father always talks fondly of you. This must have come as a shock, us being engaged but I really want you and me to become friends. I love your father very much." Fallon's mouth was set in a frozen smile and she felt a rush of jealously as she glanced at Blake's hand resting so possessively and protectively on Krystle's arm. She tensed further upon seeing the flash of Blake's sapphire engagement ring on Krystle's finger, "I can see why daddy was attracted to you. He has been singing your praises no end. Ohio must be missing such an efficient and fast worker." Fallon hoped Krystle was aware of her double meaning that she thought of her as a schemer and smiled in satisfaction when Krystle stiffened. Oblivious to the women's under currents, Blake laughed and took it a face value, "Yes Fallon, I was lucky that Krystle joined Denver Carrington. She is a true asset to the company oh and my heart."

They sat down on the lounge suite and Fallon looked Krystle up and down thinking, "Butter wouldn't melt in her mouth. She looks the part of the proper lady with her angelic face and huge innocent blue eyes. I give her that credit. But I won't let her fool me like she does daddy." Fallon raised a fine eyebrow and aloud said, "Well Krystle, don't you miss the small town life. It must have been strange for you coming to Denver." Krystle shifted uncomfortably in her seat, "Oh not really. You see I have traveled all over America with my first husband, he was a tennis pro." Fallon's eyes narrowed, "Ahhhh, the gypsy life then. How romantic. A tennis pro's wife and then a secretary, my my, you have lead an interesting life then? You must find here to be very boring." Blake interrupted Krystle's reply by suggesting they have some wine before dinner. A few minutes later Joseph came in with their wine. Joseph looked down his long nose at Krystle and Fallon thought, "Good, even Joseph can't stand her." He was about to pour the wine when Blake told him, "I'll do the honors Joseph, you may go." An annoyed Joseph left the room.

Blake poured each of them a glass of wine and asked them to stand for a toast, "To Krystle, may she feel welcome here and feel that this is her new home." Fallon said brightly, "To Krystle!" and tapped her glass hard on Krystle's so that the red rich wine splashed all over Krystle's fine lace yellow gown. Fallon tried hard not to smile in satisfaction of seeing the bright red stains, "Oops!!! So sorry Krystle. I don't know my own strength." Krystle dabbed it with a handkerchief that Blake had produced from his jacket pocket, "The little brat!!!", she thought. Aloud she said, "That's alright, it was an accident after all." Fallon took Krystle by the arm and turned to Blake, "Daddy, I'll just take Krystle upstairs. There should be something in her larger size that she could wear from the guest closet." Blake smiled at her, "You are so thoughtful, darling. It will be alright Krystle. Fallon will look after you, run along and I'll meet you both in the dining room."

Fallon dragged Krystle up the stairs and took her to one of the guest bedrooms. Krystle shook her arm off her, "You did that deliberately, didn't you?" Fallon's eyes were wide with mocking innocence, "Now why would I do such a thing." Then she laughed, "Do you think I would make it easy for some common, small town secretary like you? Oh no missy, I may not be able to change daddy's mind about you but if you intend to want to be the lady of the manor so badly, you are going to have to earn it." Krystle blinked at her in angry shock, "Fallon I may come from a poorer background but we have more manners where I come from. Did you learn that little trick from your private schooling? I really love your father. I would marry him even if he was a beggar. In fact it would be a lot simpler if he was just an ordinary man." Fallon sniffed, "Oh I'm sure you would have, huh!!! Let me tell you, if you marry daddy and I find out that you hurt him in any way or make a fool out of him....." , she treaded like a small spitting cat threateningly towards Krystle's side, took hold of her arms and dug

her fingers painfully into them, her eyes flashing, "I'll make your life here a living hell!!!! Do you hear me?" Krystle's heart was beating strongly in fear and anger and she twisted out of Fallon's hold, "I only want to make your father happy. I'll prove it to you, you will see but it would be easier if I have your support. Blake would be upset if he is torn between us." Fallon took a step back and jeered, "I'm his daughter!! How could he ever side with you over me? Oh I'll be sweet to you in front of him, don't worry, but time will tell if you are the money grabbing bitch I think you are." With that she went over to the closet and took out an old shabby housekeeper's dress that was several sizes too big for Krystle, "Here!!", she threw it at Krystle, "There are no clothes in your size and this is the only thing that seems suitable for you. After all, designer clothes must still be a novel experience." After that parting shot she flounced out the door to join her father downstairs.

Krystle swallowed her tears and screwed up the old dress and threw it on the floor, "I'm not letting you get to me Fallon. I'm not scared of your spoilt little rich girl ways." One of the maids came in as she had heard the loud voices, "Are you alright Miss Grant? Oh your beautiful dress is ruined. If you take it off I'll see that it gets cleaned." Krystle said not to worry but could the maid bring her coat up from the hall closet. Luckily it was soft and long. When it was brought to her she stripped off her soaked dress and put her coat on and belted it. She laughed at herself in the mirror, "Oh no sweet Fallon, step-daughter to be, I'm not backing down and I'm not going home, I'm going to enjoy my lunch." Then she held her head up high and was about to go downstairs when the maid came back in. Horrified that Krystle was going to have lunch in only her coat she said, "Oh Miss Grant, surely there must be something in the closet that will fit you. There are so many lovely things, didn't Miss Fallon show you?" Krystle smiled ruefully, "Um Miss Fallon couldn't find anything." The maid opened the closet and pulled out an exquisite dress, "Here Miss Grant, I can't understand how she missed this one. I insist we clean your soiled dress for you." Krystle nodded gratefully and thanked her and the maid left her to change.

Dinner was laid out on the table when Krystle appeared in the dining room. Fallon's mouth dropped opened at the sight of Krystle in the lovely smart dress. She thought she would have gone home or stayed up in the bedroom. Blake said, "How's your headache darling? Fallon said you wouldn't be down and I was just about to go check on you." Krystle stared at Fallon, "Oh it's better now that Fallon gave me something for it. You see Blake, Fallon took care of me." She walked over behind Fallon's chair and firmly held her by her shoulders and squeezed very hard, "Fallon and I have come to an understanding, haven't we Fallon." She then asserted more pressure on Fallon's shoulders. Fallon closed her mouth, gritted her teeth and nodded dumbly, stunned. She had underestimated this woman. Blake smiled and Krystle sat down and continued, "We realized we had one thing in common, your happiness. Oh and Fallon has agreed to help me with the wedding details too." Fallon's eyes widened and she quivered in indignation, "Oh round one to you Krystle.", she thought bitterly. Blake was delighted, "I'm so glad my two lovely favorite girls are getting along so well." It was a very subdued Fallon and a very triumphant Krystle who ate their meals.

About ten o'clock Blake took Krystle back to her apartment. She made him coffee and afterwards they snuggled together on her couch. Blake caressed her cheek and kissed her lips very gently, "Thank you darling for making tonight a success. I knew Fallon would like you once she met you. I was afraid she might make some trouble, she's so highly spirited and stubborn." Krystle smiled and pressed her cheek into his chest. After winning that battle with Fallon she felt she could take on the whole world to fight for Blake's love, "Don't worry Blake, I can handle Fallon. " And she knew what ever Fallon dished out to her she would give it back to her two fold. Blake murmured, "I love you Krystle. We are going to have a wonderful life together.", and Krystle said, "I love you too. Do you want to stay tonight?" Blake chuckled then pulled her more securely into his arms and carried her to bed. While Blake was placing tender seductive kisses up along Krystle's white throat, trailing kisses towards her pink pouting lips, she was content knowing that whatever dramas they may go through together that their love would see them through.

DYNASTY - SEASON ONE

"OIL" – Episode 1.1- 1.3
Original Airdate - January 12, 1981
Written by Richard and Esther Shapiro
Directed by Ralph Senensky

Guest appearances by: Jerry Ayers (Tom), Barry Cahill (Bradley Milburn), Molly Cheek (Doris), Robert Clarke (Minister), Davy Davison (Margaret), Ellen Geer (uncredited), Bebe Kelly (Alice), Stefanie Kramer (Melanie), Judy Levitt (Marion), Stephen Nichols (Flight Attendant), Julie Parrish (Secretary), Paul Sorenson (Rigger), Paul Tuerpe (Doctor) and Vernon Weddle (Mr. Afferton)

As Krystle Jennings, the former secretary to Denver's oil tycoon Blake Carrington, prepares to wed her boss, one of Blake's geologists, Matthew Blaisdel, is being escorted from a hostile Middle Eastern country along with the entire Denver-Carrington oil crew. On the plane home, Matthew runs into Blake's son Steven, who tells him he's headed for Denver to attend his father's wedding. When Matthew bumps into Krystle in Blake's office, it is clear the two were once--and perhaps still are--in love. Blake's daughter Fallon, who spends her time traveling the globe and seducing men at whim, objects to her father's suggestion of settling down with Jeff Colby, nephew of the oil-rich Cecil Colby. Krystle, uncomfortable with the opulence of her new lifestyle and angry with Blake for orchestrating her 'chance' meeting with Matthew, quarrels with her fiancé and storms out of the mansion. After several heated discussions the wedding takes place leaving Blake and Krystle ecstatic and Fallon with a new enemy.

"The Honeymoon" – Episode 1.4
Original Airdate - January 19, 1981
Written by Edward de Blasio and Chester Krumholz
Directed by Robert C. Thompson

Guest Appearances by: Jerry Ayers (Tom), Linda Dangcil (Conception), Robert Davi (Amos), Ken Martinez (Bobby), Paul Napier (Leon), Alexander Petale (Peter) and Paul Sorenson (Rigger)

While honeymooning with Krystle, Blake learns of trouble with his oil leases in the Middle East. The government is holding his tankers and he'll be ruined if he can't get the oil out of the country. Matthew and Claudia's resumed life together is off to a rocky start, as is Matthew's business: He and Walter Lankershim are having trouble with their rigs--the banks won't help them and Blake is the source of their problems. Krystle tries to adjust to her new life in the mansion; Steven, unhappy with his father, takes a job working for Matthew. Cecil Colby wants Fallon to marry his nephew, Jeff, who is in love with her: If she agrees, he'll help Blake out of his difficulties.

"The Dinner Party" – Episode 1.5
Original Airdate - January 26, 1981
Written by Chester Krumholz
Directed by Don Medford

Guest Appearances by Mace Barrett (Vince Harrison), Barbara Beckley (Marion Loomis), Bill Cort (Mr. Beaumont), Paul Jenkins (Ed), Stacy Keach Sr. (Tom Loomis), Kiva Lawrence (Tess Harrison), Ken Martinez (Bobby), Don Matheson (Frank Carter), Jennifer Nairn-Smith (Elaine Carter), Paul Napier (Leon) and Rachel Ward (Edna MacReady)

Blake continues to search for a solution to his financial crisis. Problems in the Middle East have jeopardized his oil leases. Krystle remains ill at ease with her new life in the mansion, and clashes with long-time head butler, Joseph. Although resentful of her father's new bride, Fallon gives her a few tips on how the rich behave because she doesn't want Blake embarrassed by Krystle. Blake throws an elaborate dinner party and invites Matthew Blaisdel, his former employee and Krystle's former lover. Blake needs Matthew back--with his oil leases. Fallon overhears Matthew tell Krystle he is still in love with her. Jeff struggles to hold his own with Fallon, as a bemused Michael, the chauffeur, looks on. Steven befriends a lost Claudia.

FALLON'S WEDDING – Episode 1.6
Original Airdate - February 2, 1981
Written by Edward de Blasio
Directed by Philip Leacock

Guest Appearances by Jerry Ayres (Tom), Paul Jenkins (Ed), Ken Martinez (Bobby), Cliff Murdock (Hardesty), Kathryn Leigh Scott (Jennifer) and Mark Withers (Ted Dinard)

Steven's ex-lover, Ted, arrives from New York. In an obscure diner, the two talk of their past life and love for one another. Ted wants Steven back, but Steven declines, insisting he must first find himself. The meeting is observed by Steven's fellow rigger, Amos, who tells the crew what he has heard. Steven admits his homosexuality to his boss, Matthew, and asks to stay on the job. After another reminder from Cecil Colby that he will bail Blake out of his business troubles if she marries his nephew, Fallon reluctantly flies to Las Vegas and marries Jeff. Michael, the chauffeur, attempts to bribe a banker to stop loans to Blake's rival, Matthew Blaisdel. Blake learns of the scheme and chastises the chauffeur--but later offers him more money and expanded duties to continue the work.

"The Chauffeur Tells A Secret" – Episode 1.7
Original Airdate - February 16, 1981
Written by Edward de Blasio
Directed by Ralph Senensky

Guest Appearances by Jerry Ayres (Tom), Rick Lenz (Dr. Jordan), Ben Marino (Frank), Tony O'Dell (Christopher) and Kathryn Leigh Scott (Jennifer)

Claudia and daughter Lindsay are making progress toward a closer relationship. Steven is determined to prove himself on the job, despite constant taunting by the crew because he's gay. Krystle tells Blake she wants to be more involved in his work. He counters by stating he wants a child. Fallon remains jealous of Krystle and unhappy in her marriage to Jeff. Michael, the chauffeur, learns of the terms of their union and tells Blake, who furiously confronts his daughter. Claudia tells her psychiatrist of her suspicions about Matthew's feelings for Krystle. Lindsay's friend, Christopher, makes a pass at her. Frightened, she races to the oil rig where her father's partner, Walter, consoles her. Claudia and Matthew invite Steven to dinner. Claudia advises Steven to stop trying to prove himself and do what he really wants. Moved by her compassion, Steven finds himself attracted to Claudia.

"The Bordello" – Episode 1.8
Original Airdate - February 23, 1981
Written by Edward de Blasio
Directed by Philip Leacock

Guest Appearances by Jerry Ayres (Tom), Molly Cheek (Doris), Paul Jenkins (Ed), Stephanie Kramer (Melanie), Ken Martinez (Bobby), Julie Parrish (Secretary), Tisch Raye (Sarah Pat Beecham) and Madlyn Rhue (Lucy)

As Blake's financial situation worsens--his Middle Eastern oil reserves have been seized-he attempts to save what he has from his creditors by putting everything in Krystle's name. Walter takes Steven to a bordello hoping to "make a man out of him." Steven  spends time with the prostitute watching TV. A Blaisdel-Lankershim rigger, Amos, sabotages the rig and Steven is blamed. Steven asks his father for help, promising to do anything he asks in return for his assistance--including dating the daughter of a friend. Nonetheless, Blake turns him down. Krystle pawns her diamond earrings and gives Matthew the money to get the rig repaired. At his office, the two declare their love for one another, but Krystle makes it clear that she can't give Matthew anything else that belongs to Blake.

"Krystle's Lie" – Episode 1.9
Original Airdate – March 2, 1981
Written by Edward de Blasio
Directed by Don Medford

Guest Appearances by Jerry Ayres (Tom), Robert Burton (Larry Atkins), Curtis Credel (Rancher), Ed Hooks (Man at Bar), Dawn Jeffory (Tania), Paul Jenkins (Ed), Jack Kutcher (Bartender), Rick Lenz (Dr. Jordan), Ben Marino (Frank), Ken Martinez (Bobby), Tony O'Dell (Christopher), Timothy Wayne (Desk Clerk), Mark Withers (Ted Dinard) and Patrick Wright (Buck)

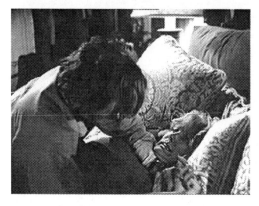

Blake is determined to find out who bankrolled Matthew's renewed drilling operation. Lindsay is shattered to learn of her illegitimacy. Blake discovers Krystle's birth control pills and flies into a rage, attacking his wife. Matthew finds that Ed, one of the riggers, tampered with his equipment and set Steven up for the blame, acting on instructions from "Carrington's people." He fires Ed, who promptly tells Claudia of her husband's affair with Krystle. Matthew then confronts Blake, who accuses him of carrying a torch for his wife. Steven receives a wire from his ex-lover Ted Dinard, who is passing through Denver. Fallon intercepts Ted at the airport and escorts him to San Francisco in the Carrington jet. On board, she cautions him to stay away from her brother.

*This was one of the few episodes that ran as a two-hour special. It was broken into two separate episodes for syndication and rerun purposes.

"The Necklace" – Episode 1.10
Original Airdate - March 2, 1981
Written by Edward de Blasio
Directed by Philip Leacock

Guest Appearances by Jerry Ayres (Tom), Robert Burton (Larry Atkins), Curtis Credel (Rancher), Ed Hooks (Man at Bar), Dawn Jeffory (Tania), Paul Jenkins (Ed), Jack Kutcher (Bartender), Rick Lenz (Dr. Jordan), Ben Marino (Frank), Ken Martinez (Bobby), Tony O'Dell (Christopher), Timothy Wayne (Desk Clerk), Mark Withers (Ted Dinard) and Patrick Wright (Buck)

Matthew receives a call from his partner Walter that their oil well is about to come in. Claudia asks to go along, but Matthew insists it's bad luck to have a woman at the rig. They argue and Claudia takes off, ending up at a singles bar where she picks up a young man. At his apartment she changes her mind and calls Steven to take her home. Blake apologizes to Krystle for his angry explosion. Michael, the chauffeur, tells Fallon he has learned that Krystle pawned a $40,000 necklace. Intrigued, Fallon asks Krystle if she may borrow the necklace and is confused when her stepmother produces a fake copy. Claudia confronts Krystle about her affair with Matthew and then follows Steven to his mountain cabin, where the two make love. When the well comes in, Matthew arrives home bearing gifts for Lindsay and Claudia, but finds his wife missing.

"The Beating" – Episode 1.11
Original Airdate – March 9, 1981
Written by Edward de Blasio
Directed by Don Medford

Guest Appearances by Brian Dennehy (District Attorney Jake Dunham), Ken Martinez (Bobby), Tony O'Dell (Christopher) and Bonwitt St. Claire (Louise Dunham)

Steven tells Blake he is moving out of the house. He has enrolled at the university to study business administration, and will come to work for Denver-Carrington. Krystle tells Matthew that Claudia knows about their affair. Michael tells Blake about Steven's involvement with Claudia. Jeff returns from Europe and tells Fallon he wants to move away. An unhappy Fallon runs to ex-lover Michael for comfort. Shortly thereafter, Michael is attacked. Fallon knows her father has orchestrated the beating. Matthew plans to take a reluctant Claudia on a second honeymoon. Lindsay follows her mother to Steven's apartment and sees the two of them together. Shattered, she runs to Walter Lankershim for comfort.

"The Birthday Party" – Episode 1.12
Original Airdate - March 16, 1981
Written by Edward de Blasio and Richard Shapiro
Directed by Burt Brinkerhoff

Guest Appearances by Barbara Beckley (Emily Laird), Larry Ellis (Waiter), Eric Lawson (Workman), Curt Lowens (Volkert), Sandra McCabe (Bethany) and Mark Withers (Ted Dinard)

Michael tells Blake that Krystle pawned her emerald necklace and gave the money to Matthew Blaisdel. Jeff learns that Blake blocked his much-wanted transfer to New Orleans and that Fallon married him only to help out her father. At a birthday party for Cecil Colby, a distraught Jeff gets drunk with his  uncle's girlfriend and throws a scene. Fallon tells Krystle she knows about the necklace, and then asks Matthew to take Krystle off her father's hands. When Matthew repays Krystle, she attempts to buy the necklace back--but finds it has been sold to a South American gentleman. Steven's former lover Ted arrives in town.

"The Separation" – Episode 1.13
Original Air Date - March 23, 1981
Written by Edward de Blasio
Directed by Gabrielle Beaumont

Guest Appearances by Ferdy Mayne (Channing) and Mark Withers (Ted Dinard)

Fallon chastises Jeff for embarrassing his uncle at the birthday dinner. He responds by throwing her, fully clothed, into the pool. Steven tells Claudia he spent the night with Ted and she leaves in tears. Krystle learns that it was Blake who bought her necklace from the pawn shop. Ted tells Claudia he is prepared to fight her for Steven. No longer able to deal with Blake's changing moods, Krystle leaves him. Steven leaves Ted a note saying goodbye and heads for the mansion to retrieve the rest of his belongings. Ted follows him and Blake catches the two in a goodbye embrace. Furious, Blake strikes Ted, who falls and hits his head against a table. As Fallon looks on, Steven accuses his father of murder.

"Blake Goes To Jail" – Episode 1.14
Original Air Date - April 13, 1981
Written by Edward de Blasio
Directed by Don Medford

Guest Appearances by Lee Bergere (Joseph), Colby Chester (Bill), Brian Dennehy (District Attorney Jake Dunham), Betty Harford (Mrs. Gunnerson), Virginia Hawkins (Jeanette Robbins), Lloyd Haynes (Judge Horatio Quinlan), Paul Jenkins (Ed) and Eugene Peterson (Natale)

Blake is taken into police custody after causing the death of Steven's lover, Ted Dinard. Krystle, who had left her husband, returns to stand by him during the ordeal. While in court, Blake learns an important board meeting has been purposely called in his absence and he sends Krystle to take his place. In a show of strength and loyalty, she defeats the opposition, forcing them to postpone further proceedings until Blake's return. At the trial, prosecutor Jake Dunham pushes for a murder conviction. Blake's attorney, Andrew Laird, argues the death was accidental. Fallon takes the stand and maintains that Ted tripped, hitting his head. Steven testifies, admitting to his affair with Ted and shocking the courtroom by accusing his sister of lying.

"The Testimony" – Episode 1.15
Original Airdate - April 20, 1981
Written by Edward de Blasio
Directed by Don Medford

Guest Appearances by Colby Chester (Bill), Brian Dennehy (District Attorney Jake Dunham), Lloyd Haynes (Judge Horatio Quinlan), Tisch Raye (Sarah Pat Beecham) and Maggie Wickman (temporary Alexis Carrington)

Fallon accosts Steven for his damning testimony against Blake, whose attorney attempts to prove the death of Ted Dinard was an accident. Against Blake's wishes, Claudia is called to the stand and tearfully testifies she and Steven had an affair. When her husband Matthew hears her statement he physically attacks Blake in the courtroom, threatening to kill him for putting Claudia through this ordeal. Matthew is summarily removed and jailed. In his cell, he learns a distraught Claudia and daughter Lindsay have been involved in a serious automobile accident. Blake takes the stand and insists he loves his son and Ted's death was accidental. The prosecution dramatically calls a surprise witness to the stand: Alexis Carrington, Blake's first wife.

SEASON TWO

"Enter Alexis" – Episode 2.1
Original Airdate - November 4, 1981
Written by Edward de Blasio
Supervising Producers Eileen and Robert Mason Pollock
Directed by Gabrielle Beaumont

Guest Appearances by Kale Brown (Doctor), Terry Burns (Clerk), Brian Dennehy (District Attorney Jake Dunham), Lloyd Haynes (Judge Horactio Quinlan) and Herman Poppe (Baliff)

At Blake's murder trial, his former wife Alexis states that years earlier, Blake caught her with a lover and crippled the man, then paid him off to keep him quiet. Blake then forced Alexis to sign a paper promising to stay away from the children. After hearing this testimony, Krystle becomes ill and leaves the courtroom. While recovering in the hospital, Claudia learns that her husband has taken off with their daughter Lindsay. Fallon tells Steven that their mother was paid $250,000 yearly to abandon them. Steven tells Alexis of his love for Ted. Fallon berates Krystle for leaving the courtroom. The jury announces they have reached a verdict.

"The Verdict" – Episode 2.2
Original Airdate - November 11, 1981
Written by Edward de Blasio
Supervising Producers Eileen and Robert Mason Pollock
Directed by Gabrielle Beaumont

Guest Appearances by Kale Brown (Doctor), Terry Burns (Clerk), Robert Clotworthy (Ty Meredith), Brian Dennehy (District Attorney Jake Dunham), Lloyd Haynes (Judge Horatio Quinlan) and Herman Poppe (Baliff)

The jury finds Blake guilty and he is sentenced to two years probation. When questioned about the effect the verdict will have on Denver-Carrington, Blake maintains that it will be business as usual. He privately wonders how long the stockholders are going to trust a man branded a killer. Krystle professes her love and returns to her husband. Fallon blames her stepmother for the guilty verdict. Claudia learns Blake has paid her hospital bills. Steven tells Claudia he loves her and is sorry for everything. Alexis urges Blake to forgive Steven. Blake accuses her of making him a "momma's boy." Blake dismisses Michael, the chauffeur, and tells Fallon to behave. Blake slaps Steven while quarreling and announces he's cutting him out of his will. A shaken Krystle suffers a fall. While waiting for the doctor to arrive, she tells Blake she may be pregnant. Despite Blake's objections, Alexis moves into her old art studio on the Carrington grounds.

"Alexis' Secret" – Episode 2.3
Original Airdate - November 18, 1981
Written by Edward de Blasio
Supervising Producers Eileen and Robert Mason Pollock
Directed by Richard Kinon

Guest Appearances by Betty Harford (Mrs. Gunnerson), Peter Mark Richman (Andrew Laird) and Jim Staszkiel (Parolee)

Krystle orders Alexis, who has reclaimed her studio on the Carrington estate, to leave the premises. Blake instructs his attorney to get Alexis out of his life and to cut Steven out of his will. Alexis insists she is staying to protect her son's interests. She stuns Steven by telling him he is Blake s only child as he did not father Fallon. Blake's attorney advises Claudia that it may be impossible to reclaim her daughter because her testimony admitting an affair with Steven will brand her an unfit mother. Distraught, Claudia tries to kill herself. At the last minute, Blake and Dr. Nick Toscanni save her. Blake moves her into the mansion where the doctor can personally care for her. The doctor also wants to exact vengeance on Blake for a past wrong. When Fallon learns of Krystle's pregnancy, she tells Jeff it's time they had a child.

"Fallon's Father" – Episode 2.4
Original Airdate - November 25, 1981
Written by Mann Rubin
Supervising Producers Eileen and Robert Mason Pollock
Directed by Bob Sweeney

Guest Appearances by Nick Angotti (Doctor)

Alexis urges Blake to make up with Steven who, she tells him, is his only child because Fallon is not his daughter. Blake learns that Cecil Colby closed a business deal without consulting him. His associates do not want to deal with an accused murderer. Alexis urges Cecil to speak with Blake so that Steven may be put back in the family will. She threatens to reveal their past affair if he doesn't. Alexis further reveals that Colby is Fallon's father. Claudia tells Dr. Nick Toscanni of her affair with Steven. Steven drunkenly falls at the mansion, hitting his head on the pool diving board. Nick pulls Steven's unconscious body from the pool and rushes him to the hospital. Steven is diagnosed with possible brain damage.

"Reconciliation" – Episode 2.5
Original Airdate – December 2, 1981
Written by Edward de Blasio
Supervising Producers Eileen and Robert Mason Pollock
Directed by Jerome Courtland

Guest Appearances by Matt Clark (Frank Dean) and Christina Hart (Bedelia)

Having reconciled with his father, Steven is taken home from the hospital to recover. Alexis remains constantly at her son's side. Krystle feels excluded. Race car driver Frank Dean, Krystle's ex-brother-in-law, sends his stepdaughter, Sammy Jo, to stay with her for a few weeks. When Sammy Jo arrives at the mansion, the 18-year old proves to be a source of amusement to a convalescing Steven. Despite treatment by Nick Toscanni, Claudia retreats more and more into her own world. She is still hopeful of being reunited with husband Matthew and daughter Lindsay. Steven asks his mother who fathered Fallon. Alexis hires a private investigator to explore Krystle's past. Cecil Colby pressures Blake to repay his $9 million loan, and offers to call off the debt in exchange for Blake's football team, which is worth $20 million. Blake refuses, vowing to somehow produce the cash.

"Viva Las Vegas" – Episode 2.6
Original Airdate – December 9, 1981
Written by Edward de Blasio
Supervising Producers Eileen and Robert Mason Pollock
Directed by Alf Kjellin

Guest Appearances by Carol Bagdasarian (Terry) and Lance LeGault (Ray Bonning)

In order to save his football team and repay the $9 million to Cecil Colby, Blake flies to Las Vegas and obtains a loan from gangster Logan Rhinewood. Nick tells his sister that Blake is to blame for the death of their kid brother, who hanged himself in jail. He intends to find proof and claim vengeance. Sammy Jo has a nightmare and goes to Steven for comfort. In the morning, Alexis sees her leaving and promptly tells Krystle that the two spent the night together. When Alexis suggests that Steven, once again his father's heir, should consider marrying, he asks Claudia to give some thought to a future together. Fallon and Nick make love. While skeet shooting, Alexis spots a pregnant Krystle riding her horse. She fires, and the frightened animal throws Krystle to the ground. She is rushed to the hospital, in danger of losing the child.

"The Miscarriage" – Episode 2.7
Original Airdate – December 16, 1981
Written by Edward de Blasio
Supervising Producers Eileen and Robert Mason Pollock
Directed by Irving J. Moore

Guest Appearances by James Carrington (Buddy), Scott Cooper (Jud), Ava Lazar (Linda), (William Prince (Dr. Miller), Kathy Rich (Debbie) and Wade Wallace (Andy)

After losing her baby due to the fall from her horse, Krystle learns she cannot have another child. Steven and Sammy Jo begin dating, but at his cabin, he finds he cannot make love to her. Jeff quits his Uncle Cecil's business and joins Denver-Carrington. Fallon continues her affair with Nick Toscanni. Steven professes his love to Claudia and asks her to marry him. She declines, stating she's still in love with her husband. Fallon interrupts Nick's visit to Krystle in the hospital and angrily assumes the worst, demanding to know if she is "another page in his appointment book." Blake's attorney, Andrew Laird, returns from Washington with news of more trouble with the Middle Eastern oil leases.

"The Mid-East Meeting" – Episode 2.8
Original Airdate – January 6, 1982
Written by Elizabeth and Richard Wilson
Supervising Producers Eileen and Robert Mason Pollock
Directed by Gabrielle Beaumont

Guest Appearances by Victoria Carroll (Dottie), Dale Johnson (Maitre D'), Andrew Masset (Aldo) and Barbara Tarbuck (Dr. Holton)

Blake and Jeff attempt to arrange a meeting with Rashid Ahmed to obtain assistance in releasing their overseas oil tankers. Alexis leaves for Rome to meet Ahmed, a former lover, under the guise of helping Blake. A despondent Krystle refuses Nick's psychiatric treatment. Claudia has recovered sufficiently to maintain her own apartment and take a job with Denver-Carrington. Cecil Colby invites her to dinner to pry company information from her. Fallon, learning she is pregnant, makes plans for an abortion and asks Jeff for a divorce. He agrees, but only after she has their baby. Fallon tells Nick she is in love with him. Alexis calls Blake to Rome, explaining she has arranged a meeting with Ahmed. Her true motive is simply to be alone with her former husband.

"The Psychiatrist" – Episode 2.9
Original Airdate – January 13, 1982
Written by Shimon Wincelberg
Supervising Producers Eileen and Robert Mason Pollock
Directed by Irving J. Moore

Guest Appearances by James Carrington (Buddy), Colby Chester (Handley), Bonnie Keith (Receptionist), Ava Lazar (Linda) and John Saxon (Rashid Ahmed)

En route to Rome to meet Rashid Ahmed, Blake calls Krystle in yet another attempt to convince his more and more despondent growing wife to make an appointment to see psychiatrist Nick Toscanni. She calls the doctor for an appointment, and Fallon is immediately jealous. Jeff begs Fallon to cancel her abortion. She confesses that she became pregnant only to compete with Krystle and further states she never loved him. Their marriage was strictly a business deal to benefit Blake. In Rome, Blake meets Alexis at Ahmed's villa. While he's rubbing suntan lotion on his ex-wife, a photographer, hired by Alexis, snaps photos. At home, a shattered Krystle sees the suggestive pictures in a gossip paper and bursts into tears. Nick comforts her and her grief soon turns to passion.

"Sammy Jo and Steven Marry" – Episode 2.10
Original Airdate – January 20, 1982
Written by Edward de Blasio
Supervising Producers Eileen and Robert Mason Pollock
Directed by Jerome Courtland

Guest Appearances by Owen Bush (Justice of the Peace), Sandy Freeman (Receptionist), Hilda Haynes (Nurse), Lance LeGault (Ray Bonning), Louise Fitch (Wife) and Viveca Lindfors (Adriana)

Nick tells Krystle he cares for her, but she refuses to jeopardize her marriage by seeing him. Fallon watches with keen interest as Krystle arrives home from Nick's apartment in the early hours. After securing the release of his oil tankers, Blake returns to Denver and learns Fallon has left to have the abortion. At the clinic, Blake finds his daughter unable to go through with the procedure. She decides to have the baby. Sammy Jo and Steven marry, and he decides to pursue a career racing cars with her help. Cecil Colby's investigators inform him that Claudia's husband and daughter have been seen in Ecuador. Although Blake swears to Krystle that nothing happened with Alexis in Rome, she refuses to believe him and dashes off.

"The Car Explosion" – Episode 2.11
Original Airdate -January 27, 1982
Written by Edward de Blasio
Supervising Producers Eileen and Robert Mason Pollock
Directed by Irving J. Moore

Guest Appearances by Joe Kapp (McAllister) and Lance LeGault (Ray Bonning)

Assuming that Fallon has gone through with the abortion, Jeff leaves the mansion. Blake tells him she will have the baby after all and persuades him to stay. Nick finally convinces Krystle to divorce Blake because she is certain he had an affair with Alexis in Rome. Steven and Sammy Jo return to the Carrington household and announce they are married. Blake, who has sold a percentage of his football team to Las Vegas racketeer Logan Rhinewood, finds himself the victim of the gangster's strong-arm tactics. As he and Jeff are leaving the office, a henchman throws dynamite at their limousine. The car bursts into flames, and although Jeff shoves Blake out of the way, Blake is blinded by the blast.

"Blake's Blindness" – Episode 2.12
Original Airdate – February 3, 1982
Written by Loraine Despres
Supervising Producers Eileen and Robert Mason Pollock
Directed by Jeff Bleckner

Guest Appearances by Lance LeGault (Ray Bonning), Percy Rodrigues (Dawson), Robert Sampson (Dr. Eggleston)

Blake's doctor informs him that although he is blinded as a result of the car explosion, there is no damage to the optic nerve. His loss of vision is attributable to severe psychological trauma. Nick begs Krystle to divorce Blake and marry him. Denver-Carrington's impounded oil is released and Blake, once again solvent, concentrates on a strategy of vengeance against his attackers. Fallon tells Alexis she is in love with Nick and plans to marry him after her baby is born. Blake has Jeff investigate Nick's past and finds he has a deceased brother whose name is familiar, although he can't quite place it. Fallon sees Nick and Krystle embrace and tells Alexis, who vows to get Krystle out of Denver for good.

"The Hearing" – Episode 2.13
Original Airdate – February 10, 1982
Written by Shimon Wincelberg
Supervising Producers Eileen and Robert Mason Pollock
Directed by Bob Sweeney

Guest Appearances by Arthur Adams (Senator Adams), Roy Andrews (Postman), John Terry Bell (Senator Brady), Angus Duncan (Linaver), Vince Ferragamo (William Hobart), Rhonda Hopkins (Saleswoman), George O. Petrie (Chairman) and Doris Singleton (Mrs. Nadia Fredericks)

Fallon tells Nick she loves him and is keeping up appearances with her husband, Jeff, solely for her father's sake. Once the baby is born, she plans to leave him. Nick, however, loves Krystle, and presses her to marry him. When Alexis intervenes on her daughter's behalf, stressing Fallon's substantial inheritance, Nick makes it clear he can't be bought. Blake, certain that Logan is responsible for the accident that blinded him, arranges to bring the Las Vegas racketeer before a crime committee hearing. When Logan's attorney manages to have the case dismissed, Blake protests heatedly and his eyesight is temporarily restored. Sammy Jo tells a stunned Alexis that she knows Fallon is not Blake's daughter. Alexis sends Blake an anonymous letter suggesting Krystle is sleeping with her psychiatrist. Blake's eyesight is restored.

"The Iago Syndrome" – Episode 2.14
Original Airdate – February 17, 1982
Written by Shimon Wincelberg
Supervising Producers Eileen and Robert Mason Pollock
Directed by Jerome Courtland and Alf Kjellin

Guest Appearances by Tim O'Connor (Thomas Crayford)

Although Blake's eyesight has been restored, he continues to act as if he is blind to suit his own purposes. Upset by Alexis's letter charging Krystle with infidelity, Blake opines to his wife that Nick is merely using her. Krystle tells Nick that it's over between them and leaves for her hometown of Dayton. Once she has gone, Nick informs Fallon that he is interested in resuming their relationship. Blake offers to adopt Jeff, who is very touched, but ultimately declines. Blake learns that Nick's half-brother, a former Denver-Carrington employee, hanged himself while in jail on drug charges. Nick finally believes Blake's explanation that he was out of the country and unable to get Nick's brother released from prison. Cecil Colby tells Claudia he knows where her daughter is and will let her know after she steals the documents outlining Denver-Carrington's oil extraction process.

"The Party" – Episode 2.15
Original Airdate -February 24, 1982
Written by Edward de Blasio
Supervising Producers Eileen and Robert Mason Pollock
Directed by Gwen Arner

Guest Appearances by Barbara Beckley (Woman Guest) and Tim O'Connor (Thomas Crayford)

To please her brother, Fallon throws a party to introduce Sammy Jo to the Carrington's social circle. After brazenly 'borrowing' Fallon's diamond and ruby necklace, a tipsy Sammy Jo appears at the party wearing a revealing dress. When Fallon asks her to behave like a Carrington, Sammy Jo spitefully  reveals that Blake is not Fallon's real father. Jeff sees Fallon kissing Nick and he leaves the party with Claudia. Nick Toscanni, once a neurosurgeon, finds he is once again able to perform surgery. Blake tells Krystle that his eyesight has been restored and the two make love. On a high-speed car ride, a distraught Fallon asks Alexis to tell her the truth about her father. When Alexis responds that she is not sure, Fallon loses control of the automobile and crashes. Her daughter unconscious, Alexis runs for help.

"The Baby"– Episode 2.16
Original Airdate – March 3, 1982
Written by Edward de Blasio
Supervising Producers Eileen and Robert Mason Pollock
Directed by Jerome Courtland

Guest Appearances by Grayce Grant (Circulating Nurse), Gail Landry (Woman Guest), Allyn Ann McLerie (Dr. Morrell), Belinda Montgomery (Jennifer) and Tim O'Connor (Thomas Crayford)

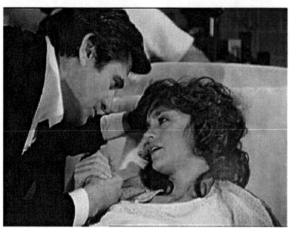

After the car crash, Fallon is taken to the hospital and gives birth to a premature son. Blake is thrilled to be a grandfather. Fallon tells Alexis that it was Sammy Jo who told her that Blake is not her real father. Alexis offers Sammy Jo $25,000 to leave Steven and she accepts. After making love to Jeff at her apartment, Claudia goes through his pockets and obtains the office keys she needs to steal the documents Cecil has demanded. Krystle learns from a grounds man that Alexis was out shooting the day she was thrown from the horse and lost her baby. When she confronts her, the two women engage in a knockdown, drag out fight. Alexis's detective reveals that Krystle's last divorce was never finalized and she is therefore not legally married to Blake. Alexis demands the detective find Krystle's husband and bring him to Denver.

"Mother and Son" – Episode 2.17
Original Airdate – March 10, 1982
Written by Edward de Blasio
Supervising Producers Eileen and Robert Mason Pollock
Directed by Lawrence Dobkin

Guest Appearances by Susannah Darrow (Nurse), Grayce Grant (Nurse) and Belinda Montgomery (Jennifer)

Since learning that Blake is not her true father, Fallon refuses to see him and also rejects her newborn son who is very ill with a heart ailment. Nick Toscanni finally persuades her to see the infant, who must undergo emergency surgery. The operation proves successful and once Fallon sees her son she  decides she cannot give him up to Jeff. Alexis admits to Blake that Cecil is Fallon's father. Jeff is falling in love with Claudia. When he catches her rifling through his office files, she explains that his Uncle Cecil promised to find her missing daughter in exchange for stealing Denver-Carrington's oil extraction formula. Claudia decides to confess her actions to Blake and then resign. Jeff learns that Claudia's daughter and husband have been lost in a Peruvian jungle and are believed dead. Upon hearing this news Claudia heads straight for her apartment and reaches for a gun.

"The Gun" – Episode 2.18
Original Airdate – March 24, 1982
Written by Edward de Blasio
Supervising Producers Eileen and Robert Mason Pollock
Directed by

Guest Appearances by Lance LeGault (Ray Bonning), Mark Thomas (Ace Hudson) and Shonda Whipple (Younger Lindsay)

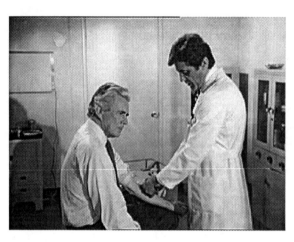

Blake submits to a blood test and the results prove he is indeed Fallon's father. Claudia confesses stealing Denver-Carrington's files and explains to Blake that Cecil promised to track down her daughter in exchange for the information. Blake forgives her and asks her to continue working at the company. Blake learns that gangster Logan Rhinewood now owns 40 percent of his firm's stock. Steven locates Sammy Jo in Hollywood where she is working as a nude model. An incoming telex advises that a jeep believed to have been carrying Matthew and Lindsay Blaisdel has been found in a Peruvian jungle with both occupants burned to death. Incensed that Cecil Colby lied to her, Claudia resolves to kill him. Krystle goes to Claudia's apartment to stop her. As the two women struggle, Nick arrives and hears a single gunshot.

"The Fragment" – Episode 2.19
Original Airdate – April 7, 1982
Written by Edward de Blasio
Supervising Producers Eileen and Robert Mason Pollock
Directed by Irving J. Moore and Ed Ledding

Guest Appearances by Fred Holliday (TV Commentator), Jan Jorden (Nurse #1), Lance LeGault (Ray Bonning), Michael McDonough (Paramedic), Tim O'Connor (Thomas Crayford), Inez Pedroza (TV Commentator), Richard Pierson (Intern), Diane Summerfield (Nurse #2), Ken Swofford (Lt. Holliman) and Aarika Wells (Hooker)

When Krystle struggled to wrestle the gun from an enraged Claudia, the weapon discharged and the bullet lodged in Claudia's head. After Nick operates, the prognosis remains uncertain, she may never be able to speak again. Logan Rhinewood continues to purchase shares of Denver-Carrington. Cecil Colby asks Alexis to marry him. The police question Krystle about the shooting incident. When Claudia regains consciousness, she screams "You stole my husband." Although Krystle explains that her affair with Matthew was years ago, Claudia is confused as to time and place. The police listen with growing interest to this exchange.

"The Shakedown" Episode 2.20
Original Airdate – April 14, 1982
Written by Daniel King Benton
Supervising Producers Eileen and Robert Mason Pollock
Directed by Philip Leacock

Guest Appearances by Fred Lerner (Arresting Officer), Steven Marachuk (Duane), Anthony Penya (Bartender) and Ken Swofford (Lt. Holliman)

Claudia is moved from the hospital to the Carrington home to recover from the gunshot wound, but she remains in a confused state: She is still unable to tell the police what happened and thereby exonerates Krystle. Alexis arranges for Tony, the gardener who saw her shoot at Krystle's horse, to leave the Carrington employ and work for Cecil Colby. Jeff presses Fallon to reconcile for the sake of their child. On his way back from Los Angeles, where he was unable to persuade Sammy Jo to come home, Steven gives a lift to a drifter named Duane. Aware of Steven's homosexual past, Duane threatens to charge him with sexual advances unless Steven pays him $500. Furious, Steven scuffles with him and the police arrive.

"The Two Princes" – Episode 2.21
Original Airdate – April 28, 1982
Written by Edward de Blasio
Supervising Producers Eileen and Robert Mason Pollock
Directed by Irving J. Moore

Guest Appearances by Christine Belford (Susan Farragut) and Rodney Saulsberry (Cop)

Steven is arrested for allegedly making homosexual advances to a drifter. Upon his release from jail, he and Blake quarrel. Steven, tired of trying to live up to his father's expectations, leaves Denver. Alexis accepts Cecil's marriage proposal. Fallon tells Nick she's going to try to make her marriage work for the sake of the baby. The news of her husband and daughter's deaths sends Claudia into shock. She reveals the truth of the shooting incident and Krystle is no longer under suspicion. Still far from well, Claudia believes that Fallon's baby is her daughter Lindsay.

"The Cliff" – Episode 2.22
Original Airdate – May 5, 1982
Written by Edward de Blasio
Supervising Producers Eileen and Robert Mason Pollock
Directed by Jerome Courtland

Guest Appearances by R.G. Armstrong (Alfred Grimes), Kabir Bedi (Farouk Ahmed), Christine Belford (Susan Farragut) and Patrick Wright (Worker)

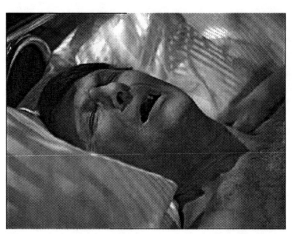

Alexis prepares for her upcoming marriage to Cecil Colby. Nick suggests that an increasingly disturbed Claudia return to the sanitarium for further treatment. Blake refuses to purchase oil leases from Middle Eastern oilmen Rashid Ahmed and his brother Farouk. Since Nick's brother died in the oilman's country, the doctor pays a visit to Farouk. Angry with Blake's refusal to do business, Farouk tells Nick that Blake was clearly responsible for his brother's death. While Krystle and Blake are vacationing at a mountain resort, Nick arrives and the two men scuffle. Nick is knocked out and Blake's horse, frightened by a rattlesnake, hurls him to the bottom of a ravine. Nick recovers and refuses to help an unconscious Blake. While making love with Alexis, Cecil suffers a heart attack.

SEASON THREE

"The Plea" – Episode 3.1
Original Airdate – September 29, 1982
Written by Edward de Blasio
Supervising Producers Eileen and Robert Mason Pollock
Directed by Irving J. Moore

Guest Appearances by Christine Belford (Susan Farragut), Nigel Bullard (TV Technician), John Carter (Dr. Osgood), Don Dubbins (Dr. Louden), David Joe Garcia (Cop), Grayce Grant (Day Nurse), Eloise Hardt (Night Nurse), Enid Kent (Nurse), Jean Le Bouvier (Care Center Woman), Tim O'Connor (Thomas Crayford), Robert Perault (Ranger), Arlen Dean Snyder (Lt. Cobb), Robert Symonds (Dr. Jonas Edwards) and Lurene Tuttle (Kate Torrance)

Krystle finds an injured Blake at the bottom of the ravine where Nick had left him to die. Blake is rushed to the hospital where he makes a complete recovery. Cecil Colby is hospitalized after suffering a massive coronary. Alexis pleads with him to go through with the wedding regardless. Fallon's baby is  kidnapped and Nick Toscanni is the prime suspect. Blake makes a televised plea for the return of his grandson. Alexis reveals the same thing happened 25 years ago when Adam, their infant son, was kidnapped and never recovered. In another part of the country, Kate Torrance, an elderly woman in poor health, watches the television appeal and tearfully tells her grandson Michael that he is in fact Adam Carrington.

"The Roof" – Episode 3.2
Original Airdate – October 6, 1982
Written by Edward de Blasio and Jeffrey Lane
Supervising Producers Eileen and Robert Mason Pollock
Directed by Gwen Arner

Guest Appearances by R.G. Armstrong (Alfred Grimes), Kabir Bedi (Farouk Ahmed), Christine Belford (Susan Farragut), Janice Heiden (Stewardess), Joanne Linville (Claire Maynard), Charles Parks (Street Cop), Rodney Saulsberry (Cop at Door), Lew Saunders (Roof Cop), Connie Sawyer (Apartment Manager), Eric Server (Rescue Expert), Michael Stearns (Investigating Officer), Robert Symonds (Dr. Jonas Edwards), Lurene Tuttle (Kate Torrance) and James Wainwright (Captain Lockwood)

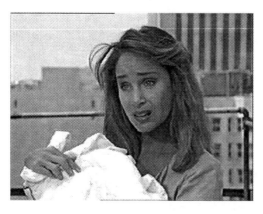

A dying Kate Torrance reveals to grandson Michael that after her son and his wife and baby were killed in an automobile accident, she stole him from a baby carriage in Denver. He is really the son of Blake and Alexis Carrington. On her deathbed, she asks Michael to return to his real parents. Claudia is discovered missing from the Carrington mansion and the police learn she is in an apartment building with a baby. When Blake, Krystle, and Fallon arrive with the officers, Claudia races to the roof, clutching the infant. Fallon pleads with her to return her son. Claudia insists the baby is her now-deceased daughter Lindsay. The disturbed woman trips, and to the crowd's horror, drops the baby to the ground. As the police pull back the blanket, they see the 'infant' is merely a doll.

"The Wedding" – Episode 2.3
Original Airdate – October 20, 1982
Written by Jeffrey Lane
Supervising Producers Eileen and Robert Mason Pollock
Directed by Irving J. Moore

Guest Appearances by R.G. Armstrong (Alfred Grimes), Christine Belford (Susan Farragut), Diana Bellamy (Nurse), Robert Clarke (Minister), Don Dubbins (Dr. Louden), Burt Edwards (Desk Clerk), Grayce Grant (I.C.U. Nurse), John Larch (Gerald Wilson), Marland Proctor (Cop) and Shirley Slater (Sanitarium Attendant)

After dropping a doll she believed to be a baby from the roof of a building, a deranged Claudia is taken to the sanitarium. Blake finally locates Fallon's baby. Nick Toscanni had paid Alfred Grimes (Roger's father) to kidnap the child. Fallon takes a job managing her father's hotel, La Mirage. Fallon runs into Michael Torrance, who is his story and sends him away. Alexis convinces Cecil to marry her in his hospital, but immediately following the ceremony, he torments Alexis with questions of her and Blake's wedding night but stresses himself so much that he suffers yet another heart attack.

"The Will" – Episode 3.4
Original Airdate – October 27, 1982
Written by Katherine Coker
Supervising Producers Eileen and Robert Mason Pollock
Directed by Gwen Arner

Guest Appearances by Bettye Ackerman (Katherine), Dennis Kirkpatrick (Newscaster), John Larch (Gerald Wilson), Louise Fitch (Mrs. Charles), Simon MacCorkindale (Billy Dawson), F. William Parker (Desk Clerk) and Marion R. Russell (Housekeeper)

Shortly after marrying Alexis, Cecil dies. When his will is read, Alexis and Jeff are named as equal beneficiaries. It is further revealed that Cecil was the mysterious 'Logan Rhinewood' who had amassed substantial Denver-Carrington stock. When Jeff refuses to grant Fallon a divorce, she insists on separate bedrooms. Having been unsuccessful in convincing Blake that he is his missing son Adam, Michael Torrance tracks down Alexis and produces a silver rattle with the initials A.A.C. Stunned, Alexis attempts to verify the serial number on the gift she had bought for her son 25 years earlier.

"The Siblings" – Episode 3.5
Original Airdate – November 3, 1982
Written by Daniel King Benton
Supervising Producers Eileen and Robert Mason Pollock
Directed by Irving J. Moore

Guest Appearances by Larry Horowitz (Brent), Hedley Mattingly (Mr. Jensen) and Robert Symonds (Dr. Jonas Edwards)

Alexis learns the silver rattle produced by Michael Torrance is indeed the same one she gave to her son Adam before he was kidnapped. Blake travels to Montana, Michael's home, and learns he is telling the truth. Blake tells Adam he believes he is his son and asks him to join Denver-Carrington. Adam declines, stating that he  will take a position with his mother's firm, Colbyco. Alexis's detectives reveal that Krystle's divorce from her husband Mark Jennings was never finalized in Mexico. Alexis meets Mark in New York. Not realizing he is her brother, Fallon finds that she is attracted to Adam. When she learns his true identity, she insists he is merely a fortune-hunting imposter.

"Mark" – Episode 3.6
Original Airdate – November 10, 1982
Written by Edward de Blasio and Philip Leacock
Supervising Producers Eileen and Robert Mason Pollock
Directed by Philip Leacock

Guest Appearances by Dee Dee Bradley (Secretary), Jeff Eagle (Attendant), John Larch (Gerald Wilson), Margaret Michaels (Tennis Player) and Ron Ray (Barber)

While working at Colbyco, Adam clashes with Jeff, who has inherited substantial stock in the firm from Cecil. To prove he is sorry for doubting his word, Blake buys Adam an expensive sports car, which Adam refuses to accept. In New York, Alexis convinces Krystle's ex-husband, Mark, a tennis instructor, to move to Denver and work at La Mirage. Fallon, attracted to Mark, refuses to hire him when she learns he was once married to Krystle. Not trusting the firm to Adam's management, Jeff resigns from Denver-Carrington and joins Colbyco, a decision which greatly disturbs Adam.

"Kirby" – Episode 3.7
Original Airdate – November 17, 1982
Written by Edward de Blasio
Supervising Producers Eileen and Robert Mason Pollock
Directed by Irving J. Moore

Guest Appearances by Bettye Ackerman (Katherine), Sally Kemp (Marcia), Ben Marino (Delivery Man) and Tom Spratley (Salesman)

Mark Jennings is hired as a tennis instructor at La Mirage. Alexis tries to persuade him to see Krystle because she wants to separate Krystle from Blake. Kirby Anders, daughter of Joseph, the Carrington's head butler, arrives in Denver from Paris. Learning that a government loan may be denied, Blake asks Congressman McVane to intervene on Denver-Carrington's behalf. Alexis attempts to block the loan. Adam suggests Colbyco loan Blake the money in exchange for his oil extraction process, but Jeff refuses. He fears Adam is trying to force Blake into a corner and then take over the company. Desperate, Adam purchases a lethal chemical compound.

"La Mirage" – Episode 3.8
Original Airdate – November 24, 1982
Written by Stephen Black and Harry Stern
Supervising Producers Eileen and Robert Mason Pollock
Directed by Irving J. Moore

Guest Appearances by France Benard (Count Pierre), Paul Burke (Congressman Neil McVane), Don Diamond (Painter), Dolores Mann (Fitter), Grayce Spence (Guest #2) and Scott Williamson (Guest #1)

At La Mirage's opening night party, Alexis promises to help ex-lover Congressman McVane with his re-election, but only if he blocks Blake's loan. Blake, however, threatens to reveal the Congressman's past indiscretions and McVane tells Alexis he's unable to accept her offer. Fallon receives a letter from Steven in Hong Kong, begging Blake to bring him home. Alexis suggests Mark fight to win Krystle back. Krystle runs into Mark, who tells her they are still legally married. Adam comes on strong with Kirby, and Jeff comes to her rescue. Mark and Fallon, both having had too much to drink, jump into the pool and kiss while the entire party looks on.

"Acapulco" – Episode 3.9
Original Airdate – December 1, 1982
Written by Leah Markus
Supervising Producers Eileen and Robert Mason Pollock
Directed by Philip Leacock

Guest Appearances by Joey Aresco (Ben Reynolds), Henry Darrow (Ramon) and Don Reid (Tom)

After learning her divorce from Mark was never finalized, Krystle heads for Acapulco to rectify the situation. Blake follows her and assures her she can obtain a Colorado divorce. He suggests they take off for Hawaii for a second honeymoon. When Krystle tells Blake that she must first speak to Mark, he storms out  of the room. Blake finally receives his government loan. Adam confesses to Alexis that his goal is to seize his father's company. Steven has been tracked down on an oil rig in Indonesia. Fallon urges her father to bring him home. Joseph warns Kirby to stay away from Jeff and return to Paris to marry her fiancé. Kirby shocks her father by stating that her fiancé is already married.

"The Locket" – Episode 3.10
Original Airdate – December 8, 1982
Written by Dick Nelson
Supervising Producers Eileen and Robert Mason Pollock
Directed by Jerome Courtland

Guest Appearances by Matt Clark (Frank Dean), John Crawford (Dan Cassidy), Wendy Kilbourne (Debbie), Elizabeth Lindsey (Stewardess) and Jennifer Wallace (Barbie)

Blake receives news of an oil rig explosion in Hong Kong. Steven is missing and presumed dead. Blake travels to Asia to learn the truth and Alexis insists on accompanying him. Mark tells Krystle he won't stand in the way of a divorce. Adam asks Kirby to dinner and is furious when she turns him down. Joseph asks Jeff to stop encouraging Kirby's attentions. Krystle's ex-brother-in-law Frank Dean returns to Denver and demands to know Sammy Jo's whereabouts. He wants to be sure she collects Steven's inheritance money. Mark sees Frank threaten Krystle and sends him away. When Blake calls from Indonesia, Fallon informs her father that Krystle is off with Mark.

"The Search" – Episode 3.11
Original Airdate – December 15, 1982
Written by Edward de Blasio
Supervising Producers Eileen and Robert Mason Pollock
Directed by Alf Kjellin

Guest Appearances by Adam Ageli (Doctor), John Crawford (Dan Cassidy), Haven Earle Haley (Salesman), Joe Horvath (Bartell), Rosie Malek (Stewardess), Don Reid (Tom) and Paul Shenar (Jason Dehner)

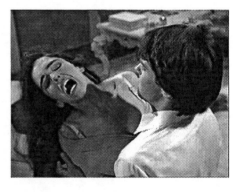

Blake and Alexis search for Steven in Indonesia. His body is not located, but his jacket is found floating in the sea. Blake refuses to believe his son is dead and hires psychic Jason Dehner to help with the search. Krystle learns Mark paid Frank Dean $1,000 to leave her alone. Kirby confesses her love to Jeff, who kisses her and accidentally calls her Fallon. Kirby dashes off in tears. Adam takes her to his apartment for consolation, but when she refuses his advances, he rapes her. Since his office has been repainted, Jeff is growing more and more disturbed. Adam secretly gloats, knowing that the paint used was poisonous.

"Samantha" – Episode 3.12
Original Airdate – December 29, 1982
Written by Edward de Blasio
Supervising Producers Eileen and Robert Mason Pollock
Directed by Bob Sweeney

Guest Appearances by Ivan Bonar (Reverend Carlton), Gary Hudson (Attendant), Janis Jamison (Massuese) and Paul Shenar (Jason Dehner)

Back in Denver, Blake continues his frantic search for Steven with the help of psychic Jason Dehner. Blake refuses to believe his son is dead, and Krystle is worried about his erratic behavior. Seeing how much she loves Blake, Fallon reconciles with Krystle. Blake refuses to attend the memorial service Alexis has arranged for their son. Alexis seduces Mark. Sammy Jo, now preferring to be called Samantha, appears at the Carrington household with a baby. The child is Steven's son.

"Danny" – Episode 3.13
Original Airdate – January 5, 1983
Written by Dick Nelson
Supervising Producers Eileen and Robert Mason Pollock
Directed by Alf Kjellin

Guest Appearances by Kieu-Chinh (Nurse Agnes), Jomes Hong (Doctor Chen Ling) and John Larch (Gerald Wilson)

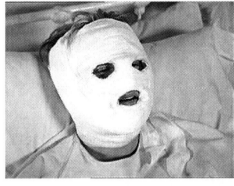

An obviously ill Jeff continues to function in a confused state. Sammy Jo announces she's headed for New York to make it big as a model and no longer wants to keep her son, Danny. Blake offers the girl $100,000 to be a mother to the child, but she declines. Alexis betters the offer and is also turned down. Krystle and Blake are overjoyed to learn Sammy Jo wants them to be Danny's adoptive parents. Alexis continues her affair with Mark. Steven, alive in a Singapore hospital with his face bandaged, regains consciousness. The doctor explains that severe burns incurred in the oil rig explosion necessitated plastic surgery.

"Madness" – Episode 3.14
Original Airdate – January 12, 1983
Written by Stephen Kandel
Supervising Producers Eileen and Robert Mason Pollock
Directed by Irving J. Moore

Guest Appearances by Kieu-Chinh (Sister Agnes), James Hong (Doctor Chen Ling), Sally Kemp (Marcia), Keith McConnell (Chester Smythe) and Linda Phillips (Ellen)

Jeff's temper continues to grow more volatile. Adam attempts to implicate Jeff in the Cecil Colby/Logan Rhinewood scandal. After learning that Blake and Krystle intend to adopt Steven's son Danny, Alexis demands custody of her grandson. Because Krystle's divorce from Mark is not yet finalized, Blake explains they must wait two months before adopting the child. Finding Fallon alone in Mark's hotel room, Jeff attacks his wife, calling her a whore. Mark arrives and rescues her. Concerned with his erratic behavior, Alexis decides to send Jeff away on vacation. Adam confesses to his mother that he's had Jeff's office painted with a lethal compound. He warns her that if she tries to remove it he'll implicate her in his scheme.

"Two Flights to Haiti" – Episode 3.15
Original Airdate -January 26, 1983
Written by Edward de Blasio
Directed by Jerome Courtland
Story by Eileen and Robert Mason Pollock

Guest Appearances by Ed Coupee (Dr. Braddock), Sandy Freeman (Divorcee), Don Reid (Tom) and Ellen Sweeney (Beth)

Although Blake begs her to postpone taking action until Jeff's violent behavior can be explained. Fallon flies to Haiti to obtain a divorce; Mark shows up unexpectedly at her hotel. Adam asks Kirby to work for him; Alexis tells Adam she cannot allow Jeff to be poisoned. In his confused state Jeff signs over his son's shares of Denver- Carrington to Colbyco, and his own voting control to Alexis: Alexis is now in a position to control Blake's company. Jeff angrily confronts Mark on the tennis court, where he collapses and is hospitalized. Alexis worries the doctors will I discover the poison in his system.

"The Mirror" – Episode 3.16
Original Airdate -February 04, 1983
Written by Edward de Blasio
Directed by Philip Leacock
Story by Eileen and Robert Mason Pollock

Guest Appearances by Kieu-Chinh (Sister Agnes), Frank Dent (Workman), James Hong (Dr. Chen Ling), John Larch (Gerald Wilson), Christopher O'Brien (Delivery Man) and Robert Symonds (Dr. Jonas Edwards)

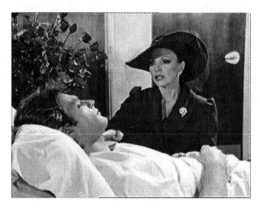

Alexis, concerned the doctors will learn the truth behind Jeff's illness, orders his office to be remodeled and the lethal paint compound removed. Mark and Fallon make love in Haiti; Blake learns Alexis is planning to orchestrate a Denver-Carrington/Colbyco merger to control both companies. Dr. Edwards, a physician who cared for Adam in his younger days, arrives in Denver to see his former patient, a one-time drug user. In the Singapore hospital, Steven's bandages are removed and he is handed a mirror. Blake is stunned to learn the hospital has found poison in Jeff's bloodstream.

"Battle Lines" – Episode 3.17
Original Airdate - February 16, 1983
Written by Edward de Blasio
Directed by Jerome Courtland
Story by Eileen and Robert Mason Pollock

Guest Appearances by Kieu-Chinh (Sister Agnes), Terry F. Cook (Desk Clerk), John Crawford (Dan Cassidy), Kelly Elias (David), James Hong (Dr. Chen Ling), Bunki Jones (Nurse) and Sally Kemp (Marcia)

Krystle suspects Alexis knows the reason for Jeff's illness and tells Blake, who is busy obtaining an injunction to prevent his ex-wife from taking over his company. Jeff is discharged from the hospital; the poison in his body still not identified. Mark and Fallon return from Haiti, and Kirby observes them kissing passionately in the mansion's entryway. Kirby fantasizes making love with Jeff. In Singapore, Steven's secretiveness continues to arouse Dr. Chen's curiosity. Blake receives a call from Singapore and learns Steven may have been found.

"Reunion in Singapore" – Episode 3.18
Original Airdate - February 25, 1983
Written by Edward de Blasio
Directed by Gwen Arner
Story by Eileen and Robert Mason Pollock

Guest Appearances by Kieu Chinh (Sister Agnes), John Crawford (Dan Cassidy), James Hong (Dr. Chen Ling), Marii Mak (Stewardess), Laurie O'Brien (Maid), Robert Parucha (Dean), Don Reid (Tom) and Michael Yama (Guard)

As Blake is departing for Singapore to identify his son, Alexis intercepts him at the airport to assure him she will not be stopped from merging their respective companies. Despite Alexis' efforts, however, Blake is assured of Congressman McVane's help in stalling official approval of the move. Jeff tells Alexis he was mistaken in signing over his stock and wants to retract the action; Adam lures Kirby to a hotel and attacks her. Jeff arrives to rescue Kirby and in a passionate moment, asks her to marry him. In Singapore, Steven tells his father he has broken from the family and will not return to Denver... until Blake tells him he is father to an infant son at the Carrington mansion.

"Fathers and Sons" Episode 3.19
Original Airdate - March 03, 1983
Written by Edward de Blasio
Directed by Jerome Courtland
Story by Eileen and Robert Mason Pollock

Guest Appearances by Claudia Bryar (Doris), Frank Cuva (Instructor), Peter Hobbs (Justice of the Peace), Sally Kemp (Marcia) and Larry Turk (Bartender)

Excitement brews in the Carrington household as preparations are made for Steven's return. It is an emotional moment as Alexis, Fallon and Krystle embrace Steven, who is introduced to his brother Adam and son Danny. Jeff and Kirby are married in Reno; plans are underway to finalize the  Denver-Carrington/Colbyco merger. Fallon and Mark continue their affair; Alexis confesses to Steven that she paid Sammy Jo to get out of Denver, and that she suspects Blake 'bought' little Danny from the girl. Steven heads to New York to find his wife.

"The Downstairs Bride" – Episode 3.20
Original Airdate - March 09, 1983
Written by Edward de Blasio
Directed by Philip Leacock
Story by Eileen and Robert Mason Pollock

Guest Appearances by Kelly Elias (David), David Hedison (Sam Dexter) and John McCook (Fred)

Upon hearing that Kirby has married Jeff, Joseph tells his daughter she has ruined her life. Blake suggests to Alexis they call a truce to their battle over Steven; Alexis offers Steven a share in Colbyco. Adam informs Fallon he doesn't consider Steven emotionally capable of handling the family business. After discussing the possibility of a reconciliation with Sammy Jo, Steven returns from New York alone. Blake disapproves of his son's plans to move out of the mansion with little Danny, but Krystle insists he let him go to prevent further alienation.

"The Vote" – Episode 3.21
Original Airdate - March 16, 1983
Written by Edward de Blasio
Directed by Glynn Turman
Story by Eileen and Robert Mason Pollock

Guest Appearances by Kelly Elias (David), David Hedison (Sam Dexter), Corinne Kason (Maid) and Charles Knapp (Galloway)

As the Board of Directors gathers to vote on the Denver-Carrington/Colbyco merger, Alexis pointedly tells the group that a nay vote will be met with immediate dismissal. The approval of the motion sends Blake into a fury. Kirby is upset to find Jeff and Fallon laughing together; Krystle comforts her, and also tries to  patch up relations between Steven and Blake. Jeff accuses Adam of falsifying reports regarding Denver-Carrington; Alexis warns Fallon of Mark's history as a gigolo. Alexis learns Congressman McVane has managed to block the merger; outraged, she spills her knowledge of his scandalous past to the press.

"The Dinner" – Episode 3.22
Original Airdate -March 30, 1983
Written by Edward de Blasio
Directed by Philip Leacock
Story by Eileen and Robert Mason Pollock

Guest Appearances by Marilyn Allen (Maid), Antonie Becker (Receptionist), Craig King (Phil) and Joanne Linville (Claire Maynard)

Blake confronts Alexis with evidence of fraudulent figures involved in the recent merger; Alexis learns Blake's lucrative oil extraction process does not extend to Colbyco. Newlyweds Jeff and Kirby have their first fight; Steven visits Claudia at the High Meadow Sanitarium. Alexis offers Mark money to leave Fallon; he refuses. Later. Fallon finds her mother in Mark's bed, undressed. Krystle arranges a dinner to improve relations between Steven and Blake; Alexis interferes and sees that Steven is out of town, unable to attend. Blake insists his absence is due to hostility and Krystle, incensed at her husband's insensitivity, storms off.

"The Threat" – Episode 3.23
Original Airdate -April 13, 1983
Written by Edward de Blasio
Directed by Bob Sweeney and Irving J. Moore
Story by Eileen and Robert Mason Pollock

Guest Appearances by Kathryn Daley (Desk Clerk #2), Jay Arlen Jones (Desk Clerk #1), Sally Kemp (Marcia), Douglas Alan Shanklin (Bernard) and Nancy Wheeler (Maid)

A scandalous newspaper headline implicates Congressman McVane with a young girl in Washington; he realizes Alexis orchestrated his downfall. Kirby finds she is pregnant; Adam is alarmed to learn that his former physician, Dr. Billings, is soon due in Denver for a convention. Krystle  and Alexis argue over Fallon, and the discussion quickly disintegrates into a brawl: The two fall into the lily pond flailing and punching. Blake approaches and pulls them apart, likening the women to 'common mud wrestlers.' Humiliated, Krystle packs her bags and checks into La Mirage. Alexis demands Joseph drain the pond and retrieve the diamond earring she lost in the scuffle, and threatens to tell Kirby the truth about her mother if he does not cooperate. A ruined McVane appears in Alexis' office after hours and threatens to kill her.

"The Cabin" – Episode 3.24
Original Airdate -April 20, 1983
Written by Edward de Blasio
Directed by Irving J. Moore
Story by Eileen and Robert Mason Pollock

Guest Appearances by Don Eitner (Dr. Richard Winfield), Judith Flanagan (Nurse), Sally Kemp (Marcia), Hank Sand (Bartender), Robert Symonds (Dr. Jonas Edwards), Nancy Wheeler (Maid) and Edward Winter (Dr. Robinson)

When Blake learns Steven's attorney Chris has moved in with his son, he vows to fight for custody of little Danny. Morgan Hess, Alexis' private investigator asks his employer for a large sum of money to payoff a gambling debt; when Alexis refuses, Hess leaves with a threat. Kirby realizes her baby was fathered by Adam. Fallon meets with Adam's former physician, Dr. Edwards, who tells her of Adam's temper and underlines his brilliance: He once won a case by proving a plant worker was poisoned and driven insane by chemical fumes. Realizing the connection to Jeff's illness, Fallon asks the hospital to investigate. Alexis tricks Krystle into meeting her at Steven's cabin, where she offers her $1 million to leave Blake. Outraged, Krystle rises to leave, but the door will not open--someone has bolted it shut from the outside, and smoke is pouring in from under the door.

SEASON FOUR

"The Arrest" – Episode 4.1
Original Airdate -September 28, 1983
Written by Edward de Blasio
Directed by Irving J. Moore
Story by Eileen and Robert Mason Pollock

Guest Appearances by David Ackroyd (Detective Lieutenant Fred Merrill), Nigel Bullard (Doctor), Virginia Gregg (Nurse), Eric Lawson (Doctor) and Robert Symonds (Dr. Jonas Edwards)

Krystle and Alexis, trapped in a burning cabin far off in the woods, find the door has been locked--from the outside. Mark, who has come to see Krystle in this remote setting, dramatically rescues the two women, who are rushed to the hospital. Blake meets with Steven to discuss the upbringing of little Danny; Blake remains convinced that a homosexual cannot provide a proper role model. A pregnant Kirby wrestles with the decision to tell Jeff he is not the father of her baby, while Fallon learns Adam is responsible for the mysterious illness that almost cost Jeff's life. Blake, suspecting that Mark's timely arrival at the burning cabin is more than coincidence, provides evidence to the police and Mark is arrested.

"The Bungalow" – Episode 4.2
Original Airdate -October 05, 1983
Written by Edward de Blasio
Directed by Alf Kjellin
Story by Eileen and Robert Mason Pollock

Guest Appearances by David Ackroyd (Detective Lieutenant Fred Merrill), Nick Eldredge (Policeman), Brenda Huggins (Nurse) and Douglas Alan Shanklin (Bernard)

Mark is charged with attempted murder and arson; Alexis tells Blake and the police his motive was revenge. The other suspects- McVane, Hess and Adam, are questioned and released. After Alexis destroys Fallon's relationship with Mark, Krystle suggests she is seeking revenge because Mark rejected her. Kirby breaks down and tells Krystle her baby is not Jeff's; an unknown man in surgical garb tries to smother Alexis. Blake and Jeff receive a frantic call from Joseph, who is muttering incoherently. At the bungalow where Kirby was born, Blake and Jeff find the disturbed butler with a gun. Before they can stop him. Joseph pulls the trigger and kills himself.

"The Note" – Episode 4.3
Original Airdate -October 19, 1983
Written by Edward de Blasio
Directed by Jerome Courtland
Story by Eileen and Robert Mason Pollock

Guest Appearances by David Ackroyd (Detective Lieutenant Fred Merrill) and Daniel Greene (Chauffeur)

Blake receives a note written by the late Joseph, stating that he indeed set the fire to kill Alexis because of the lives she's ruined with her manipulations. Alexis laughs it off, claiming she never intended to tell Kirby her mother was an "attic nympho." Blake lies to protect the girl, telling Kirby her father  was worried Alexis would take control of Denver-Carrington and tried to kill her out of loyalty to his employer. When the murder attempt failed, the butler tragically killed himself. Claudia is released from the sanitarium and she and Steven make love. When Steven learns of Blake's plan to sue for custody of little Danny, he becomes enraged. Both men lose their tempers and wrestle each other to the ground.

"The Hearing: Part One" – Episode 4.4
Original Airdate -October 26, 1983
Written by Dennis Turner
Directed by Robert Scheerer
Story by Eileen and Robert Mason Pollock

Guest Appearances by Pat Dixon (Reporter #3), Ben Marino (Bailiff), Neva Patterson (Ms. Pomeroy), John Randolph (Judge Henry Kendall), Milton Selzer (Mr. Melman) and Patrick Stack (Reporter #4)

Kirby angrily demands that Alexis divulge the real motive behind her father's murder attempt. In a fit of rage Kirby tries to strangle Alexis. Steven finds a social worker snooping around his apartment and orders her to leave. The incident later is brought up at the custody trial, and the woman describes Steven's behavior as a typical homosexual reaction. Steven's attorney and roommate Chris Deegan brings to the court's attention that Blake has previously been convicted of murdering a gay man and harbors a blind prejudice against homosexuals. Alexis testifies that Blake purchased the baby from Sammy Jo. When Blake loses his composure and lashes out at Alexis, the judge orders him to control himself and adjourns the hearing.

"The Hearing: Part Two" – Episode 4.5
Original Airdate - November 02, 1983
Written by Edward de Blasio
Directed by Irving J. Moore
Story by Eileen and Robert Mason Pollock

Guest Appearances by Ben Marino (Baliff), Nathan Purdee (Court Clerk) and John Randolph (Judge Henry Kendall)

Alexis arrives home from the trial to find her apartment ransacked. Police Lt. Merrill speculates there may be a connection between the break-in and the recent attempts on her life. Fallon testifies on Steven's behalf. When she leaves for Montana, Alexis tells Adam that if her trip  has anything to do with the poisoning incident, he's on his own. On the witness stand, Sammy Jo fabricates tales of Steven's sexual promiscuity. That night, Claudia barges into Sammy Jo's hotel room and demands she retract her courtroom statements. Claudia tells Steven she has devised a fool-proof method for him to retain custody of his son.

"Tender Comrades" – Episode 4.6
Original Airdate - November 09, 1983
Written by Edward de Blasio
Directed by Philip Leacock
Story by Eileen and Robert Mason Pollock

Guest Appearances by Royce Applegate (Jud Barrows), Anne Bellamy (Maid), Angela Black (Reporter #2), Steve Doubet (Reporter #1), Linda Foster (Reporter #3), Clark Howat (Justice), Ben Marino (Baliff), Kathleen O'Malley (Emma), John Randolph (Judge Henry Kendall) and Tyler Tyhurst (Ranch Hand)

Following through on the plan to retain custody of Danny, Steven and Claudia fly to Reno and are married. When the judge receives the assurance they will jointly rear the child, the suit is dismissed. Attempting to win Krystle back, Blake offers her a public relations job at Denver-Carrington. Adam asks Alexis to sign three routine documents, but the second and third pages are positioned so only the signature line is exposed. When alone, Adam crumples the first page and carefully places the other two in his pocket. Fallon and Jeff investigate the poisoning incident in Montana. They are stunned to learn the name of the prosecuting attorney was Michael Torrance--the name Adam used before arriving in Denver.

"Tracy" – Episode 4.7
Original Airdate -November 16, 1983
Written by Frank Salisbury
Directed by Irving J. Moore
Story by Eileen and Robert Mason Pollock

Guest Apperances by Greta Blackburn (Shelly), Art Bradley (Groom), Sally Kemp (Marcia), Thom Matthews (Male Secretary), Doug McGrath (Salesman #1), David McKnight (Salesman #2) and Peter White (Sam Rockwell)

At the store where he bought the poisonous mercuric oxide, Adam distracts the salesman and substitutes the authentic purchase order with the document Alexis unknowingly signed. Bill Rockwell, the retiring head of Denver-Carrington's public relations department, breaks the news to his disappointed assistant, Tracy that Krystle has been given the position she had planned on assuming. Mark proposes marriage to Krystle. When she refuses, he attacks her. Alexis is shocked to find her signature on the purchase order for the deadly chemical compound. She quickly realizes Adam has framed her. Blake threatens to call the press if she doesn't return Jeff's stock and cancel the corporate merger.

"Dex" – Episode 4.8
Original Airdate - November 23, 1983
Written by Dennis Turner
Directed by Lorraine Senna Ferrara
Story by Eileen and Robert Mason Pollock

Guest Appearances by Sally Kemp (Marcia), Thom Matthews (Male Secretary), Frederic Retes (Hotel Clerk) and Robert Symonds (Dr. Jonas Edwards)

Jeff storms into Alexis' office and accuses her of attempting to poison him. Her claims of innocence fall on deaf ears as Jeff forces her to sign back his Colbyco stock. After an intruder attempts to enter Alexis' apartment, Mark takes a job as her bodyguard. Adam's doctor in Montana explains to Alexis that the drugs Adam used in his youth can distort judgment. Alexis informs the board members that the sudden merger cancellation was based on her assessment of Denver-Carrington's lack of creative growth. Farnsworth "Dex" Dexter, the sharp-minded son of an important board member, surprises Alexis with a passionate kiss and suggests they form a business partnership.

"Peter DeVilbis" – Episode 4.9
Original Airdate - November 30, 1983
Written by Edward de Blasio
Directed by Jerome Courtland
Story by Eileen and Robert Mason Pollock

Guest Appearances by Ivan Bonar (McFadden), Alan Buchdahl (Race Announcer), Don Eitner (Dr. Richard Winfield), Carol Ann Henry (Irene) and Scott Leva (Waiter)

In her new position, Krystle launches a publicity campaign to counter Alexis' slanderous remarks against Denver-Carrington. Jeff rejoins Blake's firm. Dex continues his campaign to win Alexis. Jeff learns Kirby was pregnant when they wed and is shocked to learn that Adam raped her. Fallon accompanies Blake and  Krystle to L.A. to consult an architect about expanding La Mirage. While at the track, Fallon is swept off her feet by a millionaire playboy, Peter DeVilbis.

"The Proposal" – Episode 4.10
Original Airdate - December 07, 1983
Written by Dennis Turner
Directed by Curtis Harrington
Story by Eileen and Robert Mason Pollock

Guest Appearances by Marilyn Anderson (Receptionist), John Blackwood (Airline Clerk), Ben Marino (Charlie), Michael Meyer (Terry) and John J. York (Workman)

At Alexis' office, Dex discovers a confidential file marked "Tar Sands" and beats her to the contract. Later, he offers her a 60-40 split. An enraged Jeff locates Adam at the summit of the Carrington Plaza. After exchanging vicious insults and violent punches, Adam tumbles halfway over the edge. As Jeff is about to finish him off, Adam frantically explains he had no idea he fathered Kirby's child, and Jeff allows him to crawl to safety. Jeff intercepts Kirby as she is about to leave for Paris. Blake proposes marriage to Krystle, who happily accepts.

"Carousel" – Episode 4.11
Original Airdate - December 21, 1983
Written by Edward de Blasio
Directed by Philip Leacock
Story by Eileen and Robert Mason Pollock

Guest Appearances by Barbara Davis (Herself), Marvin Davis (Himself), Nancy Davis (Herself), Betty Ford (Herself), President Gerald R. Ford (Himself), Dr. Henry Kissinger (Himself), Michael Ryan (Steward) and Bunky Young (Julia)

Kirby proposes that she and Jeff divorce. Adam tells her he wants to be a father to their child. Dex and Alexis make love. Jeff is jealous to see Fallon with Peter DeVilbis. Peter's champion racehorse, Allegree, is up for sale, and Blake decides to buy the mare. At the Carousel Ball, the high point  of Denver's social season, Blake and Krystle announce their intentions to remarry. Steven warmly wishes his father the best. Blake is touched by the gesture and welcomes his son back into the family.

"The Wedding" – Episode 4.12
Original Airdate -December 28, 1983
Written by Michael Russnow
Directed by
Story by Eileen and Robert Mason Pollock

Guest Appearances by Peter Duchin (Himself), Susan Gordon (Female Guest #2), Carol Ann Henry (Irene), Robert Rothwell (Male Guest #1), Grace Simmons (Female Guest #1) and Liam Sullivan (Minister)

Nervous about leaving her new job, Krystle gives Tracy final instructions as she prepares for her honeymoon in Rio de Janeiro. Tracy persuades Krystle to give her the company credit cards as well as the keys to the confidential files. Peter arrives at La Mirage asking for Fallon, and makes a pass at Claudia. As the wedding guests arrive, Adam demands Kirby tell their child the true identity of his father. Learning she intends to divorce Jeff, Adam asks Kirby to marry him. Krystle and Blake exchange vows and are pronounced husband and wife.

"The Ring" – Episode 4.13
Original Airdate -January 04, 1984
Written by Dennis Turner
Directed by Curtis Harrington
Story by Eileen and Robert Mason Pollock

Guest Appearances by George Clifton (Joaquin Palmas), Ted Rogers (Man in Park), Sally Kemp (Marcia), Ken Lewis (Desk Clerk) and Richard Yniguez (Ernesto Pinero)

While Mrs. Gordon is walking Danny in the park, a strange man greets the child by name. Recalling little Blake's kidnapping, Claudia moves the family into the safety of the Carrington mansion. Laird discovers Tracy scanning confidential company files. Kirby and Jeff sign their divorce papers. After shelling out over $2 million to work on one of Peter's hotels, Ernesto the architect demands to know when he will be repaid. He wonders if the money is going toward Peter's "habit." Kirby's hand suddenly begins to swell uncontrollably, making it necessary to cut off her wedding ring.

"Lancelot" – Episode 4.14
Original Airdate - January 11, 1984
Written by Millee Taggart
Directed by Irving J. Moore
Story by Eileen and Robert Mason Pollock

Guest Appearances by Alan Buckdahl (Race Announcer), Don Eitner (Dr. Richard Winfield), Sally Kemp (Marcia), Paul Lawrence (Florist), Bert Ramsen (Jack Crager), Nancy Warren (Receptionist) and Gabriel York (Reporter)

Kirby is diagnosed as suffering from hypertension. Adam is startled to find her slumped against the piano. After learning she will accept his marriage proposal, Adam confesses raping her to a shocked and disgusted Blake. Peter offers Fallon cocaine. Tracy purposely misplaces an urgent business memo from Blake to Krystle. As an agitated Blake awaits his publicity director at an important meeting, Tracy cunningly shows up and 'saves the day.' Allegree the racehorse is discovered missing. Claudia receives a box of violets with a note reading, "Remember? Lancelot." Trembling with fear, she recalls that Lancelot was her late husband's nickname.

"Seizure" – Episode 4.15
Original Airdate - January 18, 1984
Written by Dennis Turner
Directed by George Sanford Brown
Story by Eileen and Robert Mason Pollock

Guest Appearances by Nigel Bullard (Reporter #2), Jane Downs (Reporter #3), Don Eitner (Dr. Richard Winfield), Theresa Hayes (Nurse), Jack Kosslyn (Reporter #1), Bert Kramer (Detective Harrison), John McLiam (Oscar Stone), Bert Remsen (Jack Crager), Matt Stetson (Waiter) and Peter White (Bill Rockwell)

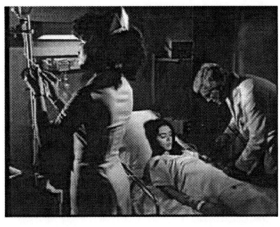

Blake receives a note requesting $2 million in diamonds for the return of his racehorse, Allegree. Peter proposes to Fallon and then makes another pass at Claudia. Dex and Alexis close a lucrative oil contract. While pouring herself a glass of water, Kirby's hand begins to tremble uncontrollably. Diagnosed as suffering from hyperreflexia, a condition that may lead to convulsions or heart failure, Kirby remains hospitalized while Adam keeps an all-night vigil in her room. Suddenly, her body becomes rigid and goes into convulsive seizure.

"A Little Girl" – Episode 4.16
Original Airdate - February 01, 1984
Written by Edward De Blasio
Directed by Irving J. Moore
Story by Eileen and Robert Mason Pollock

Guest Appearances by Don Eitner (Dr. Richard Winfield), Bert Kramer (Detective Harrison), Lorri Marlow (Night Nurse), Bert Ramsen (Jack Crager) and Cec Verrell (Surgical Nurse)

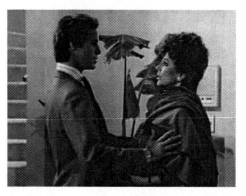

Peter has made arrangements for the ransom to be delivered to Allegree's captors. Blake grows suspicious of his refusal to call in the police and is unhappy about Fallon's decision to marry him. Kirby suffers a second seizure. To save the baby's life, the doctors decide to operate. Congressman McVane attempts to enlist Mark's help in blackmailing Alexis. Claudia receives another box of violets from 'Lancelot.' Beset with guilt, Adam confesses to Blake that he, not Alexis, attempted to poison Jeff. As Blake struggles to understand, Kirby's doctor appears to report that Kirby is alive, but they were unable to save her baby girl.

"The Accident" – Episode 4.17
Original Airdate - February 22, 1984
Written by Priscilla English
Directed by Jerome Courtland
Story by Eileen and Robert Mason Pollock

Guest Appearances by Mark Andrews (Bellboy), Richard Dano (Valet), Sally Kemp (Marcia), Chip Lucia (Jeremy Thatcher), Bert Remsen (Jack Crager) and Fred M. Waugh (The Drunk)

As Fallon plans to wed Peter, Claudia advises her of his womanizing. Fallon dismisses Claudia's concern, however, as she has with all the others who question the wisdom of her marrying Peter. Tracy sleeps with a newspaper reporter in exchange for a damaging story to scandalize Krystle. After Allegree is safely returned, Blake questions Jack Crager, the horse's trainer. After their meeting, Jack quickly phones Peter, who instructs the horse trainer to disappear until further notice. Distraught after learning that Peter has suddenly left the country, Fallon runs into the path of an oncoming car. Jeff and Blake look on in helpless disbelief.

"The Vigil" – Episode 4.18
Original Airdate - February 29, 1984
Written by Michael Russnow and Dennis Turner
Directed by Philip Leacock
Story by Eileen and Robert Mason Pollock

Guest Appearances by Bill Dearth (Hotel Security), Pat Destro (Airport Security), Diana Douglas (Mother Blaisdel), John Dresden (Airport Security), Robert Hooks (Dr. Walcott), Alan Oliney (Policeman), Lawrence Pressman (Eric Grayson) and Fred M. Waugh (The Drunk)

With the family at the hospital waiting for Fallon to regain consciousness, Blake races to the airport to intercept Peter. Passing through security, DeVilbis sets off an alarm and the guards find a cache of drugs in his brief- case. Blake blocks his escape, and Peter is taken to jail. Blake is offered an important political post. McVane informs Alexis of the appointment. He is sure she will try to topple him and wants to be there when she does…to blackmail her. Kirby accepts Adam's marriage proposal. Fallon regains consciousness and finds she is paralyzed.

"Steps" – Episode 4.19
Original Airdate - March 7, 1984
Written by Dennis Turner
Directed by Irving J. Moore
Story by Eileen and Robert Mason Pollock

Guest Appearances by Gerald Berns (Kevin), Robert Hooks (Dr. Walcott), Howard Huston (Masseur), Sally Kemp (Marcia) and Ellen Snortland (Nurse)

Fallon's doctors believe her paralysis to be psychosomatic. To prevent her from marrying Adam, Alexis offers Kirby a job in Paris. When the ploy fails, Alexis tells the girl her mother has long been confined to an institution for the criminally insane. Kirby had believed her mother to be dead. Fallon, under the care of physical  therapists and a doting family, remains unable to walk--until her child's life is in jeopardy. At a family dinner to celebrate Fallon's recovery, Claudia receives a message containing a family snapshot taken by Matthew. She determines to unravel the mystery behind her tormentors.

"The Voice: Part One" – Episode 4.20
Original Airdate - March 14, 1984
Written by Edward de Blasio
Directed by George Sanford Brown
Story by Eileen and Robert Mason Pollock

Guest Appearances by Gerald Castillo (Captain Cordillo), J. Victor Lopez (Doorman), Michael Mitz (Secretary), Dean Stewart (Frederick), Gary Wells (Waiter) and Gary Wood (Pat Dunne)

When Krystle's doctor reveals she is pregnant, both she and Blake are overjoyed. Krystle insists Blake go ahead with a scheduled business trip to Hong Kong and sends Tracy to cover for her. Upon arrival, Blake is chagrined to learn the China Seas deal is to be negotiated by Rashid Anmed, a notoriously under- handed character. Fallon begins to suffer from painful, recurring headaches. Kirby is torn between finding her mother and leaving matters as they are. Claudia and Steven visit the site of Matthew's accident in the Peruvian jungle. Seeing the wreckage, Claudia is finally satisfied her husband and daughter are dead. Once home, however, she receives a phone call from Matthew.

"The Voice: Part Two" – Episode 4.21
Original Airdate - March 21, 1984
Written by Edward de Blasio
Directed by Jerome Courtland
Story by Eileen and Robert Mason Pollock

Guest Appearances by Arnold Bankston III (Reporter #1), Natalie Core (Woman in Cemetery), Rance Howard (Gifford), May Keller (Maid), Sally Kemp (Marcia), David Muir (Reporter #2), Lawrence Pressman (Eric Grayson), Tracy Ryan (Dina), Dean Stewart (Frederick), Donald Torres (TV Commentator), Charles Walker (Security Guard), Jeff Weston (Lloyd) and Danny Wong (Bellboy)

Blake and Ahmed close their international China Seas oil deal. Alexis learns of the coup and makes plans for a counterattack. Blake confronts reporter Grayson regarding his deceptive behavior with Tracy, and then quits his political post. When Tracy makes sexual advances toward Blake, she is fired. Steven is suspicious to see Dex in Alexis' office bearing violets - the same flowers being sent mysteriously to Claudia. Kirby's search for her mother leads her to the cemetery and her mother's grave. In Hong Kong to do business with Ahmed, Alexis rekindles their former romance. Claudia receives yet another mysterious call, this time from Hess.

"The Voice: Part Three" – Episode 4.22
Original Airdate - March 28, 1984
Written by Edward de Blasio
Directed by Irving J. Moore
Story by Eileen and Robert Mason Pollock

Guest Appearances by Norman Alden (Gun Salesman), Chad Block (Sergeant), Diana Douglas (Mother Blaisdel), Sally Kemp (Marcia), Hari Rhodes (Detective) and Dean Stewart (Frederick)

Dex follows Alexis to Hong Kong and is enraged to find her with Rashid, with whom she has just concluded a business deal to ruin Blake. Kirby explores the reasons behind her father's death. After reading his suicide note, she purchases a handgun. Fallon is overcome by a seizure. Dex and Tracy make love. When the mysterious caller phones again, Krystle takes the call and realizes it is a tape recording of Matthew's voice. Matthew's mother, who had long resented Claudia, sold the tape to an unnamed buyer. Blake pays a visit to Morgan Hess and spots the tape near the phone. Hess explains he intended to frame Alexis, but Blake does not believe his story.

"The Birthday" – Episode 4.23
Original Airdate - April 4, 1984
Written by Susan Miller
Directed by Kim Friedman
Story by Eileen and Robert Mason Pollock

Guest Appearances by Nigel Bullard (Reporter #1), Jim Curley (Newscaster), Jane Downs (Reporter #2), Robert Hooks (Dr. Walcott), James J. Levine (Douglas) and Gregory Walcott (Marksman)

Tracy and Krystle exchange angry words. As Alexis monitors all of the television news programs, Mark suggests she's waiting to see some late-breaking news: news she already knows. Blake learns Kirby has unearthed the truth about her father and is anxious to demonstrate he only lied to fulfill Joseph's wishes. As little Blake's birthday party gets underway, Krystle tells a stunned Alexis that she is expecting a baby. Alexis recovers quickly and dismisses Krystle with the fact that she's been through four pregnancies. Krystle catches the slip, and Alexis explains one pregnancy miscarried. Fallon and Jeff announce their plans to remarry. The Carringtons are stunned to hear that Rashid Ahmed has created an international incident by announcing that Blake is planning a military attack on another world power involved in the China Seas oil deal.

"The Check" – Episode 4.24
Original Airdate - April 11, 1984
Written by Dennis Turner
Directed by Jerome Courtland
Story by Eileen and Robert Mason Pollock

Guest Appearances by Christopher Cary (Earl Cunningham), Alex Henteloff (Ed Linden), Bonnie Keith (Bank Officer), Peter Kwong (Mr. Lin), Adam Mills (Jerome), Dan Priest (Neighborhood Watch), Jenny Sherman (Young Woman) and Paul Tuerpe (Pilot)

As Blake confronts Alexis with his knowledge of her plot with Rashid Ahmed, Mark, on the balcony, listens with interest. Alexis is prepared to buy his silence. Blake travels to Hong Kong and learns Ahmed has left the country, leaving Denver-Carrington's money with the government. In Joseph's old bungalow, Kirby confronts Alexis, but her plan to kill her is foiled. After Mark successfully blackmails Alexis, McVane arrives and reminds him they're in this business together. Nervous that McVane will learn of his $100,000 hit on Alexis, Mark quickly opens an account at a local bank, as McVane looks on.

"The Engagement" – Episode 4.25
Original Airdate - April 18, 1984
Written by Dennis Turner
Directed by Irving J. Moore
Story by Eileen and Robert Mason Pollock

Guest Appearances by Walter Cox (Bellboy), Jonathan Goldsmith (Sergeant Cooper), Carol Ann Henry (Irene), James Karen (Avril Dawson), Tom Ohmer (Bennett) and Hari Rhodes (Taylor)

Blake's fortune now rests on the decision of a group of bankers, who will decide whether to extend his loan or call in the debt immediately. Alexis hires Tracy to obtain confidential information on Averell Dawson, Blake's banker. Shortly thereafter, Blake learns his extension has been denied. Jeff and Fallon  celebrate their engagement. Sammy Jo arrives unannounced at the mansion, claiming she's come to visit her son. Mark questions Alexis' motives for destroying Blake and is reminded he's been paid to keep his mouth shut. Not satisfied with the monetary arrangement, Mark demands she submit to him sexually. Alexis orders him from Denver. A police officer arrives and announces that Mark Jennings has died after falling from Alexis' penthouse balcony.

"New Lady in Town" – Episode 4.26
Original Airdate - May 2, 1984
Written by Edward de Blasio
Directed by Jerome Courtland
Story by Eileen and Robert Mason Pollock

Guest Appearances by Danielle Aubry (Fitter), Phillip Coccioletti (Owen Bancroft), Terry F. Cook (Desk Clerk), Jonathan Goldsmith (Sergeant Cooper), Anthony Henderson (Policeman), Alex Henteloff (Ed Linden) and Gail Landry (Couturier)

To raise the needed money, Blake sells his assets and mortgages the mansion. In a heated confrontation with Alexis, Tracy quits. Tracy tells Alexis of her ongoing affair with Dex. Alexis is again questioned by the police, who want the details of her affair with Mark. Fallon suffers another painful headache. Sammy Jo informs Steven she intends to stay in Denver and take custody of Danny. An unknown, beautiful woman, Dominique Devereaux, sweeps into La Mirage demanding the finest accommodations. When she attempts to question Fallon about Alexis, Fallon grows suspicious.

"The Nightmare" – Episode 4.27
Original Airdate - May 9, 1984
Written by
Directed by Irving J. Moore
Story by Eileen and Robert Mason Pollock

Guest Appearances by Lynn Cartwright (Inmate #1), Kent DeMarche (Hairdresser), Catherine Ferrar (Makeup Woman), Sandy Freeman (Beautician), Jonathan Goldsmith (Sergeant Cooper), Gay Hagen (Prison Matron), Marsha Haynes (Receptionist), Sally Kemp (Marcia), Lauren Levian (Dresser) and Jock McNeill (Bartender)

Alexis suffers recurring nightmares about Mark's death. Kirby again tries to kill Alexis. When she is unable to pull the trigger, Alexis offers to remain silent in exchange for Kirby's agreement to leave Adam. The truth behind the attempt to unhinge Claudia is revealed. Sammy Jo seduced Hess into handling it, and has  returned to him now to solicit his help in regaining her child. In preparation for the wedding, Alexis and Krystle visit the same beauty salon. The two women exchange words, and a mud-slinging melee ensues. While dressing for the wedding, Fallon is gripped by a seizure. She drives off as the ceremony is about to take place. The police arrive and arrest Alexis for the murder of Mark Jennings.

SEASON FIVE

"Disappearance" – Episode 5.1
Original Airdate - September 26, 1984
Written by Edward de Blasio
Directed by Irving J. Moore
Story by Camille Marchetta

Guest Appearances by Ian Abercrombie (Judge), Patty Dworkin (Matron), Bruce Gray (Liam Farley), Lenny Hicks (Paramedic), Stuart Mabray (Assistant D.A.), Ben Marino (Bailiff), James O'Sullivan (Policeman), Cynthia Steele (Lillian) and Lynne Stewart (Maid)

Following a serious traffic accident, Fallon mysteriously vanishes. Dex and Steven bail Alexis out of jail. Sammy Jo attempts to seduce Adam. Alexis flatters Adam by suggesting he work with her defense attorney, Warren Ballard. Dominique's husband Brady arrives at La Mirage and finds his wife suddenly interested in staying in Denver. Steven accuses his mother of killing Mark Jennings and ruining Blake's business. Despite her pleas, Steven tells his father everything. Steven orders Sammy Jo from the mansion. She counters by promising she'll sue for custody of Danny. After duping Adam into letting Danny ride along with her to the airport, Sammy Jo dashes off, kidnapping her son.

"The Mortgage" – Episode 5.2
Original Airdate - October 10, 1984
Written by Dennis Turner
Directed by Jerome Courtland
Story by Camille Marchetta

Guest Appearances by Philip Abbott (Lawlor), John Cedar (Sergeant Roscoe), Ellen Crawford (Woman at Phone), Bill Gratton (Truck Driver), James Karen (Avril Dawson), Clive Revill (Warren Ballard) and Stan Wojno (Morgue Attendant)

Steven accuses Adam of conspiring with Sammy Jo to kidnap Danny. Blake arranges to take out a mortgage on the mansion. He little suspects Alexis has signed the note and will become the owner if he defaults. A cross-country search for Fallon has developed few leads. Warren Ballard and Adam prepare Alexis' defense. Dominique Devereaux makes her singing debut at La Mirage, with Blake and Krystle in attendance. Krystle quickly senses Dominique's hostility toward Blake. Brady declines the Carrington's hospitality as well. Jeff finds a truck driver who gave Fallon a lift to Portland, Oregon, the night of the accident.

"Fallon" – Episode 5.3
Original Airdate - October 17, 1984
Written by Edward de Blasio
Directed by Gwen Arner
Story by Camille Marchetta

Guest Appearances by Fausto Bara (Lt. Lopez), Curtis Credel (Earl), Dana Kimmell (Emily), Kevin McCarthy (Billy Waite), John Reilly (J.J.), Clive Revill (Warren Ballard) and Liam Sullivan (Brother Leo)

To secure financing for his bankrupt company, Blake arranges to see Billy Waite, a notoriously underhanded oil man. Jeff continues his search for Fallon. Impatient with the progress her lawyer is making on her defense, Alexis fires Warren Ballard and retains Adam. Alexis visits Billy Waite in South America under the guise of concern about Blake's misfortunes. As she prepares to leave, the police arrive. She is arrested for fleeing to avoid prosecution and led away by the police. At an isolated religious retreat, Jeff learns Fallon is dead and that she died along with Peter DeVilbis.

"The Rescue" – Episode 5.4
Original Airdate - October 24, 1984
Written by Dennis Turner
Directed by Irving J. Moore
Story by Camilla Marchetta

Guest Appearances by Virginia Capers (Aunt Bessie), Linda Hoy (Matron #2), Sally Kemp (Marcia), Kevin McCarthy (Billy Waite), Carol Gordon (Matron #1) John O'Leary (Minister), Christopher Pennock (Lt. Dawes), Ted Richards (Young Cop) and Robert Rockwell (George)

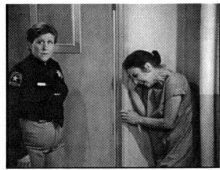

In Seattle, Jeff and Blake learn the woman who died in the plane crash with Peter DeVilbis cannot be positively identified, but the ring she was wearing is indeed Fallon's engagement ring. Blake goes to the jail and tells Alexis that Fallon is dead. Dex pulls strings and a judge allows Alexis to attend the funeral. Jeff creates a scene at Fallon's funeral. Steven meets Sammy Jo in Los Angeles, where she demands payment of $30,000 per month for Danny's return. After Claudia points out his behavior only isolates him from the family, Adam is moved to action. Adam breaks into Sammy Jo's motel room and retrieves little Danny.

"The Trial" – Episode 5.5
Original Airdate - October 31, 1984
Written by Paul Savage
Directed by Gwen Arner
Story by Joel Steiger

Guest Appearances by Lawrence Barne (Process Server), Natalie Core (Dina Hartley), Patty Dworkin (Matron), Conroy Gedeon (Bailiff), J.D. Hinton (Philip Spaulding), Basil Hoffman (Judge Drew Mayfield), Julie Inouye (Reporter), Chip Johnson (Reporter), Jeff Pomerantz (Michael Cunningham), Joan Welles (Court Clerk) and Brynja Willis (Amy)

Blake visits Dominique at La Mirage to discuss her recent revelation. She tells Blake that her mother was a long-time mistress of his father and has evidence to prove it. At Alexis' trial, a neighbor offers powerful evidence that incriminates Alexis. Along with Mark, she saw a woman on the terrace wearing a cape that has been positively identified as Alexis. Blake is called to testify and states that Alexis would indeed commit a violent act if sufficiently provoked. In a dramatic courtroom scene, Steven is called to the witness stand and he must tell what he knows or protect his mother.

"The Verdict" – Episode 5.6
Original Airdate - November 7, 1984
Written by Stephen and Elinor Karpf
Directed by Jerome Courtland
Story by Camille Marchetta and Joel Steiger

Guest Appearances by Bradford Dillman (Hal Lombard), Conroy Gedeon (Bailiff), Marlena Giovi (Matron), Basil Hoffman (Judge Drew Mayfield), Christine Kellogg (Laurie), Jeff Pomerantz (Michael Cunningham), John Reilly (J.J.), Joan Welles (Court Clerk) and Brynja Willis (Amy)

On the witness stand Steven testifies he saw Alexis push Mark to his death. Furious, hurt, and still claiming her innocence, Alexis disowns Steven. Dominique offers Blake $25 million for control of his company. Stunned, Blake offers her 40% of Denver-Carrington for $30 million. Jeff sees other women in an attempt to forget Fallon, but remains obsessed with his ex-wife. Dismissing her attorneys and deciding to represent herself, Alexis takes the stand and testifies she was not wearing the cape that incriminated her. The prosecution, however, proves it had been delivered to her and was found stuffed in a trash bin behind her building. The verdict is at last delivered: Alexis is found guilty.

"Amanda" – Episode 5.7
Original Airdate - November 14, 1984
Written by Edward de Blasio
Directed by Irving J. Moore
Story by Camille Marchetta and Joel Steiger

Guest Appearances by Barbara Allyne Bennet (Desk Sergeant), Nancy Lee Andrews (Female Socialite), Natalie Core (Dina Hartley), Jeff Crawford (Photo Lab Technician), Bradford Dillman (Hal Lombard), Patrick Dollaghan (Jerry), Linda Hoy (Matron) and Jeffrey Kaake (Male Socialite)

Adam and Dex vow to prove Alexis' innocence and begin a determined campaign. The woman who testified she had seen Alexis on the terrace with Mark had hosted a party that evening and snapped photographs. The negatives reveal it was Neal McVane who had framed Alexis for Mark's murder. Alexis is freed. Denver-Carrington is back in business. Alexis vows revenge on Dominique when she learns of her new partnership with Blake. Brady is stunned to learn of Dominique's true relationship with Blake. Upon returning home, Alexis receives a visit from a beautiful young woman named Amanda. She is Alexis' daughter.

"The Secret" – Episode 5.8
Original Airdate - November 21, 1984
Written by Dennis Turner
Directed by Jerome Courtland
Story by Camille Marchetta

Guest Appearances by Richard Hatch (Dean Caldwell), James Horan (Maxwell Allen), Dennis Howard (Dr. Harris) and Juliet Mills (Rosalind Bedford)

Amanda insists Alexis acknowledge their relationship and begs her to reveal her father's identity. Alexis tells her it was simply an anonymous ski instructor in Gstaad. Steven and Alexis reconcile and he rejoins Colbyco, where Luke Fuller, an attractive young man, has just been hired as public relations director. Claudia enters Steven's office to find Luke straightening her husband's tie. Amanda goes public with a front page story announcing she is Alexis' illegitimate daughter. Jeff meets an attractive young widow, Nicole, whose late husband was Peter DeVilbis.

"Domestic Intrigue" – Episode 5.9
Original Airdate - November 28, 1984
Written by Edward de Blasio
Directed by Irving J. Moore
Story by Camille Marchetta and Joel Steiger

Guest Appearances by Richard Hatch (Dean Caldwell), Aharon Ipale' (Colonel Saban) and Peggy Walton-Walker (Barbara)

Jeff has become involved with Nicole Simpson. Steven is jealous to find Claudia having cocktails with Dean Caldwell, and angry with himself for taking a second look at Luke Fuller. Amanda makes a pass at Dex. In Istanbul, Adam and Dominique attempt to persuade Rashid Ahmed to clear Blake's name from the messy arms deal Alexis engineered. A melee ensues and Rashid is shot dead by a guard. A pregnant Krystle hears the news and assumes the worst. As she runs from the room she tumbles down the stairs and Blake finds her unconscious.

"Krystina" – Episode 5.10
Original Airdate - December 5, 1984
Written by Will Lorin
Directed by Jerome Courtland
Story by Camille Marchetta

Guest Appearances by Pat Anderson (Nurse), Bibi Besch (Dr. Veronica Miller), Randy Hamilton (Marvin), Richard Hatch (Dean Caldwell), Dennis Howard (Dr. Harris) and Robert Parucha (Chauffeur)

Krystle goes into premature labor and delivers a baby girl, who suffers from respiratory problems. She names the child Krystina after a friend who once saved her life. Claudia is uneasy when Steven accompanies Luke on a business trip. After confiding in Dean Caldwell, he moves to hug her, and the two are soon in a passionate embrace. Amanda overhears Dex tell Alexis to stop hiding the identity of Amanda's father. Jeff finds a photo of Peter DeVilbis in Nikki's hotel room.

"Swept Away" – Episode 5.11
Original Airdate - December 12, 1984
Written by Dennis Turner
Directed by Irving J. Moore
Story by Camille Marchetta

Guest Appearances by Bibi Besch (Dr. Veronica Miller), Nigel Bullard (Reporter #1), Jane Downs (Reporter #2), Susan Gordon (Nurse), Richard Hatch (Dean Caldwell), Peter Marc (Steward), Jeffrey Orman (Waiter) and Peggy Walton-Walker (Barbara)

Upon learning that he may be Amanda's father, Blake resolves to ask Amanda to take a blood test. Nicole tells Jeff there's a chance Peter DeVilbis may have been with another woman at the time of the crash. Under the pretense of a family outing, Alexis arranges to send Dex and Amanda to a ski lodge. With the tension growing between them, Amanda and Dex begin to fight. Their fury, however, soon turns to passion. Alexis finally arrives and announces the three are bound for London, where she and Dex will marry.

"That Holiday Spirit" – Episode 5.12
Original Airdate - December 19, 1984
Written by Edward de Blasio
Directed by Curtis Harrington
Story by Camille Marchetta and Susan Baskin

Guest Appearances by Susan Gordon (Nurse), Hedley Mattingly (Vicar), Juliet Mills (Rosalind Bedford) and Alain St. Alix (La Salle)

Blake buys back his racehorse Allegree from owner Daniel Reece, who sends Krystle a gift. Furious, she demands to know how he dare approach her after what happened with her sister, Iris. Alexis and Dex are married in a small church ceremony. While they're on their honeymoon Amanda learns she is Blake's daughter. Blake, meanwhile, has contacted his father, who claims that Dominique is not his daughter. Claudia confesses her affair with Dean Caldwell to Steven.

"The Avenger" – Episode 5.13
Original Airdate - January 2, 1985
Written by Dennis Turner
Directed by Irving J. Moore
Story by Camille Marchetta and Susan Baskin

Guest Appearances by John Alderman (Businessman #2), Susan Gordon (Nurse), Preston Hanson (Businessman #1), Dennis Howard (Dr. Harris), Michael Levittan (Bartender) and Ben Marino (Stablehand)

Krystle reconciles with Daniel, who reveals that his break-up with her sister was amicable. Dominique, bitter over Blake's continued refusal to acknowledge her as a Carrington, considers a number of alternative courses, including a generous offer from Alexis for her share of Denver-Carrington. Claudia moves into La Mirage. Krystle confides to Steven that Daniel is Sammy Jo's father and therefore little Danny's grandfather. Jeff and Nicole find the missing piece of a map that DeVilbis and Fallon had shared in the hope of finding buried treasure. Blake's father suffers a heart attack.

"The Will" – Episode 5.14
Original Airdate - January 9, 1985
Written by Noreen Stone
Directed by Nancy Malone
Story by Camille Marchetta and Susan Baskin

Guest Appearances by Harry Andrews (Thomas "Tom" Fitzsimmons Carrington), Bibi Besch (Dr. Veronica Miller), Mae Hi (Nurse), Curt Lowens (Lawyer) and Peggy Walton-Walker (Barbara)

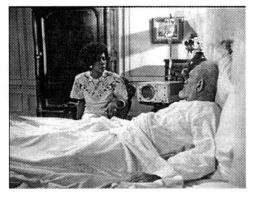

Claudia rebuffs Steven's conciliatory attempts. Tension between Dex and Amanda continues to mount. Baby Krystina is allowed to leave the hospital. Jeff remains intent upon his mission to find Fallon with the help of Nikki, who has fallen in love with him. On his deathbed, Tom Carrington makes amends with Blake, and in a final dramatic gesture, has his will changed. His vast estate is to be divided among Blake, Alexis, and his acknowledged daughter, Dominique, whom he names as executor.

"The Treasure" – Episode 5.15
Original Airdate - January 16, 1985
Written by Stephen and Elinor Karpf
Directed by Curtis Harrington
Story by Camille Marchetta and Susan Baskin

Guest Appearances by Dawn C. Abraham (Lois Dern)

Krystle begins working with Daniel. Blake is adamantly opposed and exchanges harsh words with Reece. Dex is furious with Alexis for traveling to Sumatra to see Blake's father. Alexis learns from Amanda of Dex's experience with Daniel in Vietnam. Jeff and Nikki follow the treasure map to a remote jungle location and find a statue filled with jewels, as well as a woman who has been impersonating Fallon. Jeff awakens the following day and learns that while celebrating, he and Nikki were married.

"Foreign Relations" – Episode 5.16
Original Airdate - January 23, 1985
Written by Edward de Blasio
Directed by Kim Friedman
Story by Camille Marchetta and Susan Baskin

Guest Appearances by Danielle Aubry (Maid), Alvin Ing (Mr. Huang), Kenneth Phillips (Bill) and Peggy Walton-Walker (Barbara)

Krystle launches her new business with the purchase of an Arabian horse. Sexual tension between Steven and Luke mounts. Jeff and Nikki return from Bolivia with the news of their marriage and they move into the mansion. Alexis is intrigued with Blake's recent meeting with a delegation from China. It was arranged by Lady Ashley Mitchell, an internationally known photo journalist and widow of a wealthy British lord. After Lady Ashley and Blake enjoy a lovely dinner together, she impetuously kisses him.

"Triangles" – Episode 5.17
Original Airdate - January 30, 1985
Written by Dennis Turner
Directed by Irving J. Moore
Story by Camille Marchetta and Susan Baskin

Guest Appearances by Rowena Balos (Nanny), Wolf Larson (Bruce) and Scott Perry (Vet)

Blake returns triumphant from his negotiations with the Chinese. Alexis vows to buy into the venture. Krystle, uncomfortable with Daniel's increasing attention, avoids him. Blake, absorbed in his business, is distracted by Lady Ashley. Steven's ongoing affair with Luke ends abruptly when he decides to return to Claudia. Blake invites Amanda to accompany him on a business trip to Acapulco. Alexis learns of the trip and invites herself and Lady Ashley.

"The Ball" – Episode 5.18
Original Airdate - February 6, 1985
Written by John Pleshette
Directed by Jerome Courtland
Story by Camille Marchetta and Susan Baskin

Guest Appearances by Dana Lee (Han Li Su), Dorothy Patterson (Martha) and Benita Prezia (Italian Count)

Alexis attempts to persuade the head of the Chinese delegation to hire Colbyco. Blake is surprised to learn Lady Ashley is in Acapulco. Amanda has a romantic fling with Prince Michael of Moldavia. Claudia meets with Luke, asking him to honor Steven's request that they remain apart. Krystle  makes a surprise visit to Daniel, who hurriedly hides maps and plans detailing a secret military maneuver. While riding, Krystle is thrown from her horse. Relieved she is unhurt, Daniel kisses her passionately.

"Circumstantial Evidence" – Episode 5.19
Original Airdate - February 13, 1985
Written by Edward de Blasio
Directed by Curtis Harrington
Story by Camille Marchetta and Donald R. Boyle

Guest Appearances by James Hornbeck (Reece Man #1) and Eduardo Ricard (Maitre D')

Amanda spends the night with Prince Michael and then is heartsick to learn he is engaged. Dex persuades the Chinese delegation to use his company instead of Blake's for an important drilling job. Alexis offers Blake a generous deal in the South China Seas. Although suspicious, he accepts. After Claudia spots Steven and Luke at a restaurant, she finally accepts Adam's advances. Dex decides to accompany Daniel on a top-secret military maneuver. Daniel confesses to Krystle he's been in love with her for years.

"The Collapse" – Episode 5.20
Original Airdate - February 20, 1985
Written by Donald R. Boyle
Directed by John Patterson
Story by Camille Marchetta and Donald R. Boyle

Guest Appearances by R.J. Adams (Man in Suit), Baillie Gerstein (T.V. Commentator), Santos Morales (Contra), Jeff Sanders (Secretary), Frank Schuller (Tony Nelson) and Peggy Walton-Walker (Barbara)

Tensions between Krystle and Blake mount as their suspicions of one another grow. Claudia regrets sleeping with Adam. Dominique derails Alexis' attempt to buy out her company, but is unable to stop Brady's divorce proceedings. Alexis hires a private detective to investigate the circumstances surrounding 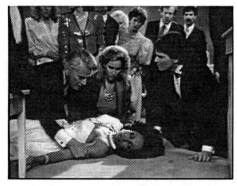 Jeff's marriage to Nikki: She learns the girl fabricated the marriage license and deluded Jeff into believing he had married her while drunk. Jeff confronts Nikki, who confesses and leaves the mansion. Dominique is suddenly seized with a violent cough and drops to the floor, unconscious.

"Life and Death" – Episode 5.21
Original Airdate - February 27, 1985
Written by Dennis Turner
Directed by Irving J. Moore
Story by Camille Marchetta and Donald R. Boyle

Guest Appearances by Toni Attell (Dr. Tully), Mark Burke (Anesthesiologist), Charles Davis (Professor), Frank Dicopoulos (Paramedic), John Findlater (Dr. Rossiter), Rick Fitts (Dr. Giddings), Bonnie Keith (Dr. Solis), Kenneth Kimmins (Dr. Chase), Halaine Lembeck (Nurse Peters) and Isabel West (Nurse Robinson)

Dominique remains in critical condition after collapsing. Luke pays an unexpected visit to Steven. Blake tells his son that he will support him regardless of his sexual persuasion. Krystle and Ashley exchange heated words. Dex returns from his secret mission quite ill, and in his feverish raving, he calls out for Amanda. Alexis calls her former lover, King Galen, a Middle Eastern monarch and Prince Michael's father. She wants to make a marriage match for Amanda and Michael.

"Parental Consent" – Episode 5.22
Original Airdate - March 6, 1985
Written by Edward de Blasio
Directed by Kim Friedman
Story by Camille Marchetta and Donald R. Boyle

Guest Appearances by Bever-Leigh Banfield (Nurse), Sam Chew Jr. (Kyle), George Skaff (Majordomo) and Gary Wells (Bellboy)

Alexis attempts to persuade King Galen to allow a marriage between Amanda and his son. She sweetens the offer by suggesting his country would receive a portion of Colbyco's revenues. Finally, she allows him to take her to bed. Steven tells Claudia that although he still loves her, he is now certain he also loves Luke. Dominique advises Krystle to reconcile with Blake or risk losing him to Ashley. Lady Ashley impulsively kisses Blake and the moment is photographed and sent to Krystle.

"Photo Finish" – Episode 5.23
Original Airdate - March 13, 1985
Written by Susan Miller
Directed by Robert Scheerer
Story by Camille Marchetta and Donald R. Boyle

Guest Appearances by Byron Michael (Secretary), Richard Hatch (Dean Caldwell), Bunky Jones (Krystle's Friend), Dorothy Patterson (Martha), Mark Schneider (Man in Bar), Peggy Walton-Walker (Barbara)

Alexis is relieved and Blake is concerned when Amanda suddenly changes her mind and decides to marry Prince Michael. Sammy Jo is revealed to be the culprit behind the compromising photographs. She realizes the scheme to split them apart is useless until she spots a woman who bears an uncanny resemblance to her aunt. Blake returns to the mansion after spending the evening with Ashley, and is surprised to find Krystle has cancelled her planned business trip. Krystle, hurt by what appears to be Blake's betrayal, immediately takes the baby and leaves the mansion.

"The Crash" – Episode 5.24
Original Airdate - March 20, 1985
Written by Dennis Turner
Directed by Irving J. Moore
Story by Camille Marchetta

Guest Appearances by Ernie Fuentes (Officer), Taylor Lacher (Burt McCann) and Dorothy Patterson (Martha)

Claudia flies to Mexico to divorce Steven. Unexpectedly, Adam appears at her hotel and they spend the night together. After Amanda embarrasses Prince Michael at Dominique's party, his patience is exhausted and he leaves her. Jeff's infatuation with Ashley grows. Dex rescues Daniel, who goes immediately to see Krystle. Relieved he's alive, she embraces him and he misinterprets her affection. Blake is enraged. While airborne with Daniel on a private plane, the men fight and knock the pilot from the cockpit, throwing the plane out of control.

"Reconciliation" – Episode 5.25
Original Airdate - March 27, 1985
Written by Edward de Blasio
Directed by Nancy Malone
Story by Camille Marchetta

Guest Appearances by Nick Angotti (Fred Mason), Nigel Bullard (Pete Davis), Stephanie Gregg (Maid), Taylor Lacher (Burt McCann), Robert Parucha (Chauffeur) and Drew Snyder (Hank Lowther)

Blake and Daniel survive the plane crash. Jeff charters a helicopter and braves hazardous conditions to finally locate the wreckage. Dominique warns Ashley not to jeopardize Blake's marriage. Krystle and Blake finally clear the air and renew their commitment to each other. Amanda reconciles with Prince Michael, and the wedding is back on. Krystle visits Daniel and tells him he is the father of her sister Iris' baby, Sammy Jo.

"Sammy Jo" – Episode 5.26
Original Airdate - April 3, 1985
Written by Dennis Turner
Directed by Irving J. Moore
Story by Camille Marchetta and Susan Baskin

Guest Appearances by Tom Everett (Vincent), Peter Marc (Steward) and Don Torres (Conrad)

Krystle accompanies Daniel to New York for his reunion with Sammy Jo, the child he's never known. While looking through photos Ashley snapped on assignment at a rock concert, Jeff is stunned to spot Fallon among the crowd. Steven's upset to see Luke having dinner with another man. Adam alters  vital information on an urgent business wire to make Jeff appear incompetent. Correcting Jeff's 'error' at the last minute, Adam gains points with Blake. Before departing for the Middle East, Daniel extracts a promise from Krystle to take care of Sammy Jo should danger befall him overseas.

"Kidnapped" – Episode 5.27
Original Airdate - April 10, 1985
Written by Dennis Turner
Directed by Jerome Courtland
Story by Camille Marchetta and Susan Baskin

Guest Appearances by Gary Clarke (Det. Sergeant), Jane Downs (Reporter #3), Michael Gregory (Nikolai), Julie Inouve (Reporter #2), Terrence McNally (Reporter #1) and Carl Strano (Yuri)

As Alexis and Amanda emerge from an exclusive bridal salon, a car suddenly screeches to a halt and Amanda is pulled inside. A high-speed chase ensues. As Dex forces the kidnapper's car onto the sidewalk, Amanda breaks free. It is clear that Yuri, the Prince's chief bodyguard, is behind the kidnap plot. Steven requests Luke accompany him to Amanda's wedding. Adam and Claudia profess their love. Dex receives a telegram bearing tragic news. At a Los Angeles police station, a young woman appears who bears a striking resemblance to Fallon.

"The Heiress" – Episode 5.28
Original Airdate - May 8, 1985
Written by Edward de Blasio
Directed by Irving J. Moore
Story by Camille Marchetta and Susan Baskin

Guest Appearances by Rowena Balos (Nanny), Michael Gregory (Nikolai) and Carl Strano (Yuri)

Dex tells a devastated Krystle that Daniel Reece is dead. Steven is outraged when Sammy Jo decides to fight for custody of her son in court. Amanda and Alexis arrive in Moldavia and are greeted by Prince Michael and his father, King Galen. Jeff proposes marriage to Ashley. Sammy Jo learns that although she's Daniel's beneficiary, her monies will be held in trust with Krystle as executor. Finding former fiancée Elena in Michael's arms, Amanda tosses her engagement ring at the prince and dashes out. Yuri watches from the shadows as Dex comforts her.

"Royal Wedding" – Episode 5.29
Original Airdate - May 15, 1985
Written by Edward de Blasio
Directed by Jerome Courtland
Story by Camille Marchetta and Susan Baskin

Guest Appearances by Ari Barak (Servant), Gary Clarke (Det. Sergeant), Dick Durock (Bodyguard), Michael Gregory (Nikolai), Carl Strano (Yuri) and John Van Deelen (Minister)

Elena confesses to Amanda that nothing happened in the bedroom with Prince Michael. Sammy Jo fits her roommate Rita with a blonde wig and has her practice duplicating Krystle's voice. Fallon has chosen a new name and heads for Denver. Dex is kidnapped by Yuri and his gang as Amanda and Michael recite their wedding vows. Dex breaks free from his captors and heads for the chapel, where terrorists have opened fire on the entire wedding party.

SEASON SIX

"The Aftermath" – Episode 6.1
Original Airdate - September 25, 1985
Written by Edward de Blasio
Directed by Robert Scheerer
Story by Diana Gould

Guest Appearances by Michael Alaimo (Dungeon Guard), Jim Alquistt (Commando B), Theodore Bikel (Warnick), Stephen Bradley (Dungeon Guard B), Miguel Fernandes (Lieutenant), Radu Gavor (Commando A), Rod Loomis (Corridor Commando), Carl Strano (Yuri), John Van Dreelen (Minister) and James Louis Watkins (Ticket Seller)

Those surviving the carnage of the bloody wedding massacre are separated and held at the palace in Moldavia to await an uncertain fate. The revolutionaries, Yuri and Warnick, have seized power and announce that King Galen is dead. Krystle, however, imprisoned in a dank dungeon along with Alexis, has seen him alive. The women are told they will not be released without meeting the terrorists' demands. In New York City, Sammy Jo reveals her plan: Rita is to impersonate Krystle in order to have her aunt removed as executrix of her father's will. While reading the newspaper, Fallon, suffering from amnesia, spots a picture of Miles Colby and is unsure why she is drawn to the name.

"The Homecoming" – Episode 6.2
Original Airdate - October 2, 1985
Written by Dennis Turner
Directed by Kim Friedman
Story by Diana Gould

Guest Appearances by Theodore Bikel (Warnick), Nigel Bullard (Reporter #1), Jane Downs (Reporter #2), Michael Keys Hall (Minister), Robin Hoff (TV Commentator), Shelby Leverington (Decorator), Louis Plante (Waiter) and Carl Strano (Yuri)

Blake pays $5 million for the release of Krystle and Alexis, and the families return to Denver from Moldavia. Steven delivers a moving eulogy at Luke's funeral. Claudia comforts him and incurs Adam's wrath. Rita's boyfriend Joel, a wheeler-dealer film director, is enthusiastic about Sammy Jo's impersonation plot-- and the money to be made. Dominique is stunned to find Alexis is no longer interested in fighting over the Sumatra Timberlands sale. She's preoccupied with worries about Galen in Moldavia. Krystle finds Sammy Jo redecorating Delta Rho Farms and demanding Krystle release more money from her trust. Michael rebuffs Blake's offer to help him begin life anew in Denver. Fallon tells Miles Colby she is suffering from amnesia.

"The Californians" – Episode 6.3
Original Airdate - October 9, 1985
Written by Edward de Blasio and Gwen Arner
Directed by Gwen Arner
Story by Diana Gould

Guest Appearances by Ben Hartigan (Butler), Charlton Heston (Jason Colby), Bonnie Keith (Babysitter), Calvin Lockhart (Jonathan Lake), Nicolas Pryor (Doctor), Leslie Rivers (Nurse), Paul Shenar (Justin Dehner), Barbara Stanwyck (Constance Colby Patterson)

After a twenty-year absence, Blake receives a visit from Jason Colby. Jason proposes the two tycoons build a joint pipeline. Although reluctant to do business with Colby because of his past shady dealings, Blake needs Jason's tankers to move his oil out of China. Jason confides to his sister Constance that he is dying. Jeff is surprised to hear from his aunt Constance, who insists it is urgent he come to California. Psychic Justin Dehner helps in the search for Fallon, who remains in California with Miles. Dex is furious with Alexis's growing obsession with Galen. Michael shuts Amanda out of his life. Gordon Barrett, assistant undersecretary of state, questions Blake about the revolution in Moldavia. In New York, Joel and Sammy Jo convince Rita to undergo plastic surgery to complete her transformation into Krystle's double.

"The Man" – Episode 6.4
Original Airdate - October 16, 1985
Written by Dennis Turner
Directed by Don Medford
Story by Diana Gould and Scott M. Hammer

Guest Appearances by Arlene Banas (Receptionist), Gary Clarke (Police Sergeant), Helen Funai (Constance's Assistant), Charlton Heston (Jason Colby), Calvin Lockhart (Jonathan Lake), Barbara Stanwyck (Constance Colby Patterson) and Peggy Walton-Walker (Barbara)

 Jason imposes a one-week deadline for Blake to decide on the pipeline proposition. Claudia heads to San Francisco to think about her relationship with Adam. Alexis turns to both Blake and Jason for help in rescuing King Galen. While riding with Miles, Fallon is surprised to learn she is an excellent horsewoman. Under the guise of a business trip, Adam tracks down Claudia for a romantic reunion in San Francisco. In Los Angeles, Constance Colby stuns Jeff--and enrages Jason--by awarding her nephew 50% of Colby Enterprises, worth over $500 million. When Krystle makes a surprise visit to Sammy Jo's apartment, Rita, who now appears to be Krystle's double following plastic surgery, hides in the bedroom. Jonathan Lake of the State Department tells Dominique they've met before--when she saved his life in Paris.

"The Gown" – Episode 6.5
Original Airdate - October 30, 1985
Written by Dennis Turner
Directed by Robert Scheerer
Story by Diana Gould and Scott M. Hammer

Guest Appearances by Theodore Bikel (Warnick), Joseph Chapman (Beaumont), Ronnie Claire Edwards (Sister Theresa) and Jack Mayhall (Waiter)

Alexis learns that Galen is alive and can be rescued if $10 million is smuggled into the Moldavian underground. Tired of competing with the king's ghost, Dex promises to help Alexis complete the mission. Joel and Sammy Jo plan to chloroform Krystle at the Charity Ball and have Rita take her place. Sammy Jo has 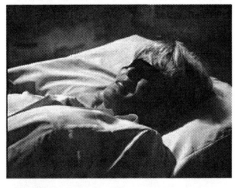 Krystle's dressmaker duplicate the gown she'll wear that evening. Jeff, now Jason Colby's partner, plans to move to California, where he believes he'll find Fallon. Michael continues to shut Amanda out of his life. In San Francisco, Adam and Claudia are married. Krystle walks in on Rita as she's practicing her imitation. Joel knocks Krystle unconscious and announces that Rita is now the new Mrs. Blake Carrington.

"Titans" – Episode 6.6
Original Airdate - November 13, 1985
Written by Edward de Blasio
Directed by Irving J. Moore
Story by Diana Gould and Scott M. Hammer

Guest Appearances by Stephanie Beacham (Sable Colby), Emile Beaucard (Guard #1), Theodore Bikel (Warnick), Frank Dicopoulos (Masseur), Robert Dowdell (Butler), Ronnie Claire Edwards (Sister Theresa), Charlton Heston (Jason Colby), Francisco Lagueruela (Guard #2), Ray Laska (Border Guard), Tom Reynolds (Alexis' Secretary), Tracy Scoggins (Monica Colby), Barbara Stanwyck (Constance Colby Patterson)

Krystle regains consciousness and finds herself locked in the attic at Delta Rho Farms while Rita is impersonating her at the mansion. Dex is caught and tortured in Moldavia. A furious Blake learns Adam lied to him by canceling a business trip to marry Claudia. Blakecuts Adam out of his will. Claudia is upset to find Michael has been appointed chairman of La Mirage. The Colby family attends Blake's party to announce the formation of the Carrington-Colby pipeline. Blake, however, continues to question Jason's integrity. One-time lovers Dominique and Garrett Boydston, Jason's chief counsel, are reunited. From his bedroom window, Jeff spots Miles Colby arriving with Fallon.

*This special two-hour episode served as the introductory showing of the *Dynasty* spinoff, *The Colby's*.

"The Decision" – Episode 6.7
Original Airdate - November 20, 1985
Written by Robert Seidenberg
Directed by Gwen Arner
Story by Diana Gould and Scott M. Hammer

Guest Appearances by Ray Laska (Border Guard #2), Duke Moosekian (Border Guard #1) and Roger Periard (Colonel)

Searching his memory for details of the moment he spotted Fallon, Jeff recalls a California license plate and realizes she was with Miles. In Moldavia, Dex overpowers his captors and rescues Galen. Disguised as a priest and a nun, Dex and Alexis transport the king out of the country amid a hail of gunfire. Little Blake overhears Rita speaking with Sammy Jo and realizes she is not his aunt Krystle, who remains bound and gagged in the attic at Delta Rho Farms. Dominique orders Garrett from her suite and then places a mysterious call to a girl's finishing school in Switzerland. As an elated Jeff heads for California to find Fallon, she and Miles make love in a roadside motel.

"The Proposal" – Episode 6.8
Original Airdate - November 27, 1985
Written by Edward de Blasio
Directed by Robert Scheerer
Story by Diana Gould and Scott M. Hammer

Guest Appearances by Freddy Chapman (Nurse), Julie Inouye (Reporter #2), Ben Marino (Security Guard #1), Terrence McNally (Reporter #1), Tracy Cunningham (Photographer), Mark Phelan (Security Guard #2) and Michael Prince (Dr. Webb)

Alexis, Dex, and Galen land in Denver amid a swarm of press. His legs paralyzed, the king is rushed to the hospital. After Rita feigns nightly headaches to avoid making love with Blake, he insists she see a doctor. Seizing the opportunity, Joel poses as Dr. Travers and makes a house call at the mansion. Blake stuns Alexis by telling her Fallon is alive in California. Claudia inherits an oil well from Walter Lankershim and moves back in with the Carringtons. Rita spikes Blake's brandy with a barbiturate to keep him sexually at bay. From his hospital bed, Galen vows to make Alexis the most powerful woman in the world.

"The Close Call" – Episode 6.9
Original Airdate - December 4, 1985
Written by Diana Gould
Directed by Irving J. Moore
Story by Diana Gould and Scott M. Hammer

Guest Appearances by David Hayward (Trainer), Bobby Mardis (Orderly), Dorothy Patterson (Martha) and Brenda Thompson (Nurse)

When Blake decides to buy Krystle a horse as a surprise gift, Sammy Jo panics at the thought of Blake going to Delta Rho. Claudia confronts Blake over Walter Lankershim's oil well, believing it was taken from her illegally. When Blake tells her he received the well through legitimate means, she schemes  with Adam to get it back. Michael and Amanda appear to grow closer as Alexis and Dex argue whether King Galen will move into their home to recuperate. Galen promises to make Alexis a powerful woman in order to use her money to regain the throne.

"The Quarrels" – Episode 6.10
Original Airdate - December 11, 1985
Written by Dennis Turner
Directed by Kim Friedman
Story by Diana Gould and Scott M. Hammer

Guest Appearances by Preston Hanson (Dr. Sidney Tyler) and Richard Pachorek (Waiter)

Rita panics when Blake tells her that he's made an appointment for her to see his physician. Dex becomes disgusted with Alexis as she pampers King Galen. Galen tells Michael that his marriage to Amanda was arranged, strengthening his own plans to regain the throne. Michael demands that he and Amanda start planning a family. Blake is enraged when Rita, posing as Krystle, runs away from his romantic advances.

"The Roadhouse" – Episode 6.11
Original Airdate - December 18, 1985
Written by Edward de Blasio
Directed by Jerome Courtland
Story by Diana Gould and Scott M. Hammer

Guest Appearances by C.J. Hunt (Male Nurse), Calvin Lockhart (Jonathan Lake), Justin Lord (TV Commentator), Eleanor Mondale (TV Anchorwoman) and Frank Zagarino (Eric)

As Blake becomes increasingly disturbed by Krystle's sexual resistance, Joel tells Rita that she has to sleep with Blake. In the meantime, Joel takes the real Krystle out for a night-on-the-town, where they are seen by an astonished Alexis and Dex. Krystle's signals for help are ignored. With Alexis' financial backing, Galen prepares to send Michael to New York to hire mercenaries for their cause. Determined to reclaim the oil well, Claudia attempts to win over Steven, believing he can persuade Blake to relinquish control. Adam offers Bart Fallmont a handsome bribe to prevent a preliminary injunction against the family enterprise.

"The Solution" – Episode 6.12
Original Airdate - December 25, 1985
Written by Robert Seidenberg
Directed by Irving J. Moore
Story by Diana Gould and Scott M. Hammer

Guest Appearances by Calvin Lockhart (Jonathan Lake)

In order to appease Blake, Rita, posing as Krystle, agrees to see a doctor. But after receiving a clean bill of health, when her evasive behavior continues Blake begins to threaten a divorce. Rita is forced to poison her unsuspecting "husband" in a frantic effort to safeguard Joel's plan. Alexis visits the still crippled Galen. After she leaves, Galen reveals his secret recovery. Amanda relives the nightmare of the wedding massacre and believes it to be an omen of Michael's impending fate when there is no word from him. Jonathan and Dominique's romantic involvement deepens, but when Jonathan announces his new association with Bart Fallmont, she severs further relations. Dominique is now left vulnerable to Garrett's attempts to rekindle an old flame.

"Suspicions" – Episode 6.13
Original Airdate - January 8, 1986
Written by Diana Gould
Directed by Nancy Malone
Story by Diana Gould and Scott M. Hammer

Guest Appearances by Calvin Lockhart (Jonathan Lake), Santos Morales (Guard) and Richard Roat (Publisher)

Blake suffers dizzy spells as Rita's slow poisoning takes effect. Anxious to secure the Carrington estate, Joel convinces Rita to administer the fatal dose. Joel professes his love to Krystle, who insincerely returns his affections in an attempt to win her freedom. When this fails, she desperately feigns illness in a second ploy to escape. An enraged Steven engages Bart Fallmont in hand-to-hand combat over the pipeline construction. Dex is granted full building rights. Claudia hastens to Oklahoma to fight for her oil well, leaving a bewildered Adam behind. Alexis receives a mysterious phone call from Caracas, Venezuela. Caress Morrell, is set free in exchange for the "Sister Dearest – The True Story of Alexis Morrell Carrington Colby Dexter". Sammy Jo discovers the empty vial of poison, and confronting an alarmed Rita, begins to suspect Joel's deadly plan.

"The Alarm" – Episode 6.14
Original Airdate - January 15, 1986
Written by Edward de Blasio
Directed by Kim Friedman
Story by Diana Gould and Scott M. Hammer

Guest Appearances by Emory Bass (Clerk), Michael Paul Chan (Lab Technician), Randy Hamilton (Bartender) and Lora Staley (Meg)

Galen plots to regain his throne while Elena, learning the counter-revolution is in jeopardy, solicits Michael's help. A mysterious woman visits Denver to conduct extensive research on Colbyco and Alexis Carrington Colby Dexter. Alexis, noting Blake's loss of faculties, is ready to pounce on Krystle for driving him to failing health. Adam has an unwitting Blake grant him power of attorney over Denver Carrington. Adam boasts to Claudia, but she is suspicious, and continues her attempt to prove rightful ownership of the oil well. Sammy Jo learns that Joel and Rita plan to poison Blake and flee to South America with Krystle. After much soul searching, Sammy Jo warns Steven, but it may be too late. Steven arrives at the mansion just after Blake, stricken with an apparent heart attack, falls down the stairs.

"The Vigil" – Episode 6.15
Original Airdate - January 22, 1986
Written by Dennis Turner
Directed by Irving J. Moore
Story by Diana Gould and Scott M. Hammer

Guest Appearances by Marilyn Raye Bradfield (Female Paramedic), Mark Flynn (Paramedic), Howard George (Man), Jason Graves (Lawyer), Calvin Lockhart (Jonathan Lake), Laurel Lockhart (Nurse), Tracy Cunningham (E.R. Nurse), Lavelle Roby (Night Nurse), David Spielberg (Dr. McNaughton) and Nina Penn (Day Nurse)

After falling down the stairs, Blake is rushed to the hospital. After verbally attacking "Krystle" (Rita), Alexis stands by Blake's bedside and promises that she won't let him die then begs him to fight to hang on. Adam realizes that he has been written out of his father's will and desperately tries to convince a delirious and barely conscious Blake to sign a new document. Blake is able to flash back to the fatal moment of his illness and realizes that Rita is not Krystle. Galen continues his deceptive charade as he requests two million dollars from an unsuspecting Alexis and Dex is incensed. Elena's father is betrayed by Yuri and thrown into a Moldavian prison. Amanda catches Elena and Michael in a consoling embrace and explodes with jealousy. Rita panics when Blake demands to know who she really is. She flees to Joel, but finds Krystle instead. A vicious struggle ensues and unexpectedly, Sammy Jo appears and helps Krystle overpower Rita. Krystle and Sammy Jo race to escape but are abruptly cut off by Joel.

"The Accident" – Episode 6.16
Original Airdate - January 29, 1986
Written by Edward de Blasio
Directed by Kim Friedman
Story by Diana Gould and Scott M. Hammer

Guest Appearances by Michael Durrell (Sergeant Landers), Rick Fitts (Second Policeman), Greg Mullavy (Editor) and Casey Sander (First Policeman)

When Joel intercepts Krystle and Sammy Jo at Delta Rho, Krystle pretends to be Rita and escapes. Rushing to the hospital, she is finally reunited with Blake. The two receive a grand welcome home, but Krystle is haunted by nightmares of Joel. Blake vows to capture the fugitives. While attacking Joel, Rita steers their car over a cliff. Both are thrown clear and reconcile in Rio de Janeiro, only to plot a future impersonating scheme. Alexis plots Krystle's demise by publishing the kidnapping story with added "facts." A neglected Dex attempts to force Galen to walk and consults doctors who can prove the king a fraud. Elena turns to Michael when her father is killed. A jealous Amanda approaches Dex for love and revenge. Dominique's daughter, Jackie, returns from Europe. Claudia calls Dr. Edwards about Adam and plans to re-establish her oil well.

"Souvenirs" – Episode 6.17
Original Airdate - February 5, 1986
Written by Diana Gould
Directed by Robert Scheerer
Story by Diana Gould and Scott M. Hammer

Guest Appearances by Maxwell Caulfield (Miles Colby), Trent Dolan (Security Guard), Anne Haney (Nanny), Ricardo Montalban (Zach Powers), Daryl Roach (Alexis' Security Guard) and Richard Roat (Publisher)

At Alexis' command, a reporter disguised as a nanny, sneaks onto the Carrington Estate to interrogate Krystle about her time with Joel. Overcome by fear and memories, Krystle returns to the attic where she was once held captive. Blake reproaches Adam for his carelessness in permitting the  malicious journalist into the mansion. Fallon returns home for consolation and support, hiding the fact that she was raped by Miles. Amanda informs a shocked Michael that she wants a divorce. Fearing damage to his own plans, Galen accidentally reveals his recovery to his son and insists that Michael save his marriage. Dex catches a "crowned" Alexis admiring herself as Moldavian queen. Amanda later finds a drunken Dex and leads him back to his room where the two make passionate love. Alexis learns that Caress is free and enlists Zach's help in preventing possible trouble.

"The Divorce" – Episode 6.18
Original Airdate - February 12, 1986
Written by Susan Baskin
Directed by Irving J. Moore
Story by Diana Gould and Scott M. Hammer

Guest Appearances by David Boyle (Night Manager), Jim Ishida (Lin), Robert Symonds (Dr. Jonas Edwards), Chuck Wagner (Man at Bar) and Corey Young (Griff)

Afraid that something may have happened to Dex, Alexis demands to be let into his hotel room, only to find Amanda and Dex in bed together. Horror stricken, she vows to disown Amanda and storms from the room. Krystle confronts Alexis for initiating false rumors to a journalist regarding her captivity. Krystle overturns a plate filled with food into a seething Alexis' lap. Galen assures Dex that he has lost Alexis forever and now she will be his queen. Alexis leaves for St. Thomas to get a divorce from Dex. Adam is dismayed to learn of Blake's plans to put Steven on the board of directors. While attending a party, Adam sees Bart Fallmont and Steven together and misinterprets it to mean something more. He immediately sets a conspiracy into motion to gather incriminating evidence against the senator. Garrett meets Jackie and after learning her age and the tragic story of having lost her father soon after her birth, Garrett suspects she might be his daughter. Back from St. Thomas, Alexis informs a forgiveness begging Dex that they are now divorced. Arriving at her penthouse, Alexis walks in on an unsuspecting Galen and overhears his scheme to use her and her money to regain the throne. She orders the despicable majesty to leave.

"The Dismissal" – Episode 6.19
Original Airdate - February 19, 1986
Written by Dennis Turner
Directed by Irving J. Moore
Story by Diana Gould and Scott M. Hammer

Guest Appearances by Michael Durrell (Sergeant Landers), Linda Graves, (Maid) and Richard Roat (Publisher)

Blake becomes obsessed with apprehending Joel and Rita. A remorseful Sammy Jo offers Krystle a prize horse in restitution and promises a hesitant Morgan Hess a small fortune for the capture of the co-conspirators. Galen is exiled to Lisbon, and a hopeful Michael returns to Amanda, only to learn that she  loves Dex. Alexis completely breaks relations with Dex, driving him back to Amanda. Blake tries to separate his daughter and Dex by tempting Amanda with a trip to Hawaii. Adam schemes to win political support by publicizing Bart Fallmont's sexual preferences. Steven protests and joins Bart for a drink. Posing as a journalist, Caress interviews Adam, and then makes a surprise visit to her sister as the final chapter of "Sister Dearest" nears completion. While having a nightmare about Dex and Galen, Alexis dreams she and Blake are in love and together again. When her attempts to make that a reality fail, she vows to destroy Blake once and for all.

"Ben" – Episode 6.20
Original Airdate - February 26, 1986
Written by Edward de Blasio
Directed by Kim Friedman
Story by Diana Gould and Scott M. Hammer

Guest Appearances by Neil Hunt (Aussie), Julie Inouye (Woman Reporter), Terrence McNally (First Reporter), Tracy Cunningham (Photographer #2), Ed Quinlan (Photographer #1), Joseph Taggart (Private Investigator), Dale Tarter (Official) and Frank Zagarino (Chauffeur)

A crisis in Hong Kong sends Blake overseas, leaving Krystle to speak beside Alexis at the joint-company dedication of Lake Colby as a preserve for Colorado's wildlife population. When Alexis publicly and willingly denounces Blake's character for his obvious failure to attend the event, a vicious argument ensues and lands the two enraged women in the mud. Although Bart and Steven cannot agree about the pipeline particulars, they are in mutual accord with their affections. Bart secretly admits that he and his old roommate were lovers, not knowing that a private investigator, hired by Adam, is also privy to the information. Garrett questions a nervous Dominique about Jackie's father. His suspicions grow when Dominique refuses to answer. Alexis learns of Ben Carrington's isolated existence in Australia. With vengeance as her inspiration, she lures the recluse back to Denver, hoping to pit the estranged brothers against one another. Upon her return, Alexis receives a housewarming gift that turns her blood cold; Caress has moved in.

"Masquerade" – Episode 6.21
Original Airdate - March 5, 1986
Written by Robert Seidenberg
Directed by Jerome Courtland
Story by Diana Gould and Scott M. Hammer

Guest Appearances by Terence Ford (Guest #1), Sandy Freeman (Betty Kingsley), Michael Lally (Guest #2) and Bob Seagren (Reporter)

Speaking at her own prearranged press conference, Alexis brashly announces a masquerade party fund-raiser at the Carrington mansion. Upon returning from Hong Kong, Blake reluctantly agrees to host the event in hopes of persuading ex-senator Buck Fallmont to re-evaluate his stand on the pipeline. Intercepting a call meant for Caress, Alexis learns of her sister's spiteful plan to write a book on her tumultuous life. Garrett confronts Dominique with the fact that Jackie's father is listed as "unknown" on her birth certificate. Dominique denies Garrett's assertions that Jackie may be his daughter. At the masquerade ball, Bart Fallmont shows Steven the newspaper headline running in the next morning's edition, which claims that Bart had a homosexual lover. Steven immediately suspects Adam's treachery and a fight ensues. Alexis then sets her plan for Blake's demise into motion when Ben removes his costume and reveals himself as Blake's long-lost baby brother.

"The Subpoenas" – Episode 6.22
Original Airdate - March 12, 1986
Written by Edward de Blasio
Directed by Irving J. Moore
Story by Diana Gould and Scott M. Hammer

Guest Appearances by Richard Roat (Publisher)

Alexis' surprise unveiling of Ben stuns Blake, but she has little time to relish her first victory when Ben threatens to be her fiercest adversary if their plans go awry. Amanda breaks down when Dex confesses that he does not love her. She later finds strength and reassurance from Steven, only to be crushed again by an unforgiving Alexis. Furious at Adam for publicizing Bart's past illicit romance, Steven instigates another battle with his brother. Blake also reprimands Adam, but the story accomplishes its purpose as ex-senator Buck Fallmont withdraws the pipeline injunction. Despite Krystle's queries, Blake refuses to discuss his estrangement from his brother. Blake is confronted by Ben, who has returned to Denver to contest their father's will. Having discovered Caress' sinister intentions, Alexis secretly buys the company contracted to publish the damaging expose. Unaware of her sister's actions, Caress continues to write and to fall prey to a merciless Alexis.

"The Trial: Part One" – Episode 6.23
Original Airdate - March 19, 1986
Written by Dennis Turner
Directed by Michael Hugo
Story by Diana Gould and Scott M. Hammer

Guest Appearances by Greta Blackburn (Jennifer), Nigel Bullard (Reporter #1), Ralph Clift (Court Clerk), Jane Downs (Reporter #2), Brion James (Hawkins), Ben Marino (Bailiff), Warren Munson (Judge Stanley Thurlowe), Tricia O'Neill (Mrs. Davis), Grant Owens (Lawyer #1), Richard Roat (Publisher), Debra Satell (Jeri), Frank Schuller (Hall), Bill Traylor (Dan Franklin), Tyler Tyhurst (Worker), Peggy Walton-Walker (Barbara) and Anthony Zerbe (Crenshaw)

After purchasing the company contracted to publish Caress' book, "Sister Dearest," Alexis savors crushing her sister's grandiose dreams of literary fame and fortune. Jackie learns that her birth certificate lists her father as "unknown." Dominique, called to testify at Blake's trial, has no time to explain and Jackie leaves in tears. Vying for the inheritance he was denied, Ben accuses Blake of maliciously turning their father against him. Blake's rise to power is exposed by the incriminating testimony of those closest to him. Despite Ben's inflammatory accusations, Blake's case remains strong until Alexis takes the stand against him and swears that Ben was in the field the day Ellen Carrington died because Blake was in bed with her.

"The Trial: Part Two" – Episode 6.24
Original Airdate - March 26, 1986
Written by Dennis Turner
Directed by Don Medford
Story by Diana Gould and Scott M. Hammer

Guest Appearances by Nigel Bullard (Reporter #1), Laurie Burton (Lawyer #2), Jane Downs (Reporter #2), Brion James (Hawkins), Ben Marino (Bailiff), Warren Munson (Judge Stanley Thurlowe), Tricia O'Neill (Mrs. Davis), Grant Owens (Lawyer #1), Debra Satell (Jeri), Frank Schuller (Hall), Bill Traylot (Dan Franklin), Tyler Tyhurst (Worker), Peggy Walton-Walker (Barbara) and Anthony Zerbe (Crenshaw)

Blake's hopes are renewed when a key witness, Franklin, admits that Alexis paid him to alter his testimony. But Franklin later arrives in court intoxicated and is unable to answer any questions. Angered by the drunken witness, the judge rules in favor of Ben, and Blake is forced to surrender one-third of the family estate. Blake vows to appeal and is determined to track down the mysterious woman who can clear his name. Bart is dropped from the senatorial race when newspaper headlines announce his homosexuality. Bart is relieved, but Steven is outraged and argues with a remorseless Adam. Bart's father, Buck, turns to Blake for advice. Dex offers Clay Fallmont a job on the pipeline. As Blake and Dex review construction particulars, a rancorous ex-employee orchestrates a potentially fatal accident. Buck Fallmont's wife, Emily, is ready to confess that she and Ben met the day of Ellen Carrington's tragic death. Fearing discovery, Ben warns Emily of the scandal that would result if she divulges the truth. Trapped, Emily remains silent while Ben and Alexis celebrate sweet revenge.

"The Vote" – Episode 6.25
Original Airdate - April 2, 1986
Written by Edward De Blasio
Directed by Irving J. Moore
Story by Diana Gould and Scott M. Hammer

Guest Appearances by Greta Blackburn (Jennifer), Tammy Brewer (Receptionist), Don Dubbins (Martin Gaines), Graydon Gould (Board Member #2), Clayton Landey (Jay Bradley), Robert Rockwell (Board Member #1) and Edson Stroll (Board Member #3)

Accused of causing his mother's death, Blake fights to prove his innocence. Blake tries to save Denver-Carrington, which has plunged in the stock market since the trial. At an emergency board meeting, Blake is temporarily asked to step down as chairman when Martin Gaines, a board member, rallies the other members against him. Blake proposes a Colbyco takeover and wins back support, with a very hesitant Steven casting the deciding vote. Dex discovers Alexis and Ben "intimately" involved in planning Blake's destruction. Caress offers Blake her help and some disturbing information that could prove Alexis' court testimony false. When Jackie runs away, a distraught Dominique turns to Garrett and acknowledges that he is Jackie's father. Amanda sinks into a dangerous depression when she is unable to find a job and is continually rejected by a cold Alexis. Hungry for a story, reporter Gordon Wales provokes Blake into a rage with talk of the trial.

"The Warning" – Episode 6.26
Original Airdate - April 9, 1986
Written by Diana Gould
Directed by Don Medford
Story by Diana Gould and Scott M. Hammer

Guest Appearances by Carole Cook (Cora Van Heusen), Tom Hallick (Winston Towers), Ron Kuhlman (Policeman), F.J. O'Neil (Bob Ashmore), Soon-Teck Oh (Kai Liu) and Concetta Tomei (Ilene)

Determined to find the identity of the mystery woman Ben was in bed with the night of his mother's death, Caress begins to piece together and when she witnesses a secret rendezvous between Emily and Ben, her suspicions are proven. In a desperate attempt to raise the money for the leveraged buy-out of Colby Co, Blake puts Denver Carrington up as collateral for a $100 million loan. The demise of Blake's empire continues when Bob Ashrnore places a congratulatory call to Ben, celebrating their successful coup over the unsuspecting Blake. As Ben's plot to ruin his brother unfolds, Alexis prepares to present the Chinese government with falsified records showing Blake to be cheating them of royalties from the China Sea leases. Claudia threatens to reveal Adam's power of attorney over Denver-Carrington unless the title to the oil well stolen from her is returned.

"The Cry" – Episode 6.27
Original Airdate - April 16, 1986
Written by Scott M. Hammer
Directed by Irving J. Moore
Story by Scott M. Hammer

Guest Appearances by Kabir Bedi (Farouk Ahmed), Woody Brown (Fred), Clint Carmichael (Worker), William Frankfather (Bartender), Richard Herd (Jim Ellison), James Hornbeck (Blanchard) and Peggy Walton-Walker (Barbara)

With his reputation destroyed after the court battle with Ben, Jim Ellison, the influential Eastern money broker, refuses to loan Blake the one billion dollars needed to rebuild Denver-Carrington. Unexpectedly, Middle Eastern financial magnate Farouk Ahrned offers to loan Blake the money for a staggering fee. Desperate for the capital, Blake accepts, not knowing that Alexis is his actual creditor. Through furtive investigations, Caress discovers that Emily Fallmont was with Ben the night of Ellen Carrington's death. She quickly relates this information to Blake, and leaves with him her expose, "Sister Dearest" as additional ammunition against Alexis. Blake confronts Emily, who breaks down and confesses her guilt. Seeing her torment, Blake promises to fight Ben without benefit of Emily's testimony. Struggling on her own, Jackie reconsiders her rash action of running away. Returning home, Jackie is shocked to learn that Garrett is her real father. Amanda becomes more and more despondent as she is continually pushed aside by family members for more important business matters. When a reporter then threatens to disclose the car accident cover-up in which she was at fault, Amanda desperately calls Alexis to beg forgiveness once more and after being curtly dismissed by her mother, swallows a bottle of pills.

"The Rescue" – Episode 6.28
Original Airdate - April 30, 1986
Written by Scott Hammer
Directed by Irving J. Moore
Story by Diana Gould and Scott M. Hammer

Guest Appearances by Michael Goodwin (Doctor), Brian Jensen (Policeman), Joaquin Martinez (Prison Official), Bob McLean (Night Manager) and Soon-Teck Oh (Kai Liu)

Feeling guilty over her cold treatment towards her youngest child, Alexis rushes to La Mirage, only to find Amanda unconscious next to an empty bottle of barbiturates. Forcing the nearly lifeless girl to walk, a remorseful Alexis begs her daughter's forgiveness. At the hospital, Alexis and Blake stand over a comatose Amanda. Even as each blames the other for their daughter's suicide attempt, they reaffirm their commitment to the other's destruction. Dominique proposes to Garrett and the two make plans to marry. Steven fears losing custody of Danny if Sammy Jo marries Clay Fallmont. Caress demands ten percent of Ben's inheritance in exchange for her silence regarding Emily Fallmont. Ben agrees, but secretly arranges to have Caress extradited to Caracas. Alexis prepares to call in her one billion dollar loan to Blake to gain control of his South China Sea leases. Calling her contact, Kai Liu, Alexis schedules a meeting with the Chinese Oil Ministry. But she is yet unaware of Ben's own scheme with Liu, who now has possession of a copy of the damaging manuscript, "Sister Dearest."

"The Triple-Cross" – Episode 6.29
Original Airdate - May 14, 1986
Written by Diana Gould
Directed by Don Medford
Story by Diana Gould and Scott M. Hammer

Guest Appearances by Michael Chong (Salesman), Andrea Howard (Saleslady), Clayton Landey (Jay Bradley) and Dana Lee (Han Li Su)

Secure that his South China Sea leases will cover him, Blake purchases tremendous amounts of Colbyco stock. Taking advantage of his precarious situation, Alexis falsifies Blake's oil production figures. Blake is faced with financial ruin when Chinese Oil Minister Han accuses him of cheating and indicates that  the leases may no longer be extended to him. Dex reveals Ben's suspicious past to Alexis. Disregarding the warning, Alexis, along with Blake, falls prey to Ben's treachery. Using the court scandal and "Sister Dearest" to blacken the reputations of the Denver-Carrington and Colbyco powers, Ben gains sole control of the South China Sea leases. Steven attempts to investigate Adam's guarded files, but the records are destroyed before he can uncover the secret he knows his brother is hiding. Dominique makes wedding plans. Passionate feelings grow when Sammy Jo and Clay spend a candlelit evening together.

"The Vendetta" – Episode 6.30
Original Airdate - May 21, 1986
Written by Edward de Blasio
Directed by Irving J. Moore
Story by Diana Gould and Scott M. Hammer

Guest Appearances by Rowena Balos (Nanny), Kabir Bedi (Farouk Ahmed), Phillip Clark (Richard Daniels), Jane Downs (Reporter), Santos Morales (Prison Guard) and F.J. O'Neill (Bob Ashmore)

Blake is completely shocked when newspaper headlines announce Ben's acquisition of the South China Sea leases. Sure of Ben and Alexis' collusion, Blake greets the co-conspirators at the airport with copies of "Sister Dearest," which he vengefully hands out to the hungry press. Claudia informs Blake that while he was ill, he gave Adam power of attorney to turn the Lankershim One oil well over to her. Disturbed that the well is nearly dry, Claudia becomes lost in a dreamlike past. Locking herself into a candlelit room at La Mirage, she accidentally sets the room ablaze. Sammy Jo and Amanda fight for Clay's affections during Dominique's engagement party. Dominique's happiness is shattered when Alexis informs her that Garrett was never married and has been lying to her for decades. After manipulating Ben into giving her half of the leases, Alexis plots her ultimate revenge. Calling in her billion dollar loan, Alexis renders a stunned Blake financially impotent. When he and Krystle arrive at the mansion, Ben greets them in the hallway as Alexis tosses Krystle's furs over the railing of the staircase ordering Blake to "take these furs and your blonde tramp and get out of my house." When she produces the paperwork giving her ownership of the mansion, Blake breaks into a fiery rage and grabs Alexis by the throat determined to kill her.

SEASON SEVEN

"The Victory" – Episode 7.1
Original Airdate - September 24, 1986
Written by Edward de Blasio
Directed by Don Medford
Story by Laurence Heath

Guest Appearances by Alan Fudge (Phil Thorpe), Kathie Gibbonie (Maid), Bennet Guillory (Captain), Stephen Landis (Fireman), James Ray (Eckland), Bob Seagren (TV Commentator), Jane Singer (Woman at Fire), Barbara Tarbuck (Dr. Holton)

Moments away from death under Blake's powerful grip, Alexis begs him to stop and her life is spared when Krystle is able to pull Blake's away from her, but not before he vows to regain the Carrington mansion. As searing flames ravage La Mirage, Amanda is rescued from the suffocating smoke by Michael Culhane, a nemesis from the Carrington's past. Phil Thorpe accuses Blake of being responsible for the death of his wife, a victim of the fire. A news crew is quick to tape the bereaved man's inflammatory remarks. The La Mirage blaze claims Claudia's life and seriously burns Jackie. Ben receives a mysterious call from a female acquaintance. Unwilling to share in her mother's "triumph", Amanda flees to live with Blake. Upon seeing news clips of the La Mirage fire, Alexis begins to form an unscrupulous scheme with Blake as the unwitting prey. Her plot unfolds as the Denver Mirror acquires a new publisher and a new headline for the morning edition--BLAKE CARRINGTON ACCUSED OF ARSON-MURDER!

"Sideswiped" – Episode 7.2
Original Airdate - October 1, 1986
Written by Edward de Blasio
Directed by Gwen Arner
Story by Laurence Heath

Guest Appearances by Norman Alden (Guard), Charles Champion (Security Guard), Paul Du Pratt (Smitty), Alan Fudge (Phil Thorpe) and Robert Rothman (Vice President)

An incensed Blake discovers the morning headlines, which accuse him of murder and arson. He rushes to the Denver Mirror only to find Alexis as the new publisher. She presents him with an ultimatum: leave Denver or face relentless persecution from her paper. Michael Culhane, the Carrington's blackmailing chauffeur from the past, persuades a reluctant Blake to reacquire his services using his rescue of Amanda as leverage. Steven offers Adam his hand in friendship to work together for their father, but Adam's true loyalties lie with Alexis and Colbyco. An unsuspecting Blake is stalked by Phil Thorpe. Sammy Jo and Clay Fallmont's romance strengthens. Alexis buys up enough stock to control Denver-Carrington, forcing Blake to relinquish his office, but not his determination to regain his company. Phil Thorpe exacts his revenge by forcing Blake's limousine off the road. From the mangled wreckage, Blake is able to drag himself free and unharmed, only to find Krystle, bloody and unconscious.

"Focus" – Episode 7.3
Original Airdate - October 15, 1986
Written by James W. Kearns
Directed by Don Medford
Story by Laurence Heath

Guest Appearances by Newell Alexander (Baines), Bever-Leigh Banfield (Reporter), Earl Boen (Reporter), Dalton Cathey (Desk Clerk), Alan Fudge (Phil Thorpe), Lorry Goldman (Assistant D.A. Ferguson), Carol Locatell (Peters), Madison Mason (Gary Tilden), Robert Pine (Lt. Calder), Elizabeth Reilly (Edmunds), Jack Stauffer (Doctor) and Curtis Taylor (Man)

Krystle lays unconscious in her hospital room, a victim of Phil Thorpe's crusade for revenge. Blake attributes the attempted murder to Alexis and vows to kill her if Krystle fails to pull through. Despite their lustful romance, Clay informs Sammy Jo he is not ready for a commitment. As Krystle makes a speedy recovery, Dominique, in a selfless display of trust, offers Blake a $50 million loan to free him from Alexis' crushing debt. Alexis threatens the Assistant D.A. with her power of the press if he doesn't prosecute Blake. Phil Thorpe gains access to the Carrington's suite and threatens her at gunpoint in retribution against Blake, but her composure and compassion persuades him to give up his maniacal scheme. Threatened by Alexis' power, the D.A. determines the La Mirage fire was deliberately set and Blake is suspect number one.

"Reward" – Episode 7.4
Original Airdate - October 22, 1986
Written by Harold Livingston
Directed by Irving J. Moore
Story by Laurence Heath

Guest Appearances by Joe Horvath (Waiter #2), Clayton Landey (Jay Bradley), Don Maxwell (Charley), Robert Pine (Lt. Calder), James Ray (Eckland), Jon Sharp (Ben Carson), Chuck E. Smith (Waiter #1) and Gary Wood (Dan Crane)

Blake discovers La Mirage manager Jay Bradley had purposely failed to tell him he hired the man believed responsible for the fire. Alexis continues her ruthless campaign against Blake, offering a $100,000 reward for information leading to the arrest and conviction of the arsonist. Michael Culhane, bent to avenge the humiliation caused him by Blake in the past, intensifies his efforts to charm Amanda. Blake and Dex agree to work together on an ambitious new drilling venture; a gamble that could win him back his empire or lose everything he ever had. Desperate to know more about their secret deal, Alexis acquires the talents of Gordon Wales, an investigative reporter with a dislike for Blake. Ben and Adam continue to distrust each other, as they are asked to prove their loyalty to Alexis. Ben bribes Jay Bradley, bitter after losing his job, to conspire against Blake. A moment of joy shared with Krystle is crushed by a warrant for Blake's arrest for murder and arson.

"The Arraignment" – Episode 7.5
Original Airdate - November 5, 1986
Written by Dennis Turner
Directed by George Sanford Brown

Guest Appearances by Lorry Goldman (Assistant D.A. Ferguson), Russell Johnson (Earl Thompson), Taylor Lacher (Captain Harris), Bryan Michael McGuire (Bailiff), Carlos Romero (Judge J. Theborn) and David White (Dr. Gavin)

Alexis learns of Ben's ploy to frame Blake with a bogus witness and reads him the riot act. Blake is denied bail and forced to await his trial behind bars. Krystle consults a doctor regarding her sudden dizzy spells and ignores his advice to slow down and rest. Adam overhears Ben nervously reject  another call from Australia, arousing his suspicions behind Ben's evasiveness. Jackie is able to tell Krystle and Dominique that the La Mirage blaze started in Claudia's room, proving Blake did not hire an arsonist. The information forces the Assistant D.A. to drop all charges against Blake. Fearing Buck's strong contempt for the Carringtons, Clay unsuccessfully tries to persuade Sammy Jo against accepting his mother's invitation to dinner. Blake receives a letter from Caress in a Caracas prison pleading for his help. He decides to attempt her freedom in exchange for her testimony against Ben. As a raging storm strands Alexis alone with Dex in his construction trailer, they banter with each other and in moment of brutal truth rekindle their romance by making passionate love.

"Romance" – Episode 7.6
Original Airdate - November 12, 1986
Written by Mart Crowley
Directed by Nancy Malone

Guest Appearances by Pamela Kosh (Embassy Official), Joaquin Martinez (Prison Official) and Madison Mason (Gary Tilden)

Blake and Krystle fly to Caracas in an attempt to free Caress. Their efforts are wasted as a prison official, bribed by Ben, denies that she's there. Alexis' renewed romance with Dex drives Ben mad with envy. After renting out an entire restaurant for a romantic evening Dex shocks Alexis with a proposal of marriage, only to have her reject his amorous bid. Blake catches Michael Culhane and Amanda in a passionate embrace. In a fit of rage, he fires his playboy chauffeur, further distancing Amanda from her over-protective father. Dominique's singing talents are pursued by Gary Tilden, a dubious character who works for a recording studio wanting to take over hers. Having had enough of Ben's conniving, Alexis kicks him out of the mansion and out of Colbyco, but not before he promises revenge. Ben threatens to expose his and Alexis' conspiracy against Blake if he isn't put back in her good favor. Nick Kimball romantically pursues Dominique, who shows little outward affection in return. Fallon returns to Denver to warn Amanda of Michael Culhane's deceptiveness. Dex agrees to Blake's plea to break Caress out of prison and use her as a weapon against Ben's evil schemes on the condition that Blake promise that he won't hurt Alexis in the process.

"The Mission" – Episode 7.7
Original Airdate - November 19, 1986
Written by Edward de Blasio
Directed by Don Medford

Guest Appearances by David Cadiente (Guard), Lorry Goldman (Assistant D.A. Ferguson), George D. Wallace (Walt Tyson) and Diana Webster (Dr. Nadine Craig)

Blake and Dex go over plans to break Caress out of prison and return her to Denver. Despite Ben's pleas to regain her trust, Alexis is well aware of his selfish motives and plays Ben's deceptive habits to her own advantage. Sammy Jo tells Krystle she is pregnant with Clay's baby and hopes he will want to settle down as a family. She warns Steven that with Clay as a husband, no court would deny her custody of Danny. Blake's former secretary, Dana confesses her love to Adam. He feigns affection in return and acquires her promise to help him obtain information from Blake's secret files. Alexis learns of Blake's bold new venture and immediately sets out to discredit his efforts. She publishes a headline proclaiming "The Crater" project as a risky speculation, causing Blake to lose vital investors. Dex and Clay Fallmont blast Caress out of her prison cell and return her to Denver. The D.A. refuses to prosecute Ben without proof he kidnapped Caress and tried to have her killed. Michael Culhane's lust for revenge drives him to call on an old and fiendish friend, Zach Powers.

"The Choice" – Episode 7.8
Original Airdate - November 26, 1986
Written by Harold Stone
Directed by Irving J. Moore

Guest Appearances by James Bartz (Assistant Manager), Ben Marino (Security Guard) and Ricardo Montalban (Zach Powers)

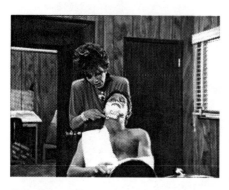

Caress vows to avenge her years of imprisonment by threatening to reveal Alexis and Ben's conspiracy behind Blake's trial unless she's paid five million dollars. Dana bitterly attacks Adam for using her to discover Blake's secret venture, "The Crater" project. An apparent reconciliation between Alexis and Caress results in a job at the Denver Mirror for Caress, and the beginning of her schemes for retribution. Michael Culhane uses Zach Powers, surreptitiously in his behalf, to offer Blake the $50 million loan he desperately needs. The transaction nets Culhane thirty percent of "The Crater" project and the perfect opportunity to crush Blake. Clay is less than ecstatic to learn Sammy Jo is pregnant. Caress promises to reveal Emily Fallmont's past with Ben unless she's paid $100,000. A devastated Emily turns to Ben for advice. As Caress enters her car, shots ring out, shattering her window, narrowly missing her and thwarting her attempted murder. Michael seduces Amanda and very much against Blake's adamant objections, Amanda moves in with the conniving chauffeur.

"The Secret" – Episode 7.9
Original Airdate - December 3, 1986
Written by Dennis Turner
Directed by Don Medford

Guest Appearances by Kimberly Beck (Claire Prentice) and Cliff Murdock (Concierge)

Caress continues her relentless extortion of Emily Fallmont, who turns to Blake, her only hope. Sammy Jo is hurt by Clay's suggestion that she have an abortion. Danny's nursery school teacher, Claire Prentice, shows Steven some of Danny's drawings showing that he's a deeply troubled little boy. Clay shows up  at Sammy Jo's door and proposes a Las Vegas wedding. Alexis uses the information she requested on Michael Culhane to expose his charade to Amanda. He pleads with Amanda to believe his love for her is real, confessing he loaned the money to her father and promising to never use it against him--as long as she keeps the information secret. Amanda forgives Michael and resumes her romance with him. Caress tells Alexis she's leaving Denver for good and begs her to watch out for Ben because he's dangerous. Suffering from the pressure of Caress' blackmailing schemes, Emily goes to Buck with the truth that she was with Ben the night of Blake's mother's death. Fleeing from Buck's drunken, verbal abuse, Emily runs blindly in front of a speeding taxi, throwing her nearly lifeless body to the pavement.

"The Letter" – Episode 7.10
Original Airdate - December 10, 1986
Written by Harold Livingston
Directed by George Sanford Brown

Kimberly Beck (Claire Prentice), Donald Jones Craig (Justice of the Peace), Cliff Murdock (Concierge), Mark Voland (Cabbie) and William J. Woff (Bellboy)

As life slowly fades from Emily's body, she whispers a loving goodbye to Buck. As Blake holds the letter she left for him, he reads as it reveals the truth behind Alexis and Ben's lies and begs him to use it to clear his name. Alexis discovers Michael Culhane secretly acquired thirty percent of The Crater project behind Blake's back. She plots to possess the shares for her own sinister deeds. Upon learning of his mother's tragic death, Clay and Sammy Jo return from their Las Vegas wedding, only to suffer the hateful wrath of Buck's drunkenness and consuming guilt. Sammy Jo renews her threat to take Danny away from Steven. Nick Kimball sweeps an unsuspecting Dominique into his arms, as the two share a moment of passion. Michael Culhane confesses his quest for revenge to Blake in hopes of winning his trust and proving his love for Amanda. An outraged Blake discounts his confession as more treachery and vows to use Emily's letter to bring Alexis and Ben to justice.

"The Ball" – Episode 7.11
Original Airdate - December 17, 1986
Written by Edward de Blasio
Directed by Nancy Malone

Guest Appearances by Carole Cook (Cora Van Heusen), Chris Cote (Randy), Madison Mason (Gary Tilden), Ed Penney (General), Bill Traylor (Dan Franklin), Diana Webster (Dr. Nadine Craig)

Armed with Emily Fallmont's incriminating letter, Blake searches for the witnesses who testified against him at his trial. Blake anticipates crashing Alexis' opulent bash and finally revealing the truth of Alexis and Ben's perjury against him. Sammy Jo's doctor informs her she is not pregnant. Disputing the diagnosis

and fearing the outcome, she keeps the news secret from Clay. Unable to buy back The Crater stocks from Michael Culhane, Blake shuts down operation on the project, fearing Alexis' determination to possess the stocks for her own vindictive schemes. At Denver's grand ball, Blake presents Alexis and Ben with signed affidavits from Dan Franklin and Cora Van Heusen, key witnesses in his murder trial. Savoring his moment of triumph, Blake challenges them to relinquish his holdings or face legal humiliation when he makes the facts public. Despite Ben's objections, Alexis knows Blake's not bluffing and reluctantly signs documents returning both the mansion and Denver Carrington immediately. He in return agrees not to prosecute them and tells Alexis that she can have one more night in the mansion and to be sure to "sleep in the master bedroom. I'm having it disinfected in the morning."

"Fear" – Episode 7.12
Original Airdate - December 31, 1986
Written by Dennis Turner
Directed by Michel Hugo

Guest Appearances by Kimberly Beck (Claire Prentice) and Frank Kahlil Wheaton (Lab Technician)

Battling Alexis for equal control of Colbyco, Ben threatens to reveal the truth behind their deceitful crusade against Blake. Blake approaches his maligned brother with an offer of reconciliation, only to have Ben vow to continue his vendetta against him. Alexis moves into a suite at The Carlton Hotel and shares a tender afternoon with Dex. Seeing how frightened she is when Ben calls barking orders, he vows to help her no matter what is wrong. Steven, recovering from a hangover induced by an old acquaintance's proposition, is forced to confide his gay lifestyle to Claire. A mutual alliance between Michael Culhane and Alexis to seek vengeance against Blake is sealed with a champagne toast. Upon reading a slanderous column in Alexis' newspaper, Dominique confronts the deflated empress and a good old cat-fight ensues. After having nightmares of being thrown in jail, Alexis calls Adam asking him to help her figure out how to get him out of their lives forever. Remembering the affects of the mysterious phone calls from Australia on Ben, Alexis sends Adam to Sydney to learn more of Ben's sordid past.

"The Rig" – Episode 7.13
Original Airdate - January 7, 1987
Written by Harold Stone
Directed by Irving J. Moore

Guest Appearances by Kimberly Beck (Claire Prentice), Philip English (Jim Wilkerson), Joy Garrett (Vera Nesbit), Dana Lee (Han Li Su), Ian Ruskin (Man in Pub), Michael Tulin (Telephone Clerk)

Sammy Jo continues to keep her false pregnancy a secret from Clay, fearing his adverse reaction upon learning the truth. Blake prepares to fly to Hong Kong with Ben and Alexis to finalize the return of his South China Sea oil leases. Krystle, concerned for her husband's safety, threatens to have Ben sent to prison if anything should happen to Blake. While in Sydney, searching for information to use against Ben, Adam happens across Ben's long lost daughter, Leslie. He discovers what he has been searching for, the mysterious woman plaguing Ben with phone calls, Vera Nesbitt. A bribe soon has her working for Adam. The name Vera Nesbitt sobers Ben into a nervous panic and he agrees to grant Alexis freedom from his demands. Upon returning from Australia, Adam goes to Dana and confesses his love to her. Michael admits to a disheartened Amanda his plans to file a lawsuit against her father over the Crater project. While inspecting his oil rig in the South China Sea, an explosion traps Blake under a steel beam. He begs Ben for help but Ben stands there watching his brother suffer and forms a slight grin as he listens to Blake's pleas.

"A Love Remembered: Part One" – Episode 7.14
Original Airdate - January 14, 1987
Written by Edward De Blasio
Directed by Robert Scheerer

Guest Appearances by Conrad Buchmann (Dr. Albans), Darrell Kunitoni (Male Nurse), Clyde Kusatsu (Dr. Chen), Khin-Kyaw Maung (Passport Clerk) and Gary Alan Wong (Houseman)

A sudden change of heart compels Ben to help his brother, and the two brothers narrowly escape the destruction of the massive explosion. Alexis waits pensively for news of Blake's condition as he is examined at a Singapore hospital. The doctor caring for him fills Alexis in on his condition and speaks of Blake suffering from memory loss, not being able to remember anything past 1964. Alexis immediately seizes the notion of using Blake's condition to get half of the South China Sea leases transferred back to her name and tells the doctor that she is Mrs. Carrington. Word of the explosion reaches Denver. Krystle and Dex, concerned for Blake's and Alexis' safety, fly to Hong Kong to search for their missing loved ones. Sammy Jo suffers a serious blow from a horse and is rushed to the hospital. Clay soon learns Sammy Jo was never pregnant and suspects her of tricking him into marrying her. Alexis' charade leads Blake to believe he has been happily married to her for the past twenty-three years and the two begin sharing old memories and wonderful moments together. Alexis melts as Blake holds her close and says he loves her and she in turn confesses her undying love for him. The following night Blake gives her the documents assigning half of the leases to her. Realizing that the leases aren't really what she wants, Alexis tears the paper in half and returns to Blake's unsuspecting arms.

"A Love Remembered: Part Two" – Episode 7.15
Original Airdate - January 21, 1987
Written by Edward de Blasio
Directed by Irving J. Moore

Guest Appearances by Jose DeVega (Private Investigator), Dian Kobayashi (Maid), Clyde Kusatsu (Dr. Chen), Helaine Lembeck (Nurse), Madison Mason (Gary Tilden) and Marcus Mukai (Administrative Clerk)

Suffering from Clay's suspicions that she tricked him into marrying her, Sammy Jo finds solace and a renewed friendship in Steven. Krystle and Dex continue their search for Blake and Alexis. Alexis' charade to take advantage of an amnesiac Blake fades into a sincere rekindling of  their past marriage and a tremendous feeling of guilt as he shares his emotions telling her that nothing will ever change between them. Dominique is confronted by Gary Tilden. Despite her adamant rejection of his business proposition, Tilden vows she hasn't heard or seen the last of him. Claiming to have given their present situation much thought, Sammy Jo shocks Clay with a request for an annulment to their marriage. Alone in her studio, Dominique is roughed-up and threatened by two hoods, until Nick Kimball surprises the thugs and comes to her rescue. Reacting to a tip, Krystle finds Alexis and demands to see Blake, only to have him fail to recognize her. The incident proves painful for Blake and he pleads with Alexis to explain what is happening to him. A tearful Alexis fills Blake in on the years he's lost and the fact that Krystle is his wife but begs him to believe that the longer they spent together the more Alexis just wanted to be near him, which is why she tore up the lease documents. An enraged Blake rejects her reasoning, causing his memory to become clearer. Blake and Krystle are finally reunited.

"The Portrait" – Episode 7.15
Original Airdate - January 21, 1987
Written by Edward de Blasio
Directed by Nancy Malone

Guest Appearances by Cathleen McVeigh (Cathy)

Krystle fears Blake's recent days with Alexis may have renewed his feelings towards her. The arrival of the portrait of Blake, done by Alexis while in Singapore, only heightens her suspicions. Following Ben's courageous act of rescuing Blake from the devastating explosion, Blake extends a sincere offer of friendship. Amanda disappears to London, leaving only a note which claims she had been unable to decide between Blake and Michael Culhane. A concerned Blake agrees not to search for his daughter. Alexis is loath to think Steven and Sammy Jo may be drawing closer together. Leslie Carrington arrives in Denver, searching for Ben. Their reunion is less than joyful, as Leslie blasts Ben for making her mother leave him. Before Ben has a chance to explain the truth, Leslie flees in tears. Clay confronts Steven concerning his motives towards Sammy Jo. A fight ensues between Clay and Steven. Sammy Jo is able to restrain the two, but Clay vows to never give her up.

"The Birthday" – Episode 7.17
Original Airdate – February 4,1987
Written by Dennis Turner
Directed by Robert Scheerer

Guest Appearances by Linda Thorson (Doctor Mansfield)

Although reluctant to end their brief marriage, Clay gives in to Sammy Jo's demands and signs their annulment papers. Sympathizing over Ben's heartfelt loss following Leslie Carrington's bitter assault on him, Blake meets with Leslie to persuade her to give Ben a second chance. Dana accepts Adam's marriage proposal.

Upon learning the good news, Alexis is quick to begin planning the entire affair. Included in her plans is the possibility of causing a rift between Blake and Krystle by having the wedding in the Carrington mansion. Having had enough of her manipulation and lies, Dex informs a stunned Alexis that he is leaving her for good. Dominique and Nick fail to realize their need for each other. Dominique and Dex are drawn together for friendship and support. As Krystina's third birthday bash draws near, she suffers a serious loss of breath and is rushed to the hospital. Krystle and Blake wait helplessly as their little girl fights for her life.

"The Test" – Episode 7.18
Original Airdate – February 11, 1987
Written by Dennis Turner
Directed by Nancy Malone

Guest Appearances by Marieta Marrow (Nurse #2), Julie Hampton (Nurse #1), Alan Haufrect (Dr. Harold Chadway), David Hess (Doctor #1) and Linda Thorson (Dr. Mansfield)

Alexis is reluctant to pursue a billion dollar venture put forth by a confident Michael Culhane. Suffering from congestive heart failure, Krystina overexerts herself and suddenly collapses again. She remains in an unconscious state until doctors are able to regain her vital signs. Krystle and Blake helplessly stand by. Dana fears something may come between her and Adam, preventing their plans of marriage. Upon hearing the news of Krystina, Alexis rushes to the hospital to see Blake. Krystle reacts bitterly to her presence, requesting Alexis to leave and stay away from her family. Despite a brave front, Alexis is badly hurt. For Danny's sake, Steven and Sammy Jo agree to assume the appearance of a normal marriage, sharing the same roof, but not the same bed. Following the incident with Krystle, Alexis flies to Los Angeles to be with Jeff and Fallon, and their new baby. Coming as a complete surprise to Alexis, Michael Culhane follows her, professing concern for her. The result of Krystina's heart biopsy reveals a serious heart ailment. Krystle and Blake learn Krystina will need a heart transplant or she will die.

"The Mothers" – Episode 7.19
Original Airdate – February 25, 1987
Written by Edward de Blasio
Directed by Irving J. Moore

Guest Appearances by Jack Axelrod (Charlie), Freddye Chapman (Nurse #1), Jane Downs (TV Director), Matthew Faison (Dr. Holland), Duncan Gamble (Boyd Curtis), Alan Haufrect (Dr. Harold Chadway), Bunky Jones (Nurse #2), Ted Lehmann (Bill), Ed Nelson (Sam Dexter), Brett Stimely (Bellman) and Barbara Whinnery (Woman in Hospital)

Krystina is flown to California to await a suitable donor for her heart transplant. Leslie arrives at the Carrington mansion, suitcases in hand, after accepting Krystle's invitation to move in. Ben takes advantage of his daughter's arrival to hopefully win back her affections. Dex and Dominique pay his father, Sam Dexter, a visit on his Wyoming ranch. As time runs out for Krystina, Blake and Krystle begin a frantic search for a heart donor by initiating a media blitz. Included, is a front-page headline in Alexis' newspaper. Dex is grieved by the news of his best friend's death, and the imminent death of his young daughter. When realizing this tragic news may offer hope for Krystina, he quickly contacts Blake. Blake flies to Wyoming to meet with Sarah Curtis, the mother of the now brain-dead little girl. In a difficult moment for both, he persuades her to allow the heart transplant that may save Krystina's life, as the good news unites the entire Carrington family. A nemesis from the Carrington past, Neil McVane, returns to Denver. He confronts Adam with evidence, acquired while serving time in prison, that will prove Adam is not a Carrington.

"The Surgery" – Episode 7.20
Original Airdate – March 4, 1987
Written by Frank V. Furino
Directed by Gwen Arner

Guest Appearances by Matthew Faison (Dr. Holland), Nancy Locke (Adam's Secretary) and Robert Symonds (Dr. Jonas Edwards)

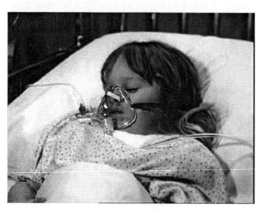

Krystle and Blake are stunned to learn the heart donor's mother, Sarah Curtis, has had second thoughts on allowing the surgery. Neil McVane carries out his promise of blackmail, as Adam receives a baby booty with his name sewn on it. This is evidence which McVane claims will prove Adam is not the Carrington baby that was kidnapped many years before. Dex, sympathizing with Sarah's plight, is able to use their friendship to persuade Sarah to give her permission for the surgery. Following the operation, a tense Krystle and Blake receive cautious optimism from the operating surgeon. Only time will tell if Krystina's body will accept the new heart. En route to ask Dex for a job, Leslie is involved in a minor traffic dispute with Clay. After being offered an apprentice job by Dex, Leslie is disheartened to learn she will be working directly with Clay. An apprehensive Adam desperately searches for clues to his childhood that will prove him to be a Carrington. Dana and Alexis begin to suspect his strange behavior.

"The Garage" – Episode 7.21
Original Airdate – March 11, 1987
Written by Dennis Turner
Directed by Don Medford

Guest Appearances by Jill Andre (Nurse Johnson), Jane Downs (Reporter #2), Matthew Faison (Dr. Holland), Chip Johnson (Reporter #1), Cleveland O'Neal (Photographer) and Robert Symonds (Dr. Jonas Edwards)

The Carrington family gathers to offer Krystina a joyous welcoming on her arrival home. Dirk Maurier, an arrogant California real estate baron, sets his sights on one of Denver's most prestigious assets, Alexis Colby. As Sarah Curtis' grief deepens, Blake and Krystle are unsuccessful in  contacting her to express their concern. Convinced that he is truly not a Carrington, Adam is forced to choke back the irony, as Blake forgives him for all his malicious past deeds and welcomes him back as his son and heir. Krystle flies to Wyoming and discovers Sarah, unconscious in a garage full of exhaust, apparently having attempted suicide. To make amends for their rocky start, Leslie and Clay have a night on the town. Neil McVane demands an invite to Alexis' party and makes an unwelcome impression. Upon Krystle's insistence, Sarah moves in to the Carrington mansion. Her presence near Krystina affects Blake with a looming uneasiness.

"The Shower" – Episode 7.22
Original Airdate – March 18, 1987
Written by Jonna Emerson
Directed by Irving J. Moore

Guest Appearances by Jill Andre (Nurse Johnson), Alan Haufrect (Dr. Harold Chadway), Ben Marino (Policeman), Renata Scott (Chambermaid) and Robert Symonds (Dr. Jonas Edwards)

Adam and Dana's relationship continues to deteriorate as a result of Adam's self-abuse over the doubts of his Carrington heritage. Alexis asks Steven to try and find what is causing Adam's destructive behavior. Dana unsuccessfully questions Dr. Edwards on Adam's mysterious past. Furious at Alexis' dismissal of their personal and professional relationship, Michael joins forces with Neal McVane to exact revenge. Ben is leery of Leslie's growing fondness for Clay, fearing he may be his illegitimate son with Emily. Returning from an encounter with Neal, Adam is arrested for drunk driving and incarcerated. Blake and Dex notice the unnatural attachment Sarah is forming with Krystina. When Krystle is forced to fire the nurse looking over Krystina, Sarah is quick to volunteer her services. Following a surprise wedding shower for Dana, Adam cruelly decides to call off the wedding.

"The Dress" – Episode 7.23
Original Airdate – March 25, 1987
Written by Frank V. Furino
Directed by Gwen Arner

Guest Appearances by Nancy Locke (Adam's Secretary), Viviane Lord (Nurse), Natalia Nogulich (April), Hale Porter (Bartender) and Frank Schuller (Private Detective)

Krystle and Blake fear the worst upon discovering Krystina missing from her room. Their worries are quickly relieved when they find her sleeping, cradled in Sarah's arms. Blake is suspicious of Adam's motives for canceling his and Dana's wedding. Blake hires a private investigator to  find the cause of Adam's irrational behavior. Adam's despair grows as he reluctantly agrees to involve Neal McVane in an illegal insider-trading scheme with one of Alexis' companies. Greatly disturbed by the loss of her own little girl, Sarah makes Krystina a dress that is an exact copy of one worn by her daughter. Sammy Jo and Steven share a night by an intimate fire and their passionate feelings drawing them together. Leslie and Clay encounter Buck Fallmont and after discovering Leslie to be a Carrington, his drunken rage heightens. Leslie is mystified by his father's offensive outbursts. Ben confronts Buck, but is bitterly rebuffed by his unrelenting hatred.

"Valez" – Episode 7.24
Original Airdate – April 1, 1987
Written by Dennis Turner and Rita Lakin
Directed by Nancy Malone

Guest Appearances by Janet Adams (Liz), Blake Conway (Vet), Gary Costello (Jay), Bunky Jones (Maid) and Madeleine Sherwood (Tenant)

Steven questions his love for Sammy Jo and his homosexuality. As usual, Alexis disregards Dex's warning of Dirk Maurier's unscrupulous business practices, agreeing to a partnership in his plans for a subversive takeover of Trouville Industries. Leslie and Clay's bond turns to passionate love. Dominique discovers Sarah's photo album, revealing the bereaved mother's attempts to make Krystina resemble her own deceased little girl. Convinced Adam is in serious trouble, Blake promises to find what is causing his son's suddenly volatile behavior. Venting his frustration by riding Danny's horse at a dangerously fast pace, Steven is thrown, resulting in serious injuries to the horse. Reeling from his inner conflict, Steven moves out of the ranch, claiming to be leaving those he is hurting the most. Krystle, aware of Sarah's psychologically unbalanced attachment to Krystina, asks her to leave the mansion. Unable to part from the little girl, Sarah kidnaps Krystina, disappearing without a trace.

"The Sublet" – Episode 7.25
Original Airdate – April 8, 1987
Written by Edward de Blasio
Directed by Don Medford

Guest Appearances by Richard Caine (Butler), Ala Haufrect (Dr. Harold Chadway), J.J. Johnston (Gym Manager), Damu King (Policeman), Jeff O'Haco (Fighter), Mark Sisson (Bellman), John Howard Swain (Sergeant Benson) and Dianne Turley Travis (Woman on the Phone)

Blake and Krystle wait helplessly as an all-points-bulletin is put out for Sarah and Krystina. Adam betrays Alexis' trust by tipping Neal McVane off to her and Dirk Maurier's stock buyout of Trouville Industries. Hiding out in a leased apartment, Sarah convinces herself Krystina is her little girl. 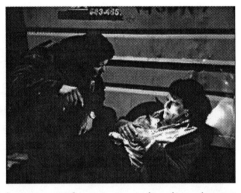 Krystina, missing her family and home, refuses to take her heart medicine, resulting in a dangerous risk of rejecting her new heart. Having reaped the benefits of three very successful oil wells, Nick Kimball jets Dominique off to San Francisco for dinner, and caps the evening off with a proposal of marriage. In a drunken haze, Adam wanders the streets looking for the abuse he feels he deserves. Krystle finds an address circled in the newspaper. At the apartment, Krystle persuades Sarah to open the door, reuniting mother and daughter.

"The Confession" – Episode 7.26
Original Airdate – April 22, 1987
Written by A. J. Russell
Directed by Irving J. Moore

Guest Appearances by Janet Adams (Secretary), JoAnne Astrow (Dr. Miller), Will Carney (Bellman), Michelle Davison (Sergeant), Neil Dickson (Gavin Maurier), Alan Haufrect (Dr. Harold Chadway), Barry Pierce (Manager), Geof Prysirr (Concierge) and John Howard Swain (Sergeant Benson)

Following the stock plunge of Trouville Industries and his large financial loss as a result, Dirk Maurier confronts Alexis. He accuses Adam of being responsible for the insider-trading scheme. Krystle and Blake drop all charges against Sarah and place her under private psychiatric care. Adam, unable to tolerate Neal McVane's blackmail any longer, confesses his true identity to Blake and Alexis, leaving them stunned. Wanting to free them of his deceptive lies, Adam leaves, vowing to never return. Waiting to give Nick Kimball an answer to his marriage proposal, Dominique is surprised by Jackie's return to Denver, and her news that Garrett is still very much in love with her. Adam returns to Denver following a visit to his mother's grave in Montana. Putting aside the past, Dana passionately welcomes Adam back into her life. As Dana and Adam prepare to leave Denver, Blake persuades Adam to believe he will always be his son and a Carrington. Gavin Maurier, nephew of Dirk, arrives in Denver, searching for Alexis and her money, to pick up where his uncle's failures left off.

"The Affair" – Episode 7.27
Original Airdate – April 29, 1987
Written by Frank V. Furino
Directed by Don Medford

Guest Appearances by JoAnne Astrow (Dr. Miller), Neil Dickson (Gavin Maurier) and Randy Olea (Workman)

Blake is stunned by Buck Fallmont's claim that Clay may be Ben's son. Concerned for Clay and Leslie's well being, Blake tells Clay the shocking news. Hoping to reunite her mother and father, Jackie asks Nick to stay away from Dominique. When her efforts fail, Jackie makes plans to  return to her father. Krystle attempts to bring Sarah to face the reality of her baby's death by bringing her to the gravesite. The realization proves painful for both Sarah and Krystle, as Sarah is finally able to accept the tragic loss of her baby. Fearing that Ben may be his father, Clay confides in Leslie the possibility that they may be brother and sister. Leslie responds with rage towards Ben for not telling her sooner. Gavin Maurier treats Alexis to an unusual date on the back of a motorcycle, which leaves Alexis intrigued by the mysterious and younger Maurier. Krystle is angered to find a workman lingering after the completion of alterations for Adam and Dana's wedding. As surprisingly as the man appeared, he vanishes through an open door, leaving Krystle concerned over the encounter.

"Shadow Play" – Episode 7.28
Original Airdate – May 6, 1987
Written by Edward de Blasio
Directed by Irving J. Moore

Guest Appearances by Robert Balderson (Alfred), Neil Dickson (Gavin Maurier), Ray Genadry (Stranger #1), Russell Johnson (Earl Thompson), Fredrick Lopez (Stranger #2), Ron Rescaner (Will) and Darrell Zwerling (Minister)

Krystle is haunted by an eerie sense of foreboding following the appearance of mysterious shadows beneath her window. A blood test to determine the identity of Clay's real father proves inconclusive, causing Clay and Ben's decision to leave Denver. Steven's decision to leave Denver results in further pain and confusion for those that love him the most. Adam is awed and overjoyed by Blake and Alexis' demonstration of love by officially adopting him. Swept away by the romance and splendor of Adam and Dana's wedding, Dominique accepts Nick's proposal of marriage. Struggling with her loneliness following the wedding, Alexis flees in a state of emotional duress. Her car plunges off a bridge and falls into the river. The joyous atmosphere of the wedding is shattered as mysterious men besiege the mansion and round up the Carrington family. Krystle's ominous suspicions are confirmed when she recognizes one of the men as Matthew Blaisdel, who has returned for her.

SEASON EIGHT

"The Siege: Part One" – Episode 8.1
Original Airdate – September 23, 1987
Written by Edward de Blasio
Directed by Don Medford

Guest Appearances by Wren Brown (Policeman), Ray Genadry (Stranger #2), Chip Johnson (Dr. Wilton), Fredrick Lopez (Stranger #1), Don Matheson (Commander), Michael McGuire (Chief McHenry), Greg Mullavey (Sheriff) and Mark Phelan (SWAT Captain)

Being held captive by Matthew, the Carrington family tries to figure out a way to escape Witnessing Alexis' car plunge into the river, a handsome and mysterious stranger rescues her from the rushing current. Unaware of the tragedies that face their family, Adam and Dana are on their private jet, en route to their honeymoon paradise. Fallon's car is found abandoned in the desert. Receiving word of his wife's disappearance, Jeff rushes to the scene. Searching several miles from the car, Jeff finds her unconscious by the side of the road. Allowed to leave the mansion to secure a fortune in cash for Blaisdel's trip back to Peru, Blake overpowers his guard and goes for help. Determined to thank her mysterious rescuer, Alexis finds the man she feels indebted to, but is dismayed by his casual acceptance of her gratitude. Protecting Leslie after she tries to escape, Dex lunges at Matthew. In the ensuing fight, Dex finds an opportunity to run out the door and across the grounds for help. Blaisdel's accomplice steadies his gun and shoots Dex. Returning to the mansion, with a SWAT team covering him, Blake is terrified to find the mansion empty, except for the shredded remains of Krystina's doll.

"The Siege: Part Two" – Episode 8.2
Original Airdate – September 30, 1987
Written by Edward de Blasio
Directed by Don Medford

Guest Appearances by Robert Crow (First Aid Doctor), Ray Genadry (Stranger #2), Richard Kuhlman (SWAT Officer), Fredrick Lopez (Stranger #1), Michael McGuire (Chief McHenry), Mark Phelan (SWAT Captain), Reid Smith (Larry) and Milt Tarver (Dr. Ganton)

Dex is rushed to the hospital while a search party scrambles to locate the missing Carringtons, who are being held captive in a bunkhouse. Fear of the deranged Matthew forces Krystle to pretend that she still has feelings for him. Fallon insists she wants to go home to Denver after Jeff finds her unconscious in the desert. Adam's plans to have a child surprise Dana on their honeymoon. After discovering that her family is being held captive, Alexis joins Blake and the SWAT team covering the compound when the family is being held hostage. When he discovers that Matthew has rigged the cottage with explosives and Blake and Krystle are inside the house with him, Steven rushes to the rescue. He stabs Matthew in self-defense and the family's ordeal is over.

"The Aftermath" – Episode 8.3
Original Airdate – October 7, 1987
Written by Frank V. Furino
Directed by Irving J. Moore

Guest Appearances by Jordan Charney (Bill Cochran), Michael McGuire (Chief McHenry), Ray Stricklyn (Dr. Parris) and Steven Whiteford (Reporter)

The incident in the bunkhouse leaves Steven emotionally scarred. The police urge him to seek psychiatric help to deal with the trauma but Steven refuses to accept any even after Blake, Krystle and Alexis all try to get him to open up about the ordeal. Jeff and Fallon's unexpected homecoming helps everyone  put the tragedy behind them but Blake suspects that there is something troubling his daughter. Adam is suspicious when Dana keeps changing the subject when it comes to having children. Alexis is completely determined to find the mystery man who saved her life and asks Morgan Hess to locate him. Fallon confesses her experience to Jeff, but he doesn't know how to handle it. Blake emerges as a candidate in Colorado's gubernatorial race.

"The Announcement" – Episode 8.4
Original Airdate – October 14, 1987
Written by Frank V. Furino
Directed by Don Medford

Guest Appearances by Ian Abercrombie (Tom Bowman), Jordan Charney (Bill Cochran), Lisa Hilboldt (Rebecca Payne) and Thomas Ryan (Dr. Davis)

Blake asks Steven to be his campaign manager. He is deeply disappointed when Steven declines his offer, expressing no interest in exposing his private life to public scrutiny. Attributing Jeff and Fallon's intimacy with Blake to their giving him grandchildren, Adam continues to pressure Dana into starting a family. Alone, following Alexis' surprise catered dinner Sean Rowan carefully studies an old news clip of Blake's custody trial for Steven's son, Danny. Alexis is hounded by a reporter, Rebecca Payne, from an unscrupulous tabloid. Rebecca is seeking a comment on Alexis' recent decline in support for her gubernatorial candidacy. Sammy Jo is saddened by the realization that her and Steven's relationship will never have the closeness she has longed for. Taking up Alexis offer of a place to stay, Sean Rowan shows up at her Carlton hotel suite. Giving in to lust, they are drawn together in heated passion. Jeff is surprised by Blake's request to have him as his campaign manager. Intrigued by the offer, Jeff waits for Fallon's reaction before giving Blake an answer. Learning of Dana's appointment with her doctor, Adam rushes to his office, hoping for good news. His dreams of starting a family are crushed when he overhears Dana's doctor inform her she is unable to have children. Alexis contemplates the means at her disposal to thwart Blake's gubernatorial bid. With his own secret reasons for Blake's demise, Sean Rowan eagerly awaits Alexis' next move.

"The Surrogate: Part One" – Episode 8.5
Original Airdate – October 28, 1987
Written by James Harmon Brown and Barbara Esensten
Directed by Don Medford

Guest Appearances by Jane Downs (Mother), Fred Holliday (TV Host), Gary Hudson (Skip Maitland), Matt Stetson (Father) and Robert Symonds (Dr. Jonas Edwards)

Intrigued by Sean's unaccounted for mysterious interludes during the day, Alexis hires Morgan Hess to follow her enigmatic lover. But when he catches Hess spying on him, Sean returns to Alexis, informing her of his decision to leave Denver. Pleading with him to stay, Alexis offers him a job. Tortured by a secret from her past explaining her inability to bear children, Dana struggles about whether to tell Adam, and risk losing his love. Jeff accepts Blake's request to be his campaign manager, after learning Fallon has sent for L.B. Detained at Blake's fundraiser, Jeff cancels his and Fallon's reconciliation dinner further weakening their fragile marriage. Alexis commits Colbyco to fight Blake's proposal of saving valuable timberland as a national park, depriving her of a resource for her newspaper. Accepting Alexis' job offer, Sean asserts Adam's involvement is a conflict of interest, persuading her to let him take over control of the matter. Steven asks Blake to sell him the Denver Monarch's football team. Asking the team's quarterback, Josh Harris, to the ranch, Steven offers him a lucrative contract if he can pull the team together. Shaking hands on the deal, Sammy Jo walks in, immediately feeling attracted to the roguish quarterback. Tormented by Adam's desire to have children, Dana is filled with renewed hope after learning of the successes of surrogate mothers.

"The Surrogate: Part Two" – Episode 8.6
Original Airdate – November 4, 1987
Written by James Harmon Brown and Barbara Esensten
Directed by Don Medford

Guest Appearances by Mark S. Porro (Waiter), Mark Roberts (Harry Donalds) and Frank Schuller (Houser)

Stunned by the morning paper's praise for Blake's stand on conservation Alexis takes Sean's advice about pointing out another slant to the story. Using Blake's campaign pledge of saving the acres as depriving the state of badly needed jobs, Alexis sets out to undermine the public's opinion of Colorado's candidate. Researching the possibility of a surrogate mother, Dana sets up a meeting for her and Adam with a prospective candidate, Karen Atkinson. All of Adam's doubts to using a surrogate vanish when he sees her. A beautiful, single mother of two gorgeous children, Dana becomes jealous of Adam's obvious interest in her. Seeking more from life than what working for Dex has to offer, Leslie accepts Alexis' job proposition. Sensing the hostility between Jeff and Fallon, Blake invites them to dinner. Sharing a terse glance, they decline his offer. Jeff retreats to the study to work on countering Alexis' viperous editorial against Blake. Working late, he gives in to Leslie's playful persuasion. Following the artificial insemination, and the doctor's optimism that Karen may be pregnant, Adam embraces her, leaving Dana outcast and afraid. After he brings flowers as a peace offering for his brutish behavior, Sammy Jo allows Josh to kiss her. Witnessing the heated interlude, Steven breaks up their lustful encounter, as he is filled with a slow burning rage.

"The Primary" – Episode 8.7
Original Airdate – November 18, 1987
Written by Edward de Blasio
Directed by Irving J. Moore

Guest Appearances by Jeff Crawford (Stage Manager), Michelle Davison (Mrs. Johnson), Sandy McPeak (Arthur Whitcomb), Carlos Rivas (Justice of the Peace), Vernon Weddle (Mr. Alpert) and William S. Woff (TV Reporter)

Distraught over Blake's meteoric rise in pre-election popularity, Alexis gives in to Sean's persuasions, and he flies her off to a remote cabin on the Pacific coast of Mexico. Entranced by his romanticism, Alexis accepts his impromptu offer of marriage. Reacting to Steven's indifference and preoccupation with business, Sammy Jo gives in to Josh's passionate advances. Blake meets with Arthur Whitcomb, hoping to persuade him against selling the timberland leases to Alexis. Whitcomb has a change of heart and gives Blake the leases. Attending a support group for those who have encountered space aliens, Jeff finds the discussion too unbelievable and leaves without Fallon. Leslie offers Jeff a good luck kiss before the primary elections, as Fallon and Dex observe the moment with hurt feelings. Weary of Leslie's selfish ambitions, Dex tells Fallon it was Leslie who told him about her extraterrestrial encounter. Adam is overjoyed to learn Karen is pregnant with his child, as Dana feels left out of his excitement. Adam brings home an exquisite pair of earrings, lifting Dana out of her gloom, until she realizes they are for Karen. At Blake's election victory party, a jubilant Adam informs Blake he will have another grandchild. Doing her best to share the happiness, Dana offers her brightest smile, covering her emotional pain.

"The Testing" – Episode 8.8
Original Airdate – November 25, 1987
Written by Edward de Blasio
Directed by Don Medford

Guest Appearances by Will Carney (Pilot), Gary Hudson (Skip Maitland), Patricia McPherson (Victoria Anders), Maggie Roswell (Miss Penelope Shane) and Gilles Savard (Maitre D')

Forced to divest interests in Denver-Carrington to avoid conflict with his political career, Blake struggles to decide who in the family will assume power. Taking full advantage of Jeff's marital problems and vulnerability, Leslie shows up on the Carrington jet and flies with him to New York under the pretext of doing business for Alexis. Taking Dex's advice to call Jeff in an effort to save their marriage, Fallon is devastated when Leslie answers the phone. Blake walks in on Steven as he is reprimanding Josh Harris for his declining performance on the field. Impressed, Blake makes note of Steven's decisiveness in handling the situation. Sammy Jo is confused by her lingering feelings for Steven and her yearning feelings for Josh. Soon after Sammy Jo leaves, Skip Maitland, the original quarterback for the Monarchs, shows up at Josh's door with a vial of cocaine. Distraught by Fallon's coldness, Jeff takes Leslie to his room, asking her to stay the night. Blake asks Steven to run Denver-Carrington. Sean vows to avenge the suicide of his father, Joseph Anders, and the rape of his sister, Kirby. Blaming Alexis for his father's death, Sean promises to crush her and her family by using his influence on her to turn the family against themselves.

"The Setup" – Episode 8.9
Original Airdate – December 2, 1987
Written by James Harmon Brown and Barbara Esensten
Directed by Harry Falk

Guest Appearances by Michael Canavan (Editor), Carole Cook (Cora Van Heusen), Shannon Eubanks (Hooker), Jerome Front (Reporter #1), James Haskins (Reporter #2), Meta King (Reporter #3), Cynthia Leake (Anna Gregory) and John McCann (Football Coach)

Prodded on by Alexis' incessant questioning, Dana reluctantly explains the reason for her infertility was due to a botched abortion many years before. Suspecting Dana is manipulating Adam to selfishly benefit her own future, Alexis schemes to prevent Dana from legally becoming the mother of Adam's surrogate child.  Seeking to undermine Steven's position of power at Denver-Carrington, Adam anonymously informs the press of Skip Maitland's arrest for dealing drugs to players on Steven's football team. Returning from New York guilt stricken by his weekend affair with Leslie, Jeff hopes to work out his problems with Fallon. Concerned by his poor playing performance, Steven requests Josh Harris have a physical. Fearing his drug use will be detected Josh quits the team. After Alexis informs Sean of Dana's ill-fated abortion, he develops a strategy to use Dana to his advantage. Flying to Billings, Montana, Sean meets with a schoolmate of Dana's, discovering the father of her aborted child was Adam. Alexis invites Krystle and Blake to an Olde English Fair to benefit Krystle's drug rehabilitation program. Expecting a turnout of influential people affecting Blake's campaign, Alexis prepares a special surprise to hinder his political goals.

"The Fair" – Episode 8.10
Original Airdate – December 9, 1987
Written by James Harmon Brown and Barbara Esensten
Directed by Don Medford

Guest Appearances by Terrence Beasor (Beefeater), James "Gypsy" Haake (Caterer), Nick Lewin (Shell Game Man), Eric Magerum (Jester), Jim Piper (Magician), Ann Walker (Representative)

As Alexis' grand fair draws near, Sean assures her that all is going according to plan. Sean threatens to blackmail Dana with the truth about her abortion if she does not gather secret information on the Carringtons. After misinterpreting Sammy Jo's plea for him to not quit the team as meaning something more, Josh asks her to marry him. Devastated by her rejection, Josh reverts to his alcohol and drug addiction. While preparing to attend Alexis' Olde English Fair, Fallon informs Jeff of her decision to file for a divorce. Stunned by her sudden desire to end their marriage, Jeff storms from the room. Passing Leslie on his way out, a vulnerable Jeff is tempted by her offer to stop by her suite at the Carlton. Participating in the merriment of the Olde English Fair, Alexis and Krystle are chosen for a tug-of-war contest. Strung out between a pool of slosh, Alexis and Krystle pull ferociously until Alexis falls face first into the oozing mud. Conceding the first round to Krystle, Alexis promises more surprises to come. Climaxing the evening with a campaign film of Blake and Krystle touring the rehabilitation center, Alexis and Sean unveil their sinister scheme. Spliced into the film are scenes of Blake visiting Cora Van Heusen's brothel, the partygoers are stunned by the insinuation of Blake's infidelity.

"The New Moguls" – Episode 8.11
Original Airdate – December 23, 1987
Written by Frank V. Furino
Directed by Irving J. Moore

Guest Appearances by Carole Cook (Cora Van Heusen), Daniel Davis (Harry Thresher), Mike Garibaldi (Jeffrey Ames), Gary Hudson (Skip Maitland), John McCann (Football Coach), Cis Rundle (Hooker), Kirk Scott (Editor) and Anthony Winters (Vitron Secretary)

Krystle asks Cora Van Husen to relinquish information on the scandalous video of Blake in her brothel. Though reluctant at first, Cora hands a copy of the tape over. Calling a press conference to prove the tap had been tampered with, Blake is finally vindicated. A seething Alexis vows never to give up her campaign to destroy Blake. Dex accepts Fallon's request to check out a questionable oil deal in West Africa before she approves committing Denver- Carrington to a contract. Discovering the man in charge of the operation, Harry Thresher, is somehow tied in with Sean Rowan, Dex decides to stick around to find answers to the unraveling mystery. Jeff's pleas to work their problems out have no affect on Fallon. Finally admitting their relationship has fallen apart, Jeff agrees to see his lawyer. The realization that their marriage is lost fills Fallon with a deep sadness. Learning of Josh's cocaine addiction from Skip Maitland, Steven offers him a chance to take a drug test and get help for his self-destructive binge, or else be kicked off the team. Outraged by the ultimatum, Josh quits. Concerned when she can't reach him at his apartment, Sammy Jo stops by and finds Josh unconscious from a drug overdose.

"The Spoiler" – Episode 8.12
Original Airdate – December 30, 1987
Written by Frank V. Furino
Directed by Nancy Malone

Guest Appearances by Brian Avery (Ralph Dunbar), William Bassett (R. D. Fleming), Daniel Davis (Harry Thresher), Trent Dolan (Lieutenant), Mark Drexler (Photographer), Mike Horton (Mike), J.N. Houck (Coroner), Chris Hubbell (Man), Anthony Jackson (Bartender), Keith Jones (Keith), John McCann (Football Coach), Doug Simpson (Doug) and Charles Summers (Maitre D')

Following Josh Harris' drug overdose death, Sammy Jo carries a burden of guilt. Realizing her obsession to be with Steven is depriving her of an intimate relationship, Sammy Jo asks Steven to move out of her Delta Rho ranch. Steven is pressured by the press and Jeff to administer drug testing on his team. Troubled by crisis in his personal and professional life, Steven welcomes the surprise visit of his old friend, Chris Deegan. Steven is shocked by the team's decision to volunteer for the tests in order to alleviate the stress it has placed on Steven and on Blake's campaign. After Dex returns from Natumbe, Steven reprimands him and Fallon for going against his orders. Sean's amorous moves are shot down by a brooding Alexis. Alexis' indifference sends Sean looking for affection in Leslie's hotel suite. Jeff asks Sammy Jo to accompany Danny, L.B., and him on a weekend skiing trip. Before leaving, Jeff is presented with Fallon's divorce papers. Discovering a new angle for destroying Blake's campaign, Alexis calls a late night press conference to declare herself an independent candidate for governor.

"The Interview" – Episode 8.13
Original Airdate – January 6, 1988
Written by Edward De Blasio
Directed by Harry Falk

Guest Appearances by Jordan Charney (Bill Cochran), Nathan Haas (Aide), Robert Harland (James Rayford), Chris Kriesa (Dan) and James Mackrell (Deselles)

Following a night of lovemaking with Leslie, Sean hears a news report announcing Alexis' bid for governor. Seeing an opportunity to avenge his father's death, Sean returns to Alexis in order to get back into her good favor. Alexis asks Sean to assume control of Colbyco so she can  concentrate on the election. At the mountain cabin with Jeff and the kids, Sammy Jo contemplates her failed marriage and her inadequacies as a mother. Jeff comforts Sammy Jo and a new bond forms between them. Karen urges Dana to tell Adam that he was the father of the baby she aborted in high school. Adam is bitter when Dana finally tells him and he accuses her of murdering his child. Adam turns to Karen for solace and confides his worry that the baby she's carrying will come to a bad end. Karen reassures Adam and gives him an innocent kiss which Dana witnesses and misinterprets. Alexis sabotages Blake's televised debate and then tries to steal his thunder. Krystle fills in for Blake and capably defends him against Alexis' political insults. Trying to think of a way to get back at Alexis, Krystle remembers Alexis' hasty marriage to Cecil Colby before he died. Krystle wonders if she can prove that he didn't die from natural causes and somehow implicate Alexis.

"Images" – Episode 8.14
Original Airdate – January 13, 1988
Written by Frank V. Furino and Jeff Ryder
Directed by Harry Falk

Guest Appearances by Paul Cavonis (Drunk), Robert I. Clarke (Minister), Daniel Davis (Harry Thresher), Glenn Dixon (Caretaker), Don Dubbins (Dr. Louden), Michael Goodwin (Russ Kelton), John Larch (Gerald Wilson), Lavelle Roby (Nurse) and Bradley Thomas (Bellboy)

Ignoring Blake's objections, Krystle continues her investigation into Alexis' deathbed marriage to Cecil Colby. Krystle learns Alexis wielded her influence over the hospital administrators to persuade Cecil's doctor to allow the highly unusual wedding. Leslie follows Sean to his father's gravesite and discovers his true identity as Joseph Anders' son. Threatening to reveal his charade, Leslie coerces Sean to accept her as an equal partner in his scheme. Heeding Sammy Jo's advice, Dana returns to Adam. Realizing he almost her forever, Adam holds Dana in a desperate embrace. After Dana tells Adam of Sean's blackmail, he calls Sean, promising to kill him if he hurts Dana again. Fallon and Dex fly to Natumbe to check out the Vitron oil deal. Satisfied with what Harry Thresher has to show her, Fallon decides to fight Steven in favor of the deal. Celebrating her affirmative stance, a very drunk Fallon is carried out of a local club by Dex, as an enterprising bartender catches the moment on film. Krystle promises to reveal the findings from her investigation to the press if Alexis does not withdraw from the election. Hoping that Krystle is bluffing, Alexis watches in horror as Krystle challenges her to call her bluff, before turning and confidently walking from the room.

"The Rifle" – Episode 8.15
Original Airdate – January 20, 1988
Written by Frank V. Furino
Directed by Irving J. Moore

Guest Appearances by Peter Crook (Reporter), Daniel Davis (Harry Thresher), Robert Harland (James Rayford), John Larch (Gerald Wilson) and Josef Rainer (Moderator)

Alexis begins having nightmares about Cecil's death and fears about Blake. Sean prepares to leave for Natumbe to finalize his deal with Harry Thrasher. Leslie convinces Sean to let her join him on the trip. Alexis tries to persuade Gerald Wilson, Cecil's personal lawyer, to  work for Colbyco. Instead of helping Alexis, Gerald gives Krystle a copy of Cecil's original will. Krystle learns the will was changed soon after Cecil and Alexis were married. Krystle thinks she finally has solid evidence against Alexis. Steven is outvoted and reluctantly authorizes the Vitron oil deal. Sean's vendetta against Alexis and the Carringtons is put into effect. Alexis has second thoughts about running for governor when a reporter hints at a scandal behind her marriage to Cecil. Realizing that Alexis running for governor is crucial to his revenge scheme, Sean tries to convince her to remain in the race. As she prepares to debate against Blake, Alexis questions whether or not she should run. In the rafters, a rifleman trains a gun below. Blake begins the debate unaware that a rifle is trained on his heart. Alexis stands with the intention of withdrawing from the debate and she unwittingly stands in front of Blake and takes the bullet meant for him.

"The Bracelet" – Episode 8.16
Original Airdate – January 27, 1988
Written by James Harmon Brown and Barbara Esensten
Directed by Don Medford

Guest Appearances by Beau Billingslea (Doctor), Jordan Charney (Bill Cochran), Michael Goodwin (Russ Kelton), Michael Gray (Photographer), Robert Harland (James Rayford), Marykate Harris (Reporter #2), Mark High (Uniformed Policeman), Karen Ragan (Tenant), Josef Rainer (Moderator), Chuck Sloan (Reporter #1) and Robert Wilson (Tony)

As Blake holds a bleeding Alexis, Sean scrambles because he's hit the wrong person. Recovering from her wounds, Alexis tells Blake she has decided to withdraw from the election. But when she becomes aware of her sudden rise in popularity, she reconsiders. Determined to unleash his frustrated sexual energy on Leslie, Sean drags her into Alexis' bedroom. Struggling against him, Leslie's bracelet falls off and rolls unseen under the bed. Deciding to speed his plan up, he flies to Natumbe. Thinking Sean is skimming profits off the top of the Vitron oil deal, Leslie follows him, demanding a piece of the action. Karen's husband, Jesse, shows up and tells her he never signed the final divorce papers, making them still legally married. After Jeff bails Sammy Jo out of her financial debts, Steven offers him a warning to stay away from his ex-wife. Saving Sammy Jo from an attempted rape, Jeff stays with her for the night. Dex shows Alexis a picture he found in Harry Thresher's desk, revealing Sean and Thresher to be good friends. After finding Leslie's bracelet under her bed, Alexis knows Sean and Leslie are together in Natumbe.

"The Warning" – Episode 8.17
Original Airdate – February 3, 1988
Written by James Harmon Brown and Barbara Esensten
Directed by Don Medford

Guest Appearances by Reed Armstrong (Bellhop), Michael Goodwin (Russ Kelton), Bill Holloway (Reporter), Kimberly Holman (Kelly), Richard Jacobs (Reporter), Marybeth Manning (Lillian) and Pamela Roberts (Reporter)

Suspecting that Alexis knows about her and Sean's passionate rendezvous, Leslie vows to take Sean down with her if she loses her job. Outraged by her threat, Sean plants a venomous snake in her hotel room. Arriving just in time, he grabs the snake and holds it close to her, emphasizing his distaste for  the game she is playing. Fearful that Jesse will complicate the legal procedures for taking custody of Karen's surrogate baby, Adam bribes him to leave town. Finding out about the bribe, Karen loses all faith in Jesse and his promise that he has changed. Realizing his mistake, Jesse gives the money back. After hearing Jesse tell Adam all he wants is Karen, Sean warns him to keep their bargain to make Adam's life a living hell by suing for custody of Karen's child. Despite the attempt to ignore her feelings for Jeff by putting her energies into Delta Rho, Sammy Jo can't stop herself from falling in love with him. Concerned about the recent purchase of Denver-Carrington stock, Steve, Fallon, and Adam are stunned to learn Jeff is the one buying his influence into the company. Threatening to initiate a proxy fight for control of the company, Jeff demands a seat on the executive committee for all pipeline business, with Dex heading up the project.

"Adam's Son" – Episode 8.18
Original Airdate – February 10, 1988
Written by Edward de Blasio and Jeff Ryder
Directed by Nancy Malone

Guest Appearances by Danielle Aubry (Maid), Bruce Berman (Campaign Worker), Kathleen Holly (Doctor) and Robert Pucci (Campaign Worker)

After walking in on Adam and Jesse locked in a bitter fight, Karen is shoved into a chair and the impact puts her into labor. Waiting pensively at the hospital, neither Adam nor Jesse can let go of their overwhelming resentment for each other. Jeff resigns as Blake's campaign manager after Blake voices his displeasure over Jeff's tactics in maneuvering into Denver- Carrington. Reconfirming his alliance to Blake, Jeff turns down Alexis' offer to come to work for her. Accompanying Sammy Jo to Los Angeles for a horse auction, Jeff stops by her hotel suite after spending the day together at the beach. Feeling herself falling in love with Jeff, she allows herself to surrender to his passionate kisses. Sean threatens to kill Leslie if she quits her job at Colbyco, fearing it would confirm Alexis' suspicions about their affair. Scared for her own safety, Leslie turns to Dex, telling him she knows Sean's true identity. Suspecting Sean is seeking vengeance for his father's suicide, Dex warns Alexis. Not wanting to believe that Sean is trying to destroy her, Alexis wonders with horror if Dex's accusations are true. Overjoyed by the birth of his son, Adam holds the baby in his arms. But his and Dana's jubilation is shattered when Karen asks for the baby back and with tears in her eyes, tells them she can't give up her baby.

"The Scandal" – Episode 8.19
Original Airdate – March 2, 1988
Written by Edward de Blasio
Directed by Irving J. Moore

Guest Appearances by Ian Abercrombie (Tom Bradfield), Danielle Aubry (Maid), John Boehnke (Campaign Worker), Paul Burke (Neal McVane), Daniel Davis (Harry Thresher), Ben Marino (Process Server), John Milford (Captain Lard Nordstrom) and George Murdock (Charlie Braddock)

Certain Sean is intent on exacting revenge for his father's death, Alexis warns Blake that their family may be at risk. Taking Dex with him, Blake leaves for Natumbe to uncover Sean's mysterious dealings with the Vitron oil deal. Uncertain of her future with Jeff, and not wanting to get hurt, Sammy  Jo asks him to keep their romance a secret until they know for certain what they are feeling is permanent. Returning to Denver to capitalize on Alexis' bid for political office, Neal McVane is paid an unexpected visit from Adam. Forcing McVane to name his source on the Carrington kidnapping, Adam finds him and questions him on what he knows. To his great satisfaction, Adam learns that he truly was the Carrington baby that was kidnapped. His elation is short lived, however, when he is served papers for Karen's custody suit to keep the baby. Blake and Dex discover the illegal arms shipment, but they are locked in the hold of the tanker. Seconds before Sean sets the tanker ablaze in a thunderous explosion, Dex blasts their way to safety using grenades from the arms shipment. Certain that Sean was killed in the explosion, Blake contacts Alexis to tell her, as Sean's shadowy figure slips away to safety.

"The Trial" – Episode 8.20
Original Airdate – March 9, 1988
Written by James Harmon Brown and Barbara Esensten
Directed by Ray Danton

Guest Appearances by Fran Bennett (Gloria Wilby), Robert Cornthwaite (Judge Edward P. Langdon), Garrett Davis (Minister), Michael Ensign (William Todd), Nancy Renee (Reporter #2), Patty Tiffany (Reporter #1) and Bradley White (Alfred Sorenson)

Following his near fatal brush with death in Natumbe, Blake returns to Colorado facing accusations that he was involved in an illegal weapons deal. Concerned that the bad press will harm his campaign, Fallon and Steven fly to Natumbe to find proof that will clear their father's name. As Karen's custody suit draws near, Alexis discovers proof that Sean paid Jesse to return to Denver. Bringing the evidence into the courtroom, Alexis proves Jesse acted out of greed in influencing Karen's decision to keep the baby. Tortured by the pain the custody suit has caused everyone, Dana blurts out that Karen is the rightful mother. Devastated by her outburst, Adam moves out of their bedroom. After Leslie discovers Jeff's divorce is final, she throws herself at him. But after he abruptly puts an end to their relationship, Leslie is left broken hearted. Jeff stops by Blake's campaign headquarters to patch up their differences. Mutually regretful for their separation, Jeff asks to return as Blake's manager. Steven and Fallon return to Denver with documents that prove Sean was behind the arms shipment. Alexis tries to conceal her terror when she is told the body assumed to be Sean is Harry Thresher's. Despite Dex's assurance that no man could have survived the explosion in Natumbe, Alexis can't suppress her ominous suspicion that Sean is still alive.

"The Proposal" – Episode 8.21
Original Airdate – March 16, 1988
Written by Frank V. Furino
Directed by Don Medford

Guest Appearances by Brandyn Artis (Nurse #1), Fran Bennett (Gloria Wilby), Jordan Charney (Bill Cochran), Robert Cornthwaite (Judge Edward P. Langdon), Michael Ensign (William Todd), Michael Goodwin (Russ Kelton), George Hirschmann (Bailiff), Roger Nolan (Reporter), Kathryn White (Nurse #2) and Kenneth Wilson (Floor Manager)

Dana tries desperately to convince Adam how much she wants their son. She proposes that if they were a loving couple again, the judge would find in their favor. Still hurting from her outburst in court, Adam is cold to her pleas. Out of a job and money, Leslie comes to Alexis, asking for forgiveness. Amused by her change of heart but unmoved to compassion, Alexis sends Leslie away. Waiting pensively for the judge's decision on his son's custody, Adam is stung by Jesse and Karen's in-court announcement that they are going to reconcile their marriage. Sammy Jo is caught off guard by Jeff's marriage proposal. Turning to Krystle for advice, she is blunt in reminding Sammy Jo how uncomfortable their marriage would be for the family. Unable to tolerate Adam's abuse, Dana firmly places the blame on him for their failing marriage. Dana leaves Adam, making Jesse and Karen probable winners in their custody suit. Sean returns to Alexis' apartment to kill her, but sneaks out when Dex arrives to console her on her apparent loss in the governor's race. Accepting her projected defeat, Alexis leaves to congratulate Blake. But when a late poll shows Alexis gaining votes, she retracts her concession and leaves Blake stunned by the sudden turnaround. One day before the final custody hearing, Karen and Jesse visit the baby. Upon opening the door to the maternity nursery, they are horror stricken when they discover the baby is gone.

"Colorado Roulette" – Episode 8.22
Original Airdate – March 30, 1988
Written by Edward de Blasio
Directed by Irving J. Moore

Guest Appearances by Robert Cornthwaite (Judge Edward P. Langdon), Kathryn Daley (TV Commentator), Ronald R. Foster (Sheriff), George Hirschmann (Bailiff), James Parkes (Burell), Ken Swofford (Lieutenant) and Chuck Walling (Plainclothes Policeman)

Adam is absolved of suspicion in the kidnapping of his son when Leslie calls him to say that Sean has taken the baby and is holding her captive. They find Leslie badly beaten, but Sean has already taken the baby. Chasing after him, Adam and Steven find him and get back the baby, but not before Sean is able to escape. Jealous that Jeff has fallen in love with Sammy Jo, Fallon stops by Jeff's apartment. When a heated argument turns passionate, their lust for each other becomes uncontrollable. Answering a knock at his door after he and Fallon have made love, Jeff is stunned to find Sammy Jo with champagne, ready to toast her decision to marry him. Sean returns to Alexis' apartment to kill her and take revenge for his father's suicide. Grappling with all the uncertainty in his life and Sammy Jo's current love affair with Jeff, Steven decides to leave Denver. Confident the judge will find custody in his favor after he saved his son's life, Adam is mortified when custody is awarded to Karen. Dex bursts into Alexis' apartment and fights with Sean. The gun Sean is carrying goes off as Alexis watches in horror. Concerned about Krystle's sudden headaches, Blake places a call to her doctor. Returning to the Carrington mansion, he finds their room a total mess, and Krystle gone. Blake realizes that Krystle's mysterious headaches are related to her sudden disappearance.

SEASON NINE

"Broken Krystle" – Episode 9.1
Original Airdate – November 2, 1988
Written by James Harmon Brown and Barbara Esensten
Directed by James Harmon Brown and Irving J. Moore

Guest Appearances by Jack Bannon (Dennis Champlin), Carl Ciarfalio (Truck Driver), Marsha Clark (Doctor Susan Aames), Mitchell Edmonds (Detective Coe), M.E. Loree (Cindy), Ben Mittelman (Jerry), Marcus Mukai (Sam), Jack Murdock (Janitor) and Ben Piazza (Dr. Charles Hampton)

Recovering from Sean's attempted murder on her life and his subsequent death, Alexis and Dex flee to Los Angeles. There, they regain the passion they once had. Jeff tries to keep Sammy Jo from entering his room after he and Fallon have just made love. To Jeff's relief, Fallon has put on her clothes and slipped out,  undetected. Following Krystle's bizarre disappearance, Blake searches frantically for her. Adam withdraws into a drunken stupor, alienating his family and Dana. Intent on using Dana to help him regain his son, he apologizes for his behavior. But when Dana packs her things and leaves him, he suddenly realizes how much he truly loves her. Sammy Jo broods over Fallon's influence on Jeff's life and after leaving unanswered messages on his machine, she pays him an unexpected early morning visit. Groggy after spending most the night making calls to help find Krystle, he tells her about Krystle's disappearance. Sammy Jo mentions Krystle's favorite hideaway, an out of the way lake. Sensing she may have gone there, Jeff and Sammy Jo go after her. Finding tracks and Krystle's diary near the lake, they spot something floating in the water. Investigating closer, they are stunned when they discover a dead body.

"A Touch of Sable" – Episode 9.2
Original Airdate – November 10, 1988
Written by Ron Renauld
Directed by Irving J. Moore

Guest Appearances by Jesse D. Goins (Detective Jack Lyons), Jon Greene (Officer), Christopher Neame (Hamilton Stone) and Jonathan Perpich (Detective Pete McWhorter)

Sammy Jo and Jeff are relieved to discover the body they found in the lake is not Krystle, but the mystery of how she is involved still haunts them. Krystle's car is found in Harmon Springs and the man responsible for stealing it is a convicted murderer. Frustrated by the bizarre elements involved in Krystle's disappearance, Blake is both relieved and confused when Krystle's sister, Virginia, informs him that Krystle is with her. Finding a sealed farewell letter to Blake and Sammy Jo from Steven, Adam tosses it in the fire. Fallon comes across the partially charred remains, and immediately suspects her brother of treachery. After Dex expresses his unwillingness to help Alexis strengthen her empire, she takes advantage of Sable's unexpected return and her political and financially affluent friend, Hamilton Stone. Alexis persuades Stone to help her get her ships back from Natumbe, while Sable contemplates how she can benefit from their budding relationship. Blake flies to Dayton, Krystle's hometown. Meeting Virginia, he learns that Krystle's memory has regressed back to her earlier life of growing up in Dayton. Virginia confides in Blake that Krystle had mentioned she was on the run from someone who was trying to kill her. Listening in shock, Blake is further stunned when she tells him Krystle confessed to having killed a man.

"She's Back" – Episode 9.3
Original Airdate – December 1, 1988
Written by James Harmon Brown and Barbara Esensten
Directed by Nancy Malone

Guest Appearances by Don Baker (Chauffeur), Jack Bannon (Dennis Champlin), John Brandon (Detective William Handler), Jesse D. Goins (Detective Jack Lyons), Jon Greene (Officer), Stella Hall (Claire Tennyson), Tom Lahm (Waiter), Tom McGreevey (Butler), Eddie Quinlan (Clarence) and Del Zamora (Janitor)

Finding Krystle and her cousin, Virginia, talking, Blake is pleased to see Krystle well, but remains distressed when she has no recollection of how she got to Dayton. Fearing she will react badly to the news that she may be involved with a murder, Blake keeps the truth from her when they  return to Denver. Adam persuades Steven's secretary, Claire Tennyson, to work for him, hoping she will reveal some of Steven's secrets. Claire eagerly accepts, having her own devious reasons for doing so. With Alexis in Natumbe with Hamilton Stone, Sable pours her seductive charms on Dex, who is only amused by her passes. Krystle is overcome by a painful migraine, as the reason for her attacks continues to frustrate her. Finding out from Sgt. Zorelli that she is a suspect in a murder, Kryslte accuses Blake of lying to her. Needing to know what happened at the lake, Krystle goes to Sammy Jo, demanding to be told the truth. Finding out about the body in the lake, she convinces Blake to take her to the morgue to see the corpse. Pulling back the sheet, Krystle does not recognize the face. But when Blake looks, he cringes with the recognition of who it is.

"Body Trouble" – Episode 9.4
Original Airdate – December 8, 1988
Written by Tita Bell and Robert Wolfe
Directed by Dwight Adair

Guest Appearances by Mary Baldwin (Florence), Robert Alan Beuth (Morgue Assistant), Michael Fairman (Dr. Westhaven), Jesse D. Goins (Detective Jack Lyons), Stella Hall (Claire Tennyson), Richmond Harrison (Brunner), Tom McGreevey (Butler), Ben Piazza (Dr. Charles Hampton), Malcolm Smith (William) and Stephanie Williams (Pamela)

Devastated by Blake's reliance on Jeff, Adam schemes to gain control of Denver-Carrington. Making light of Sammy Jo's objections to him working closely with Fallon, Jeff playfully teases her. Krystle awakens screaming after a nightmare reveals a horrifying glimpse into her clouded memory. Arriving in Los Angeles to meet with Dr. Hampton, Blake tells Krystle that her headaches are a result of complications from the fall she took off her horse several years before. Accompanying Sgt. Zorelli to the morgue to identify the body, Fallon privately thinks that the dead man looks familiar. Sharing her thoughts with Blake upon his return, he admits the young man looks like someone he knew many years ago. Blake goes through photographs dating back to 1963, showing the man and Blake together. While mingling with guests at a party for Blake's friends and supporters, Krystle is gripped by a painful headache. Losing control, she flings dishes at the guests until Blake is able to calm her. Arriving at the party unexpected, Sgt. Zorelli informs Krystle she is no longer suspected of murder after an autopsy showed the body to be dead for over twenty years.

"Alexis in Blunderland" – Episode 9.5
Original Airdate – December 15, 1988
Written by Ron Renauld
Directed by Nancy Malone

Guest Appearances by Marie Berry (Marie), Lorelle Brina (Mother), Joe Elrady (Youth), Stella Hall (Claire Tennyson), Kathy McCullen (Sable's Secretary), John Rixey Moore (Buck Howser), Christopher Neame (Hamilton Stone) and Patrick Omeirs (Nate Pencroft)

Returning from her trip to Natumbe, Alexis is greeted by Dex and his gloomy prognosis for Colbyco. Desperate to liquefy her assets, she makes plans to sell the Carlton Hotel and the Vitron tankers, as the realization she may lose everything finally hits her. Finding out about Fallon's one night stand with Jeff, Sammy Jo squares off with Fallon. Wrestling with each other, they fall into a water trough and then take a roll through the mud, before they finally realize they are fighting over a man neither wants anymore. Adam plots to double cross Jeff by reading Steven's confidential notes on the pipeline. Fallon questions Dex on what he knows about the man-made lake where the body was found. Uneasy about discussing the subject, Dex admits the lake was made after a project had gone bad between Blake, the Colbys, and Dexter's family. Sable is delighted to hear Hamilton Stone has succeeded in winning Alexis' trust. With Stone's inside knowledge of Colbyco's business dealings, Sable schemes to take Alexis' oil tankers. Blake receives a bad news call from Krystle's doctor. Seeing the pain on Blake's face, Fallon barges into the library demanding to know what is going on. Finding Krystle crying in Blake's arms, he asks Fallon to gather the family.

"Every Picture Tells A Story" – Episode 9.6
Original Airdate – December 21, 1988
Written by James Harmon Brown and Barbara Esensten
Directed by Bruce Bilson

Guest Appearances by Carey Eidel (Security Guard), Rocky Giordani (Arnie), Stella Hall (Claire Tennyson), Ben Piazza (Dr. Charles Hampton) and Jack Slaster (Workman)

Taking the picture of Blake standing with the young man found floating in the lake, Fallon sets up an appointment with Sergeant Zorelli to view the corpse. Krystle undergoes more tests to determine her reaction to a new drug. Virginia joins Blake and Krystle at the hospital. Blake and Virginia develop a special bond of friendship. After sleeping with Claire, Adam tells her it's best she find another job. Following her tests, Krystle has a new resolve to live. Sammy Jo and Fallon put their differences aside and develop a friendship. Dex asks Jeff to help him find more out about Fritz Heath, Colbyco's comptroller. A seething Alexis berates Dex for unwittingly selling the Carlton to Sable. Unable to view the corpse, Zorelli sets Fallon up in a room and gives her a picture. Unaware that a camera is focused on her, she pulls out Blake's picture and compares photographs, as Zorelli watches. Virginia is awestruck by the opulence of the Carrington mansion as she returns to Denver with Blake and Krystle. Finding out about the picture, Sable goes to Blake to let him know that when the story gets out, he can count on her as an ally. Taking Sable's suggestion to ask her mother about the man in the picture, Fallon goes to Alexis for answers. Recognizing the man to be Roger Grimes, a man Blake discovered her having an affair with, she accuses Blake of murdering him twenty five years ago.

"The Last Hurrah" – Episode 9.7
Original Airdate – January 4, 1989
Written by Tita Bell and Robert Wolfe
Directed by Dwight Adair

Guest Appearances by Marque Gritta (Waiter), Ben Piazza (Dr. Charles Hampton), Joe Verroca (Guy) and Stephanie Williams (Pamela)

Blake is furious at Fallon for showing the picture of Roger Grimes to Alexis. Overhearing his tirade, Krystle is uncertain why Blake is so concerned by the picture. After Alexis vows to make Blake suffer for killing Roger Grimes, Dex is convinced that she still harbors feelings for Roger. Deciding not to be Alexis' toy lover any longer, Dex pays an amorous visit to Joanna Sills, Sable's personal assistant. While visiting the seedy part of town with Sammy Jo and Virginia, Krystle looks for ways she can help the unfortunate. Approached by a man with a knife, Virginia attacks him with a viciousness that makes Sammy Jo think she may be more street wise than she wants people to think. Krystle is told her only chance for survival is an operation with a marginal chance of success. Alexis is outraged by her discovery that Hamilton Stone only got two of her ships out of Natumbe. Finding out about Alexis' vendetta against Blake, Krystle barges into her apartment. Krystle threatens to use her recent mental illness as a justifiable excuse to kill Alexis if she carries out her plans to accuse Blake of Roger Grimes murder.

"The Wedding" – Episode 9.8
Original Airdate – January 11, 1989
Written by Tita Bell and Robert Wolfe
Directed by Jerry Jameson

Guest Appearances by Gene Butler (Painter), Gene Knight (Maitre D') and Stan Sells (Gibson)

Krystle agrees to the operation only after Blake reluctantly signs her divorce papers and living will, to be enacted if the surgery is not a success. Virginia tells Krystle of her troubled youth after their mother left her. Krystle invites Sable to dinner and their friendship continues to grow. Fallon is haunted by a recurring dream of Roger Grimes. Dex hires a Vietnam buddy, Painter, to investigate Colbyco's controller. Krystle recognizes one of the caterers at her dinner party, Gibson, as the same man she sees coming out of the lake in her haunting nightmare. Fearing Krystle will put the puzzle together, Sable tells Gibson to discontinue his dives into the lake. Those are the same dives that originally uncovered the body of Roger Grimes. Thinking he has discovered an underwater passageway, Gibson is hesitant to abandon his search. Virginia reacts very strangely when she is introduced to Dex. Following the reaffirmation of their wedding vows, Blake is forced to cancel his and Krystle's second honeymoon. Krystle and Blake leave immediately for Switzerland so she can have the high risk operation.

"Ginger Snaps" – Episode 9.9
Original Airdate – January 25, 1989
Written by Clyde Ware
Directed by Kate Swofford Tilley

Guest Appearances by John Brandon (Captain William Handler), Gene Butler (Painter), Jay Kerr (Clint), Ben Piazza (Dr. Charles Hampton) and Stan Sells (Gibson)

Despite orders from his Captain to drop the search for Roger Grimes murderer, Zorelli continues his investigation. Virginia's obsession with Dex intensifies. While looking at the phone numbers Heath has called over the past months, Dex notices one of them belongs to Joanna Sills, Sable's personal assistant. Hearing  noises in the barn, Sammy Jo investigates and is knocked unconscious by an unseen assailant. Sneaking out, he drops his knife. Dex questions Joanna about Heath. A grieving Blake returns to Denver following Krystle's unsuccessful operation and her subsequent lapse into a coma. Dex suspects someone may be letting Heath know he is being watched. Blake asks for Dex's help in keeping Alexis from bringing up any Colby, Dexter, and Carrington family secrets relating to their joint mining venture. Jeff warns Sable to stay away from Blake now that Krystle may be gone forever. Virginia stuns Dex with the revelation that he knew her long ag0 when she went by the name of Ginger.

"Delta Woe" – Episode 9.10
Original Airdate – February 1, 1989
Written by Don Heckman
Directed by Dwight Adair

Guest Appearances by Laurel Adams (Secretary), Chloe Amateau (Waitress), Jon Greene (Officer), Jack Heller (Aly Samarkian) and Stan Sells (Gibson)

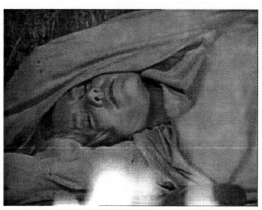

Following their passionate love making, Zorelli suspects Fallon is merely trying to influence him to drop the Roger Grimes case. After Virginia storms from Dex's room, leaving behind pictures of them together from a happier time, Dex is left stunned by the uncanny turn of events. Blake orders Zorelli to stay away from Fallon. To avoid having their family secret revealed, Blake vows to take the rap for Grime's murder. Fallon continues to be haunted by the memory of Grimes. Sable discovers Gibson left his knife in Sammy Jo's barn. Confronting Gibson, she warns him to leave Denver or face her wrath. Zorelli receives a blown up photograph of Grimes with Blake, proving Blake knows more than he is letting on. Learning that Heath is a regular gambler at her friend's casino, Sable follows him there. Surprised to discover Dex has also followed Heath, Sable uses the opportunity to toy with Dex. Arousing his interest, Sable then turns him off like a cold shower. Alone in her barn, Sammy Jo hears noises and takes her shotgun to investigate. Gibson jumps her and she gets off a shot that hits Gibson. As Gibson drags himself out of the barn, a raging fire traps Sammy Jo inside.

"Tankers, Cadavers to Chance" – Episode 9.11
Original Airdate – February 8, 1989
Written by Roberto Loiederman
Directed by Kate Swofford Tilley

Guest Appearances by Fredric Arnold (Surgeon), Patrick Johnson (Paramedic), Rodger LaRue (Williams), Billy Long (Hank), Albert Lord (Maitre D'), Walt Scott (Pete) and Stan Sells (Gibson)

Jeff pulls Sammy Jo from the burning barn, and Gibson is taken into custody. Sammy Jo recognizes Gibson as the man Krystle saw in her nightmares. Blake worries that Gibson is involved in trying to uncover his family secret. Dex gives Virginia a letter explaining his side of the story. She  tears it up but later pieces it back together and gets teary as she reads it. Blake gives Dex an audio tape and documents relating to their secret for safe keeping. Loathing the thought of Sable winning over Dex, Alexis reignites his passion. Alexis fears the work she did to secure her ships in Natumbe may have run afoul. Adam snoops through Virginia's room and discovers the letter from Dex. Adam seduces Virginia and wins her trust. Gibson threatens Sable to get him out of jail. Zorelli storms into the Carrington mansion, accusing Blake of having him pulled off the Grimes case. Denying it, Blake has him thrown out. Torn between her father and her lover, Fallon leaves with Zorelli. Sable terrorizes Alexis with the news that she has undone all her work in Natumbe and gained possession of Alexis' tankers.

"All Hands on Dex" – Episode 9.12
Original Airdate – February 15, 1989
Written by Don Heckman
Directed by Dwight Adair

Guest Appearances by John Brandon (Captain William Handler), Jed Gillin (Officer Hansen), Ed Marinaro (Creighton Boyd), Christopher Neame (Hamilton Stone), Stan Sells (Gibson) and Stephanie Williams (Pamela)

Irate after Sable gains control of her ships, Alexis hires one of Adam's college friends, the handsome and intriguing Crey Boyd, to get them back. Running into Hamilton Stone at the Carlton, Alexis promises to make him pay dearly for double crossing her. Shaken by her threats, Stone ponders the damage she could cause. Sammy Jo is mistaken for a sixteen year-old runaway by Tanner McBride, a teen counselor. Apologizing and embarrassed, Tanner is attracted to Sammy Jo. Zorelli pleads with his captain for a second chance, only to be sternly denied. Dex begins to doubt his and Alexis' relationship can survive. Jeff reprimands Adam for neglecting his loyalties to Blake. Stung by his reproach, Adam swings wildly at Jeff. After several missed blows, Adam orders Jeff out of the house. Blake confronts Gibson. Offering to help him if he talks, Gibson tells Blake Sable hired him. Accusing Sable of working for Jason, Blake lashes out at her. Before Sable can explain, Alexis walks in on their fight, renewing her vow to crush them both. Sable finds reason to rejoice when Joanna gives her Fritz Heath's marker, indebting him for over two-hundred thousand dollars to her. Dex walks in on Sable's jubilation and she throws herself into his arms, taking him and Joanna by surprise.

"Virginia Reels" – Episode 9.13
Original Airdate – February 22, 1989
Written by James Harmon Brown and Barbara Esensten
Directed by Bruce Bilson

Guest Appearances by Robert L. Benwitt (Waiter), Robert Neary (Officer), Leonard Ross (Pit Boss), Stan Sells (Gibson), Arlen Dean Snyder (Property Clerk) and George Wilbur (Security Guard)

Sable meets with Blake and Dex to explain she was searching the lake to discover what her ex-husband, Jason, was determined to keep hidden. She assures them that she had no idea Blake and Dex would be harmed by uncovering the secret that lay hidden there. Dex is  intrigued by her honesty. Sammy Jo helps Tanner McBride persuade an official to let him retain temporary custody of one of his runaways. Appreciative of her efforts, Tanner brings her a rose and leaves his number for her to call if she ever wants to talk. Sable threatens to reveal Heath's embezzling money from Colbyco unless he helps her obtain damaging information on Alexis. Dex learns that Adam took advantage of Virginia after reading the letter he wrote. Outraged, he attacks Adam, threatening to kill him. Jealous of Dex's interest in Sable, Joanna accepts Adam's offer to get better acquainted. Going against orders, Zorelli copies a map taken from Gibson outlining the lake and Delta Rho. Fallon discovers the picture Zorelli took of her holding the picture of Blake with Roger Grimes, and suspects he is using her to get information on Blake. Blake is saddened by Virginia's decision to leave Denver. Sable is amused by Heath's demand for 5 million dollars for the information on Alexis. Pulling out a gun, Heath nervously aims it at Sable.

"House of the Falling Son" – Episode 9.14
Original Airdate – March 1, 1989
Written by Ron Renauld
Directed by Alan Myerson

Guest Appearances by Judy Jean Berns (Maid), Dick Durock (Jimbo) and Ed Marinaro (Creighton Boyd)

Sable is able to maintain a calm facade and convince Heath to put the gun down so they can talk. Agreeing, and feeling more at ease, Heath talks about how Sable can ruin Colbyco. After Heath leaves, Sable is still in shock from her close encounter with death. Needing to be with someone, she goes to Dex. Blake questions Dex about what Adam did to Virginia to make her want to leave. Hearing the truth, Blake kicks Adam out of the house, as Blake feels his family slip away from him. Alexis goes to Paris to check on Boyd's commando operation. Alexis finds herself wanting Boyd. Fallon moves in with Sammy Jo. Zorelli asks Fallon to explain why she is suddenly cold to him. Joanna confronts Sable for stepping in between her and Dex, causing Sable to suspect Joanna's loyalty. Joanna tries to seduce Dex but he turns down her advances. Sable meets with Dex to apologize for their night together, promising she respects his love for Alexis. Despite their polite insistence that the whole affair meant nothing, they feel a burning desire for each other. Unable to resist, they go back to her suite and make passionate love. Before Boyd leaves for his dangerous mission, Alexis gives in to her own lust, as she allows Boyd to take her into his arms.

"The Son Also Rises" – Episode 9.15
Original Airdate – March 15, 1989
Written by Roberto Loiederman
Directed by Ron Satlof

Guest Appearances by Lou Hancock (Heidi)

Seeing the disarray of Denver-Carrington, Blake resumes control of the company. His first act is to fire Adam. Appreciating Joanna's knowledge of Sable's affairs, Adam tries to charm her into working for him and Alexis. Sable watches as Adam enters Joanna's suite, confirming her suspicions of Joanna's disloyalty. Zorelli realizes that Fallon saw the picture he stole of Blake and Grimes, explaining why she suddenly became hostile towards him. Sable asks Dex if he will be able to turn against Alexis if she pursues her vendetta against Blake. Tanner McBride stops by Delta Rho to make Sammy Jo and Fallon dinner. Fallon notices Sammy Jo's obvious attraction to him. Sable's daughter, Monica, comes to Denver to visit her mother. Knowing Joanna can no longer be trusted, Sable convinces Monica to stay in Denver and help her with her campaign to destroy Alexis. Zorelli tells Fallon that he is in love with her, and that he never meant to use her to get at Blake. Confused by her feelings for him, Fallon slaps Zorelli and orders him to leave. Zorelli offers her the only copy of the picture to prove he is not using her. Joanna accepts Adam's offer to work for Alexis. Jeff shows Blake an ad in Alexis' newspaper asking for information on Roger Grimes. Blake hardens his resolve to stop Alexis once and for all.

"Grimes and Punishment" – Episode 9.16
Original Airdate – March 22, 1989
Written by Tita Bell and Robert Wolfe
Directed by Nancy Malone

Guest Appearances by John Brandon (Captain William Handler), Tony DeCarlo (Mechanic), Lezlie Deane (Phoenix Chisolm), Pierrino Mascarino (Father Shea) and John McLiam (Elsworth Chisolm)

Joanna agrees to tell Adam everything she knows about Sable. Upon Alexis' return to Denver, Blake confronts her about the ad asking for information on Roger Grimes. She reasserts her vow to see him pay for Grimes' murder. Fearing Alexis may get a warrant to search the lake, Blake asks Dex to dive into the lake and make sure everything that needs to be hidden stays that way. Zorelli promises his commanding officer, Capt. Handler, that he will drop the Grimes case and is given his old job back. Sable is pleased when Monica moves in with her. But Sable's joy is short-lived when Alexis and Adam tell her the tankers have been destroyed. Sammy Jo offers Tanner a check for his home for runaways. She grows increasingly fond of him, unaware that he is married. Blake goes to Delta Rho to make amends with Fallon, and finds the picture Zorelli left behind. With all his faith in Fallon destroyed, Blake storms out. Dex goes to Alexis' penthouse to talk about her vendetta against Blake. With guilt written all over his face, she realizes he slept with Sable. Devastated, Alexis kicks Dex out. With a war clearly brewing between Alexis and Sable, Monica tries to persuade Jeff to take Sable's side. Alexis' grief over losing Dex is diverted when Adam tells her he has found a man who knows who killed Grimes. Elsworth Chisolm tells Alexis he saw Blake carry Grimes' body out of the mine he was working on.

"Sins of the Father" – Episode 9.17
Original Airdate – March 29, 1989
Written by James Harmon Brown and Barbara Esensten
Directed by Bruce Bilson

Guest Appearances by Timothy Dale Agee (Waiter), Leslie Arnett (Maid), Tony DeCarlo (Boy), Lezlie Deane (Phoenix Chisolm), Joleen Lutz (Girl), Pierrino Mascarino (Father Shea), Patricia Mullins (Maid), Jack Stauffer (Hotel Manager) and Susan Wolf (Waitress)

Alexis is emotionally crushed by Dex's affair with Sable. She sends Adam to try and make up with Blake, so she can have a set of ears in his camp. Blake and Sable renew their bonds of friendship. Adam meets with Chisolm's granddaughter, Phoenix. She tells Adam that there was another secret project going on at the mine. Alexis rummages through a box of Roger Grimes' things and she comes across a picture he gave her. Sable sees the picture and suddenly realizes what Blake's secret is. Blake confesses to Dex and Sable that the secret beneath the lake is a Nazi treasure of precious art innocently obtained by his father. Blake vows to keep the treasure and his father's involvement a secret for fear it would ruin his family name. Blake tells them his father killed Grimes because he discovered the treasure and was trying to make his fortune from it. Sammy Jo gets a rude awakening when she discovers Tanner McBride is a priest, married to the church. Adam tells Blake that Alexis has a witness who saw him murder Grimes. Fallon realizes that her grandfather, Tom Carrington is also in her nightmares. She tells Zorelli that she remembers her grandfather taking her into dark tunnels. Dex dives into the lake and discovers the seal to the mine entrance is open. Zorelli watches from the shore.

"Tale of the Tape" – Episode 9.18
Original Airdate – April 5, 1989
Written by Roberto Loiederman
Directed by Dwight Adair

Guest Appearances by John Brandon (Captain William Handler), Mark Costello (Head Marshall), Lezlie Deane (Phoenix Chisolm), Al Fann (Charles Matthews), John McLiam (Elsworth Chisolm), Patricia Mullins (Maid), Marguerite Ray (Jane Matthews) and Stephanie Williams (Pamela)

Blake and Jeff are stunned when Dex finds the hidden vault beneath the lake completely empty. Blake asks Sable to try and find out any information Alexis may know about the vanished treasure. Having a passkey to Alexis' suite, Sable waits for the right time to sneak in and take the painting Roger Grime's stole from the hidden Nazi treasure. Alexis tells Captain Handler about her eyewitness to Roger Grimes' murder. Meeting Dominique's uncle, Charles Matthews, Zorelli puts a bug in his house and learns Matthews knows more about Grime's murder than he is letting on. Jeff warns Blake that he doesn't think Sable can be trusted. Federal Marshals burst into Alexis' suite to seize Colbyco records, as Sable unleashes her lawsuit to bring Alexis to her knees. Alexis leaves for Switzerland to protect her assets. Adam phones Blake and tells him where he can find Elsworth Chisolm. While Fallon opens up to Zorelli about her grandfather and the mine beneath the lake, she doesn't know her conversation is being recorded. Chisolm makes a deal with Blake to tell him everything he knows about the secret tunnels beneath the lake. Someone watches them from a narrowly opened door. Adam pulls up just as Blake is leaving to get money for Chisolm. Going inside Chisolm's house, Adam finds him dead.

"No Bones About It" – Episode 9.19
Original Airdate – April 19, 1989
Written by Tita Bell and Robert Wolfe
Directed by Michael Lange

Guest Appearances by Judy Jean Berns (Maid), John Brandon (Captain William Handler), Lezlie Deane (Phoenix Chisolm), Al Fann (Charles Matthews), Stephanie Menuez (Photographer), Marguerite Ray (Jane Matthews) and Joris Stuyck (Edward Prusky)

Captain Handler, suspecting Blake may have killed Chisolm, puts Zorelli back on the Grimes case, despite Zorelli's belief that Blake is innocent. Blake accuses Adam of setting him up to look like he killed Chisolm. Learning that Alexis is having her painting appraised, Sable convinces the appraiser to tell Alexis the painting is worthless. Sable learns someone has been searching for a Frederick Stahl painting. Adam has a hotel photographer shoot pictures of Monica and Jeff together. Charles Matthews warns Blake that Zorelli has been asking them questions. When Blake tells Fallon that Zorelli has been using her to get information about Matthews, her love for Zorelli turns to contempt. Tanner's feelings for Sammy Jo make him question his priestly vows. Finding a diagram with his father's things that Charles Matthews dropped off, Blake discovers that it is for a tunnel system originating from the basement of the mansion. Adam visits Phoenix Chisolm and in her grief, she blurts out that her grandfather knew about the tunnels under Blake's mansion. Acquiring a listening device that detects tunnels, Dex, Jeff, and Blake search the basement for a tunnel entrance. Finding it, they crawl into the dark space and discover a human skeleton.

"Here Comes the Son" – Episode 9.20
Original Airdate – April 26, 1989
Written by James Harmon Brown and Barbara Esensten
Directed by Jerry Jameson

Guest Appearances by Laurel Adams (Blake's Secretary), John Brandon (Captain William Handler), Michael Collins (Goon), John Considine (David Prescott), Tony DeCarlo (Boy), Lezlie Deane (Phoenix Chisolm), Harvey Jason (Ray Montana), Jeff Kaake (Dennis Grimes), Marlyn Mason (Emily Grimes), Ron Perkins (Middle Aged Man) and Oz Tortora (Jack)

Another skeleton is discovered buried in the tunnel beneath the mansion. He gives Dex and Jeff one week to meet with Roger Grimes' widow, Emily, before he reveals their tangled secret to the police. To prove his loyalty to Fallon, Zorelli quits the police department. Sable learns she is pregnant, but is unable to tell Dex he is the father. Fallon decides to move into an abandoned cottage on Blake's property. Adam retouches the photograph he had taken of Jeff and Monica to appear as if their relationship may be incestuous. He then submits it to a sleazy tabloid for publication. Outraged, Jeff storms into the tabloid's office and begins attacking the reporter. A photographer captures the assault on film. Fallon recognizes a lullaby she hears Krystina sing. Setting up house in her cottage, she is haunted by the lullaby. Afraid her mind is playing tricks on her, Fallon thinks she sees Roger Grimes staring at her through the window. Desperate for answers, Blake goes to see Phoenix Chisolm. She refuses to let him in, creating a commotion that brings the neighbors out. They recognize Blake as the man who was with Elsworth before he was murdered. Emily Grimes tells Jeff and Dex that Roger had a son, Dennis. Seeing his picture, they are shocked by his resemblance to Roger. Outside Fallon's cottage window, Dennis Grimes watches her.

"Blasts from the Past" – Episode 9.21
Original Airdate – May 3, 1989
Written by Tita Bell and Robert Wolfe
Directed by David Paulsen

Guest Appearances by John Brandon (Captain William Handler), Al Fann (Charles Matthews), John Gowans (Fred Hughes), Jeff Kaake (Dennis Grimes), Fred Lerner (Officer), Pierrino Mascarino (Father Shea), Stephanie Menuez (Debbie), Marguerite Ray (Jane Matthews) and Spike Silver (Officer)

Convinced that someone is trying to frame him for Chisolm's murder, Blake turns to Charles Matthews for answers to his father's mysterious past. Zorelli finds a bug in his apartment, which Dennis Grimes, and Captain Handler planted. Jeff finds out that Adam was responsible for the story that accused him and Monica of being involved in an incestuous affair. Jeff confronts Adam and a serious brawl ensues. Walking in on the fight, while Sable and Monica watch, helplessly, Alexis uses the moment to announce that Jason Colby is not Monica's father. Outraged by Alexis' betrayal, Sable hurls herself atop of Alexis, pummeling her wildly. Adam tells Alexis that the painting Grimes gave her is a Fredrick Stahl. Putting the connection together, Alexis realizes Blake is hiding a treasure plundered by the Nazis. Sammy Jo tells Tanner that she loves him. Sable tells Dex that he is the father of her baby. Sable turns to Blake for solace over the children and confides in him that the reason she had been raped. Handler blackmails Blake, telling him to cooperate in giving him the treasure or face a prison sentence. Alexis meets Fallon at the cottage to help release the childhood memories locked inside of her. Fallon flashes back, remembering how she shot Grimes to stop him from beating Alexis.

"Cache 22" – Episode 9.22
Original Airdate – May 10, 1989
Written by Samuel J. Pelovitz
Directed by David Paulsen

Guest Appearances by John Brandon (Captain William Handler), Ron Burke (Officer), Tony DeCarlo (Rick), Jeff Kaake (Dennis Grimes), Ben Marino (Officer), Patricia Mullens (Angela) and Robert Pescovitz (Desk Sergeant)

Blake tells Alexis that his father, Tom Carrington, covered up the incident. Alexis blackmails Blake for half of the plundered Nazi treasure. Fallon dreams of the lullaby she heard Krystina singing to her dolls then remembers the lullaby came from a music box that was part of the treasure. Alexis offers to give up her claim for half of the treasure, sparing Blake public scorn, if Sable withdraws her lawsuit against Colbyco. Sable agrees. Krystina leads Fallon into a secret tunnel passage and to the hidden treasure, unaware that Dennis Grimes has followed them. Grimes takes Fallon and Krystina hostage inside the tunnel. Handler and several police officers raid Blake's mansion. Handler informs Blake that he has the treasure and has taken Fallon and Krystina hostage to insure his cooperation. Blake and Jeff overpower Handler. Handler breaks free and reaches for his gun. Blake and Handler exchange bullets. Both take hits and fall to the ground. Fallon shoots Dennis Grimes, sending the tunnel caving in on the entrance, trapping all three inside. Fallon tries to get out unaware that Dennis Grimes is trying to pull himself up. Dex and Adam get into a fight over comments about Sable's baby. Dex is hurled into Alexis, sending them crashing over a rail and onto the landing below.

DYNASTY THE REUNION

A Two-Part Miniseries
Original Airdates – October 20 and 22, 1991

Written by Esther Shapiro, Richard Shapiro, Robert Mason Pollock, Eileen Pollock and Edward de Blasio
Directed by Irving J. Moore

Starring: John Forsythe, Linda Evans, Joan Collins, John James, Heather Locklear, Emma Samms, Kathleen Beller, Al Corley, Maxwell Caulfield, Michael Brandon (Arlen Marshall), Robin Sachs (Adam Carrington) and Jeroen Krabbe' (Jeremy Van Dorn)

Supporting Cast Members: William Beckley, Brandon Bluhm, Orlando Bonner, Justin Burnette, Natalie Core, Alphonsia Emmanuel, Evelyn Guerrero, Betty Harford, Virginia Hawkins, Tony Jay, Emily Kuroda, Wendie Malick, Michael A. Nickles, Jeff O'Haco, Jessica Player, Ray Reinhardt, Richard Roat, Sam Sako, Eric Sinclair, Brittany Alyse Smith, Cameron Watson and Keone Young

As a result of the death of Captain Handler, Blake has spent the past three years in federal prison. Jeff has been working feverishly to prove Blake was innocent and after all this time, the governor grants Blake a full pardon. While he's been in prison, Blake has been trying to gather information  about the consortium that has taken over Denver Carrington and all of his other holdings. He is convinced that the entire Handler situation was a conspiracy from the beginning to get him out of his company. In the process, this said consortium also managed to get their hands on the Nazi plunder from under the tunnels under the mansion. Blake feels he's in danger and goes to Washington D.C.

In Switzerland, Krystle has emerged from her coma and is in the process of being programmed. The doctor treating her is one of the members of the Consortium and they figured who better to kill Blake than his newly recovered wife. A nurse worries about the plot and tells Krystle to go home immediately.

Meanwhile, in Denver, there is a public auction being held at the Carrington mansion. Everything in it and the house itself are being auctioned to the highest bidder. As Krystle gets to the house, she's stunned to see the group of people walking around looking at all of the items for sale. She's also surprised by the fact that the entire house has been gutted and remodeled. As she walks up the staircase she asks a couple about Blake and the rest of the family. The woman proceeds to tell her that Blake's just gotten out of prison, Fallon and Krystina were saved from maniac Dennis Grimes

 and that Dex didn't fare very well from the fall over the balcony, but that Alexis is there.

When the auction is over, Alexis is shocked to see Krystle standing in front of her. She tells her that Sammy Jo is broke, Blake's lost everything and Krystina is living with Fallon in Los Angeles. Krystle waits for a taxi and then heads for California.

Blake visits Steven and asks him to help him arrange for a congressional hearing to discuss the Consortium's existence and how to end it. He also asks his son if he is happy living with Bart. Steven says they are perfectly fine together and for once, Blake approves.

Alexis is approached by a powerful businessman named Jeremy Van Dorn. Unbeknownst to her, Jeremy is the leader of the Consortium. He tells her that "they" (the Consortium) want her to take over a designer fashion line called 'Fashion Fury'. They want Arlen Marshall out of the way and are giving the opportunity to Alexis as a test. She accepts the challenge, especially after discovering that Sammy Jo is the company's lead model. Alexis finds a great deal of pleasure in the fact that she gets to personally fire Sammy Jo.

Krystle arrives at Fallon's house in Malibu and shares a tear-filled reunion with Krystina. While staying with Fallon and the children, Krystle is filled in on everything that's taken place since she's been gone. She and Krystina spend hours on the beach.

Jeff is in Switzerland trying to find out where Krystle is. He's about to get the entire story from her nurse when a speeding car runs over and kills her instantly. The Consortium kidnaps Jeff and holds him hostage. They group tries to make him cooperate with them and give up Blake's location but they get nowhere with him. Frustrated, they beat him and throw him in a cell.

Blake gets word from Fallon that Krystle is alive and with her so he immediately goes to Malibu. They are both so relieved to see each other but Blake knows she too is now in danger. They leave California and move to a small house in Virginia while they wait for word of the congressional hearing.

Fallon is worried about the fact that Jeff hasn't come back from Switzerland nor has he called to check in on the children. She asks Miles to fly to Switzerland to look for him. Miles reluctantly agrees and leaves. He's rather surprised to run into Adam and tries to make him see that the Consortium is an evil organization. Finally convincing him, the two plot to rescue Jeff. Adam is pleased when he runs into Kirby Anders. He asks her to dinner and at first she refuses. He persists and she changes her mind. Turns out she's been working for the Consortium as well as a translator. When Adam tells her about the plans to get Jeff back, Kirby volunteers to help. After quite a bit of fighting and creative maneuvering, they manage to break Jeff out and all of them escape. Kirby agrees to go back to the United States with Adam. They arrive at Blake's to let him know what is happening with the Consortium. Adam and Blake bury the hatchet again and agree to try forging a true father/son relationship. Adam also asks Kirby to marry him and to his surprise, she accepts the proposal.

Krystle is acting very strangely when she hears the sound of a ceiling fan. It is the trigger that she has been programmed with. She takes the gun she was given and waits in the front yard of the house. Since it's the middle of the night, Blake gets up to see where she is. He's shocked to see her aiming a gun at him and with a tremendous amount of talking, manages to get the gun away from her. He takes her to a psychiatrist who manages to deprogram her.

Blake is pleased that he's getting his congressional hearing. He knows he's going to win the support of Congress and regain everything that is rightfully his. Jeremy Van Dorn has other thoughts on that topic and tells Alexis that the Consortium wants her to go to the hearing and make sure she does everything she can to ruin Blake's chances with the officials. When she resists he tells her that she must pass the test. Reluctantly she goes and is accompanied by several members of the group.

It would appear that Blake is losing his case and in a last ditch effort tries to make the committee members understand that there was a mole at Denver Carrington. Everyone in the hearing is stunned to hear Adam admit to being that person. He then fills in the committee on all of the activities the Consortium is currently involved with. Alexis listens in dismay and Blake is overjoyed when the mansion and Denver Carrington are ordered to be returned immediately.

As the family gathers in Denver for a reunion celebration, Alexis and Jeremy are on a plane headed for a business meeting. Jeremy sees the expression on her face when she talks about the events taking place that evening and tells her that they're going to be there. She reminds him that she's not one of Blake's favorite people and he tells her not to worry, that he and Blake are good friends. When they arrive at the mansion, Blake has no idea who Jeremy is. Alexis makes an excuse for him and they leave. Once outside, she confronts him with his lie and finally figures out who he is. Grabbing her, he takes her to the tool shed, ties her ankles and wrists, gags her with his handkerchief and starts a power mower. He leaves her there with carbon monoxide filling the room. Going back into the mansion, Jeremy interrupts the video presentation the family is watching. Blake tells Krystle to keep watching the family movies while he finds out what Jeremy wants. Jeff recognizes the voice as the head of the Consortium, gets Steven and Adam and head for the library.

Jeremy is holding a gun on Blake. Blake tells him that the boys are behind him but Jeremy doesn't believe Blake. That is, not until he turns around. The men begin to fight and Jeremy makes a run for it. As they go after him, each of the men goes a different direction. Adam runs around to the driveway and finds Alexis' purse lying on the ground. He hears sounds coming from the shed and finds her just before she loses consciousness. Blake and Steven watch as Jeremy is put into a police car and is taken away. Little do they know that the car is being driven by two more members of the Consortium.

A few hours later, the entire family is gathered in the dining room. Blake proposes a toast to all of them and thanks them for their love and support. Krystle joins the toast and talks about how wonderful it is to be home. Always one to have the last word, Alexis joins them at the head of the table and thanks everyone for including her in their lives. As the evening winds down, Blake and Krystle stand in the ballroom and promise to never leave each other again.

COULD I HAVE THIS DANCE
THE FINAL CHAPTER OF THE CARRINGTON DYNASTY
Copyright 1995 – Judith A. Moose

As the curtain closed on the Dynasty era, fans were left wondering what had happened to their favorite characters. Those questions were answered three years later with "Dynasty - The Reunion" in which everyone lives happily ever after --- well almost everyone. Now four years later the story continues for Alexis, Blake, and the rest of the Carrington and Colby clans... and the realization of a dream coming true...

As the sun rises over Denver Alexis lays sleeping in her goose-feathered bed. Suddenly, she sits up, frightened, looking around the room. There are shadows in the corners of the room the light has yet to flood. She glances at the clock. It's 5:45. Alexis wonders why she is so uneasy. Then she remembers... the date is September 29, 1995. Her mind starts to wander back in time to 38 years ago on this day. This was the day her precious baby Adam was kidnapped and also the beginning of a cold and empty existence, for not only did she lose her son, but the love and attention of the only person who ever mattered - Blake.

She lay back down and closed her eyes thinking this feeling would surely go away. But the longer she lay there, the emptier she felt. Alexis looked at the clock again and read 5:57. "Well so much for sleep", she said as she got out of bed. The sunlight had completely engulfed the room. As Alexis lowers herself to sit at the vanity she surveys her body in the mirror. "Not bad for 57", she says with a smile. The smile soon disappears and staring back from the mirror is the picture of a bitter, lonely, old woman. The sparkling green eyes are glassy with dark circles underneath them. "Too much Champagne, too many tears", the words seem to flow from her mouth. Her mouth, the lips and smile that could charm the world now turn downward as Alexis tries to think of a reason to smile. "What is wrong with you?" the English beauty asks the image in the mirror. "What have you got to be depressed over? You've got four children who love you and you love them, you run a billion dollar empire, and you're one of the most powerful, respected women in the world. What more could you want?"...

On the outskirts of Denver, the house is bustling with the sound of people. Blake has just emerged from his bedroom and begins downstairs for breakfast. He says good morning to his children and grandchildren, and then looks to the end of the table. The chair is unoccupied. Blake shakes his head in despair for that is where his beloved Krystle used to be. He still can't believe Krystle's decision to divorce him, take Krystina, and move into the city. Blake sips his coffee and wonders what lies ahead...

Today won't be easy. A board meeting of both Denver Carrington and Colbyco is to be held at 11:00. The two companies have taken major financial hits and this will be a brainstorm session. Adam, Steven, Fallon, and Jeff have all been racking their brains to come up with a way to get Blake and Alexis to work together. But how? There simply has to be a way.

The board members begin to arrive at Denver Carrington. It is a somber mood as they take their seats for what could be the last time. As Blake and the children arrive they are greeted with an unenthusiastic hello from each member. Alexis arrives a few moments later, mumbles regards to the members, glares at Blake, and kisses her children good morning before settling into her chair.

"All right Blake, you got us into this mess, now how are we going to get out of it?" Alexis asks with her usual sarcasm.

"Alexis," Blake says with an aggravated edge in his voice, "You know perfectly well this was a Colbyco investment from the beginning and it's not my fault the deal went bad!"

"Don't give me that Blake. Every time anything has ever gone wrong in business or personal matters you always manage to find a way to blame me for causing it. Well this time, it's not my fault. Denver Carrington was in charge of administrating the financing, so if you want someone to blame, go stand in front of a mirror!"

"It's very easy to blame you for most of what happens because every time I suspect you of creating or causing a problem, you usually do something. I do expect the worst from you and so far I've never been disappointed!"

"Okay that's enough!" Fallon interjects, attempting to sound like she has authority. "For the past fifteen years we have all sat here watching the two of you rip each other apart. Well I for one have had enough. All our lives we've been told to behave, never step out of line, and above all else - act like Carringtons. When exactly are the two of you planning to do so?"

"Fallon's right," Steven says, "For years Dad has been telling me to act like a Carrington, be a real man, but right now I wish I were someone else, if only so I didn't have to be Blake and Alexis Carrington's son. We have a problem with the potential to send both of these companies into bankruptcy and instead of figuring a way out of this, the two of you are too stubborn or maybe too pig-headed to swallow your pride, admit you were wrong, and work together. You built Denver Carrington together whether you want to admit it or not. Are you really willing to let everything you spent your lives building go because you're too hard-headed to say I'm sorry and start over again?"

Blake and Alexis are stunned that their children would say such things to them and in front of Denver Carrington and Colbyco's boards. They glowered disgusted expressions at each other, nodded their heads in agreement, and went to work.

At 6 p.m. the board members left with very little to work with. Jeff, Fallon, Steven, and Adam left about a half hour later. By 8:30 p.m., Blake and Alexis were still sitting at the table, grasping at straws and coming up with nothing but air.

Blake muttered: "I knew this would be a nightmare."

"No more of one than being married to you." Alexis shot back at him.

"Thank God that's over. I'd probably be dead by now..." Blake threw in.

Alexis, having quite enough says, "Look, you think you have it all. Blake Carrington's perfect little world. Well look around, your precious Krystle has left you and taken Krystina with her, your company is in ruin, your children are embarrassed to be related to you, and here you are, the mighty giant, all washed up. You probably couldn't even get a lady of the evening excited..."

"Well at least she'd be a lady. The best you ever got was underrated slut!"

"How dare you, you pompous, arrogant, excuse for a man! If you were ever half the man you claim to be, I never would have had to sleep with anyone else..." Alexis shouts as she slaps his angry face. "If you ever really loved me you never would have thrown me in as "part of the deal"."

Blake grabbed Alexis' arms and violently shook her. "If you ever, ever say anything about Krystle or my private life, I swear you'll never see the children or the light of day again!"

"Oh no Blake, you stole my children once and you'll never take them from again! Never!" Alexis says with fury. Blake grabs her again and suddenly jerks her body next to his and kisses her. Thirty years of hatred quickly dissolves into passion as they sink to the office floor.

"Blake," Alexis gasps, "Blake, I hope you're not waiting for me to stop you."

"Alexis, for once in your life, shut up..." Blake whispers as he begins unbuttoning her blouse and kisses her again.

Alexis closes her eyes and lays back. She feels a teardrop on her cheek. Thirty years of waiting for this moment are finally over. Blake is in her arms, the long-awaited dream is coming true.

As they lie in the office basking in the afterglow of their moment of passion, Blake and Alexis are a little uneasy. Blake looks at Alexis, she seems lost in thought. "What are you thinking?" Blake asks.

"I was just thinking of how surprised the children would be if they walked in and saw us like this," she answers. She couldn't bring herself to say that what she was really doing is wondering if Blake had just made love to her or to memories of Krystle.

Blake laughs in agreement, "Yes, that would be rather amusing, wouldn't it? Perhaps we should think about calling it a night." Alexis agrees and they rearrange their clothes, fix their hair, and sneak out past security. They have another brainstorm session in the morning.

Back in her penthouse, Alexis lays in bed, lost in a dream. She and Blake are back in Singapore but this time they really are Mr. and Mrs. Carrington. As a band plays, they start dancing, reminiscing of the way they met, fell in love, and got married. Then the band begins to play "Bewitched, Bothered, and Bewildered". It was the first song they ever danced to. As the music played, Blake held her closer and whispered "I love you" into her ear.

Meanwhile, Blake is unable to sleep, so he goes downstairs to the library. He pours himself a brandy, sits down, and sighs. He's at a loss, trying to put the last few hours into perspective. He never intended for anything like that to ever happen. It was just when Alexis' eyes flashed with fury, all he saw was her beauty. Blake finished his drink, left the snifter on the table, and went upstairs determined to sleep and to never repeat this night again.

The next morning, Blake arrives at Denver Carrington and is surprised to see Alexis is already there waiting for him and begins talking. "Blake, I think we should talk about what happened last night"...

Blake looks apprehensive as he sits down and says: "Yes, I think you're right. What happened last night was a mistake. We both got a little out of hand and got up in a moment. I apologize for my actions and promise it will never happen again."

Alexis' smile begins to fade. That wasn't the reaction she was hoping for. She fought back a tear as she said: "I'm sorry too, Blake. It was just a flashback in time. It happened, it's over, now let's forget it and move on. The board members must be arriving by now. Let's get to work."

Assembled in the boardroom once again, the talking seemed to go forever. Blake was still uncomfortable about last night, but tried to push it out of his mind. Alexis appeared to be a million miles away. Her eyes remain fixed on a corner of the room, the corner were less than twelve hours ago, she and Blake had made love. And it is love, at least for her. "I need a break," she thought to herself, "maybe a few weeks away". After the meeting broke up she said good-bye to her children and headed for a place in the sun. How she wished she weren't going alone.

While Alexis locked herself away in a villa, Blake carried on with business as usual. There was still a feeling nagging at him, a feeling he hadn't had in a very long time. He missed Alexis. He missed her voice, her perfume, her beguiling smile, even her snide remarks, though he could live without those. His mind drifted back to that night in the boardroom. She was right; his world was falling down around him. Blake shook his head and told himself to stop. He still loved Krystle and getting involved with Alexis would only end up hurting him again.

Two weeks later Alexis emerged from her airplane and was greeted by Adam. "Hello Mother, you look well rested. Good trip?"

"Yes darling, how's everything here?" Alexis inquired.

"Fine, business as usual Mother," Adam replied.

"Business as usual", Alexis thought. How could she be nonchalant around Blake when all she wants to do is love him? The only thing she accomplished in Barbados was the realization that what she needed was Blake, in business and in private. Cecil, Dex, and Sean, husbands two, three and four were right. Her heart and soul have always belonged to Blake. Though she truly did love Dex, there was always a soft spot for Blake that even Dex couldn't come close to.

"By the way, there's another meeting scheduled for the day after tomorrow," Adam continued. Alexis nodded her head in acknowledgment, climbed into the car, and quietly thought of what to do now.

The board meeting is a success. Finally, a plan to save the companies is to be put into action. Blake and Alexis will have to fly to Washington, DC to address the SEC. It would be a quick trip; they should be gone for a day. They leave tomorrow.

It is an exhausting day of arguing but Blake and Alexis emerge victorious. Walking out of the building, they see it has begun snowing again. The nation's capital is already covered...more was the last thing it needed. In the cab to the plane, the radio DJ announces that the airport is closed until the blizzard condition warning is lifted. Blake and Alexis look at each other and asks the driver to take them to a hotel. The driver leaves them at the front entrance. Blake looks up and jokingly says: "Oh how appropriate, Alexis we're staying at the Watergate."

"Shh Blake, don't tell anyone, it's a conspiracy." Alexis laughs. They walk to the front desk and are informed that there is only one room left. Stranded, they take the room. They have no luggage since they were only supposed to be gone for the day. Blake calls home and tells a housekeeper that they've been snowed in for the night, and then asks Alexis if she'd like to have dinner downstairs or have room service bring something up. Alexis opts for room service and tells Blake she's going to take a shower while they wait.

Back in Denver, the children have come home expecting to hear about the meeting. Instead they hear about Blake and Alexis being snowed in together.

Adam smirks and says: "I would pay to be there to see what they're doing."

"Are you kidding, Adam..." Jeff sarcastically replies. "I wouldn't want to be within a hundred miles of them tonight. Knowing the two of them, they are pulling their hair out, screaming at the top of their lungs, and probably trying to kill each other."

Steven laughs and adds: "Well nothing to worry about then. They hate each other as much as they always have. They're probably shouting at each other right now."

Alexis comes out of the bathroom and laughs when she sees Blake hanging a quilt from the ceiling down to the center of the bed. "Well it worked for Gable didn't it?" He said as hammered with his shoe for the last time. "There that should do it."

Drying her hair with a towel Alexis bats her eyes and asks: "What's for dinner?"

"Ah, lobster in garlic sauce, a freshly tossed salad, asparagus spears, and for dessert...raspberry truffle cheesecake. Oh, almost forgot, we'll be drinking Chateau Marmot 1961."

"My favorite vintage," Alexis says smiling, "You remembered."

After dinner they decided to go to sleep. As they both lay there, the quilt hanging between them, Blake asks: "What are you thinking?"

"Nothing", she answers.

"Want to know what I'm thinking?" Blake inquires.

"I KNOW what you're thinking." Alexis emphasizes knows.

"What do you think?" Blake presses on.

"About what you're thinking?" she asks.

"About what I'm thinking," he continues.

"What if what you're thinking isn't what I think you're thinking?" she replies.

"Live dangerously. What do you think?" he says coyly.

"I think," Alexis hesitates, "Oh what the hell..." The blanket comes down as they meet in the middle of the bed to spend another night in each other's arms.

Alexis awoke the next morning to the sounds of snowplows fighting their way through the streets. She lay in bed staring at Blake as he slept. It had been nearly thirty years since she had watched Blake wake up and she savored every moment. His eyes began to flutter, and then slowly open. Blake looked at her smiling face, smiled back and said: "Good morning" as he leaned over to kiss her.

"Not only is it a good morning Blake, it's probably the most beautiful morning Washington DC has ever seen," Alexis says with enthusiasm. Her eyes appear luminously bright and happy. A wonderful lightheartedness is coming over her as she gazes into his eyes. Alexis is in love.

The plane ride home is a bumpy one, not only the turbulence, but Blake's mood as well. His mind keeps wandering back to Krystle and the good times they had. He glances at Alexis, and then begins reading a paper. Maybe he was wrong about letting Krystle go; maybe he was wrong about getting involved with Alexis again. If only he knew what to do. Blake spends the rest of the flight trying to sort out his thoughts. He decides to talk to Krystle.

As the plane lands in Denver, Blake and Alexis try to come up with a way not to answer their children's questions about what happened last night. It will be hard to avoid them asking questions, as Alexis is radiantly glowing. The plane comes to a stop at the hangar and as expected, Adam, Steven, and Fallon are waiting.

"Blake, you were right, they are here," Alexis says. "Perhaps we should just tell them about last night. One thing we can say is that our children aren't stupid. They're bound to figure out that something happened, so why don't we save them the time of giving us the third degree. They'll need to get used to the idea that we're an item, as it were," she says with a smile.

Blake hesitates and suggests: "Alexis, I don't think we should involve the children yet. Why don't we just take our time and when the moment is right we'll talk to the kids? Okay?"

"Okay Blake, but I think it would be better coming from us than from gossip on the street. But if it makes you happy, I won't say anything."

They get off the plane acting as if they couldn't wait to get away from each other. Each of them hugs the children and express how happy they are to be home. Adam, Steven, and Fallon came together; so all five of them ride back into town.

Adam can't help but notice that Alexis has a definite change in her. He can't quite figure out what it is but there's something different about his mother. She seems carefree as she and Blake are telling them about the SEC meeting. The driver drops Alexis off at her penthouse. She tells Blake she'll call him soon so they can pick up where they left off on the plane.

Blake asks his driver to drop him off at Krystle's apartment. He tells the children that he wants to see Krystina and he'll meet them at the office later. He knocks on Krystle's door and is shocked to see a man answer. The mystery man quickly says good-bye and leaves. Blake has a jealous feeling as he watches him go. He turns to Krystle and asks, "Well, he certainly left in a hurry. What's wrong, something I said?"

Krystle gives Blake a very disapproving look and says, "You could have called before you came over. I would have saved you the trip. Krystina's spending the night at a friend's and I have other places to be, so if you'll excuse me, I have to get ready to go." She walks to the door and opens it. "I'd like you to leave."

"Krystle, I'm sorry. I didn't mean for this visit to be like this. I didn't come here just to see Krystina; I wanted to talk to you. There are so many things I want to say to you. Please, can we sit down and talk for a while?"

Krystle closes the door, walks over and sits down on the sofa. "Okay Blake, let's talk. What do you want to talk about?"

"I want to talk about us," he begins.

She interrupts him by saying, "Blake there is no us. We said goodbye. Why can't you just leave it at that?"

"Because I still love you and as long as I live I'll never understand why we aren't together. Until the day I die, you're the last person I want to see at night and the first one in the morning. I've spent so many nights awake wondering why we grew apart. Krystle, I'm here to beg you for one more chance. We had something too rare and too beautiful to let it go without a fight. Can you honestly tell me you feel nothing for me anymore?"

"Of course I still have feelings for you Blake. You're Krystina's father and we'll always have that bond. I have to admit that I do still love you too, but I don't know where we stand. I think we need to give ourselves time to think about where to go from here."

Blake nods his head in acknowledgment and turns to go. He looks back at Krystle and asks her if she would consider joining him at the Carousel Ball at the end of the week. Krystle accepts as Blake leaves. On the way to his office, Blake has a feeling of relief and joy. He will win Krystle back... he knows it. His joy is short lived. The car phone rings. It's Alexis.

"Just thought I'd call to say hello. I'm at my office buried in paperwork and I figured if I didn't call you now, I probably wouldn't get to hear your voice for days. It could take that long to get out of here." she says with a joking laugh.

Blake hesitates for a moment and then says, "Alexis, it's very important that I talk to you. I need to see you sometime today. Do you think you can find the time?"

"I always have time to talk to you. Shall we say 8:00 at my place?"

"That will be fine. I'll see you then," he answers.

Alexis smiles while she thinks, "He wants to see me. I wonder what could be so important." Her mind starts to drift to tonight. She and Blake will have dinner, talk for a while, perhaps make love again, and fall asleep wrapped in each other's arms. What a glorious way to spend an evening.

Wearing her most beautiful outfit and Blake's favorite perfume, Alexis waits for him to arrive. She glances at the table where a candlelight dinner is set and the champagne is chilling. She has a sense of exhilaration, a wonderful anticipation just to hear his voice. A few moments later there is a knock on the door.

"Good evening Blake. My goodness, don't you look overly solemn. Wait, I know you've forgotten your smile at the office. That's all right, I'll see if I can find you another one. Perhaps a glass of champagne?"

Blake shakes his head no, takes a deep breath, and looks at her smiling face. She can see that something is wrong with him.

"My God Blake, are you all right? Has something happened to one of the children? What is it?"

"No, no there's nothing wrong with the children. Alexis, please sit down. There's something you need to know. I don't know quite how to say this and I want you to know that nothing will change the past few months or what we've shared."

"Blake, we've always been totally honest with each other. You don't have to be concerned with what the world will think. Do you remember the tango we did on the night we met? We made time stand still. I fell in love with you that very moment and after all that's happened between us, I love you just as much right now. We've finally found that what we need in this world is each other."

"Alexis, what I'm trying to tell you is that I've already found the person I need in this world. I have and I always will love Krystle. It's taken her leaving me to make me realize just how much I do love and need her in my life."

Alexis is stunned. This was not at all what she was expecting to hear him say. She closed her eyes and bit her bottom lip to keep herself from crying. Blake continues talking, "I'm sorry if this hurts you. I never meant to do that. We never should have let it go this far. We were just two lonely people looking for someone to hold. My heart belongs to Krystle, and I can't change that, not even for you. I think I should go." He stands up and walks to the door. As he opens the door to go, Blake turns around and sees the table with the candles flickering. "I'm sorry," he says as he walks out the door.

Alexis watches the door close behind him. Her world has just walked out the door. "This can't be happening. I can't have just lost him twice."... She pours herself a drink and turns toward the table. Leaning over, she blows the candles out one by one. Looking out the window, she sees Blake's car moving into the distance. Walking back into her empty bedroom, Alexis sits down at her vanity and starts taking off her jewelry. She looks at herself in the mirror and once again sees a bitter, lonely, old woman. "Why Blake, why can't you love me?" she asks as the tears start to fall.

A board meeting has been called to discuss the details of Blake and Alexis' trip to Washington. Assembled in the boardroom once again, they sit at opposite ends of the table. There is a definite coolness in Alexis' mannerism. After the meeting adjourns, Fallon asks her mother if she will join her on a shopping spree. She needs to find her gown for the Carousel Ball on Friday.

"You will be there, won't you Mother?"

"I don't know darling, I'm not in a party mood these days."

"I've noticed. Mother, what is it? One day you're walking on sunshine and now you look as if you've lost your best friend. I know we've sometimes had our problems, but it hurts me to see you in pain. Please, tell me what's wrong."

"You don't know how much it means to me to hear you say that, Fallon. I don't understand this game called life. Why is it that when you think you have life so well controlled, it slips away, and the years of your life just melt before your eyes. When you're a child, you sit there on your Daddy's knee and dream about the future. You grow up, get married, and dream about the future. You watch your children grow up and have children of their own and dream about the future. Then you wake up one morning and you realize that the future you dreamed so much of is now nothing more than your past and all the dreams are gone. If life was meant to be a fairy tale like the stories your Daddy used to tell, then I'm afraid my knight in shining armor has rode into the sunset without me. I've spent so long dreaming about the future, I never got to enjoy the present. Does that make any sense?"

"Yes it does, Mother, but why do think you have to stop dreaming? Your knight in shining armor could be searching for you right now, or at the Carousel Ball. But how will you ever know if the dreams are gone unless you give your heart and mind the chance to let that knight into them?"

Alexis smiles at her beautiful daughter and says, "What did I ever do that was so good I got you? The Carousel Ball, huh? Good thing I don't have anything else planned for that evening. I'll have to find something suitable for riding into the sunset to wear." She and Fallon spend the rest of the day laughing, shopping, and enjoying the present.

The crowd has begun to gather outside the auditorium, waiting to see Denver's elite as they arrive for the social event of the year. The crowd erupts in applause as Blake and Krystle arrive. Inside they begin to mingle among the crowd. Steven and Sammy Jo are already on the dance floor. Adam and Kirby decide to join them. Blake notices that Jeff and Fallon have yet to arrive, but he doesn't let it bother him. He's there with his beloved Krystle on his arm and that's the only thing that matters.

A few minutes later Jeff and Fallon arrive with Alexis. It is a rare occasion as Alexis came without a date. This is one of those times she wished Dex were still here. Whenever she needed someone she could always count on Dex. She reaches for a glass of champagne, determined to enjoy herself no matter what...

The room is buzzing with gossip. Alexis Colby without an escort! How shocking, considering she's usually surrounded by men. Alexis is aware of the rumors circulating, but she tries not to let it bother her. Just as she takes her seat with Jeff and Fallon, a waiter comes to the table. Carrying a sprig of heather, the waiter hands it to Alexis and says: "From the gentleman at the bar." Alexis turns around and the mystery man raises his glass and smiles. She smiles back and mouths "Thank you".

His eyes never leave her. They follow her wherever she goes. Finally, Alexis excuses herself from the table.

"Mother, where are you going?" Fallon asks.

"To find out why he keeps staring at me." Alexis answers.

"Maybe he's afraid to talk to you. You being Alexis Colby and all. Although I will say one thing...He's gorgeous!"

"Fairy tales and knights. I think I'll go see if he has a white horse." Alexis laughs as she walks toward him.

He turns around again and looks at her. Alexis looks up into his eyes and sighs. They are sapphire blue. She smiles and says, "Well you've been staring at me so long, you might as well know my name..."

"I know your name, but apparently you don't know mine. I'm...sorry, my beeper's going off. Will you excuse me please, I must take care of this." and with that her mystery man walks away, leaving Alexis infatuated and intrigued.

Alexis walks back over to the table. Fallon asks, "So who is he?"

"I don't know, darling, but I do intend to find out..." Alexis says with a lustful determination. As they continue talking Blake and Krystle walk to the table.

Blake begins, "Good evening. Lovely party isn't it?"

Fallon answers, "Yes Daddy, it is. Krystle you look wonderful tonight."

"Thank you Fallon, so do you. Alexis, no date? What's wrong no one would fly into your web?" Krystle sarcastically says.

Alexis glares at Krystle..."That's very good Krystle. I see you've been practicing. Too bad you haven't practiced your taste in clothing. Pastels make you look so mousy. You know what that dress needs...a little splash of color..." She picks up a glass of red wine and splatters Krystle's white gown. "There that looks much better." and with that Alexis picks up her purse, laughs, and walks out the door.

Alexis walks through the door of her penthouse feeling a mixture of guilt and satisfaction. "Imagine Krystle thinking for one moment that she could take Blake away from me and not have to suffer for the rest of her life," Alexis laughs to herself. Going into her bedroom, Alexis is outraged when she sees the mystery man from the Ball in her bed.

"Who the hell are you and how did you get in here?" Alexis shouts.

"I've been waiting for you my darling... Don't be afraid, come to bed..."

"Come to...come to bed? I'm not going to bed with you! I don't even know who the hell you are! I want you out of my bed and out of my penthouse now or I'm calling security."

"Fine, call security, and I'll tell them we were having a lover's quarrel. They'll never know the difference. From what I hear you should have a revolving door added to your bedroom. I'll go tonight my love, but I will see you...ALL of you...again." He gets out of bed, dresses, and starts to leave. He turns around one last time and adds, "By the way, you can call me Jonathon."

The telephone rings at 7 a.m., Alexis answers the phone, it's Fallon. "Mother, I can't believe what you did last night! After all these years you would think you and Krystle could at least be civil in public.

Why do you always have to do something to embarrass Daddy?"

Alexis has a rough edge in her voice as she answers. "Embarrass your father! Fallon believe it or not your father has a lot more to worry about than me pouring a glass of wine over his beloved Krystle. If you think for one minute that I'm going to stand by while that oh so transparent gold-digger sinks her claws back into your father, you're all in for a very rude awakening. Now I love you and the others more than anything else in the world, but I'll be damned if she's going to have your father. And darling, do yourself a favor, don't call me before 9:00 again unless it's an emergency. Goodbye Fallon." She hangs up the phone, sits up, and swears she'll get Blake, even if it's the last thing she ever does.

Blake wakes up in Krystle's bed. He glances across the room and sees her holding her gown. "They'll never be able to get this out.," she says looking at the wine stain. Blake gets out of bed and walks over to see the damage.

"I'm going over to talk to her today. It's time she learns once and for all that I want her out of our lives and that I won't stand for her tantrums anymore." Blake angrily says.

Adam and Alexis get off the elevator on the 22nd floor of Colbyco's building and begin toward their offices. Alexis is informed by her secretary that Blake is waiting in her office. Alexis swings open the door, strolls over to her desk, sits down and looks up at Blake's angry face.

"And what, prey tell, can I do for you?" she asks.

"What you can do is explain that little stunt last night! You had no right to do anything like that to Krystle. When are you going to leave her alone?"

"When that blonde tramp is on a bus back to Ohio or where ever the hell she's from. I'm tired of her using you and our children to get what she wants. She's the paragon of truth and happiness in everyone's eyes but by damned, she's never fooled me. She's using our children and the Carrington name as her stepping-stone to a fortune. Well they're our children, our family name, and our family home. Up until now I've only toyed with her because I found it amusing, but she plays a deadly game and I'm going to stop her. When will I leave Krystle alone? When they start serving ice cream in hell! Now I have work to do, so get out of here please."

Blake angrily turns to go but changes his mind and sits down. "You know, I'm looking at a woman that I used to know better than anyone else. I remember a beautiful English girl with emerald eyes that I fell madly in love with. Now I see a cold, unfeeling, ruthless woman who contaminates and destroys everything she touches. What happened to my Alexis?"

Alexis looks up at him with pure hatred in her eyes. "As you're leaving, think back about thirty years, and look in the mirror. You'll see the monster that made me this way. Now please go..."

Blake reaches for the door, turns and says: "I pity you Alexis. It must be a horrible feeling to know that you're all alone, but that's the story of your life and it's all in the dedication - To Alexis - with all my love."

"I've been lonelier with men than I've ever been by myself, so save your pity if that's all you've got left. I don't need you Blake; I don't need you or anyone else. I was a fool to think we could stand a chance again. So tuck your tail in between your legs and run back to Krystle if that's what you want. And don't bother to look behind your back, because when I finally get what I want, I'll be standing there to see your face. Now for the last time, get out!"

He shakes his head and slams the door behind himself. Alexis reaches for the phone and tells her secretary, "Get me Morgan Hess on the phone." The buzzer rings, she picks up the phone and starts talking. "Mr. Hess its Alexis Colby calling. Put on your tacky blazer and get over to my office. I have a job for you."

Blake walks into his office shaking his head and cursing the day he ever met Alexis. Steven asks what's wrong when he sees Blake's face. Blake looks at him and replies, "What's wrong? The same thing that's been wrong for forty years! That twisted barracuda you call mother... I swear I would like nothing more than to see her drop off the face of the Earth. At least then I might get some peace!"

"Dad, is this about last night? Don't you think you're overreacting a little?"

"No, no I don't. For thirty years, that woman has been trying to ruin my life, she's made Krystle's life a living hell and I'm tired of it. God help you all because she is your mother, but she is without a doubt the most self-centered, egotistical, person in the world. Sometimes I wonder if she really is a person, because no one could possibly do what she does and feel nothing for doing it! I'm going to teach her a lesson in life she's never going to forget."

Adam knocks on his mother's office door and comes in. He can see that Alexis is very disturbed. "What was that all about, Mother?"

"That was about the mighty giant and his damned beloved tramp."

"Ah, so father came to chastise you for the red wine incident last night. Do you really think it was necessary to do that to Krystle?"

"Krystle, Krystle, always Krystle! I am so tired of constantly hearing about Krystle, and Krystle's feelings. I don't give a damn about Krystle's feelings. I wish I could drop her out of an airplane and forget to pack the parachute! Adam, I swear I'm not going to rest until that blonde barracuda is out of your father's life once and for all! Maybe then I'll get some peace."

"You know Dad will be watching every move you make, so what are you going to do?"

"I'm not sure yet, but your right, your father will be watching. I want him to be watching. I 'm going to teach that man a lesson he will never forget..."

Adam begins to laugh and says "I'll bet father is saying the exact same thing about you right now." The intercom on Alexis' desk buzzes and her secretary announces, "Mr. Hess to see you Mrs. Colby."

"Thank you, send him in." Adam looks at his mother and asks, "What's he doing here?"

"Just a little personal business darling. You get back to work and I'll fill you in on the plan later." Adam leaves as Mr. Hess is coming in. "Mr. Hess," Alexis begins, "Close the door and sit down. The reason I've called you here is of a personal nature. Remember when I sent you out to find Sean Rowan? I want you to do that again. There is a man whom I saw at the Carousel Ball. He followed me all night long, and when I got home he was in my apartment. The only things I can tell you about him are that he's tall, handsome; he has blue eyes and dark grayish hair. His name is Jonathon. I don't know his last name or anything else about him."

Morgan Hess leaned over in his chair and said, "That's not exactly a lot to go with Mrs. Colby. This could take a while."

"This can't take a while, Mr. Hess. I don't have the time for you take your time doing this. I want it done soon. And the amount of time we've spent discussing this, you could already be out there earning your fee. Good day Mr. Hess." He leaves and Alexis begins thinking to herself. "Now, what to do about Blake and that damned woman. There has got to be something or someone I've missed along the way. I just have to find it. Your days are numbered Krystle; I hope you've polished up on your stenography skills. You're going to need them by the time I'm done with you.

Meanwhile, at Denver Carrington, Blake and Krystle are having lunch together and are discussing the morning's events. "Blake, I can't believe that Alexis is going to back away and leave us alone."

"If I know Alexis, you're right she won't. I don't know what it is that makes her do the things she does. You know, she wasn't always like this. The Alexis I married was a young, beautiful, loving person who wanted nothing more from life than a home and children. There was always that determined drive in her, but never like this. It was that drive that I loved the most about her then. Isn't it funny that it's the thing I hate the most now."

"Blake, I know there have always been a lot of hard feelings between the two of you, but you would think she'd try to be civil at least for her children's sake. Maybe all she needs is to find someone else to take her mind off us."

Blake looks at Krystle and gently smiles. His mind drifts back to a few weeks ago, when he told Alexis that there was no chance for them. "Maybe you're right. At least when Dex was alive, she could always turn to him and he'd be waiting there with open arms. I tried so hard to stop him from getting involved with her in the beginning, but he was so much in love with Alexis, he wouldn't listen. In a way, I'm glad he didn't. I think somewhere in the back of her mind, Alexis just might have loved him too."

As the sun sets in Denver, Alexis walks into her penthouse. A fire is lit in the fireplace, champagne is chilling, and music is playing. She recognizes the tune immediately, it's "Bewitched, Bothered, and Bewildered". Alexis looks toward the open terrace doors and sees a man on the balcony. "Blake? Is that you?" she asks.

The man turns around. It's Jonathon... "No my love, it's not Blake. In fact, why don't you forget about Blake Carrington? You're never going to have him, and besides, why would you want him when you could have me?" He looks at her face. The expression is a mixture of anger and surprise. "I know, how did I get in here? How did I know this was yours and Blake's song? How do I know that the champagne that's chilling is the same vintage that you drank on your wedding night? I make it a habit to know everything about the women in my life. I know when you're up, when you're down, when caviar excites you, and when you'd rather have popcorn. I know about Switzerland and Amanda, Adam's breakdown, Steven's present gay lover, and Fallon's affair with Miles Colby. I even know about your cousin's affair with Dex Dexter. Do you want me to tell you what color dress you were wearing the first night you and Blake made love?"

"How could you possibly know something like that? No one should know things like that. Who are you and what exactly do you want from me?" Alexis asks with a hint of fear in her voice.

"Who am I? I told you my name is Jonathon. I've already said that I like to know everything about my women and as far as I'm concerned, you are my only woman. What do I want? I want to take you to new and exciting heights. I want to feel you in my arms as I make love to you all night. I want to spend the rest of our lives together as one. And someday I want you to be Mrs. Jonathon Chase."

Jonathon reached out and took Alexis in his arms. He pressed his lips next to hers and began to kiss her. She could feel herself giving in to the feeling of his strong arms around her. Before she knew it, he had picked her up and carried her to bed. They spent the entire night making love. When she woke up the next morning, he was gone. There was a photo album on the table. The page was turned to a picture of her and Dex. A note was lying next to the picture, "He's the next one I'll replace".

Alexis sat down and looked at the picture. It was their first anniversary. She picked up the phone and called her pilot. "Eric, could you please have the plane ready for takeoff in a hour. I want to fly to Wyoming. Thank you."

Three hours later, the Colbyco plane landed in Laramie, Wyoming. Alexis took a taxi to a remote place. It was large; all the flowers were in bloom. She walked over to a bench under a tree and sat down. She raised her head slightly to see the stone in front of her. It read Farnsworth "Dex" Dexter 1952 - 1989, may he always rest in peace. "Dex, darling I'm sorry it's taken me so long to come. I couldn't be here when they buried you and it's taken me this long to be able to face myself much less forgive myself for what happened. I never meant to hurt you. It was just when I found out about you and Sable, all I could think of was how much you hurt me. I never stopped to think about why you felt you had to hurt me. It never occurred to me that I hurt you too. I wish there were some way I could turn back the clock and make it all better. I need you here so much. You were my best friend, you were the only one who could understand me and love me for who I am. If you're up there somewhere, please keep an eye on me. I need to know that there's still someone in the world I can turn to when I need to talk. I'd give up everything I have if I could just hear your voice and feel your arms around me one more time. I love you." She leaned down and kissed the top of the stone. Walking away in tears, there was a sudden roll of thunder. She looked toward the sky and saw a bright rainbow appear, and a rose from one of the bushes fell at her feet. Alexis picked up the flower, held it to her lips and kissed it. Looking back to the sky and then to the grave, she smiled and said "Thank you my darling."...

Meanwhile, back in Denver, Blake is busy planning a party to celebrate his reunion with Krystle. He wants the entire world to know that they're back together. The party will be held at the Carrington mansion next weekend. Adam asks if there's anything he can do to help.

"Yes Adam, there is something you can do... You can make sure your mother stays as far away as possible. The last thing I need is to have to deal with one of her tantrums. This is going to be a very special night for Krystle and me and I want everything to be perfect."

"Father, how in the world do you think I'm going to be able to do anything about Mother? You know she's going to do whatever she wants to and no one has been able to stop her yet. You were married for eleven years, did she ever behave herself then?"

Blake looked up at Adam and laughed, "There was a time when your mother was much more human than she is now. All I know is that I want the Ice Queen as far away as I can get her."

Adam lowered his head and sat down. He glanced back at Blake. "You know there are some times when I think that Mother's not the cause of all your problems. I've thought about it a few times. You're always the first one to attack her, whether she's done anything or not. Why do you always assume that her only goal in life is to destroy you?"

"Adam, I know you love your mother, and in her own peculiar way she may actually love you. Though quite honestly, I don't think she could ever love anyone except herself. She has done nothing for the last twenty-five years but try to bring me to my knees. She's done things that are completely unforgivable that you know nothing about. Your Mother and I have been fighting for a long, long time and I don't think we'll ever stop, so don't worry about who's left when the war is over."

"You're right Father, Mother has done some really horrible things in her day. I know about Krystle losing your first child because Mother fired a gun while Krystle was horseback riding. I know about Roger Grimes and all the other affairs she had while you away. I know she attacks you every chance she gets, but have you ever stopped to think about why she does it?"

"She does it because she's a piranha, and she's not going to stop until I'm dead and buried. She'll probably stomp on my grave a few times a week just to make sure I'm in there."

"Father, has it occurred to you that the reason she does those things is because she knows it will make you angry? Every time you get angry, you go over to confront her. It seems to be the only way she ever gets your attention. It doesn't seem to matter if you're yelling at her for five minutes or five hours, she has your undivided attention. As far as Krystle's miscarriage goes, we were the one thing that only she had given you. You even had one child you knew nothing about, the thought of someone else giving you a child threatened Mother's only link to you. When you divorced, she didn't leave you, you threw her away. I know you don't want to hear this but I truly think she's jealous of Krystle. Think about it for a minute Father. Here Krystle is, with all four of Mother's children and grandchildren living with her, in a house you had built for Mother, and she has you. You know Mother has actually said that under different circumstances she and Krystle might have been good friends, her only mistake was marrying you and for that she'd pay dearly. Hell would freeze over before she admits it but Mother is now and always has been head over heels in love with you. The two of you are the only ones too blind to see it." Adam leaves for the office.

Blake begins thinking about what Adam said. Alexis in love with anyone other than herself. He shrugs his shoulders and goes back to work on the guest list for the party.

Adam heads straight for Alexis' office. "Mother, Father's throwing a reconciliation party for Krystle and himself and I've been ordered to keep you as far away as I can."

Alexis looks up from her paperwork. "Really, how very interesting. He's throwing a party to welcome home his concubine. Let me guess, he doesn't want me anywhere near it, so it's at the mansion. Don't worry darling I'll stay at least five feet away from him the entire night. Wish I could say the same for Krystle. I know just the person to accompany me to the party. His name is Jonathon Chase. Good work darling, I knew I could always count on you. What ever will I wear?"

"Mother, he's serious. He doesn't want you there."

"Like I live to obey his every command. See you at the party." She gets up from her chair and leaves the office. Adam shakes his head as he watches her go. Somehow this is not going to be a quiet party.

The guests arrive at the mansion for Blake and Krystle's party. Adam, Fallon, and Steven all look wary, wondering what Alexis is going to try tonight. Alexis and Jonathon make their entrance, she smiles coyly at her children as she reaches for a glass of champagne. Taking Jonathon by the arm, she says, "Come darling, there are some people you must meet."

Blake and Krystle come down the hallway and see Alexis and Jonathon standing there. Blake is visibly annoyed as he looks at Alexis. Krystle is stunned when she sees Jonathon on Alexis' arm. Blake begins, "Alexis, you're not welcome here."

"Oh Blake, calm down and have some champagne. I just want to toast your happiness." Alexis says sweetly. She looks at Jonathon. "Darling, I must show you the garden." Walking away, Alexis looks back at Krystle and says, "Krystle dear, have Blake get you a bottle of hair color. Your stenographer roots are showing."

Blake watches them go out onto the terrace. As they go he feels a little pang of jealousy as he thinks of Alexis with someone else. Then he remembers the face. "I know that man", he says. "I can't place it, but I've seen him somewhere before." Krystle stands there next to him and thinks to herself, "Yes, I know his face too. What is he doing here with her? He said he loved me." She watches as

Jonathon leans down and kisses Alexis. Krystle's eyes begin to tear. "My God, Jonathon, no."....

It's been two days since the party. Krystle is still trying to figure out what Jonathon was doing with Alexis. She calls his hotel again. Still no answer, Krystle leaves another message. Where could he be?

His arm rests across her body; she can feel its weight as she breathes. He moves closer and begins to nibble on her ear. Still lost in a dream, Alexis mumbles, "Oh Blake, I love it when you do that." Jonathon leans closer and bites down on her ear. Alexis screams in pain and sits up. "What are you doing?" she shouts at him.

"What am I doing? What were you and Blake doing a minute ago?" Jonathon shouts back at her.

"I don't know what you're talking about!"

"Really, well let me refresh your memory! Oh Blake, I love it when you do that! Don't try to tell me I'm imagining things. I know what I heard and I told you a long time ago that I was going to be the only man you ever have again!". He takes her by the arms and shoves her back down on the bed. Alexis winces and says, "Jonathon stop, you're hurting me..." He keeps going. "Stop please... I think you had better leave before you do something you'll regret".

"No Alexis, you'll be the one with regrets. Because you're never going to have Blake Carrington, you're never going to love anyone; no one's ever going to love you. Blake doesn't love you, your other three husbands had to die to get away from you. You're like a black widow, dark and mysterious while weaving your web, but touch and get devoured. Well lady, you can keep your fantasies. I hope they keep you warm at night." Now dressed, Jonathon storms out of the penthouse, leaving Alexis shaken and hurt.

Blake stands behind his desk at Denver Carrington, looking out the window. He is disturbed because he still hasn't remembered where he's seen Jonathon before. The part he really can't figure out is why Krystle's mood changed so drastically after Alexis and Jonathon arrived. Granted, Alexis being there would strain the evening, but she was almost on her best behavior. There's something Krystle's not telling him. Blake picks up the phone and calls Krystle's apartment. She answers..."Hello..."

"Krystle, darling, it's Blake. I was just sitting all alone in my office and I thought I would invite the prettiest lady I know out to lunch. I don't suppose you would be free?"

Krystle hesitates before she answers, "Actually Blake, I'm a little busy today and I don't think I can make it to lunch. I was just leaving. I'll call you later, okay?"

"All right, I'll talk to you soon. Goodbye." He hangs up the phone. Something is definitely wrong. But what? He turns back to the window and gazes out.

Jonathon slams the door to his room as he reads the messages from the front desk. There are five from Krystle. He decides to call her back. "Krystle, it's Jonathon. Why so many messages?"

"Why so many messages? Jonathon what were you doing at that party? Not to mention what were you doing there with Alexis Colby of all people? I know you were angry that I decided to give Blake one more chance, but I always thought you had enough sense than to get involved with that viper."

"What's wrong Krystle, a little jealous?" Jonathon snidely says.

"Jealous of Alexis? Please, I know her a lot better than you do. She'll eat you up and spit you out. Is that what you want?"

"Look Krystle, I'm not going to discuss Alexis or anything else with you until you make up your mind which one of us it's going to be...me or the mighty Blake Carrington. You can't have us both."

"I know...I just don't know what to do...I need to see you, can we have lunch today?"

"I don't know Krystle..."

"Please, meet me at the Saint Dennis Club at 12:30...Jonathon please."

"Okay, I'll see you at 12:30." Jonathon hangs up and wonders what he'll say when he sees her.

Alexis calls her office and tells Adam she won't be in. "Mother, I thought you wanted to discuss the SEC problems."

"Adam, darling I'm not feeling overly wonderful and I just don't want to come in today. That's the beauty of owning the company. I can take a day off without having to explain it to the boss."

"Okay Mother, I'll call you later to see how you're feeling. Get some rest." He hangs up the phone, worried. She sounds very, very upset.

Alexis sits on the sofa in her penthouse, looking at an old photo album. She turns the pages and her eyes fill with tears as she looks at a portrait of her and Blake. It was taken at Adam and Dana's wedding. It was just after that week in Singapore. They were so happy then. She turns another page and sees Cecil, herself, and Blake at a party back in the old days. "They did love me," she thinks to herself. "I know Dex loved me, I just never gave him the chance to love me after his affair with Sable. Maybe if I had he'd still be here"..."Cecil always loved me. If it weren't for Cecil I never would have met Blake. He always said Blake stole me from him. It's not my fault he died before we had a chance to build a life together. How dare Jonathon say they never loved me!"

Her mind drifts back to the day Gerald Wilson read Cecil's will. "If he didn't love me, he never would have left me everything, he wouldn't have hated Blake so much." Alexis decides to go over to the Colby mansion. She hasn't set foot in it in all these years, yet Cecil loved it so much. "David, bring my car around, I'm going out."

She hangs up the phone thinking, "I'll show him who loves who."

The car pulls up to the front of the mansion. It is in slight disrepair, as no one has lived there for nearly fifteen years. Alexis unlocks the door and goes inside. She looks around the dusty room and wonders where to begin. She walks down the grand hallway, surveying the paintings on the walls. Entering a room, Alexis has an eerie feeling. It's almost as if Cecil were watching every move she makes. Going down the hall once again, she goes into library. Thousands of books are lined up on the shelves, first editions, leather bound; nothing was too good for Cecil. "This place has possibilities," she thought as she starts up the staircase. Opening the doors, she peered into each room like a child playing hide and seek. Finally, coming to the end of the hallway Alexis stood before a set of double doors. Again, she had an eerie feeling but pushed the doors open anyway. It was Cecil's room. The bed was made; the closet still contained his clothes. It wasn't dusty in this room. She could feel his presence in that room. It was stronger than it had been. Becoming slightly frightened, she turns to leave, but stops when an open lock box catches her eye.

The box is filled with photos and clippings of her and Blake. Their marriage, the divorce, Blake's trial, even Adam's kidnapping. "Why on earth would Cecil have saved all of this?" Alexis thinks to herself. Her curiosity fully peaked, Alexis pulls another stack of papers out of the box, but this time she gets the shock of her life. One of the letters falls open to the ground. As Alexis picks it up she begins to read the letter. "Mrs. Torrance, please find enclosed a cashier's check for $250,000 to make your and the baby's life a little easier. It almost didn't work, his mother wasn't going to let him out today, but we all convinced her that Adam needed to stick to his daily routine. Job well done Kate. Remember, no ransom note, no phone calls, nothing... I don't ever want Blake or Alexis to know if he's dead or alive. Cecil Colby." Her hands shaking, Alexis drops the letter as she looks around the room in disbelief. Cecil paid to have her baby stolen! How could he do that to her! He always said he loved her, why would he want to hurt her so badly?

She stuffs the letter back into the box, but not before she sees a cancelled check made out to Roger Grimes dated the same day Blake found them in bed. "God no Cecil, how the hell could you," She shouted out in the empty room. Alexis read the note attached to the check. "Don't forget Blake will be home at 3:30. Make sure you've got her in bed. I don't care how you get her there, but just in case she gives you any problems, slip one of the pills I gave you into her drink. I've been dropping hints to Blake for so long, but he doesn't believe it. Today will be the day I've waited eleven years for: the fall of Blake's Camelot, and the beginning of my life with Alexis. I'll be in touch." With tears streaming down her face, Alexis picks up the box and runs out of the room, down the stairs, and out of the house.

The chauffeur begins to drive her back to her penthouse. Alexis, almost hysterical, calls Blake's office. Blake picks up the phone. "Hello..."

"Blake, it's Alexis." she says with a quivering voice.

"Alexis, what's wrong?" Blake asks with concern.

"Blake, I have to see you. Please, I don't know what to do, I have no one else to turn to, and right now I just want to die. Please Blake, please..." Alexis answers while crying.

"Okay, okay, calm down. It's 12:15; I'll meet you in fifteen minutes at the Saint Dennis Club. You sound like you could use a drink."

"Thank you Blake, I'll be there." She hangs up the phone and tries to stop crying. "How is Blake going to react to this?" she wonders. Maybe this will be the thing that finally makes him realize how wrong he was about divorcing her.

As she waits in the bar, Blake walks in the door. He sees her there and begins to go to her. Suddenly, out of the corner of his eye, he sees Jonathon sitting at a table in the dining room. He still can't place where he's seen him. It becomes clear when Krystle arrives and goes to Jonathon's table. "That's it!" Blake remembers... "It was the man coming out of Krystle's apartment that day... What the devil is going on?"

Krystle sits down, the waiter goes over, and she orders a drink. Jonathon begins talking, "So, what is so important?"...

Krystle replies, "You, me, us, whether there is an us. I don't know what to do. I love you but I love Blake too. He is Krystina's father and she missed him so much. And I know he still loves me..."

"I love you too Krystle. There is nothing in the world that I wouldn't do for you, you know that don't you?" Jonathon reaches for her hand. She pulls it away.

"If you love me so much, why are you involved with Alexis?" Krystle inquires.

"I'm not involved with Alexis Colby. Look, we were lonely, I was hurt and she was perfectly willing to accommodate my every desire. I don't love Alexis; I don't even really like Alexis. Why can't we just forget anything ever happened and go back to the way it was before the mighty Blake Carrington rode in on his horse and carried off my love?"

"Oh Jonathon, if only it was that easy." Krystle says with despair.

In the bar, Blake is busy trying to calm Alexis enough for her to tell him what is wrong. "Blake, how could he, how could he possibly be so hateful?" Alexis keeps saying through her tears...

Blake shakes his head and again asks, "How can who be so hateful? Alexis, how am I supposed to make you feel better if I don't know what's wrong? Who hurt you?"

"It's not just me; it's you and our family, our lives... Jonathon and I had a fight this morning. He said none of my husbands ever loved me. I wanted so desperately to prove him wrong, so I went over to Cecil's mansion. I was looking around and I found this..." Alexis hands Blake the lockbox and continues to talk while crying, "I can't believe it. He said he loved me... All those years that he stood there and held my hand while I cried for my baby and he said nothing!"

Blake reads the note to Kate Torrance and shakes his head in disbelief. "Cecil Colby did this, my best friend in the world arranged to have our son stolen! My god, I can't believe this... What other nasty little secrets are hidden in this box?" He reaches in and opens the next letter. It's the letter to Roger Grimes. As Blake reads it, he glances up at Alexis and then back to the note. He suddenly realizes that Alexis was telling the truth when she swore she wasn't having an affair. Blake opens another letter from Roger to Cecil, it describes how delirious the pills make Alexis and how he's having a great time, because she thinks she's in bed with Blake and is more than happy to do whatever I want her to. Blake lowers his head and says; "I think I should take you home. We have to put this into some kind of perspective."

Alexis wipes her eyes and nods her head okay. Blake takes her by the hand and leads her to the door. He glances back over his shoulder to the dining room. Krystle appears to be getting ready to leave. Jonathon stands up, pulls her closer to him, and kisses her. She returns the kiss as Blake stands there watching. Turning around, he takes Alexis by the hand and walks out the door. As the chauffeur drives them to Alexis' penthouse, Blake thinks to himself, "Now what is going on between Krystle and Jonathon, and why was Jonathon at the party with Alexis?"

The elevator door opens and Blake leads Alexis into the living room. She's still a little shaky, but has stopped crying. Blake is still in shock, not only about Cecil but by Krystle as well. He goes to the bar, gets them both a drink, and then sits down on the sofa beside Alexis. She takes the drink and says "Thank you Blake, I don't know how I would have made it without you."

Blake gently smiles and takes her hand. "I still can't believe Cecil would do something like this. All of the years I knew him, I called him one of my best friends, and all the time he lied. He had our son stolen and then told us how sorry he was that Adam was missing! How in God's name could one person be so calculating and cruel?"

"I don't know Blake. Isn't it strange though, you've been saying the same thing about me for years." Alexis says almost joking. "Blake," she now says very seriously, "perhaps this is actually a good thing."

Blake looks at her in dismay. "How on earth could this be a good thing?"

"Well if nothing else, it proves that I wasn't lying to you for all that time. But maybe, just maybe, it proves it's not too late for us."

"Alexis please, we've been through this before. I love Krystle and I always will. There has been too much hurt and pain between you and me for so long, there's no way to make it all better. You've got to understand that."

Alexis shakes her head. "The only thing I'll ever understand is that I love you Blake. I've always loved you. You and I had a love that will never be broken and will always survive the test of time. I know I've said I'd never need any man, but I was wrong. I need you Blake. I need you more than anything in the world."

Blake looks at her and rises from the sofa. "I think I had better be going now."

Alexis reaches for his hand as he stands up. "Blake, don't leave me. I need you so much; I need to have your arms around me for just a little while. I need to know that everything's going to be okay. Stay with me tonight."

The sky in Denver is ominous; the rain hits the window of Alexis' bedroom. A bolt of lightning flashes, there is a roll of thunder. Alexis restlessly tosses and turns. She opens her eyes and looks to the other side of the bed. Her hand reaches for the pillow. As Alexis hugs the pillow she thinks of last night. Blake left rather uncomfortably after she asked him to stay. She closes her eyes and tries to put yesterday out of her mind.

Blake sits alone in the library listening to the rain come down. There's an open box on the desk in front of him. He pulls out a stack of photos. As he looks at the pictures he lightly smiles. The smile fades when he comes across a picture of Alexis and himself. It was their wedding day. Blake closes his eyes and thinks of last night. "I' m sorry", he says to the picture. "There's so much I'm sorry for." His thoughts are interrupted when the telephone rings. Gerard comes in and informs Blake that Krystle is on the phone.

"Good morning Krystle, what can I do for you?" he asks with a tone of apprehension.

Krystle sensing the tone says, "I just called to apologize for missing lunch yesterday and I was hoping we could have dinner tonight.".

"Dinner tonight, okay. I'll pick you up at seven".

"Blake, is something wrong?" she asks.

"What could be wrong Krystle?" Blake answers.

"I don't know. I guess I' m just hearing things. I'll see you at seven. Bye Blake."

Blake hangs up the phone. "What's wrong," he thinks, "I think his name is Jonathon." Blake takes a sip of his coffee and starts reading the morning paper.

Krystle looks at Jonathon and says "There's something wrong with Blake. There's something odd about his voice."

Jonathon shrugs his shoulders and grins. "Maybe he saw us yesterday at lunch." he says laughing.

"It's not funny. I don't even think something like that. I told you last night that I want to try again with Blake. Why can't you get that through your head?" Krystle replies.

"So you've chosen the pitiful giant and his little kingdom. Okay fine, we can both play this game..." he says angrily.

"What's that supposed to mean?" Krystle shouts back.

"You'll see..." Jonathon slams the door as he leaves. Krystle sits down and tries to figure out what he meant.

Steven knocks on Alexis' office door and goes inside. "Good morning Mother."

She glances up from her paperwork. "Is it?" Alexis replies solemnly.

"Something wrong Mother? You seem upset."

"I'm all right darling. Man troubles again, it's nothing. What's the occasion for a visit?" she says with a light smile.

"Something very special, an invitation to take my beautiful mother out for dinner... What do you say?" Steven asks with a boyish grin.

"Steven, that's very sweet of you, but I wouldn't be very good company tonight. I'll take a rain check, okay?"

Steven walks over to her chair, leans down and kisses her forehead. "Okay, rain check it is. I'll call you soon," he says as he's leaving. Jonathon is coming in as Steven goes. He comes into the office, closes and locks the door behind himself.

"What are you doing here?" Alexis asks with an aggravated tone.

"I know you're probably angry with me, but I had to see you..."

"I have nothing to say to you Jonathon, so please leave."

Jonathon walks to the side of her desk and continues talking, "But there's something I need to say to you. I'm sorry about yesterday morning. I know what I said and did was wrong and I'm truly sorry if I hurt you. I'm a very jealous man when it comes to the woman I love..."

Alexis rolls her eyes, sighs, and says, "Love? Please Jonathon, give me some credit... Yesterday you're shouting that no man will ever love me and now you stand here pouring out your heart, swearing your undying devotion. Give me a break..."

"Believe what you want, Alexis, but it's the truth. I've been miserable without you. I can't eat, I can't sleep, all I can do is think of you. I've never felt like this before and it's a feeling I don't want to give up." Jonathon pleads.

Still unconvinced, Alexis begins to laugh. "You know you're really something. You think that all you have to do is waltz in here, say I'm sorry, confess your uncontrollable passion, and think I'm going to throw my arms around you and say it's okay... Well it doesn't work that way. You said things that were totally unforgivable and because of those things I learned something that destroyed every feeling of love I've ever had. So do yourself a favor and get out while you can, because Alexis Morrell Carrington Colby Dexter Rowan doesn't give a damn anymore."

Jonathon opens the door to go. He looks back to Alexis. "I'm going to make it up to you. I promise, I will." The door closes, leaving Alexis lonelier than ever.

Krystle sits in her apartment. It's 6:55; Blake should be there any minute. She's apprehensive because of Blake's tone this morning and because of Jonathon's abrupt departure earlier. There is a knock on the door. Krystle goes to the door and Blake comes in. He is about to ask about her connection to Jonathon, but Krystle begins talking... "Blake, I'm sorry about missing lunch yesterday, but it really couldn't be helped. It doesn't matter though because we're together now and in your arms is where I want to be." Krystle reaches out and hugs Blake. "I love you so much and I want to be together forever."

Blake wraps his arms around her and returns the hug. "So do I Krystle, so do I." They separate and gaze into each other's eyes.

Jonathon is sitting on the sofa at Alexis' penthouse. She walks through the door and sees him there. "You don't listen very well do you?" she says snidely.

"I told you I would make it up to you and I know just the way to do it..." he says with a devilish grin.

"I'll bet you do." Alexis coyly replies. "Too bad I'm not interested."

"Don't you even want to know what I'm going to do?" Jonathon asks.

"Not really, but if my listening will make you leave, go ahead and tell me."

He takes her by the hand and leads her to the sofa. Instead of sitting next to her, Jonathon goes to the bar and pours them both a glass of champagne. He hands her a glass and says "To you my beauty, my life, my love."

Alexis sips the champagne and looks at him. "Could you please get on with it? I'm really tired and I want a long bath before I go to bed. Alone!"

Unswayed by her lack of enthusiasm, Jonathon proceeds with his conversation. "I spent the entire day wondering what I could do or say to show you how much I really do love you. I finally came up with this." He reaches into his pocket and pulls out a small box. Opening it, the box contains a diamond ring. "I know it's not nearly grand enough, but it is sincere. I love you and I would be honored to have you as my wife."

Alexis shakes her head in disbelief. "Marry you? Have you completely gone mad? I've gone through that four times, thank you, and I'll never make that mistake again. Well, like I said, I'm tired. I'm sure you know the way out." She gets up and walks upstairs.

As Jonathon picks up his jacket, he yells up to her. "I'm leaving the ring, just in case you change your mind." Getting into the elevator Jonathon thinks to himself, "You have to change your mind Alexis. Maybe then I'll show Krystle how it feels to be betrayed."...

Fallon and Lauren arrive at Alexis' just before 9A.M. They are going Christmas shopping and Lauren wants Alexis to come along. As they put down their coats Fallon sees the ring on the end table. Lauren starts upstairs. She opens the bedroom door. Seeing Alexis is sleeping, Lauren tiptoes to the side of the bed.

"Gramma," the seven-year-old whispers. "Gramma, wake up."

Alexis slowly opens her eyes and sees Lauren's smiling face. "Hi baby what are you doing here?"

"Mommy and me are going shopping. Can you come too Gramma? Please?"

"Sweetheart, I have an awful lot of work to do today. Maybe you'd better go without me."

Lauren's smile fades and she begins to pout. Fallon walks into the room and asks, "What's going on up here?"

"I was just explaining to my granddaughter that I am a little busy today and that I can't go shopping with you."

Alexis looks at Lauren and continues "But how about if I meet you for lunch around one."

Lauren smiles at Alexis. "Okay Gramma, we'll meet you at the ice cream store." She turns around and runs out the door. Fallon looks at her mother and asks, "Mother, where did that ring on the table downstairs come from?"

Alexis feigns confusion. "Ring on what table? Oh I remember, Jonathon proposed last night. Nothing important. I laughed and told him no."

"Mother why did you do that? It's obvious he adores you, why don't you give him a chance?"

"Why don't you just take my granddaughter shopping and I'll see you at one." Alexis answers coyly.

Fallon shakes her head and leaves. Alexis decides to pay Blake a visit. They need to discuss the other night.

Blake sits on the edge of the bed watching Krystle sleep. He still can't get rid of the curiosity over Jonathon. "Why would she be kissing Jonathon and saying she loves me at the same time?" Blake thinks to himself. "Why would he be kissing Krystle and romancing Alexis?" The thought of Jonathon with Krystle is bad enough but to have him with Alexis too is more than Blake can handle. He gets out of bed, showers, and leaves for the office hoping for a better day.

Blake gets off the elevator walks to his office and opens the door. He is surprised when he sees Alexis sitting in the chair in front of his desk. Blake takes a deep breath and says "Good morning Alexis. To what do I owe this visit?"

Alexis smiles as he sits down. "Well, I wanted to apologize about the other night. I know I made you really uncomfortable and I'm sorry. I must have had too much to drink."

He lightly sighs and agrees, "Perhaps we both had a little too much the other night."

"Blake, there's something I need to know. Why did you leave me alone after I asked you to stay?"

Blake lowers his head. "Because if I didn't leave then, I never would have."

"Would that have really been so bad? I meant everything I said about always loving you. Isn't that enough?"

"No I'm afraid it isn't. We had something very special, but it was a lifetime ago and no matter how hard we try we'll never get that back. You were then..."

"And Krystle's now?"

"Yes... Alexis you are a beautiful, magnificent woman that any man would cherish more than anything in the world." The intercom buzzes and Blake's secretary reminds him of his board meeting. "I'm sorry I have to go."

Alexis stands up and begins to leave. She hears Blake's words again. "A woman any man would cherish... Any man but you, Blake" she thinks to herself. Her mind wanders back to last night. "Maybe Jonathon was right. Blake doesn't love me. But do you

Jonathon?" She glances at her watch and leaves to meet Fallon and Lauren for lunch.

The sun has set again in Denver. The penthouse is empty when Alexis gets home. She was actually hoping to see Jonathon sitting there. Instead all she sees is a lonely room. Sitting down on the sofa, she sees the ring on the table. "Alexis, you must be crazy to even think about marrying him. You don't even really know him. Course, you only knew Blake for three days before you agreed to marry him. No, absolutely not, you are not getting married again! But do you really want to spend the rest of your life alone? Maybe this will make Blake want me." she mumbles. Then suddenly she says, "Yes I think I will marry Jonathon."

"What did you say?" a voice behind her says. She turns around startled and sees Jonathon standing there.

"I said I will marry you Mr. Chase." Alexis says with a smile. He rushes over to her, sweeps her up in his arms and kisses her. He carries her upstairs to bed. After making love to her again, Jonathon goes downstairs and makes himself a drink. As he stands there in the shadows of the night, he begins laughing. "I'll show you Krystle. You'll see how it feels." He picks up the phone and calls the Denver Mirror newspaper and tells the editor to place an engagement announcement for tomorrow's paper. Still reveling in his victory, he finishes the drink and begins back upstairs.

Blake and Krystle are having breakfast. Blake is reading the financial section while Krystle is skimming through the rest of the paper. Her eyes come to a stop and her mouth falls open as she sees the headline. "Alexis Colby to wed Mr. Jonathon Chase". Blake looks up from the paper "Krystle, is something wrong?" he asks. She hands him the paper. He reads the headline and grins, "Well looks like she's at it again." Krystle gets up from the table and goes to take a shower. Blake looks at the paper again, but this time there is no smile. He finishes his coffee and leaves.

Alexis walks into her office to see all of her children standing there. "Good morning." she says as she makes her way to her desk.

"Mother," Steven begins, "Don't you think you have a little explaining to do?"

"No darling, I don't have any explaining to do. You all knew I was seeing Jonathon. He asked me to marry him and I said yes. It's not the first time I've done this you know."

"So when's the big day?" Fallon inquires.

"Well Jonathon is in a hurry for some reason, so he insists that it's going to be at noon on New Year's Eve. He says he wants to begin the year with a new life. I think it's rather sweet of him."

"It's something..." Adam thinks.

There is a knock on the door. Jonathon goes over and answers it. He is delighted to see Krystle standing before him. "Krystle, what a surprise... Come on in." He closes the door behind her. "Can I offer you cup of coffee?"

"No I don't want coffee. I want an explanation. Have you lost your mind? Are you so upset that I went back to Blake that you have to run off and marry the Queen of Bitches?"

"Krystle, I gave you a chance. I told you I love you and that I need you and you made your choice. I am marrying Alexis Colby on New Years Eve whether you like it or not. In fact, just so you do believe it, why don't you and the old man come to the wedding? I'm sure Alexis won't mind." Krystle storms out of the room. Jonathon shakes his head and smiles. All is going exactly as planned.

Adam, Fallon, and Steven sit in the limousine staring at each other. Adam shrugs his shoulders, "I don't know what to say. Mother is going to marry Jonathon Chase. The man is a gold-digger. Didn't she learn anything after Sean Rowan? We have got to stop her."

"What's wrong Adam, Afraid you're going to lose part of your inheritance?" Fallon asks. "Why don't you just leave her alone and let her do what she wants."

"Because, what Mother wants isn't Jonathon Chase. I don't care about the money, I care about my mother." Adam answers with an edge in his voice.

Steven sighs and adds, "Maybe she's tired of being alone. Mother has a wall of steel around her, but underneath is a wonderful person who has a heart of gold and no one to love. If Jonathon is going to make her happy, than let her be happy."

Adam looks at his younger brother and sister in disbelief. He thinks to himself, "I'll stop this disaster. I will find a way to stop this if it's the last thing I do."

Alexis sits at her desk, looking at the pictures on the table behind her. Her four beautiful children. "Too bad Amanda isn't here", she thinks. The door slowly opens, she turns around.

"Your secretary is away from his desk, may I come in?" Blake asks.

"Of course, come in, sit down." Alexis answers with a light smile. She's not really surprised to see him. "What can I do for you, Mr. Carrington?"

"I came by to congratulate you on your engagement. He's a very lucky man."

"Yes he is. But that's not the only reason you're here is it Blake? I know what you're thinking. It's the same thing the children are thinking. I hardly know this man, why on earth am I going to marry him? That is what you came here to find out isn't it?"

Blake lowers his head and then looks back at her. "Yes, that is why I'm here. Alexis, you need to know a few things about Jonathon before you commit to the rest of your life."

Alexis has an aggravated tone as she says, "I can't believe you. Here you are trying to stop me from having a little bit of happiness in my life. You think you can come in here and tell me not to marry Jonathon and then say something to make me change my mind.

Well, the only thing that would ever change my mind is you down on bended knee with a ring in your hand. But since you went back to the ever-so-sterling Krystle, you have no right to even suggest that I not marry Jonathon. I don't care about whatever it is you've dreamed up about him. I am getting married on New Year's Eve whether you or the children like it or not. It's my life and you gave up any rights to it about thirty years ago. Now I'm very busy with my wedding plans so could you please close the door on your way out." Without another word, Blake turns around and leaves. Alexis swings her chair back around to face the window. "It is my life," she mumbles. "I will be happy, they'll all see," Alexis says with an unconvincing tone.

The holidays come and go very quickly as Jonathon puts the final touches on his wedding plans. To his surprise there is an R.S.V.P. from Blake and Krystle. He hands it to Alexis. "Jonathon, I don't understand why you invited Blake and her to our wedding."

"Because my love, I want the whole world to see how happy we are and he is your children's father. I would think you would want him there, if for nothing else, so you can show him what real love is all about." He leans over and kisses her cheek. "I better be going, it's bad luck to see the bride before her wedding. See you soon darling."

The church is filled with people. "Jonathon must have invited all of Denver" Alexis thinks to herself as she walks up the aisle. She stops at the altar where Jonathon is waiting. They turn to face the minister.

"Dearly beloved, we are gathered here today to witness and bless this union. The union of marriage is not to be taken lightly, but reverently, wholeheartedly, and in accordance with God's wishes. Into this holy union, Jonathon and Alexis now come to be joined. If there is anyone who has just reason why these two cannot be joined, let him speak now or forever hold their peace..." From the center of the church, voices ring out "Wait... There is a reason"... As everyone turns around in shock, the minister says, "Perhaps we should take a moment to resolve this interruption." Jonathon and Alexis agree...

About fifteen minutes later assembled before the altar once again, the minister asks, "May we proceed?" They nod their heads yes and the ceremony continues. After a wonderful reception, they leave for their honeymoon... The sky is clear and full of stars. They stand together on a balcony gazing at the moonlight. His arms wrapped around her waist, he leans over to kiss her. A band on the terrace below begins to play... She puts her arms around his body and slowly starts to sway to the music. Suddenly, she steps back, looks up and closes her eyes.

"What are you doing?" he asks.

"I was just wishing on a star. They say there's magic in the air tonight."

"There's magic anywhere you are..."

"You know I waited a lifetime to hear those words." Alexis gazes into his eyes and smiles. "I love you".

He returns the smile, holds her closer, and kisses her. As the music plays he leans over and whispers "I love you too, Mrs. Carrington." Alexis rests her head on Blake's shoulder. Finally, the dream has come true.

Chapter Eleven

They're Coming To Take Me Away

"Who knows, if we'd thought of the flying saucer earlier and put some of our so-called big stars into it, we might have been top of the ratings today." – Aaron Spelling telling his senior executives that The Colbys has been cancelled.

Columnist Robert Mackenzie described his impressions of The Colbys in a review that ran in the April 19, 1986 issue of TV Guide. With a build-up like this, how could this show go from the most welcome newcomer to ending with an alien kidnapping?

DYNASTY II: THE COLBYS

"The Authoritiy of Wealth, the Passions of Love and the Intrigues of Willful Sensuality Ignite the Interrelationships of the Dynamic, Strong-willed Colby Family ... "

That's how an early press release described The Colbys and by golly you've got to admire the publicist who packed that whole ball of wackos into one practically readable sentence.

The Carringtons of Dynasty and the Colbys are sort of related. Best we could figure out is that Fallon Carrington Colby (now played by Emma Samms) was married to, divorced from, and about to remarry Jeff Colby (John James) when she contracted a severe case of multi-episode amnesia and wound up as the wife of Miles Colby (Maxwell Caulfield). Jeff, heir apparent to the Colby oil holdings, is the son of Francesca Scott Colby Hamilton Langdon (Katharine Ross), widow of Philip Colby, the nogoodnik brother of Jason Colby. Jason is commonly referred to as the "patriarch" of the family, and for good reason, he is played by Charlton Heston, who can patriarch with the best of them.

We haven't got all day here. Last we saw, Fallon and Jeff were getting remarried after she and Jeff went through their young son's near-fatal illness together and their love was rekindled at the very least. The heavy in this one is Jason's wife, Sable (Stephanie Beacham), an English-accented yenta who meddles and plots to help her three children by Jason: the twins, Miles and Monica (Tracy Scoggins) and young Bliss (Claire Yarlett). You also see a lot of Jason's sister Constance (Barbara Stanwyck); her rugged but noble boyfriend Hutch Corrigan (Joseph Campanella); Garrett Boydston (Ken Howard); the company lawyer who has eyes for Dominique Devereaux (Diahann Carroll, on loan from Dynasty); and a dastardly, smooth-talking villain out to do the Colbys no good, Zachary Powers (Ricardo Montalban).

Since this is a product of Richard and Esther Shapiro and Robert and Eileen Pollock, the elite among soap-opera professionals, The Colbys is well-written and impeccably produced. There is a tasteful lack of ostentation about the lush sets. What acting is called for, with the veterans noted above setting the tone, is as competent as any on television.

Still, there are the needs and the limitations of soap opera. A large cast must be utilized and egos satisfied. The music must be ominous. The pauses must be pregnant. The looks must be arch, meaningful or soulful. The stories must concern greed, lust, jealousy, hate, betrayal and other deplorable human foibles that lead to misery. Humor, which might relieve some of the overwhelming aura of depression that permeates these shows, is nowhere in evidence.

In that sense, The Colbys, like all the other nighttime and daytime soap operas, is not true to life. Somehow no matter how unhappy a situation in real life, we always try to find a way to relieve the tension by finding some humor in it. Not so the folks who inhabit these shows. Gloom and doom hang over everything; meals, evenings out, bedrooms. One wants to shout, "Enjoy something, for goodness' sake. Cheer up!"

LADIES AND GENTLEMEN: THE COLBYS

JASON COLBY
Portrayed by Charlton Heston

Jason is the patriarch of the Colby family. The brother of Cecil Colby, Jason runs the family business Colby Enterprises in Los Angeles, California. Founded by their father Andrew, Colby Enterprises was equally given to Jason and his sister Constance upon their father's death. He rules Colby Enterprises with an iron fist and his family in the same way.

In the early 1960s Jason married Sabella "Sable" Scott. Sable is the first cousin of Alexis Morrell Carrington Colby Dexter Rowan. Jason also had an affair with Sable's younger sister Francesca. Unbeknownst to Jason, that affair resulted in the birth of Jeffrey Broderick Colby; who was raised to believe that he was brother's son. He raised three children with Sable; Monica, Miles and Bliss.

Jason is forced to take stock of his life when he is mistakenly told that he is dying. When Francesca returns to Los Angeles and tells him that she still loves him, Jason leaves Sable to pursue the true love of his life. After a tremendously expensive settlement and endless tribulations, he divorces Sable and focuses his attention on Francesca.

When his presumed dead brother arrives in Los Angeles, Jason becomes involved in a scandal that threatens the very foundation of the Colby family…

SABELLA "SABLE" SCOTT COLBY
Portrayed by Stephanie Beacham

Sable Scott Colby is fiercely protective of everything hers. That includes her children, her husband and her own personal greed. The first cousin of Alexis Carrington Colby, Sable found herself on the losing side of the stick when her younger sister Francesca descended on the Colby household and staked her claim to Sable's husband Jason.

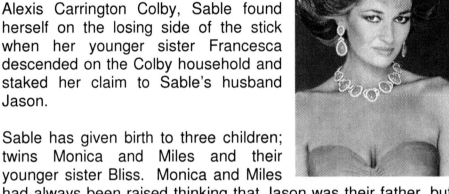

Sable has given birth to three children; twins Monica and Miles and their younger sister Bliss. Monica and Miles had always been raised thinking that Jason was their father, but in reality they are the result of an unfortunate rape early in Sable and Jason's marriage. He was so thrilled about the idea of being a father she didn't have the heart to tell him the truth.

Never one to hold her tongue, Sable doesn't hide her dislike for Jeff or his aunt Constance and makes a point of telling them so. After discovering the paternity of her sister's son, Sable insists on divorcing Jason, despite the fact that she's still madly in love with him. After a nasty divorce and a few hundred million dollars, Sable moves to Denver to inflict revenge on her cousin Alexis. Alexis' crime was telling Jason that Monica and Miles aren't his children and for that Sable will make her pay dearly. She tries to befriend Blake and ends up sleeping with Dex. Unfortunately, Sable discovered that revenge sometimes comes with repercussions: she manages to become pregnant with Dex's child.

CONSTANCE COLBY PATTERSON
Portrayed by Barbara Stanwyck

Constance Colby Patterson is the epitome of elegance and class. She's sharp-tongued when she needs to be and incredibly understand and gentle at the same time. Despite her inability to have children of her own, Constance lavished her brother, nieces and nephews with love and attention. With her brother Jason, she owned half of Colby Enterprises and stunned everyone when she presented the majority of her holdings to her nephew Jeff.

Constance has always been protective of "little brother" Jason and has taken on his wife Sable on more than one occasion. She was nearly committed when Sable tried to make her believe she was losing her mind. Always the optimist, Constance managed to find love twice in her life. Her first husband died and it took decades for her to meet another man who made her feel alive again. That man was Hutch Corrigan.

While traveling abroad with Hutch, Constance boarded a small plane bound for India. The plane crashed somewhere on the way and despite her body having never been found, Constance was declared dead. She left behind a legacy of love.

FRANCESCA "FRANKIE" SCOTT COLBY HAMILTON LANGDON
Portrayed by Katharine Ross

Frankie is an interesting woman. First she marries Philip Colby then she sleeps with his brother Jason Colby. After giving birth to Jason's son Jeff, she tells everyone that he's Philip's son. Then three years after Jeff was born, she gives Jeff to their brother Cecil Colby and doesn't reappear until he's in his early 30's.

Despite that, Frankie is a down-to-earth woman who wants nothing more from life than a happy home and someone to love. After her many years of searching for love, she finds it with Lord Roger Langdon or so she thinks. She marries Roger despite the fact that she's in love with her sister Sable's husband Jason. After revealing her true feelings, Roger allows her to divorce him so she can pursue her dream of being Mrs. Jason Colby. So after descending on her sister's family and causing a nasty break-up, Frankie is finally getting that dream wedding. But before she has the chance to say "I do," her first husband Philip Colby miraculously has risen from the dead just in time to stop the ceremony.

Her relationship with Jeff has been mended and everyone knows Jeff is Jason's son. So you would think Frankie would be happy but think again. Turns out she's decided she actually doesn't want to be with Jason, she wants to be with Philip. What she didn't know was that Philip wasn't nearly that wonderful man she fell in love with and instead is a kidnapper who, after driving off a cliff, left her for dead.

MONICA SCOTT COLBY
Portrayed by Tracy Scoggins

Monica spent her entire life believing that she was the eldest daughter of Jason Colby and his wife Sable. While she certainly is Sable's daughter, it turns out she's not Jason's. Unbeknownst to her, her mother was brutally raped and that's how she and her twin brother Miles were conceived.

Monica is a lovely woman with a good head on her shoulders. She was encouraged as a child by her mother to be anything she wanted to, so Monica chose to become an attorney. After passing the bar, she went to work at Colby Enterprises but wasn't happy with the fact that she was treated like "daddy's princess" and was continuously subjected to sexist attitudes about her abilities. Finally having had enough, she quit Colby Enterprises when Dominique Devereaux offered her the top spot at Titania Records. It was there that Monica would meet Neil Kittridge and Wayne Masterson. Both men would eventually have affairs with her but neither would last.

When Jason hires a Senator to assist with a project being developed for the space program, Monica must again deal with demons. The Senator is not only a former lover but the father of her son. She had become pregnant and with Constance's help, managed to conceal the pregnancy from the entire family and then gave the baby up for adoption. It is later revealed that her son is living with his father.

After being cut out of Jason's life, Monica turned up in Denver to live with her mother and assumed the role of Sable's doting daughter and co-conspirator in the revenge plot against Alexis.

MILES ANDREW COLBY
Portrayed by Maxwell Caulfield

Miles is a complicated man. He grew up with the attitude of a playboy: fast cars, polo ponies, loose women and no sense of professional ambition. Despite Jason's insistence, Miles would rather be anywhere than at work or a family function. Born five minutes after his twin sister Monica, Miles is clearly his mother's favorite child. Even his younger sister Bliss doesn't get the attention that he does.

His attitude changes dramatically when he meets and falls in love with a woman named Randall. That's not really her name but she liked it when she saw it on a street sign. Randall was suffering from amnesia and had no clue that she was actually Fallon Carrington Colby. After a whirlwind courtship, Miles and Randall were married. Upon their return to Los Angeles, Miles was stunned when Jeff told him that Randall is his missing fiancé Fallon.

When Fallon had regained her memory, she asked Miles to step aside so she could be with Jeff. Miles furiously raped her and proceeded to torture both her and Jeff throughout Fallon's entire pregnancy. He was crushed when Fallon's daughter turned out to be Jeff's.

While sulking about life's problems he met Channing Carter. She was sent to gather information about the Colby family for her uncle but soon found herself falling for Miles. They married and after several tumultuous months, a pregnant Channing left him.

BLISS COLBY
Portrayed by Claire Yarlett

Bliss is the youngest child of Jason and Sable Colby. She was born with the proverbial "silver spoon" in her mouth and never fails to take advantage of that whenever the situation warrants. She has a roving eye but a good heart.

Her relationship with Sean McAllister began at the request of his uncle, Zach Powers. He was to dig for information about the Colby family but the plan backfired when Sean claimed to have fallen in love with her. The two were to be married but the plans were called off and he left Los Angeles to move to Florida.

Her next conquest was a Russian ballet dancer named Nikolai Rustov. She chased him for months and begged her father to find a way to keep Nikolai from having to return to Russia. After assisting him to defect to the United States, Jason and Sable watched as their daughter became more captivated with this man. When Nikolai moved to New York to head his own company, he proposed and Bliss happily accepted. They announced their engagement and left Los Angeles together.

CHANNING CARTER COLBY
Portrayed by Kim Morgan Greene

Carter Channing was sent to the Colby mansion to for one purpose: to get information for her Uncle Lucas so he could destroy Jason Colby. Sometimes, things don't always work out as planned.

Channing met Miles at the Excelsior Hotel and was attracted to him. She was welcomed by Sable and soon moved into the Colby mansion. Not long after that, Channing and Miles were married.

She had a feeling that Miles would never be completely hers because he was still in love with Fallon. Despite pressure from him and the Colby family, Channing refused to have a child. Not that she didn't want one, but because she was frightened. Her mother had died while giving birth to her brother and she was terrified that the same would happen to her. After Miles discovered that Fallon's newborn daughter wasn't his, Channing felt sorry for him and decided to give motherhood a chance. Unfortunately, the pressure and fear became too much for Channing to handle. She left Miles and told him that she would be filing for divorce and terminating her pregnancy.

PHILIP COLBY
Portrayed by Michael Parks

The prodigal son, Philip Colby was married to Francesca Scott. Despite her insistence that he was Jeff's father, Philip always knew that wasn't the truth because he was sterile. Shortly after making that revelation in a letter to his brother Cecil, Philip was sent to fight in the Vietnam War. Word came that he had been killed and Frankie led Jeff to believe that Philip was his father.

Decades later, Philip contacted his sister Constance and asked for two million dollars to avoid being killed for gunrunning. He had assumed the name of a fellow soldier (who was killed in the war) and proceeded to carve out a not-so-savory life for himself. Shortly after receiving the funds, Philip a.k.a. Hoyt Parker bid his sister farewell. It would be the last time Constance would be seen alive.

He returned to Los Angeles determined to rekindle his marriage to Francesca but discovered that she was to marry Jason. What's a brother to do but crash the wedding? Endlessly pursuing her, it appeared that Jason held her heart. In a last ditch effort, Philip kidnapped Frankie but lost control of his car and flipped it over a cliff. His whereabouts and fate are unknown.

GARRETT BOYDSTON
Portrayed by Ken Howard

Garrett Boydston is the Chief Legal Counsel for Colby Enterprises as well as a personal friend of Jason Colby's. Garrett may seem like a mild-mannered, straight-laced man but he kept a secret that came back to haunt him. While traveling through Europe, he met and fell in love with Dominique Devereaux. When Dominique wanted to settle down and get married, Garrett confessed that he was already married to a woman  named Jessica. Dominique was hurt but understanding and let Garrett live his life.

When they met again in Denver, Dominique and Garrett rekindled their affair. Garrett told her that Jessica was now out of his life and that they could be married. Dominique was pleased but Garrett was speechless when he discovered that they had a daughter, Jackie. Garrett's best-kept secret was revealed by Alexis Colby at his and Dominique's engagement party. Jessica is definitely out of his life and in fact always has been; she never existed in the first place. Unable to cope with his deception and the fact that Dominique split up with him, Garrett asked Jason to allow him to take on a new position within Colby Enterprises and moved to New York.

Although Dominique has accepted his apology, she refused to attempt reconciling again. Garrett spends the majority of his free time with their daughter Jackie, who was holding out hope that her parents would marry. Dominique married Nick Kimball thus leaving Garrett alone once again.

HENRY "HUTCH" CORRIGAN
Portrayed by Joseph Campanella

Accused of being a con-man out for Constance's money, Hutch becomes a pawn in Sable's plan to have Constance declared mentally incompetent. A cowboy with a heart of gold, Hutch had no idea of the wealth Constance possessed and was offended at the suggestion that he was after her for her money. When he discovered that she hadn't told him who she really was, his pride was wounded and he ended their relationship.

Feeling guilty for the way things ended, Hutch came to the hospital to visit Constance after Sable ran her over. He explained his feelings and she apologized for not being truthful with him from the beginning. The two reconciled and set out for an adventurous trip around the world. He and Constance would never be seen again and a few weeks later, both were presumed dead.

ZACHARY "ZACH" POWERS
Portrayed by Ricardo Montalban

Shipping tycoon Zach Powers is a ruthless man who, at one time or another, has managed to sleep with Sable, Alexis and her sister Cassandra. Zach has held a vengeful spirit against Jason and the Colby family since his father committed suicide. Zach has always blamed Jason for his father's death and will do anything to inflict pain in Jason's life.

When Jason and Sable split, Sable sought solace with Zach. He proposed marriage and admitted he loved her, but the marriage was never to take place. Zach joyfully continues to make Jason squirm every chance he gets.

ADDITIONAL SUPPORTING CAST MEMBERS

Lisa Aliff - Gail Kittridge
Ivan Bonar - Henderson Palmer
Peter Browne – Fielding
Ashley Mutrux - Blake "L.B." Jeffrey Carrington Colby (1985-1986)
Brandon Bluhm - Blake "LB" Jeffrey Carrington Colby (1986-1987)
Jenny Pharris – Lauren Constance Colby

SEASON ONE

"The Celebration" - Episode 1.1
Original Airdate - November 20, 1985

Guest Appearances by Gary Hudson (Drunk Man), Barbara Bingham (Miles' Receptionist), Phyllis Hamlin (Woman Reporter), Richard Garrison (Reporter #1), Charles Van Eman (Sean McAllister) and Sam Hennings (Reporter #2)

Jason Colby, head of one of the most powerful financial empires in the world, has just entered into a huge oil pipeline contract with Denver Carrington and ColbyCo Oil. His family life is nowhere as easy to deal with as his business is. Constance, his sister, elevates their nephew Jeff to share Jason's throne by giving him her half-share of Colby Enterprises by telling him that the shares should have been his father's anyway. Jason's wife Sable worries that their children (Miles, Monica and Bliss) are being disinherited in the process. When Jeff arrives from Denver, Jason tries to send him on an errand to Hong Kong but Jeff immediately shows his uncle that he cannot be ordered around. He may have gotten his shares from his Aunt Constance but Jeff has every intention of making sure Colby Enterprises holds up its end of the pipeline contract. Monica offers to go to Hong Kong to handle the business but Jason refuses, especially after finding out that Zach Powers is behind the damaging rumors against Colby Enterprises. Constance is having a fling with Hutch Corrigan (who doesn't know of her vast wealth). Sable enlists the assistance of her sister Frankie to talk to Jeff and tell her son to take it easy. Returning from his trip to Denver, Miles makes the unexpected announcement that he's just gotten married. He introduces the family to his new bride, "Randall," a woman who is currently suffering from amnesia. Jeff nearly falls over as he looks at his "cousin's" new wife. "Randall" is Fallon.

"Conspiracy of Silence" - Episode 1.2
Original Airdate – November 27, 1985

Guest Appearances by John Forsythe (Blake Carrington), Ray Stricklyn (Dr. James "Jimmy Lee" Parris), David Lain Baker (Angello), Ed Lottimer (George) and Rick Partlow (Chauffeur)

The family is stunned at Miles' marriage especially when Sable and Jason also realize that their new daughter-in-law is Blake and Alexis' daughter Fallon. Jeff immediately calls Denver and tells Blake that he's found Fallon and that she's at Jason's house in Los Angeles. Blake wastes  no time getting to Los Angeles but is extremely disappointed when he arrives. When "Randall" doesn't recognize anyone, including her father, Constance asks psychiatrist Dr. Jimmy Parris for help. After examining Fallon, Dr. Parris recommends the family not try to push her to regain her memory and that it will come back on its own in time. Jeff's mother Frankie arrives in Los Angeles and has to face her son for the first time in decades. Jeff shares his resentment with his mother for her giving him to his uncle Cecil when he was three. Jason continues to try to get Miles to go to Hong Kong, which would mean leaving "Randall" (Fallon) behind. Blake asks Jason to keep a watchful eye on his daughter and to let him know immediately if there's any change in her condition. In the meantime it is discovered that Jason will probably need to use Zach Powers' supertankers for the transport of the oil to the pipeline. As a gesture of his love, Jeff gets all of Fallon's jewelry back for her. She had pawned it when she got to Los Angeles. As she thanks him for his kindness, Miles orders Jeff to stay away from his wife.

"Moment of Truth" – Episode 1.3
Original Airdate – November 28, 1985

Guest Appearances by Nicholas Pryor (Dr. Maurice Boland), Reid Shelton (Oliver Baines), Charles Van Eman (Sean McAllister), Ed Lottimer (George) and Kira Lawrence (Denise)

On Thanksgiving Day, Jason is informed he has only six more months to live. With this in mind, Jason gives Miles and "Randall" ten percent of Colby Enterprises as a wedding gift but says nothing about his current condition. Frankie offers to help Jeff get Fallon back but Jeff is suspicious of her intentions. Wanting to have a permanent hold on her, Sable approaches Fallon about trying to have children. Fallon flatly refuses to consider having a child until she has regained her memory. Zach and Miles discuss business affairs concerning 'Powers Shipping' with Jason. Jason warns Bliss' boyfriend Sean McAllister not to use his daughter for his own political gain. Sable also wants Jeff out of the mansion but Constance points out that the house is the Colby family home and that Jeff is a Colby. Sable will simply have to get used to having him there. Jason and Frankie run into each other and reminisce about the brief affair they had years before. Sable discovers Jason's lab reports giving him only six months to live and is positively crushed. While she is crying her eyes out, Jason is informed by his doctor that it was all a computer error and he is not dying after all.

"Family Album" – Episode 1.4
Original Airdate – December 5, 1985

Guest Appearances by John Forsythe (Blake Carrington), Diahann Carroll (Dominique Devereaux), Arlene Banas (Sharen), Orly Kate Sitowitz (Katie), Peter White (Arthur Cates) and Carol Ann Henry (Mrs. Wrigley)

Miles interrupts Fallon and Jeff's discussion as Jeff is in the process of telling her that she is his former wife and the mother of their son. Zach continues to try to do business with Jason to ship Blake's oil with Jason ordering Zach to stay away from his son. Meanwhile, Monica must face the fact

that her father believes only a man can take care of business when she offers to go to China on business for him. Sable tries to talk to Constance about taking back her shares of Colby Enterprises but Constance won't consider such an idea. Attorney Arthur Cates tells Sable that the only way to have Constance's gift rescinded, Constance would have to be declared mentally incompetent. Blake brings Fallon's son (L.B.) from Denver and she does not recognize him either. Frankie tries to get close to her grandson but Jeff doesn't want to encourage a relationship between them. Garrett Boydston has bought stock in Titania Records and offers Monica the chance to head the company. Sable starts putting her plan to prove Constance is losing her mind into motion. Bliss tries to get Jason to give Sean the benefit of the doubt about their relationship. While L.B. and Fallon are going through the family photo album, Fallon discovers photos of herself. Obviously in shock, she blames both Miles and Jeff for their deception and wanting to be away from everyone speeds off in one of the cars.

"Shadow of the Past" – Episode 1.5
Original Airdate – December 12, 1985

Guest Appearances by David Lain Baker (Angelo), Ray Stricklyn (Dr. James L. "Jimmy Lee" Parris), Philip Brown (Neil Kittridge) and Gordon Thomson (Adam Carrington)

While looking for Fallon, Miles and Jeff continue to blame one another and decide to let Dr. Parris know about her disappearance. Jason becomes upset when he finds out that Adam Carrington has approached Zach Powers regarding the use of his tankers and tells Adam that in the future he is to check with him first. Fallon goes to Dr. Parris on her own for help and during the treatment, remembers the day she was raped by someone and runs away. Sable encourages Miles to create his own life with Fallon despite anything Jeff says or does. Frankie tells Jeff that Cecil "forced" her to leave Jeff with him. Monica steps down from Colby Enterprises and starts over as an executive at Titania Records. Jason isn't happy with her decision to leave but she explains to him that she's tired of being "daddy's princess" and is only thought of as the spoiled girl who got a job because daddy owns the company. At Titania Records, her predecessor Neil Kittridge isn't exactly thrilled to meet her as he knows he's being replaced. Bliss is upset because she thinks she's the only Colby child without any special talents. When Miles picks her up from Dr. Parris' office and gets Fallon back to the mansion, she runs into Adam. Seeing Adam immediately brings back horrible memories of the night she left Denver because she claims he is the man who raped her.

"A House Divided" – Episode 1.6
Original Airdate – December 19, 1985

Guest Appearances by Gordon Thomson (Adam Carrington), Alain Saint-Alix (Fabrice), Dawson Mays (Bill Cochran), Ray Stricklyn (Dr. James L. "Jimmy Lee" Parris), Charles Van Eman (Sean McAllister), Lauren Levian (Wardrobe), Catherine Ferras (Makeup Lady) and Kent DeMarche (Hairdresser)

With Dr. Parris' help, Fallon finally remembers it wasn't Adam who raped her (This coming after Jeff and Adam get into a fight, forcing Adam to return to Denver). Sable keeps trying to convince Jason something is wrong with Constance and tells everyone that Constance is involved with a con-man who is trying to extort money from her. Jason complains to Frankie that he wishes Sable would back off and he doesn't understand why she's become so self-absorbed. Zach reminds his nephew Sean that he's only supposed to be pretending to like Bliss while getting information on Colby Enterprises but he's being met with opposition because Sean has fallen for the youngest Colby daughter. Hutch is offended and surprised when Constance gives him the two hundred thousand dollars he spent on his motor-home. Sable gets wind of the large transaction and plans to somehow add that into her plot. Miles tries to make Fallon decide if she wants to be with him or with Jeff. She begs them to simply give her a little space to work things out for herself. Zach and Jason finally sign a contract in case Jason can't ship all of the Carrington oil. Jason is furious when Sable tells him she's taken the first steps to have Constance declared incompetent.

"The Reunion" – Episode 1.7
Original Airdate – December 26. 1985

Guest Appearances by John Forsythe (Blake Carrington), Diahann Carroll (Dominique Devereaux), Titos Vandis (Nikos Livadas), Read Morgan (Curtis), Peter White (Arthur Cates) and Philip Brown (Neil Kittridge)

Frankie doesn't want to disturb her sister's marriage to Jason despite the fact that he's making advances and asking to renew their old romance. Due to Miles' impatience and her feelings for Jeff, Fallon considers returning to her family home in Denver and letting her father know that she has gotten her memory back. Jason moves out of his and Sable's bedroom after telling Sable he will fight for Constance. Monica and Neil Kittridge (whose position she now holds) continue to have disagreements concerning the running of Titania Records. Dominique walks into the office in the middle of one of the disagreements and is very disturbed with what she sees. When Monica accuses Hutch of extortion, he finds out who Constance really is. Hutch is highly insulted and angrily tells her to leave and never come back. Constance receives a summons to court and although furious, Garrett tells her not to lose her cool or it could be playing into Sable's hands. Dominique and Garrett are enjoying their romance and time together but there's still a secret Dominique won't share. Zach blackmails one of Jason's tanker captains. Blake and Jason discover there is trouble on both ends of the pipeline. After quite a bit of soul searching, Miles offers Fallon an annulment then witnesses a scene between Jason and Frankie, where Jason comments that he married the wrong sister and declares his love for her.

"Fallen Idol" – Episode 1.8
Original Airdate – January 2, 1986

Guest Appearances by Gary Morris (Wayne Masterson), Titus Vandis (Nikos Livadas), Arlene Banas (Sharen), Philip Brown (Neil Kittridge), Mickey Jones (Bubba) and Read Morgan (Curtis)

After their talk at the Five Oaks Inn, in which Jason pledges his continuous love, Frankie decides to return to London. As a way to get Sable off her back, Jeff offers to return his shares of Colby Enterprises to his aunt Constance, who immediately dismisses the entire idea. Colby Enterprises must face  the fact the oil spill was probably caused by one of their tankers. Zach continues to blackmail Captain Livadas who responds with threatening to take Zach down with him. Monica meets and records the blind singer, Wayne Masterson. When she presents him to Neil, Neil doesn't share her enthusiasm for Wayne. Miles is extremely jealous of the attention Fallon gives to Jeff and again tries to force her into deciding who she wants to be with. Even though Frankie has returned to London, Jason leaves Sable when he discovers she is unwilling to stop her crusade against Constance. Monica apologizes to Constance for ruining her relationship with Hutch. Constance tells Monica that everything will be fine and not to worry about it. Monica also tries to convince Hutch to give his relationship with Constance another try but Hutch's pride is wounded and he refuses to consider it. Constance tells Jeff there is a letter that Philip wrote to Cecil that will undeniably prove that Jeff is entitled to his share of Colby Enterprises. Colby Enterprises receives and injunction against the pipeline since it appears they are responsible for the oil spill. When Jason decides to go to London to track down Frankie, Miles accuses him of betraying the family and that as far as he's concerned Jason no longer has a son.

"The Letter" – Episode 1.9
Original Airdate - January 9, 1986

Guest Appearances by Gordon Thomson (Adam Carrington), David Hedison (Lord Roger Langdon), John Marion (Auctioneer), Barbara Pallenberg (Verna) and Paul Sinclair (Paramedic)

Constance is insistent that Jeff find the letter from Philip. Jeff enlists Alexis to help him but she calls and says she hasn't found anything in Cecil's private files yet. A little later, Adam calls and tells Jeff he has found the letters proving Jeff's entitlement in Cecil's files and that for some odd reason his uncle had put them in his Logan Rhinewood file. Miles continues to try to talk Sable out of going to New York. Frankie accepts Roger's proposal just as Jason shows up. Jason assures Adam and Blake that he has everything control and Monica starts working with Wayne. Sable is furious at being outbid for the Matisse and even more so when she finds out Zach Powers is the buyer. Adam arrives with not only brought the letter Jeff needed, but also another which insinuates that Jeff is not Philip's son. When Constance attempts to burn the letter, she fails to notice it was not destroyed as she thought. Sable returns from the auction and Constance wishes to have a conversation with her. While trying to catch up with her, Constance walks in front of Sable's car and is accidentally run over. Jason is furious, Constance could be seriously injured and Sable is beside herself with guilt. Going into the mansion, Sable looks at the fireplace and sees the note Constance had thrown in. She retrieves it and proceeds to read the potentially damaging information.

"The Turning Point" – Episode 1.10
Original Airdate – January 16, 1986

Guest Appearances by Ed Lottimer (George), John Carlyle (Maitre d'), Steve Eastin (Bill Mahoney), June Lockhart (Dr. Sylvia Heywood), Paul Sinclair (Paramedic), David Hedison (Lord Roger Langdon), Charles Van Eman (Sean MacAllister) and Healy Cunningham (Polly Trumble)

Thankfully Constance was extremely lucky and only suffered a concussion. Sable feels so completely guilty that she drops the entire competency suit against Constance. Jeff feels incredibly guilty for showing the letter to Constance and decides to visit his mother in Rome as she is the only one who can  tell him the truth. Jason assures Sable it is too late to reconcile because of all the things that's happened between them recently. Zach has turned up with the Matisse and Sable tells him to take it back and leave her alone. Miles and one of the pump men (William Mahoney) go out on a fishing expedition. During their evening out both men have too much to drink and end up in an argument. The argument leads to a fight. When Sean quits working for his uncle in order to marry Bliss, Jason promises to stop the marriage. Constance opts not to tell Jason about Philip's letter for fear that he would use it against Jeff. Sable accidentally learns of Miles' concerns over Frankie and Jason's relationship. When Sable tries to force Jason not to divorce her, he leaves her. That wasn't quite what Sable had in mind…

"Thursday's Child" – Episode 1.11
Original Airdate – January 30, 1986

Guest Appearances by Gary Morris (Wayne Masterson), Charles Van Eman (Sean MacAllister), Anthony DeFonte (Inspector Verlakis), June Lockhart (Dr. Sylvia Heywood), Father George Venetos (Greek Orthodox Priest), Jimmy Stathis (Director), Peter White (Arthur Cates), Philip Brown (Neil Kittridge) and Nelson Welch (Cyril)

Sable shows Jason the letter that Constance had tried to burn saying that Jeff isn't Philip's son. Jason tries to reach Frankie to tell her that Jeff is extremely upset and that Sable has the letter. Frankie is able to sit Jeff down and convince him that he is indeed Philip's son but and then she warns him about Sable and the fact that she's capable of anything when pushed up against a wall. When Jeff arrives in Athens to investigate the idea that Zach could be behind the oil spill he finds the murdered body of Captain Livadas. Sable is advised to get Philip's will authenticated as soon as possible because it is stipulated in Andrew's will that only blood relatives are to be shareholders in Colby Enterprises. Hutch visits Constance when he learns of condition after the car accident and asks for another chance. Neil is very jealous of Wayne, who likes Monica. Bliss and others feel used and deceived when they learn of Sean's relationship to Zach. Fallon is appalled when Miles suggests that he should adopt L.B. and raise him together. When the annulment papers arrive Miles is filled with rage and loses control. He rapes Fallon and she takes L.B. and heads for Denver. Despite her better judgment, Sable is finding herself attracted to Zach. When Frankie arrives from London, Jason asks her if Jeff is their son.

"The Pact" – Episode 1.12
Original Airdate - February 6, 1986

Guest Appearances by Diahann Carroll (Dominique Devereaux), Robert Loring (Maitre d'), Philip Brown (Neil Kittridge), Gary Morris (Wayne Masterson), Carol Ann Henry (Mrs. Wrigley) and Richard McKenzie (Dr. Leonard Jamison)

Despite what the letter from Philip says and the fact that it is authentic, Frankie is still standing by her insistence that Jeff is Philip's son and not Jason's. Sable, wanting to protect Miles, threatens to use the letter against Jeff if he doesn't back away from Fallon and allow her to remain married to Miles. When Fallon and L.B.

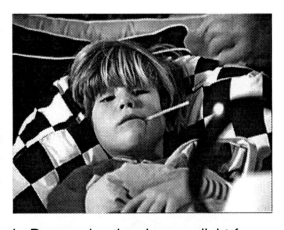

return from visiting the family in Denver, he develops a slight fever. The fever worsens and he is taken to the emergency room. The doctors explain to Jeff and Fallon that L.B. has contracted a life-threatening strain of meningitis and he is hospitalized in extremely serious condition. Dominique is introduced to Wayne Masterson and is impressed by his talent. Sable gets Jason to agree to a pact, they don't divorce, and there will be no trial against Jeff. Dominique tells Monica her lover is already married. Jason, Miles and Jeff continue to try to prove that Zach actually caused the oil spill that has halted any progress on the pipeline. Despite coming back from Denver with the realization that she loves both Miles and Jeff, Fallon sits in the hospital chapel and while praying for her son's recovery, swears that she will never leave her son or Jeff if L.B. pulls through this crisis.

"Fallon's Choice" – Episode 1.13
Original Airdate – February 6, 1986

Guest Appearances by Gary Morris (Wayne Masterson), Philip Brown (Neil Kittridge), Charles Van Eman (Sean MacAllister), Salome Jens (Mrs. McAllister), Meta King (Nurse #3), Arlene Banas (Sharen), Bill Washington (Resident), Barney McFadden (Lt. Olsen), Cam Clarke (Young Man), Orly Kate Sitowitz (Katie), Tamar Cooper (Nurse #2) and Richard McKenzie (Dr. Leonard Jamison)

Miles feels like he isn't a part of anything as he watches Fallon and Jeff supporting each other. Jason calls Blake and tells him about his grandson's illness. The doctors treating L.B. tells the family that all anyone can do is wait and pray that the medication saves him. Jeff calls Frankie and Constance tells Hutch, disappointing him again. Monica is less than supportive when Miles confides that he's hoping to get Fallon back. She tries to reason with him but he doesn't seem to want to listen to her. The police have found William Mahoney dead in the harbor. As soon as L.B. recovers Jeff asks Fallon to marry him and is delighted when she accepts. Sean takes Bliss to the hospital to see his mother, explaining he owed Zach for paying for everything. Constance discovers Sable has been playing tricks, trying to make her think she was losing her mind. Fallon tells Miles she has chosen Jeff. When Sable shows Miles the letter from Philip, he decides to use it against Jeff. Neil interferes when Wayne and Monica start getting close so she confronts him about the fact that he's married. Constance goes back to work at Colby Enterprises. Roger surprises Frankie with the news that he has been appointed vice-counsel at the British Consulate in Los Angeles.

"The Trial" - Episode 1.14
Original Airdate - February 20, 1986

Guest Appearances by Philip Abbott (Judge Barham), David Hedison (Lord Roger Langdon), Philip Brown (Neil Kittridge), Robert Hogan (Timothy Holmes), Sam Melville (Michael Grogan), Guy Dolman (Peter Hackford), Harriet Medin (Mary Hackford), Vernon Weddle (Gregory Farnsworth), Vanessa Bell Calloway (Lowell Sherman), Harold Harris (Butler), Charles Van Eman (Sean MacAllister), Peter White (Arthur Cates) and Richard Garrison (Reporter #3)

Miles has filed suit against Jeff claiming that he isn't eligible to hold stock and a seat on the board of Colby Enterprises and he's using Philip's letter as evidence to back up his claim. Jason is not terribly happy with his son when he receives a summons to appear in court. Jason informs Jeff that because of the stipulations in Andrew's will, he won't be allowed to keep the shares if the letter Philip wrote Cecil is authentic and Jeff's not Philip's son. Frankie tells her son not to worry and that she'll be there to testify on his behalf. Constance offers Miles her personal voting power if he simply drops the suit but Miles asks her for understanding instead. Constance hires Garrett Boydston to represent Jeff's claim to his father's estate. Roger is concerned over what may come out when Frankie testifies and asks Jason to stay away from her. Sable publicly calls Frankie a slut. Bliss reconciles with Sean. Arthur is hard on Frankie while she is on the stand. Frankie still maintains her story and keeps swearing that she was always faithful to Philip. As a surprise witness, Arthur brings in a doctor from Saigon who testifies that Philip was sterile.

"Burden of Proof" – Episode 1.15
Original Airdate - February 27, 1986

Guest Appearances by David Hedison (Lord Roger Langdon), Philip Abbot (Judge Barham), Robert Hogan (Timothy Holmes), Peter White (Arthur Cates), Harold Harris (Butler) and Reid Smith (Worker #2)

Arthur continues to badger Frankie on the stand and despite admitting that she had an affair, she still insists that Jeff is a Colby. Finally having seen enough, Jason shocks the entire courtroom by announcing that Jeff is not Philip's son but is actually his son. Completely taken by surprise, Miles leaves the courtroom and is in a car accident but comes out of it uninjured. Roger is upset when Frankie agrees to see Jason even though she won't let Roger comfort her. Jeff is totally dumbstruck by the realization that Jason is his father and that Frankie lied to him for his entire life. Constance tells Jason to give Jeff time to adjust to the shocking news he's just been delivered. Constance then gets into an argument with Sable and tells Sable that everything is her fault to begin with. Sable is emotionally crushed at the news and after telling Jason that she'll never forgive him, runs to Zach, who is waiting for her with open arms. Wayne plans to have eye surgery and is annoyed with Monica for postponing his concert tour. Fallon finds a note Miles left when he snuck into her bedroom while she was asleep that professed his undying love for her and begging her for another chance. After returning from a walk on the beach with Fallon, Jeff and Miles get into yet another fight. Jeff slips when one of the balustrades on the beach cracks and breaks, sending Jeff tumbling down the rocks.

"My Father's House" – Episode 1.16
Original Airdate - March 6, 1986

Guest Appearances by David Hedison (Lord Roger Langdon), Gary Morris (Wayne Masterson), Nick Cavanaugh (Mover #2), William Bogert (Harold Jessup), Carol Ann Henry (Mrs. Wrigley), Ben Hartigan (Donald), Gareth McClain (Mover #9) and Lynn Herring (Lena)

Thankfully, Jeff hasn't been seriously injured in the fall and despite his anger level, Miles rescues Jeff from the side of the cliff. Miles is also not sorry that Jeff fell over the cliff. After quite a bit of consideration, Sable and Jason realize that Frankie's revelation about the affair and Jeff's paternity is the end of their marriage. The two agree to file for divorce. Jeff wants to return to Denver to get married and live but Fallon insists on getting married in Bel Air instead. Frankie makes an attempt to reconcile with Sable but her sister makes it very clear that her actions are unforgivable. Miles refuses to go to New York when his father suggests him getting away for a while to clear his mind. Sable insists on Jason giving her the house in the divorce. Jason reminds her that Constance owns half of the estate so Sable approaches Constance, offering to buy her out. Constance dismisses Sable's offer and tells her that the house is the Colby family home and she will see to it that it remains that way. Sable stays in Zach's penthouse while Constance's private investigator is watching her every move. Roger is transferred to Singapore (courtesy of a few pulled strings by Zach) while Frankie stays in California. Jason and Sable are supposed to be looking after L.B. but end up arguing over the house and divorce. They're in the heat of battle when they realize L.B. is nowhere to be found.

"The Outcast" – Episode 1.17
Original Airdate - March 13, 1986

Guest Appearances by Diahann Carroll (Dominique Devereaux), Jack Coleman (Steven Carrington), Ingrid Anderson (Valerie), Philip Brown (Neil Kittridge) and William Bogert (Harold Jessup)

After a frantic search through the house and on the grounds, Jason finds L.B. hiding in a trunk in the attic. Jason asks Jeff to understand that he didn't know he was Jeff's father and asks him to give their newfound relationship a chance. Jeff agrees to try and says he and Fallon will be married in Los Angeles. Miles confronts his mother about staying the night at Zach's so Sable tries to explain. She also tells him about the upcoming wedding. Dominique is upset that Monica didn't consult her before getting rid of Neil and orders Monica to rehire him immediately. Sable and Fallon argue about the wedding plans. Miles accuses of Fallon of planning the wedding in Los Angeles to get back at him for raping her. Garrett tells Jason to reconsider the divorce because it would be too expensive for Colby Enterprises. The private investigator gives Constance the tape in which Sable tells Zach that they have to be reasonable regarding their relationship. Miles discusses the Mahoney case with Zach and the two reach an agreement: Zach will help with the case against Miles and Miles won't tell Jason about Sable spending the night. Fallon and Jeff are upset that Blake, Krystle and Alexis couldn't be at their engagement party but are determined to make the best of the evening. Miles turns up to the party falling-down drunk to wish Fallon and Jeff good luck, but adds that he has no intention of ever giving up on getting Fallon back.

"The Wedding" – Episode 1.18
Original Airdate - March 20, 1986

Guest Appearances by John Forsythe (Blake Carrington), Jack Coleman (Steven Carrington), Diahann Carroll (Dominique Devereaux), Ray Wise (Spiro Koralis), Charles Van Eman (Sean MacAllister), Ian Abercrombie (The Minister), and John Considine (Lt. Braden)

The last minute details and arrangements for the wedding are well underway. There is good news and bad news out of Denver. A blizzard has moved through the area causing the Denver airport to be closed, making it impossible for Alexis or Krystle to fly out in time for the wedding. Blake and Steven had arrived a few days early. They're trying to figure a way around the pipeline injunction and how to clean up the controversy surrounding the oil spill. Miles asks the police to conduct an examination of the body (William Mahoney). Fallon is furious with Alexis when she finds out about the fact that she's brought Ben to Denver to force Blake into court. Dominique apologizes to Jeff for all of the times she tried to make him believe that Fallon was dead. Jeff forgives her and is optimistic that this time he and Fallon are going to be happy no matter what happens. Completely against Sable's wishes, Zach attends the wedding and Miles also participates in the festivities. Jason surprises himself when he realizes that he still finds Sable attractive. Blake happily welcomes his son-in-law back into the family. The wedding takes place and inspires Bliss and Sean to agree to secretly marry. Moments after Jeff and Fallon leave for their honeymoon, the police arrive and arrest Miles for murder.

"The Honeymoon" – Episode 1.19
Original Airdate - March 27, 1986

Guest Appearances by Mabel King (Fortune Teller), Charles Van Eman (Sean MacAllister), Gary Morris (Wayne Masterson) and Donald Torres (Newscaster)

Fallon and Jeff enjoy their honeymoon in Jamaica and reminisce about their first impulsive Vegas wedding. While on the island they are told of a frightening prophecy by a fortune teller. After hearing the news of Miles' arrest, Bliss and Sean return to Los Angeles and cancel their plans to marry in Las Vegas. Sable is frightened for her son and turns to Jason for comfort and reassurance. Monica visits Miles in jail and tells him that he'll have to stay put for at least one more day while they wait for his bail hearing to take place. Roger offers to let Frankie go after she confesses that she's still in love with Jason. Frankie accepts Constance's invitation to stay in the pool house and is placed directly in the line of Sable's wrath. Monica tells Sable that she's at a loss because Miles is shutting her out and won't talk to her about the impending charges. Frankie accuses Jason of being behind Roger's transfer but he denies it emphatically, causing Frankie to verbally attack Sable, not knowing that Sable had no part in the transfer either. Miles admits to his mother that he had suffered a blackout and honestly doesn't know if he killed William Mahoney or not. Unfortunately for him, the police say they have the murder weapon and there are fingerprints all over it; they belong to Miles.

"Double Jeopardy" – Episode 1.20
Original Airdate - April 10, 1986

Guest Appearances by Helen Funai (Min), Ed Lottimer (George Samuels), Donn Whyte (Federal Marshal), Ray Wise (Spiro Koralis), Vincent Baggetta (Lt. John Moretti), Gary Morris (Wayne Masterson), Philip Brown (Neil Kittridge) and Rita Taggart (Brenda)

Fallon and Jeff receive word of the trouble Miles is in and cut their honeymoon short to return to Los Angeles and help him. Frankie leaves for Mexico to divorce Roger and vows she won't come back until Jason's divorce is final and he is a free man. Lt. Moretti comments that Jeff was in  Greece at the same time Captain Livadas was murdered. Jason convinces Garrett to file a claim for disclosure of all evidence against Miles, despite Garrett's desire to wait until the preliminary hearing. Sable starts planning to win Jason back and uses the current trouble Miles is in as a stepping stone to his heart. Monica continues her affair with Neil despite the fact that he's married. Sean breaks up with Bliss after accusing her of using him to make her father angry. He then tells Zach that he is no longer willing to participate in his plan and is moving to Florida. Zach persuades Sable to keep the Matisse even though she's going back to Jason. Sable begs Zach not to come to the opening night of the gallery's new wing because Jason will be present and it would be uncomfortable for all of them. Frankie calls Constance to let her know that her divorce is final. Both women are unaware that Sable is listening in on another line. Despite Sable's pleas, Zach shows up at the gallery opening anyway. The evening is interrupted by Lt. Moretti. This time he has a warrant for Jeff's arrest for the murder of Captain Livdas.

"A Family Affair" – Episode 1.21
Original Airdate - April 17, 1986

Guest Appearances by Vincent Baggetta (Lt. John Moretti), Ray Wise (Spiro Koralis), Evelyn Guerrero (Jane), Mark McIntire (Clerk) and Michael Yhuelo (Maitre d')

While he and Garrett are working to get Jeff freed, Jason claims Lt. Moretti is trying to obtain revenge by arresting Jeff for a murder that he didn't commit. Constance calls Frankie in Mexico to let her know what is going with Jeff and Frankie insists on coming back to Los Angeles. After spending a night making love to Jason, Sable witnesses a phone call between Jason and Frankie. Garrett manages to get Jeff out on bail and Miles vows to stand by his brother and help in any way he can. Constance asks Monica whether audio tapes in court are of any use or relevance on a case and is told that they are usually not admissible. Despite Jason's belief that Zach is the person behind Jeff and Miles' current legal troubles, he makes a deal. Jason offers to allow Zach to transport all the Carrington oil on the provision that the cases against both of his sons disappear. Zach swears he is not behind the problems, but later admits that he hates the Colby family because his father committed suicide after being financially ruined when living in Greece. Zach instructs Spiro to find out everything he can on the Mahoney case and begins devising a plan. Suspecting that there is far more to this case than meets the eye, Sable books herself on the same flight to Greece as Jason and Frankie are on.

"The Reckoning" – Episode 1.22
Original Airdate - May 1, 1986

Guest Appearances by Gary Morris (Wayne Masterson), Stefan Gierasch (Koulermous), Jo Ann Pflug (Judge Veronica Payne), Ray Stricklyn (Dr. James L. "Jimmy Lee" Parris), Jack Bruskoff (Kostas), Healy Cunningham (Polly) Zitto Kazann (Viachos) and Clayton Norcross (Steward)

Sable is bent on making Frankie's life a living hell. While the three of them are in Greece, Sable never misses an opportunity to try to convince Frankie that she and Jason are once again husband and wife and proceeds to share details of their lovemaking. When he mysteriously disappears, the family and police assume that Miles has jumped bail, when in actuality he has gone to see Dr. Parris in the hopes that the doctor may be able to help him remember anything during his blackout. With both Miles and Jeff in horrible trouble, Fallon remembers the Jamaican fortune teller's prediction and becomes extremely frightened. Zach is in hot water after Jason discovers that the witness in Athens was a hoax from the beginning and that Jeff is totally in the clear. Monica is worried but relieved when Wayne comes out of surgery able to see. Finally having had more than enough of Sable's games, Constance gives Jason the tape of Sable and Zach talking about how careful they have to handle their relationship. Frankie accuses Jason of not being serious about their relationship and if he were, Sable would already be out of the house. After arriving to his court hearing late, Miles is forced to admit that Dr. Parris was of little assistance and that the hammer used to kill William is definitely his.

"Anniversary Waltz" – Episode 1.23
Original Airdate - May 8, 1986

Guest Appearances by Michael Greene (Fowler), Philip Brown (Neil Kittridge), Fran Ryan (Helen Webster). Ray Wise (Spiro Koralis), Georgann Johnson (Dr. Waverly) and Christopher Lofton (Gilman)

That old saying about the "best laid plans" is coming true as Sable is planning a surprise anniversary party for her and Jason. She is determined that this will be just the thing to finally get them back together once and for all. Little does she know, Jason has the tape and is trying to figure out just what to do about his scheming wife. Jeff and Miles discover that Miles didn't have possession of the murder weapon when it was used on Mahoney. Neil gives Monica a key to his apartment and when Wayne finds out about their relationship, he not only decides to leave 'Titania Records', but he also leaves Los Angeles. Spiro thinks his stepfather is responsible for this mother's fatal accident and sets out to try to prove it. Fallon tells Constance and Hutch that she may be pregnant and thanks them for everything they've done for her. Jeff and Miles find the original hammer. When Jason finds out about the anniversary dinner, he informs Sable that he has the tape and as far as he's concerned their attempt at reconciliation and their marriage is over. Sable then runs to Zach for comfort and is in disbelief when she learns that Zach has always hated the entire Colby family. With the original hammer in hand, Jason heads for Zach's penthouse, where he nearly finds Spiro and Bliss in bed and heads for Zach's yacht instead. When he gets to the yacht, Jason angrily confronts Zach with the evidence. Zach pulls a gun to force Jason to leave. The gun accidentally goes off while the two of them are fighting with the bullet hitting Sable in the head.

"Checkmate" – Episode 1.24
Original Airdate – May 22, 1986

Guest Appearances by Vincent Baggetta (Lt. John Moretti), Lisa Ailiff (Gail Kittridge), Tom Fuccello (Surgeon), June Christopher (Night Nurse), Steve Dart (Police Officer), Helen Funai (Min) and Christopher Lofton (Lt. Gilman)

Sable is rushed to the hospital and undergoes surgery to remove the bullet from the side of her head and relieve the pressure a blood clot is placing on her brain. Jason and Zach are both filled with guilt when the doctors say she may lose her eyesight. Fallon is in the process of telling Jeff  that she might be pregnant when Monica bursts in with the news of the shooting. Zach admits that he is in love with Sable, but she had been refusing to sleep with him. The family is relieved to learn that Sable is going to be alright and isn't going to be blinded. Zach orders Spiro to stay away from Bliss. When Jason gives Moretti proof of Miles' innocence, Moretti proceeds on to the next case: Sable's accident. Miles confesses he is still in love with Fallon. Zach found out Spiro set up the wrong witness in Athens, and throws him out. Monica finds Neil in bed with his wife and flies off in her plane, which crashes shortly after taking off. Out of the hospital and still determined to get Jason back, Sable follows Jason and Frankie to try to stop their trip to the Dominion Republic but she trips and falls down the staircase. When she regains consciousness, Sable tells Moretti that Jason tried to kill her. Just before boarding the plane Jason is placed under arrest for attempted murder.

SEASON TWO

"The Gathering Storm" – Episode 2.1
Original Airdate – September 18, 1986

Guest Appearances by Vincent Baggetta (Lt. John Moretti), Peter White (Arthur Cates) and Bill Zuckert (Forest Ranger)

As her small plane burns, Monica is rescued just before a massive explosion destroys the aircraft. Moretti is feeling an odd, almost perverted sense of satisfaction as he throws Jason in jail for trying to kill Sable. Jason insists that he had nothing to do with Sable's fall but Moretti doesn't believe him. Frankie visits Jason and pledges her undying love for him and promises that nothing will ever tear them apart again. Frankie then proceeds to order Sable to drop the charges. Sable enjoys watching her sister's tantrum and refuses to comply with the order. Fallon's pregnancy is confirmed but now she is faced with the problem of not knowing whether Jeff or Miles is her child's father. Sable tries to blackmail Jason by telling him that she'll drop the attempted murder charges if he'll forget about the divorce plans. Jason holds his ground and tells her that he'll take his chances in court. Miles makes a dinner date with Channing Carter, a woman he met at the Excelsior Hotel. Fallon questions Frankie about her relationship with Jason and her feelings for Philip but won't say why. Out on bail, Jason finds comfort in Frankie's arms. Sable decides she needs reinforcements for Jason's hearing and sleeps with Zach as a way to convince him to lie on the stand for her. Too bad he decides to tell the truth anyway.

"No Exit" – Episode 2.2
Original Airdate – September 25, 1986

Guest Appearances by Diahann Carroll (Dominique Devereaux), Kevin McCarthy (Lucas Carter) and Vincent Baggetta (Lt. John Moretti)

When no one will go along with Sable's version of the "attempted murder", she realizes she has no choice but to drop the charges but when she tells Moretti that she falsified the charges, he tells her that it's either Jason or her that will be serving time in jail. With the feeling that everyone has abandoned her, Sable withdraws into a deep depression and claims that she was mentally unstable at the time she accused Jason of harming her. Jason and Frankie begin making plans as they celebrate their new life together. Fallon has nightmares about her unborn child's paternity and finally confides her fears in Jeff along with the news that Miles had raped her. Dominique has decided to sell 'Titania Records' in order to help Blake fend off Alexis and Ben. Before returning to Denver, Dominique tells Garrett that because of his life-long lie about being previously married, they no longer have any type of future. Garrett then transfers to Colby Enterprises' New York office. Channing (on orders from her uncle) proposes an article on Sable in Modern Design Magazine as a way to gather information on the family and its business affairs. Jason decides enough is enough and once and for all orders Sable out of the mansion. As she's reluctantly leaving, Sable conveniently faints in the doorway.

"Jason's Choice" – Episode 2.3
Original Airdate – October 2, 1986

Guest Appearances by Diahann Carroll (Dominique Devereaux)

Sable has the last laugh again as the doctor orders her to stay in bed for a least a week. Jason is beside himself for being so hard on her and tries to make her comfortable while she recuperates. Frankie is also hard on herself but warns Jason not to fall for Sable's "poor little me" act. Monica quits when she discovers that Dominique has sold 'Titania Records' and her holdings in the hotel to Zach. Sable accepts the idea of the magazine article and Channing moves into the mansion. While she and Miles are getting closer, she's on the defensive when she's caught going through desk drawers. Dominique asks Jason to help Blake in his fight against Alexis. Jason refuses to become involved in their personal attacks on each other. Fallon and Jeff take a miniature vacation to get away from the constant stress in their lives. Bliss talks Sable out of leaving the mansion. One by one, each of Sable's children goes to Jason to plead her case. Miles plans a romantic evening with Channing. The two make love but Channing can sense that Miles is still in love with Fallon. After being ganged up on by his children, Jason finally gives in and tells Sable she can remain in the mansion on one condition: that she immediately grants him an uncontested, uncomplicated divorce. He's going to marry her sister. Pushed in a corner with no way around it, Sable reluctantly agrees to his demand.

"The Matchmaker" – Episode 2.4
Original Airdate – October 16, 1986

Guest Appearances by Kevin McCarthy (Lucas Carter), Anna Levine (Anna Rustov) and Adrian Paul (Nikolai Rustov)

Jason hand delivers the divorce papers to Sable and informs her that although she is staying, Frankie is now the lady of the house and will have full run of the household. Sable cringes as she thinks of her husband and her sister being happy with each other. Sable is even less thrilled when in the heat of an argument, Frankie lets it slip that Jason has set up a ten million dollar trust fund for Jeff and Fallon's new baby. Channing lets it be known that she is interested in Miles while looking at the Colby Collection. Monica is less than forthcoming with information about her plane crash while talking to Jason. After accepting a public relations job for a new dance company, Bliss meets a Russian dancer to whom she is immediately attracted. Monica takes over Garrett's position as General Counsel for Colby Enterprises. Fallon refuses to have a paternity test conducted until after the baby has been born. Miles is having a case of sibling rivalry and complains that Jason cares more about Jeff than he does any of his other children. After finishing his transaction with Dominique, Zach presents Sable with The Excelsior Hotel and tells her that he will teach her to use her divorce settlement to gain money and power. Channing and Miles take off for Vegas to elope with Lucas and Sable close behind, hoping to get there in time to stop the wedding.

"Something Old, Something New" – Episode 2.5
Original Airdate – October 23, 1986

Guest Appearances by Anna Levine (Anna Rustov), Adrian Paul (Nikolai Rustov), Judson Earney Scott (Sacha Malenkov), Randi Brooks (Mrs. Mahoney), Michael Paul Chan (Reporter), James Houghton (Senator Cash Cassidy) and Kevin McCarthy (Lucas Carter)

Channing is informed that Lucas and Sable are on their way to Las Vegas so she convinces Miles not to wait and the two are married within a few hours later. Upon their return to Los Angeles, Sable warns Channing not to hurt Miles and if she did Sable would see to it that her life was miserable. Monica finally tells Jason about her affair with Neil and the circumstances of her plane crash. Jason is less than thrilled when he receives a phone call from former Senator Cash Cassidy but his mood changes when he hears that the government has decided to back his 'I.M.O.S.' project. Upon hearing about Miles' marriage, Jason too tells Channing to be very careful. Bliss finds out that the dance troupe's choreographer is a KGB agent who has been ordered to keep Nikolai and his sister away from Americans. Monica is still bent on nailing Zach for his wrongdoings and visits William Mahoney's widow in the hopes of obtaining incriminating information. Jeff questions Frankie about her feelings when she realized that he was Jason's child instead of Philip's but wouldn't tell anyone why he wanted to know. Jason offers Miles an executive position in the Aerospace Division of Colby Enterprises as a wedding gift. Cash crashes the reception that Sable holds to celebrate Miles and Channing's marriage. Monica places a desperate phone call to Constance to tell her of Cash's return.

"The Gala" – Episode 2.6
Original Airdate – October 30, 1986

Guest Appearances by James Houghton (Senator Cash Cassidy), Peter White (Arthur Cates), Anna Levine (Anna Rustov), Adrian Paul (Nikolai Rustov) and Judson Earney Scott (Sacha Malenkov)

Jason is finding himself getting a tremendous amount of pressure from all sides of the family. Sable is insisting that he give Miles a seat on Colby Enterprises' board, Monica is flatly refusing to work on anything that Cash is involved with and Miles informs him that Zach has just purchased a tremendous amount of stock in the Japanese company Onishy Electronics, which is the company largely responsible for building part of the system used in Jason's new satellite program. Monica is increasingly anxious about Cash's return and receives a note from Constance telling her not to worry because the past is just that. Monica later confides in Arthur Cates that she is concerned over what would happen if Cash ever discovered that she had given birth to his child. As Sable prepares for the dance troupe's opening, Frankie offers her assistance but is flatly refused. Miles and Jeff end up in another argument after Miles gives Fallon a gift for the baby. In an attempt to show Jason that he is serious about settling down, Miles urges Channing to start a family but she says no thinking that he's just trying to compete with Jeff for Jason's attention. Zach urges Sable to have her lawyer insist on Colby Enterprises stock as part of the divorce settlement. Channing has nightmares about her mother's death during childbirth and hides the truth from the Colby family.

"Bloodlines" – Episode 2.7
Original Airdate – November 6, 1986

Guest Appearances by Georgann Johnson (Dr. Waverly), Adrian Paul (Nikolai Rustov), Judson Earney Scott (Sacha Malenkov) and Shanna Reed (Adrienne Cassidy)

Jason is forced to allow Frankie to work on the satellite project (IMOS) after she insists that she can handle both the job and family. Channing is taking birth control pills to avoid becoming pregnant but tells Miles that she had an abortion years earlier that left her unable to have children. Sable, concerned over Miles' indifference about the things happening in his life, asks Channing for an explanation. Channing repeats the abortion story to Sable, who insists that she see Dr. Waverly for a new examination. Bliss is becoming more infatuated with Nikolai but he becomes withdrawn after being threatened by Sasha. Monica runs into Adrienne Cassidy (Cash's wife) who reminds her of the agreement they had made many years before. Sable accompanies Channing to Dr. Waverly's office and while Channing is being examined, Sable sneaks a look at Fallon's chart. She is stunned when she reads the line "paternity unknown". Sable puts the chart back and after thinking back to the day that Fallon ran out of the mansion and angrily went to Denver, realizes that Fallon could very well be carrying her grandchild. In the meantime, Channing is told that there's no reason why she couldn't conceive a baby. She swears the doctor to secrecy and continues taking the birth control pills.

"Deceptions" – Episode 2.8
Original Airdate – November 13, 1986

Guest Appearances by Peter White (Arthur Cates), Anna Levine (Anna Rustov), Adrian Paul (Nikolai Rustov), Judson Earney Scott (Sacha Malenkov), James Houghton (Senator Cash Cassidy)

Fallon threatens to have an abortion because of the problems her child's unknown paternity is causing. Sable is secretly having meetings with Arthur Cates to determine what rights Miles would have if he is proven the baby's father. She then proceeds to drop hints to Fallon about custodial rights causing Fallon to wonder what Sable knows. Miles confirms Sable's suspicions when he tells her about the night he raped Fallon five months earlier. In the meantime, Jason is trying to convince Miles that he and Channing should adopt a child. Bliss is forced to follow Anna's advice to stay away from Nikolai for fear that Sacha may report the relationship to his superiors. Channing fears she's losing Miles to his quest to get Fallon back. Monica is having a difficult time masking her feelings for Cash, especially after he tries to convince her that he's married "in name only". In yet another of their tense moments, Jeff and Miles get into a fight on the helicopter pad of Colby Enterprises. Danger lurks as the two reach the edge of the building and because it's raining, Miles slips over the side.

"And Baby Makes Four" – Episode 2.9
Original Airdate – November 21, 1986

Guest Appearances by James Houghton (Senator Cash Cassidy), Adrian Paul (Nikolai Rustov), Shanna Reed (Adrienne Cassidy), Coleby Lombardo (Scott Cassidy) and Peter White (Arthur Cates)

Security guards arrive on the roof and manage to pull Miles to safety. Both men are sorry that the fight went as far as it did but it also caused Fallon to once again threaten to have an abortion. Miles tells Sable about Fallon's threat and she instructs him to speak with Arthur Cates regarding his rights as the potential father. After leveling threats back and forth, Miles, Jeff and Fallon agree not to go to court over the paternity and give Miles father-to-be rights. Miles and Channing's marriage is becoming more strained because of his obsession with Fallon's baby. Jason and Frankie admit the entire situation sounds vaguely familiar as it is the same premise of their relationship and Jeff's paternity. Nikolai is banished from Bliss' life by Jason after he's caught in her bedroom after breaking into the Colby mansion. In a chance meeting, Monica runs into Cash, Adrienne and meets their young son Scott. Adrienne tries to keep Scott at a distance but he and Monica become fast friends. Monica is completely unaware that Scott is the child she gave up for adoption so many years before and forbids Cash from ever telling her that Scott is her son or that Constance insisted that they take the baby or she would have Cash removed from his Senate seat. Zach watches the meeting with a great deal of interest and then visits Arthur Cates to try to get more information on the Senator and his Colby connection.

"Bid For Freedom" – Episode 2.10
Original Airdate – November 28, 1986

Guest Appearances by Adrian Paul (Nikolai Rustov), James Houghton (Senator Cash Cassidy), Shanna Reed (Adrienne Cassidy), Coleby Lombardo (Scott Cassidy), Anna Levine (Anna Rustov) and Judson Earney Scott (Sacha Malenkov)

Fallon and Jeff are having problems because of Miles' claim to the baby and instead of fighting about it they decide to take a break at the Colby cabin in Lake Arrowhead. Miles is suspicious that the two of them are planning an "accidental miscarriage" so he tricks Channing into also  going to the cabin for the weekend. It becomes an even worse situation when bad weather prevents anyone from leaving. Frankie, Sable and Bliss are all upset and angry with Jason for the way he handled the situation with Nikolai. Bliss is rebels and tells her father that she is in love with Nikolai so to smooth things over Jason agrees to help Nikolai and his sister obtain asylum in the United States. As they are being given the good news, Sacha and other KGB operatives chase Nikolai and Bliss through the halls of a hotel until they are trapped on one of the upper floors. Meanwhile, Monica has invited Scott to join her and Cash while they watch a rocket take off and is nearly told about her relationship to the boy. Adrienne is furious and goes to Jason to insist that he remove Cash from the entire project but Jason refuses to interfere in personal matters. Zach decides he is in love with Sable and asks her to marry him. Anna is captured by the KGB and Nikolai jumps from a balcony as the agents close in.

Guest Appearances by Adrian Paul (Nikolai Rustov), Judson Earney Scott (Sacha Malenkov), Anna Levine (Anna Rustov), Joames Houghton (Senator Cash Cassidy), Shanna Reed (Adrienne Cassidy), Coleby Lombardo (Scott Cassidy), John Dehner (Billy Joe Erskine) and Peter White (Arthur Cates)

Nikolai manages to escape and asks for political asylum in the United States. When get finally gets to talk to Anna, she tells him that she's going to return to Russia to live with and protect their mother. Sacha decides to cooperate with the newly defected dancer's wishes only after Jason threatens to bring in the media. At the cabin, Fallon begins experiencing severe pain and while Jeff and Miles scramble for someone to provide assistance, a furious Channing is left to care for Fallon. Her pains get worse leading everyone to suspect that she may be going into premature labor. Finally reaching the mansion by telephone, Frankie arranges for a helicopter to retrieve all of them from the cabin and take Fallon to the hospital. It is a false alarm but one that makes Frankie advise Fallon to be cautious of Channing's motives. Zach knows the truth about Scott and tries to blackmail Cash into leaving the IMOS program. Knowing that Zach will carry out his threat, Cash decides to beat him to it but doesn't make it in time. Zach drops more than a few hints that lead Monica to call Constance. Constance tells Monica the entire sordid story and confirms that Scott is indeed her son. Monica is furious and takes out her anger on Cash when he arrives to tell her the truth.

"Sanctuary" – Episode 2.12
Original Airdate – December 18, 1986

Guest Appearances by Adrian Paul (Nikolai Rustov), James Houghton (Senator Cash Cassidy), Coleby Lombardo (Scott Cassidy) and John Dehner (Sam "Billy Joe" Erskine)

Monica is suffering from nightmares about Scott being her child but refuses to talk to Jason or Sable about her recent discovery. She becomes deeply depressed and insists that Jason accept her resignation from Colby Enterprises. Jason refuses to do so and keeps trying to  get her to open up about what's bothering her. Frankie again tells Fallon not to turn her back on Channing because there's something that just doesn't seem right. Frankie suspects Channing had something to do with the dead phone line at the cabin. Bliss tells Jason that Nikolai is being denied basic rights so Jason agrees to rethink a meeting between himself and the Soviets. Zach once again threatens to expose Cash's secret of Scott's paternity but Cash tells him that Monica already knows everything. Sable is stunned when Zach informs her that she's a grandmother and that her grandson is Scott Cassidy. Channing refuses to spy on the family for her Uncle Lucas and then tells Miles that she's looking forward to helping him raise Fallon's baby because she loves him. Constance appears to be missing despite a two million dollar withdrawl made from her New York bank account and a message for Jason to fly to New Delhi, India to meet with her. Jeff and Miles take off for India after discovering that Constance and Hutch were on a small chartered plane that has completely disappeared.

"Power Plays" – Episode 2.13
Original Airdate – January 1, 1987

Guest Appearances by Shanna Reed (Adrienne Cassidy), John Dehner (Billy Joe Erskine), Bruce David (David Soames), Kavi Raz (Prased), Nana Visitor (Georgina Sinclair) and Adrian Paul (Nikolai Rustov)

Jeff and Miles frantically continue their search for Constance and at the same time Jason is named "Man of the Year". Preparing for the agreed upon meeting with the Soviets, Jason asks Frankie to join him on the trip. Sable is noticeably jealous of their relationship and as a diversion, calls Adrienne Cassidy to ask her to lunch. During their lunch conversation, Sable tells Adrienne that she wants Scott to be raised as a Colby. Adrienne furiously refuses to give up "her" son and storms out of the restaurant. Fallon confronts Channing about the dead phone line at the cabin and insinuates that Channing was actually hoping that she would have a miscarriage. Channing denies Fallon's accusations but secretly acknowledges that it is the truth. Nikolai is given a new dance partner. She is Georgina Sinclair, a dancer from New York with whom Nikolai is familiar. Jason is furious when Sable shows up at the Colby Enterprises board meeting and announces that she, Zach and Jason are equal partners in Onishy Electronics. Jeff and Miles are told that Constance and Hutch were last seen boarding a plane for Katmandu, Nepal so they head for the small nation. Once there, they're told that she met with a man by the name of Hoyt Parker. While Jason is trying to reason with Zach about Sable's newfound wealth and power, he is interrupted by a phone call from Jeff with the news that Constance has died.

"The Legacy" – Episode 2.14
Original Airdate – January 8, 1987

Guest Appearances by Adrian Paul (Nikolai Rustov), Robert Sampson (Henry Marlis), Nana Visitor (Georgina Sinclair), James Houghton (Senator Cash Cassidy), Coleby Lombadro (Scott Cassidy) and Shanna Reed (Adrienne Cassidy)

Although there are no bodies, the Colby family and friends gather for a memorial service in Los Angeles to honor Constance and Hutch, who have apparently died in a plane crash. Jason is inconsolable and withdraws from everyone including Frankie. Sable offers her condolences to Jason and apologizes for the  problems that she and Constance had in the past. Channing is making waves again telling Miles that Fallon is refusing to be friendly much less civil to her. Adrienne is heavily drinking and tells Scott that his father doesn't love her anymore and only wants Monica. Scott goes to Monica and says he never wants to see her again. Sable is pleased and the rest of the family is surprised when Constance's will is read and she leaves her seat on Colby Enterprises' board along with her voting power to Miles. Miles, reveling in his newly inherited position, tells Jeff that he's going to get back everything that Jeff "stole" from him and that includes Fallon and their child. The mysterious Hoyt Parker arrives in Los Angeles. Jason is receiving threatening letters stemming from newspaper articles in which Jason is accused of favoring the Soviets. Sable is upset that Jason pulled out of Onishy Electronics, thus leaving her with "nothing" as she tells Zach. Frankie suggests that she and Jason take a miniature vacation at the Colby ranch in Eureka, California but their peaceful break is destroyed when they are attacked by a stranger with a gun.

"The Home-Wrecker" – Episode 2.15
Original Airdate – January 15, 1987

Guest Appearances by John Dehner (Billy Joe Erskine), Nana Visitor (Georgina Sinclair), Adrian Paul (Nikolai Rustov), James Houghton (Senator Cash Cassidy), Shanna Reed (Adrienne Cassidy), Coleby Lombardo (Scott Cassidy) and Kevin McCarthy (Lucas Carter)

Hoyt Parker is responsible for terrorizing Jason and Frankie. Jason, not knowing who the man is, manages to scare him off before he could cause major damage. With the threatening letters still arriving and in light of this new incident, Jeff suggests Jason get bodyguards. Jeff also has Fallon to contend with when she decides she wants to find a job to occupy her time with. Channing is feeling wealthier since Lucas released her trust fund to her but is still refusing to cooperate in any of his schemes to investigate and blackmail the Colby family and instead tells Jason that her uncle is ruthlessly dangerous. Jeff suspects Zach is involved in the murder attempt on Jason and Frankie. Nikolai denies having an affair with Georgina and swears there's nothing going on so he and Bliss reunite but split up again after Georgina arranges a little surprise for Bliss. Monica is getting a tremendous amount of pressure from Sable to tell Jason that Scott is his grandson. Monica threatens to cut Sable out of her life completely if she breathes a word of this secret to Jason. Sable accuses Zach of trying to destroy Jason and the company, which is the same as destroying her. Zach counters her attack with a marriage proposal and rather large engagement ring that Sable accepts but then says she wants more time to make up her mind and explore her feelings. Scott runs away from home causing Adrienne to tell Jason and Frankie to have Monica find him, especially since she's his mother.

"Manhunt" – Episode 2.16
Original Airdate – January 22, 1987

Guest Appearances by Eileen Barnett (TV Reporter), Michael Paul Chan (Reporter #2), John Dehner (Billy Joe Erskine), Susan French (Mrs. Parker), Nana Visitor (Georgina Sinclair), Adrian Paul (Nikolai Rustov), James Houghton (Senator Cash Cassidy), Shanna Reed (Adrienne Cassidy) and Coleby Lombardo (Scott Cassidy)

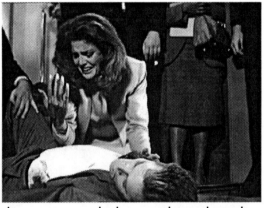

Jason confronts Monica with the news of Scott being his grandson and the fact that he's missing. Everyone is frantically searching for the child and Monica finally figures out that he may be at the observatory. They find him there but Scott tells Monica to leave him alone. Cash tries to convince Monica that her son needs her and so does he, but Monica doesn't want to listen to anything he has to say. Jason is upset that Constance had arranged such a deal and Sable is equally upset that they hadn't paid more attention to Monica. Maybe if they had, she wouldn't have been in this situation at all. Adrienne tells Cash that she'll lose custody of Scott if he tries to leave her. Sable tries to convince Bliss that Nikolai isn't cheating on her with Gina but Bliss doesn't believe it. Jeff is determined to track down Hoyt Parker and in an attempt to do so, visits his mother in Idaho. A furious Miles tries to force Billy Joe to run an article retracting the accusations against Jason. Monica is being pressured by Sable to fight for custody of Scott and points out Adrienne's drinking and suicide attempts as grounds for the fight. Following a meeting for the IMOS project, Jason is shot at but the gunman misses him and hits Cash instead, with a very frightened Monica by his side.

"All Fall Down" – Episode 2.17
Original Airdate – January 29, 1987

Guest Appearances by Christopher Coffey (Arnold), Lou Felder (Dr. Ames), Liam Sullivan (Mr. Rollings), James Houghton (Senator Cash Cassidy), Shanna Reed (Adrienne Cassidy), Coleby Lombardo (Scott Cassidy), Nina Visitor (Georgina Sinclair) and Adrian Paul (Nikolai Rustov)

Although seriously injured, Cash is operated on and will survive. While he's coming out of the anesthesia he repeatedly asks for Monica. Scott apologizes to Monica for the things he said to her the night he ran away. Sable is getting pressured by Zach to give him an answer regarding his marriage proposal and finally gives her 24 hours to make up her mind. Police capture the gunman and find a ticket to Eureka in his pocket, thus making them think he was also the person who shot at Jason and Frankie. After seeing the story of the shooting in the newspaper, Sable tries to convince Jason that she's still in love with him but is stunned to discover that Jason has proposed to Frankie. Hoyt Parker invests two million dollars in Colby Enterprises stock. Channing tries to convince Jeff that Miles is still in love with Fallon and Fallon is furious over the entire situation. She and Jeff argue and Jeff walks out of the room. Fallon follows him, Channing follows her and watches when Fallon loses her balance at falls down the staircase just as Miles enters the house. He frantically runs to Fallon's side and while looking up sees Channing standing at the top of the stairs.

Guest Appearances by Peter Haskell (Dr. Bill Banks) and Adrian Paul (Nikolai Rustov)

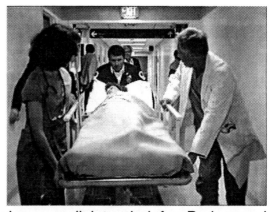

The fall has caused Fallon to go into premature labor and fearing injury to the baby, the doctors perform an emergency cesarean section. They deliver a baby girl and she is immediately rushed to the neonatal intensive care unit. Jeff is at the Excelsior Hotel where he unknowingly sits next to Hoyt Parker. He takes a call intended for Parker and recognizes Zach's voice on the other end and attempts to chase Parker but is stopped by the police for speeding. He has no idea that Fallon has just given birth. When he reaches the hospital, Jeff tells Jason and Miles about Parker and Zach's apparent involvement in the scheme to kill Jason. Jason is further convinced that Zach had something to do with Constance's death. Sable and Frankie briefly make peace with each other as they worry about the fate of Fallon's tiny baby. Channing begs Miles to believe her when she swears she had nothing to do with Fallon's fall. Jason threatens to kill Zach if he had anything to do with Constance's death. Monica and Sable share a mother/daughter moment and finally discuss Monica's pregnancy and what's going to happen with Scott's possible future as a Colby heir. After he returns to the hospital, Jason talks to Fallon and is emotionally touched when she asks if he would mind is she gives her daughter the middle name Constance. Miles finally believes Channing after L.B. tells him that he left marbles on the stairs and Fallon tripped on them. The family is summoned back to the hospital. Lauren Constance Colby is having difficulty breathing and is not expected to live.

"Fallon's Baby" – Episode 2.19
Original Airdate – February 12, 1987

Guest Appearances by Mary Cadorette (Researcher), Peter Haskell (Dr. Banks), Adrian Paul (Nikolai Rustov), Shanna Reed (Adrienne Cassidy), James Houghton (Senator Cash Cassidy) and Coleby Lombardo (Scott Cassidy)

The Colby family waits terrified that Lauren will die as doctors tell them there's nothing more they can do. After several tense days of waiting and worrying, Fallon receives the good news that her little girl is going to live. She tells Frankie and Jason that they should move ahead with their wedding plans. Sable is having Adrienne Cassidy investigated in the hopes of gaining more damaging information that could be used in a custody battle after witnessing a scene in which Adrienne tells Cash that she's returning to Washington and taking Scott with her. Zach tells Sable to give up her dreams of ever getting back together with Jason. Miles verbally attacks Jeff in Channing's defense and informs him that L.B. is responsible for Fallon's accident. Frankie is concerned about Sable still living at the mansion after she marries Jason. Hoyt Parker begins gathering information about the Colby family. Bliss wants to get married immediately but Nikolai isn't sure if he's made the right decision and says he isn't ready. Cash tells Monica that they can never have a future together because he doesn't want to hurt Scott by divorcing Adrienne. The paternity tests are performed and to their delight and Fallon's relief, Lauren is Jeff's daughter.

"Answered Prayers" – Episode 2.20
Original Airdate – February 26, 1987

Guest Appearances by Peter Haskell (Dr. Banks) and Robert Sampson (Henry Marlis)

Jeff and Fallon are thrilled with the news of Lauren's paternity but Miles refuses to believe the baby isn't his. Jeff tells him that he brought all of this on himself and to stay out of Fallon's life. Channing gets the brunt of Miles' disappointment and he lashes out at her for never  wanting him to be Lauren's father and then later apologizes for his behavior. Channing decides to throw away her birth control pills and try to give Miles a child. Miles doesn't believe that Sable wants to marry Zach Powers. Jason and Sable sign their divorce papers and agree to part as friends. Frankie tries to make amends with her sister and is told in no uncertain terms that Sable will never forgive her for destroying her life. Miles and Monica are worried that Zach may be using Sable as a way to get back at Jason for bad business dealings. Sable and Zach are in Marrakech, Morocco while Frankie is scheduled to be marrying Jason and shortly before the ceremony is to begin Sable and Zach both wish on a shooting star. Meanwhile, back in Los Angeles, the family and friends are gathered for Jason and Frankie's wedding. Frankie faints during the ceremony when a man stops the wedding and she realizes that one of the guests is her presumed dead first husband Philip Colby. What no one realizes is that Philip Colby and Hoyt Parker are one and the same person.

"Return Engagement" – Episode 2.21
Original Airdate – March 5, 1987

Guest Appearances by Georgann Johnson (Dr. Waverly), Adrian Paul (Nikolai Rustov), Anna Levine (Anna Rustov) and Shanna Reed (Adrienne Cassidy)

There are quite a few shocked people when they discover that the mystery guest is Philip Colby, particularly since he's been presumed dead for four decades. Jason wonders why he's come back on his and Frankie's wedding day of all times but Philip insists he came home because of Constance's death. Jason offers to let him stay at the mansion, which doesn't sit well with Frankie. Jeff and Philip hit it off immediately, which also bothers Jason and Frankie. Sable gets on the first plane back to Los Angeles after Monica calls and tells her the news of the postponed wedding. Zach is furious with Sable for leaving him the day before their wedding to once again try to get back together with Jason. A maid finds Channing's birth control pills and gives them to Miles. Miles furiously attacks her for deceiving him and tells her to leave. Zach tells Adrienne that they can both work out their problems with the Colby family together. Jason realizes Philip's handwriting matches Hoyt Parker's and becomes upset when Jeff tells him that he plans to offer Philip part of his shares of Colby Enterprises. Nikolai receives a call from his sister Anna informing him that their mother is ill but then lets it slip that it's a set-up by the KGB to get him back in the country. Jeff and Fallon happily bring Lauren home from the hospital. As Philip visits Frankie and tries to explain where he's been and why he returned, the two get caught up in the moment and share a passionate kiss, unaware of the fact that Sable is standing outside watching the whole thing.

"Devil's Advocate" – Episode 2.22
Original Airdate – March 12, 1987

Guest Appearances by Bianca Jagger (Maya Kumara), David Hedison (Lord Roger Langdon), Shanna Reed (Adrienne Cassidy), Coleby Lombardo (Scott Cassidy) and Adrian Paul (Nikolai Rustov)

Sable meets with Philip to discuss his feelings for Frankie and he admits he's still in love with her and will do anything he can to get her back. Jason still isn't sure about his decision to allow Philip to stay at the house and Frankie is dead set against the idea. Monica listens in on a phone conversation Philip is having and unbeknownst to him, she speaks and understands Chinese fluently. Monica reports to Jason that Philip talked about needing two million dollars. Jeff is a bit upset when Fallon says she doesn't want to buy a new home for their family because she thinks he's just trying to get back at Jason for the way he's treating Philip. Jason gets confirmation that Philip's handwriting is the same as Hoyt Parker's and heads to Singapore, where he meets Frankie's ex-husband Roger. Roger sends him to see Maya Kumara for more information about Hoyt Parker. Maya fills Jason in on Philip's gunrunning life and how all of his business associates thought he was dead. Channing tells Miles about her mother dying during childbirth but Miles isn't sure he can ever believe anything she says. Bliss asks Sable not to allow Nikolai to break his contract because he'll move to New York and she'll lose him forever. During an argument between Monica and Adrienne, Scott overhears that he is Monica's child. Frankie and Philip share another passionate moment that results in Frankie running away because she still has feelings for him. When Jason returns from Singapore he confronts Philip with the evidence he has against him and then introduces Maya, who identifies Philip as Hoyt Parker.

"Betrayals" – Episode 2.23
Original Airdate – March 19, 1987

Guest Appearances by Bianca Jagger (Maya Kumara), James Houghton (Senator Cash Cassidy), Adrian Paul (Nikolai Rustov) and Shanna Reed (Adrienne Cassidy)

The family is shocked that Hoyt Parker and Philip Colby are one and the same. Jason corners his brother and accuses him of killing Constance but Philip emphatically denies having any part of her death. He tells Jason that he used the name of a war buddy who died and asked Constance for two million dollars so he could repay the money for a gun purchase gone bad. Jason orders him out of the house, which causes more friction between him and Jeff. Jeff offers Philip three hundred thousand to help him out and although he's taking it, Philip also strikes a deal with Zach to supply information on Jason's business dealings in exchange for three million. Monica fills Sable in on all of Zach's threats regarding Scott. Sable proceeds to return his engagement ring and tells him she never wants to see him again. Scott promises Adrienne that he'll never leave her. Sable releases Nikolai from his contract despite Bliss' request but he counters by proposing marriage. Frankie admits that she hasn't set another wedding date because of Philip's presence. Cash is told that he can have a divorce if he wants one but that he can never have his son. Sable watches as Philip sneaks his way out to the pool house and seduces Frankie. As if by a miracle, Jason comes home early and Sable seizes the moment. She halfheartedly tries to keep Jason from going out to the pool house but doesn't stop him from doing so. When he opens the door Jason is floored as he discovers Frankie in bed with Philip.

"Dead End" – Episode 2.24
Original Airdate – March 26, 1987

Guest Appearances by Kevin McCarthy (Lucas Carter), James Houghton (Senator Cash Cassidy) and Shanna Reed (Adrienne Cassidy)

Jason hits the roof when he sees his brother and his fiancé in bed together. Despite Sable trying to keep things calm, Jason and Philip proceed to beat each other to a pulp. Sable tells Frankie that her behavior has been completely unforgivable and that Jason is crushed. After  admitting that she's still in love with Philip, Frankie runs away to a beach hotel to try and escape from her feelings. Bliss and Nikolai announce their engagement to the family before they leave for New York. Sable is trying to get closer to Jason and refuses to help Philip try to get back into Jason's good graces so when she briefly leaves, he steals her access card into Colby Enterprises. Channing discovers she's pregnant and tells Lucas that she's not doing anything to upset the Colby family again. Zach comes to Sable professing his love for her but she tells him that she accepts his apology but doesn't really love him and they have no future. Philip takes photos of the IMOS project and turns the material over to Zach. While Philip was taking the photos, Zach was doing a little investigating and finds the gun used in the Eureka shooting in Philip's hotel room. Jason is determined to talk to Frankie one more time but can't find her. Jeff figures out that she may be at the beach hotel and goes to talk to her. When he doesn't find her in her room, Jeff goes to the beach and is terrified when he sees her in the ocean gasping for air.

"Crossroads" – Episode 2.25
Original Airdate – April 3, 1987

Guest Appearances by Coleby Lomardo (Scott Cassidy)

Jeff reaches his mother in time to save her from drowning. Frankie tells him that she intentionally tried to commit suicide. Jeff immediately blames Jason for his mother's frame of mind and asks Fallon to come to the hotel to keep an eye on her while he tries to find Jason. During the course of the evening, Fallon sees a very odd light in the sky. Frankie leaves the hotel despite Fallon telling her not to. Channing tells Miles she's pregnant and he is thrilled about the news. Unfortunately, Channing is still being haunted by her mother's death and caves under the pressure. She calls Miles and tells him that she can no longer handle everything so she's filing for divorce and having an abortion. Sable again tries to get Monica to fight for custody of her son but Monica again refuses. Zach drops a bombshell on Sable when he tells her that Philip tried to kill Jason and Frankie in Eureka and that he can prove it. Sable tells Jason about the gun which leads him to the hotel to retrieve it from Philip's room. Not happy with her daughter's thinking, Sable kidnaps Scott from his school not knowing that Zach watched her do it. Philip takes Frankie hostage and heads for the Mexican border while Jeff and Jason are following them. Frankie and Philip argue and with his attention distracted, the car swerves and flips down a hill. When Jason and Jeff reach the wreckage they can't find Philip but Frankie is gravely injured. As Jason holds her in his arms, she begs him to forgive Sable for everything. Fallon is on her way back to the mansion when her car stalls and won't restart. Her cell phone is dead too so she gets out of the car. As she slowly starts to walk, the bright light returns and looking up to the sky Fallon sees a UFO. The spacecraft lands and a dark, mysterious figure holds out a hand as Fallon steps onboard.

THE CREW OF THE COLBYS

PRODUCERS

Aaron Spelling – Executive Producer
Esther Shapiro – Executive Producer / Creator
Richard Shapiro – Executive Producer / Creator
Douglas S. Cramer – Executive Producer
E. Duke Vincent – Executive Producer
Eileen Pollock – Supervising Producer / Creator
Robert Mason Pollock – Supervising Producer / Creator
William Bast – Producer
Dennis Hammer - Producer
Paul Huson – Producer
Christopher Morgan – Producer
Ursula Alexander – Associate Producer
Shelley Hull – Associate Producer
Marko Joelson – Associate Producer
Stephen K. Rose – Associate Producer

DIRECTORS

Gwen Arner
Gabrielle Beaumont
Roy Campanella
Jerome Courtland
Harry Falk
Kim Friedman
Curtis Harrington
Richard Kinon
Don Medford
Robert Scheerer
Richard T. Schor – First Assistant Director
Wendy Shear – Assistant Director

WRITERS

William Bast
Bruce Bilson
Oliver Clark
Mart Crowley
Rick Edelstein
Frank V. Furino
Paul Huson
Maryanne Kasica
Elliott Lewis
Charles Pratt, Jr.
Donald Paul Roos
Carol Saraceno
Michael Scheff
E. Doris Silverton
Jeffrey Smith
Dennis Turner

EDITORS

Chuck McClelland
Chuck Montgomery
Larry Strong, A.C.E.

DIRECTOR OF PHOTOGRAPHY

Richard L. Rawlings, A.S.C.
Tony Askins

ART DEPARTMENT

Jack Chilberg – Art Director
Olga Lehmann – Portrait Artist

SET DESIGN

Deborah Siegel

SOUND

John S. Coffey – Sound Mixer
Richard LeGrand, Jr. – Sound Editor

MUSIC

Bill Conti – Theme Composer
John E. Davis
Ken Harrison
Dennis McCarthy
Greig McRitchie
Angela Morley
Peter Myers

COSTUMES

Nolan Miller

STUNTS

Larry Holt – Stunt Performer

SPECIAL EFFECTS

Gary Zink

Chapter Twelve

Out And About With The Cast Of Dynasty

There are quite a few candid photos of assorted Dynasty and The Colbys cast members, which only goes to prove that there really was life during and after Dynasty!

"Even pretending to have a marriage with John has been heaven. It's so wonderful to be able to come in and express that part of myself and act it out. To be involved in marriage forever" – Linda Evans

July 16, 1983
John Forsythe with Jack Lemmon
Celebrity Night at Dodger Stadium

July 16, 1983
John Forsythe with
Annette Funicello
Celebrity Night at
Dodger Stadium

October 1, 1985
John Forsythe launching Carrington
cologne at Marshall Fields in
Chicago, Illinois

October 1, 1985
Preparing to sign boxes of
Carrington cologne at
Marshall Fields in Chicago

October 9, 1988
John Forsythe and wife Julie with
Pamela Bellwood at the Dynasty
clothing line fashion show

October 9, 1988
Another great shot of John
at the Dynasty fashion show

March 07, 1999
John arriving at the Screen Actors
Guild Awards

October 22, 2000
John with Nicole Carter
Charlie's Angels Movie
Premiere

July 25, 2002
Mr. and Mrs. John Forsythe
John and Nicole on their
wedding day

July 13, 2003
John going out for dinner in
Los Angeles, California

"This is a beautiful romantic whose passion for life and laughs has been balanced by her terrific business sense and her compassion for others. She's had the brilliance to understand her own limitations and the character to take both her successes and disappointments with grace and dignity. She's given us all countless hours of viewing pleasure and whether she's making us mad or exciting our libidos, she always does it great style and class. I wish her another million years of making us happy." – Geraldo Rivera

January 01, 1983
Joan teaching daughter Katy
how to serve.

August 12, 1985
Joan with pop culture artist
Andy Warhol

March 17, 1989
Joan with her wax figure at
Madame Tussaud's in London

December 13, 1994
Joan hanging out with a few
friends at a movie theater
opening in London

February 12, 2000
Joan Collins with Nolan Miller
and Sophia Loren at the
International Designer Awards

July 9, 1995

Joan and Linda Evans at
Valentino's Fall & Winter Line
Fashion Show

July 25, 2000
Joan with daughters Tara and
Katy at the London premiere of
*The Flintstones in
Viva Rock Vegas*

January 20, 2001
Joan with *These Old Broads*
Co-stars Debbie Reynolds and
Shirley MacLaine at the
Nevada Ballet Theatre Honors
in Las Vegas.

October 19, 2001
Joan with Frank Langella in the
London stage production
Over The Moon

December 18, 2002
Joan with husband Percy Gibson
at opening night of *Chicago*

"She has such a natural way of working that she makes it look easy. But it isn't. The subtlety of "natural" acting, without it becoming strident, is very, very difficult to achieve. I would love to work with Linda some day in something other than Dynasty. I hope we can..." – Stephanie Beacham

April 04, 1981
Linda competing in the ABC
television series
Battle of the Network Stars

April 20, 1986
Linda with Heather Locklear at
Bruno's in Los Angeles for
Dynasty's season wrap party

October 9, 1988
Linda at the Dynasty clothing
line fashion show

November 24, 1987
Linda and Larry Hagman at the
Annual Bud Grant Dinner
in Los Angeles

May 19, 2001
Linda at the Cannes Film
Festival Opening Night

January 11, 2004
Linda arriving at the People's
Choice Awards ceremony

"When a virgin blushes, she already knows too much..."
– Gordon Thomson

October 09, 1988
Gordon Thomson at the Dynasty
clothing line fashion show

April 06, 2002
Gordon and John James at the
Starlight Foundation's Annual
Gala Fundraiser

"There's that little glimmer of devilment in the corner of her eye, and the later the hour, the bigger it gets. It makes her day to break me up." – John James

March 20, 1983
Pamela Sue Martin at the opening of *Dreamgirls*

March 03, 1987
Pamela with Alex Cord at the opening of *American Ballet*

"It's very hard to find acting jobs that don't conflict with being a full-time mother" – Emma Samms

April 06, 2002
Emma and John James at the Starlight Foundation's Annual Gala Fundraiser

March 13, 2004
Emma at A Night of Comedy Benefit for Children

"When Dynasty started in 1980, John James and I used to spend our time talking about women. In 1991, we talked about baby strollers..." – Al Corley

May 17, 2002
Al Corley with producers Gene Musso and Bart Rosenblatt at the Cannes Film Festival

November 09, 2004
Al at the premiere of his newest feature film production *Noel*

"Jack's got a world of charm, but unfortunately he hasn't gotten a chance to show it on this series." – John Forsythe

May 29, 1987
Jack Coleman and Heather Locklear at the premiere of *The Common Pursuit*

April 06, 2002
Jack with his wife Beth Toussaint at the Starlight Foundation's Annual Gala Fundraiser

"Joan Collins made up pet names for her and myself; 'Big Bitch and Little Bitch'." – Catherine Oxenberg

January 24, 1986
Catherine Oxenberg and
Diahann Carroll arriving at the
Golden Globe Awards

October 06, 1988
Catherine and Nicolette
Sheridan competing in the Kauai
Celebrity Sports Invitational

July 08, 2000
Catherine and her husband
Casper Van Dien at the Video
Software Dealer's Association
convention in Las Vegas

August 13, 2003
Catherine and Linda Gray at the
premiere of *Grind*

"He presents a nice guy image on the outside, then comes the shell. That shell has preserved the fact he's a nice guy."
– Stephanie Beacham

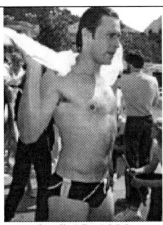

April 15, 1982
John James competing in the
ABC television series
Battle of the Network Stars

November 12, 2002
John at the book signing event
for the launch of Joan Collins'
new book *Star Quality*

"Egotism - usually just a case of mistaken nonentity."
– Barbara Stanwyck

January 24, 1986
Barbara Stanwyck and
Kirk Douglas at the
Golden Globe Awards

December 21, 1988
Barbara arriving at a Christmas
party at the Beverly Hills Hotel

"I've played three presidents, three saints and two geniuses - and that's probably enough for any man." – Charlton Heston

August 09, 2002
Portrait taken of Charlton Heston on the day he announced he has Alzheimer's

July 23, 2003
Charlton receives the Medal of Freedom from President George W. Bush

"I'm not a fighter. I usually smile and then go into my room and cry my eyes out." – Diahann Carroll

June 06, 1996
Diahann arriving at the Tony Awards

March 19, 2005
Diahann Carroll and Sidney Poitier pose for the NAACP Awards Portraits

"Now I think everyone should ask, 'Am I going to be able to be the person I want to be in this relationship?'"

— Ali MacGraw

October 26, 1999
Ali MacGraw at the Night of
Stars Salute to Film and Fashion

March 24, 2002
Ali and Ryan O'Neal at the
Vanity Fair Oscar Party

"My career hasn't turned out to be anything like I expected it would." — Maxwell Caulfield

August 15, 1986
Maxwell Caulfield and Kim
Morgan Greene at the wrap
party for The Colbys

March 16, 2002
Maxwell and wife Juliet Mills
attending Liza Minnelli's
New York wedding

"It's a show about foreplay… It's just titillating the audience to keep them coming back." – Pamela Bellwood

July 12, 2005
Pamela at the premiere of the movie *Going Shopping*

July 12, 2005
Pamela Bellwood and sons at the premiere of the movie
Going Shopping

"It is to TV that I owe my freedom from bondage of the Latin lover roles." – Ricardo Montalban

October 19, 2003
Ricardo Montalban attending the Catholics in Media Association Awards Gala

May 11, 2004
Peter Mark Richman attending the premiere of
Elaine Stritch at Liberty

"I was thinking the other day. Could I be friends with Sable? Yes, I suppose I could cope with her, but I don't think Sable would give me another look." – Stephanie Beacham

May 08, 2005
Stephanie Beacham arriving at the British Soap Opera Awards

January 15, 2005
Katharine Ross attending the Penfolds Gala Black Tie Dinner

"I think I've always been good so God wouldn't strike me dead." – Heather Locklear

March 15, 1987
Heather Locklear, Leann Hunley and Terri Garber at the People's Choice Awards

June 13, 2005
Heather at the premiere of her new film *The Perfect Man*

"Style With An All-American Spin..." - Tracy Scoggins

September 29, 1984
Tracy Scoggins, Heather
Locklear and Jamie Lyn Bauer
compete in the
ABC television series
Battle of the Network Stars

July 11, 2004
Tracy attending the Jim Thorpe
Sports Awards

"I really missed performing but you can't do it all."
– Susan Scannell

November 3, 2003
Susan Scannell prepares to
open in the stage production
Love Jokes

June 11, 2004
Claire Yarlett attending the
premiere of the movie
De-Lovely

"Two bits, four bits, six bits, a peso. All for Zorro stand up and say so!" – George Hamilton in Zorro The Gay Blade

January 27, 2005
George Hamilton attends the Vanity Fair Oscar Party in Beverly Hills

March 30, 2005
John Saxon attends the opening of *The Masters of H*

"If I ain't perfect, that's OK as long as I keep the process going." – Michael Nader

September 9, 1984
Michael Nader taking a break on the set of Dynasty

March 19, 2004
Studio portrait for a new magazine layout

"Aaron Spelling is the P.T. Barnum of television."

— *Joan Collins*

January 28, 1997
Joan and Aaron at a cast party after she
joined his new series Pacific Palisades

March 16, 2005
Joan Collins, Luke Perry and Tori Spelling listen as Aaron Spelling
receives the Pioneer Award for fifty years of television production

Chapter Thirteen

What Were They Thinking?

ABC Television Network – Press Release – Entertainment
December 8, 2004

**"DYNASTY: THE MAKING OF A GUILTY PLEASURE"
TO AIR
SUNDAY, JANUARY 2 ON THE ABC TELEVISION NETWORK**

Before "Desperate Housewives," ABC-TV had one of the original guilty pleasures – "Dynasty," the phenomenally successful show which ran from 1981-1989 and reflected the Reagan years of excess and glamour. The ABC Premiere Event, "Dynasty: The Making of a Guilty Pleasure," a two-hour dramatization with a behind-the-scenes look at the hit '80s primetime soap opera, will air SUNDAY, JANUARY 2 (9:00-11:00 p.m. ET) on the ABC Television Network.

"Dynasty: The Making of a Guilty Pleasure" offers a satirical yet poignant look at how "Dynasty," the television series, evolved. The show did not begin as an instant hit. In fact its creators, Esther and Richard Shapiro, initially set out on a noble mission to explore the effect of wealth on the American family and other important social issues. But despite an inauspicious start, the series eventually dazzled audiences around the world with one of TV history's most notoriously wicked female characters, Alexis Carrington; revolutionized the term "cat fight," as Alexis and Krystle went at it through lily pond and mud puddle; inspired millions of women to beef up their shoulder pads; and allowed people to forget about their own ordinary lives and drink in the champagne and caviar existence of a TV family dripping in jewels, but a little short on basic morality.

Yet behind-the-scenes, success had some side effects – some of the stars began demanding bigger and bigger salaries, and the show's budget ballooned, making it one of the most expensive television programs at the time. "Dynasty: The Making of a Guilty Pleasure" tells of the sometimes desperate and frequently hilarious efforts to keep the series at the top of the ratings. No plotline was too outrageous – a royal wedding interrupted by revolutionary commandos crashing through church windows! – or too inconceivable – while the "real" Krystle is locked in a dungeon, her "evil twin" beds Blake!

As the country began reeling from the excesses of the decade, the show began its own decline in the ratings. Ultimately "Dynasty" was cancelled, but not before leaving an indelible imprint on the 80s.

Unforgettable, classic television moments will be seen – including the cat fights between Alexis and Krystle, the Moldavian Massacre and an on-screen kiss between Linda Evans and Rock Hudson's characters that sent shockwaves through Hollywood.

The movie stars Pamela Reed ("Proof of Life," "Kindergarten Cop") as Esther Shapiro and Ritchie Singer as Richard Shapiro. Portraying the actors who became household names as members of the wealthy and dysfunctional Carrington Family are Bart John as John Forsythe, Alice Krige ("The Mystery of Natalie Wood") as Joan Collins and Melora Hardin ("Hot Chick") as Linda Evans. Also starring are Holly Brisley as Heather Locklear, Nicolas Hammond as Aaron Spelling, Red Hunt as Al Corley, Rachael Taylor as Catherine Oxenberg and Rory Williamson as Michael Nader.

The executive producers of "Dynasty: The Making of a Guilty Pleasure" are Greg Gugliotta, Robert M. Sertner, Frank von Zerneck, Stanley M. Brooks and Damian Ganczewski. The director and writer of the screenplay is Matthew Miller, and the producer is Randy Sutter. The movie, filmed in Sydney, Australia, is produced by Village Roadshow Dynasty Productions Pty. Ltd., Nitelite Entertainment, Inc. and Once Upon A Time Films, Ltd.

This dramatization includes time compression and composite and fictionalized characters and incidents. This program carries a TV-PG,L,S parental guideline.

ABC Media Relations

When reading the press release for this movie the first thing that comes to mind is FINALLY – the true story of what happened on the set of Dynasty. WRONG!!! This movie was anything but the "true" story and instead of having an opening disclaimer stating that there are time compressions, etc... it should have started with something more to the effect of:

"What you are about to see is complete and utter fiction. The characters and content of this film have been stretched so far beyond the imagination of reasonable people that even the cast, crew and creators of the original series wouldn't be able to recognize themselves or the circumstances being passed off as truth. If you're willing to sit through the next two hours of trashy innuendo please join us but if you're a fan of the original series and wish to view depictions of events that actually took place, please turn your television to a different channel because you won't be seeing any tonight. Thank you."

Throughout the United States as well as a good portion of the countries around the World, the thoughts of journalists and viewers were the same – What were these people thinking? They took the most popular series of the entire 1980s decade and actually made it campier than it was to begin with! Unfortunately for the "Guilty Pleasure" creators, the original stars of the series were asked for their opinions on the film and actors portraying them and they didn't hold back.

To borrow a quote from one of Joan Collins' reviews of a former co-star early in her career, "To say that his performance was wooden would be unkind to a tree." That statement would perfectly describe Bart John's portrayal of John Forsythe. John is originally presented as a washed-up, unshaven actor reduced to doing voice-over work on the series "Charlie's Angels". When he joins the cast of Dynasty, he's suddenly a humorless, stick-in-the-mud complaining about his hair and stupid storylines.

"Of course I worried about the scripts and storylines. That's what a responsible actor does when one is starring in a long-running TV show. And being the member of the cast with the most seniority, experience and long-standing history with Aaron Spelling, I would proudly and yes, sometimes defiantly take my concerns to the executive producers for discussion." - John Forsythe

Alice Krige's performance as Joan Collins was about as lackluster as a floor that hadn't been polished in a few hundred years. There was no Collins magic, no sparkle, nothing but an imitation of a grown woman trying to play dress-up and attempt learning to speak with a British accent. Matthew Miller even went as far as to completely fictionalize the circumstances on how Joan actually accepted the part of Alexis. For the record, when did Joan change her youngest daughter's name from Katy? That's not what they called her in the movie and since they're supposed to be telling the "truth" you would think they'd at least get names right!

Perhaps the furthest from the truth cast portrayal was Melora Hardin as Linda Evans. Matthew Miller obviously got sucked in by the sweetness and light that Krystle used to portray, because he missed Linda Evans by a mile! Linda is anything but the air-headed, brownie baking, crybaby they made her out to be.

"There were no brownies. No cookies. Most all of this stupid, satirical stuff is completely untrue. There was without exception so much love between most of the cast." – Linda Evans through her manager Mike Greenfield.

There are just far too many mistakes to attempt to list them all but just off the top of my head let's start with the opening scene. The scene shows Linda, Joan and John at a department store opening of the Dynasty clothing line. The store then gets mobbed and the actors are rushed out. Well that did happen but with an exception. The entire cast of Dynasty was there with the exception of Joan.

Next up would be the "car accident" that Catherine Oxenberg was in shortly before being replaced by Karen Cellini. Perhaps the writers simply forgot that Amanda's transformation took place at La Mirage while it burned down and it was Pamela Sue Martin that left via an automobile.

How could anyone leave out one of the more crucial elements, commonly known as The Moldavia Massacre. Does anyone else find it at all odd that Sammy Jo was at the wedding in Moldavia? Especially since she was in New York City training Rita to replace Auntie Krystle!

What the Guilty cast had to say...

"This is not a put-down," explains Pamela Reed, who plays "Dynasty" creator Esther Shapiro. "That is not what this is. This is about how a show comes alive, and then how a show that has a soapish quality to it goes through the machinations to stay alive, and then its demise. It is a metaphor of the '80s and the excess that we went through, and then how we paid for it and are still paying for it."

Neither Reed, nor Krige watched much "Dynasty" in its heyday: Reed, because she worked nights in theater in New York, and Krige, because she grew up without a television.

"I was a 'Dynasty' virgin," Krige admits. "I have done as much research as I had time to do. I found two interviews with Miss Collins that I pretty much know by heart, and I have watched a lot of 'Dynasty' as I had a lot of ground to cover, and I have read both of her biographies and beauty books, so I am getting up to speed."

Still Krige says that the task of playing Collins is terrifying, because the actress is a great icon. "The most fun I am having is to inhabit her confidence as a human being," Krige shares, "and what is marvelous are the frocks."

Getting Krige, who doesn't resemble Collins, into costume is a team effort for the hair, makeup and wardrobe staff. But also a great deal of fun. "I would say the engineering that is required to produce my figure is fairly outrageous," she says with a laugh. "If a bra strap were to pop, the entire thing would collapse."

The two-hour movie dramatization of the hit '80s primetime soap opera spoofs unforgettable, classic television moments, including the cat fights between Alexis and Krystle, the above-mentioned Moldavian Massacre and the on-screen kiss between Linda Evans' and Rock Hudson's characters that sent shockwaves through Hollywood.

That said, the film is not cartoonish. "What drew me to this script is that it is very funny," says Reed. "It is very smart and sassy."

If they say so...

Of course the most amusing part of the entire film that actually DID take place happened behind the scenes when ABC's Publicity Department actually announced that Joan Collins herself would be available to do a PR tour to promote this movie. What really happened was that Joan was presented with a copy of the script and after reading it, turned them down flat. Thank goodness Joanie hasn't lost her marbles yet!

Let's not leave out the critics who actually get paid to watch things like this. The Chicago Sun Times critic described the movie perfectly.

A slap in the face for stars, fans of 'Dynasty'

If you're going to exploit the popularity of a hit series, here's a tip: It's best you don't have contempt for its cast and creators, the network executives who shepherded it and especially the folks who watched. Having seen NBC and CBS churn out campy TV movies about old ABC shows such as "Three's Company," "Charlie's Angels" and "Batman," ABC is finally raiding its own history with Sunday night's "Dynasty: The Making of a Guilty Pleasure."

Regrettably, the film seems to be at a loss to explain why anyone ever liked the show and depicts the millions who did as sheep, albeit sheep who range from unkempt slobs to fastidious drag queens. Writer-director Matthew Miller does look out for long-gone ABC execs, changing their identities. But everyone else -- including Linda Evans (Melora Hardin), Joan Collins (Alice Krige), Heather Locklear (Holly Brisley) and producers Esther Shapiro (Pamela Reed) and Aaron Spelling (Nicholas Hammond), who can't grasp the appeal of "Thirtysomething" -- is ridiculed by name. - Chicago Sun Times

Bottom line: We pretty much get a collection of "Dynasty" actors who are even less dimensional than their characters.

Barry Garron of the Hollywood Reporter obviously wasn't terribly impressed with the imitation cast and blunders. Just read on…

This tell-not-quite-all movie and its subject, the glitzy primetime soap of the 1980s, have at least one thing in common -- they both owe their existence to producers and networks only too eager to imitate success elsewhere. In the case of "Dynasty," the Aaron Spelling-produced, Esther Shapiro-managed series that took greed and excess to dizzying, make that unfathomable, heights, the model was "Dallas," which had shown that deceit among the wealthy could attract a big audience. In the case of this lackluster film, the model is recent telefilms, like NBC's "Behind the Camera" franchise, which purported to tell the inside story of "Charlie's Angels."

Although the success of "Dynasty," particularly in seasons two through five, is hard to dispute, its lingering fascination for viewers is highly debatable. While "Charlie's Angels" enjoys a camp nostalgic gloss, "Dynasty" enjoys no such luster. And without that, this tale of supposedly fascinating inside information has a built-in "who cares" factor to overcome. It never does, by the way.

Credit Pamela Reed for rising above the trite dialogue and unimaginative storytelling and somehow turning Shapiro into a flesh-and-blood character. As for the others, we pretty much get a collection of "Dynasty" actors who are even less dimensional than their characters. Also, while it might be fun to watch all of the banality and unctuousness of network executives compressed into a single character (ABC's fictional Vince Peterson, played by John Terry), the suggestion that Esther's husband Richard (Ritchie Singer) wrote every word of every episode is both untrue and a little too much to swallow. Principal blame for the production rests with director-writer Matthew Miller, as well as Village Roadshow Dynasty Productions Pty. Ltd., Nitelite Entertainment Inc. and Once Upon A Time Films Ltd.

Chapter Fourteen

I'm Coming Out...

GET OUT YOUR SHOULDER PADS – DYNASTY IS BEING RELEASED ON DVD!

The Ultimate 80's TV Series schemes, cheats and seduces audiences with its four-disc DVD set debut on April 19, 2005 from Fox Home Entertainment.

Century City, CA – Relive all the suspense, glamour and the biggest shoulder pads in Denver when the *"Dynasty" Season One DVD Collection* debuts just in time for Mother's Day as a four-disc DVD set on April 19, 2005 from Fox Home Entertainment.

Fueled by an all-star cast including John Forsythe, Heather Locklear, Linda Evans, Al Corley, Pamela Sue Martin and later, Joan Collins, the groundbreaking and trendsetting 80's phenomenon follows the saga of the wealthy oil-business family, The Carringtons. From legendary producer Aaron Spelling (*Charmed, Melrose Place*) and the show's creator, producer and writer team Esther and Richard Shapiro, "*Dynasty*" steamed up the small screen as one of the first ever prime time soap operas.

Delivering unforgettable bouts between Alexis and Krystle, scandalous romances and fantastic fashion statements during its nine season run on ABC from 1981-1989, "*Dynasty*" now sizzles for the first time ever on DVD with all 15 episodes from the first season, optional commentary, a "Family, Furs and Fun: Creating "*Dynasty*" featurette, Character Profiles on Fallon Carrington Colby, Blake Carrington, Steven Carrington and more. They *"Dynasty" Season One DVD Collection* will be available for the suggested retail price of $39.98 U.S./$54.98 Canada.

DVD Special Features:

The *"Dynasty" Season One DVD Collection* showcases the full first season of unforgettable "*Dynasty*" episodes, optional commentary from the show creator Esther Shapiro, Al Corley and Pamela Sue Martin, a special "*Dynasty*" overview, family tree profiles and outtakes. Presented in Widescreen aspect radio 1:33:1 and Dolby Surround, the series is dubbed in English, Spanish and French and offers English and Spanish subtitles. The following episodes and special features are exclusive to each disc.

Disc 1 – Side 1:
- "Oil" Part 1 and Part 2
- Optional commentary by Esther Shapiro

Disc 1 – Side 2:
- "Oil" Part 3
- "The Honeymoon"

Disc 2 – Side 1:
- "The Dinner Party"
- "Fallon's Wedding"

Disc 2 – Side 2:
- "The Chauffeur Tells A Secret"
- "The Bordello"

Disc 3 – Side 1:
- "Krystle's Lie"
- "The Necklace"

Disc 3 – Side 2
- "The Beating"
- "The Birthday Party"

Disc 4 – Side 1
- "The Separation"
- "Blake Goes To Jail"

Disc 4 – Side 2:
- "The Testimony"
- Optional commentary by Esther Shapiro
- "Dynasty" Overview
- Family Tree: Pamela Sue Martin Profile
- Family Tree: Al Corley Profile
- Outtakes

A recognized industry leader, Twentieth Century Fox Home Entertainment is the marketing sales and distribution company for all Fox film and television programming on VHS and DVD as well as video acquisitions and original productions for the U.S. and Canada. Each year the Company introduces hundreds of new and newly repackaged products, which it services to more than 70,000 retail outlets – from mass merchants and warehouse clubs to specialty stores and e-commerce – throughout North America. Twentieth Century Fox Home Entertainment is a unit of Fox Filmed Entertainment, a New Corporation company.

Chapter Fifteen

A Word From Our Sponsor

Remember when you could never watch a television show without the station taking a break for commercials? This is a book based on a television series so why not add a few commercials? The pages to follow contain information on the current and upcoming projects of a few members of the *Dynasty* cast.

The logos on the bottom of the page are my companies, so if you would like to take a moment to send questions or comments, please feel free to do so.

One piece of advice if I may... If you get the chance to see any of the cast in person, don't forget to take this with you for autographs. You might just end up with a great piece of memorabilia!

For all of you shoppers out there, there's also a list of books and other items being promoted by assorted cast members. Have fun!

www.jmmediagroup.com

For the little bit of Hollywood in all of us...

www.signingstars.net

Changing the perceptions of Independent Publishing one book at a time...

Legends! A Comedy by Tony award-winner James Kirkwood (*A Chorus Line*) centers on Sylvia (Joan Collins) and Leatrice (Linda Evans), two fading and somewhat desperate movie stars. The actresses reluctantly agree to star together in a Broadway show, despite the fact that they have hated each other for decades. The resulting full-blown comic confrontation is played to the hilt by two real-life stars that the world will always know as "rivals to the death" from the international television phenomenon *Dynasty*.

TOUR SCHEDULE

September 13 – October 23, 2006 – Toronto, Canada
October 25 – November 6, 2006 – Chicago, Illinois
November 8 – 13, 2006 – Dallas, Texas
November 15 – 20, 2006 – Hartford, Connecticut
November 22 – December 4, 2006 – Washington D.C.
December 6 – 11, 2006 – Fort Myers, Florida
December 13 – 18, 2006 – Fort Lauderdale, Florida
January 10 – 15, 2007 – San Diego, California
January 17 – 29, 2007 – Los Angeles, California
January 31 – February 5, 2007 – Phoenix, Arizona
February 7 – 19, 2007 – Denver, Colorado
February 28 – March 5, 2007 – Boston, Massachusetts
March 7 – 19, 2007 – Philadelphia, Pennsylvania
March 21 – April 2, 2007 – Cleveland, Ohio
April 4 – 9, 2007 – Forth Worth, Texas
April 11 – 16, 2007 – Fayetteville, North Carolina
April 18 – 23, 2007 – Memphis, Tennessee
April 25 – 30, 2007 – Milwaukee, Wisconsin
May 2 – 7, 2007 – Raleigh, North Carolina

**BUCKS COUNTY PLAYHOUSE
PROUDLY PRESENTS**

GORDON THOMSON
AS
DRACULA

Bram Stoker's original novel has been re-created and is better than ever! The undead Count arranges to move from his home in Transylvania to Whitby, and once there, a reign of terror on the residents begins...

PERFORMANCE SCHEDULE

October 12th - 2:00 PM and 8:00 PM
October 13th - 2:00 PM and 8:00 PM
October 14th - 8:00 PM
October 15th - 4:00 PM and 8:00 PM
October 16th - 2:00 PM

October 19th - 2:00 PM and 8:00 PM
October 20th - 2:00 PM and 8:00 PM
October 21st - 8:00 PM
October 22nd - 4:00 PM and 8:00 PM
October 23rd - 2:00 PM

For more information or to purchase tickets contact:

Bucks County Playhouse
70 South Main Street
New Hope, PA 18939
or call 215-862-2041

COMING TO SELECT THEATERS ON
NOVEMBER 04, 2005

Adam is a college senior - and an aspiring singer/songwriter. He meets Eve - a beautiful, bright, talented college girl. They begin dating and he quickly learns that, hard as it is to believe of such a hot girl in today's campus world, Eve is still a virgin.

For her it's not about religion, or waiting to wedlock, but about waiting until it feels "right". This begins a relationship that is at once sexy, romantic, sometimes painful, and often hilarious, as Adam, Eve and all their friends wait for Eve to be ready. If you think virginity is not a laughing matter... think again.

Starring: Cameron Douglas, Emmanuelle Chriqui, Courtney Peldon, George Dzundza, Terri Garber, Brianna Brown, Dan Gunther, Jake Hoffman and Branden Williams.

Visit the official website at www.nationallampoon.com/adam&eve

Terri Garber can also be seen in her role as Iris on the CBS soap opera *As The World Turns*. For more information visit the show's website at www.cbs.com/daytime/atwt or www.soapcity.com.

A LITTLE SHOPPING ANYONE?

Linda Evans presents the official workout of her namesake exercise center. Includes three levels of varying intensity, adjustable to suit differing levels of fitness.

Join Linda Evans and fitness professional Kari Anderson as she leads you through a 45-minute gentle, low-impact workout in three progressive phases.

Released: Nov 18, 1997
Company: BMG Video

* Although no longer in print, this item can be ordered through Amazon.com.

To compliment the workout video you can also find the audio cassettes of Linda's complete guide to nutrition. It will guide you on your path to creating a healthier eating pattern. The cassettes are titled *"Welcome to My World"* and *"Write Your Own Script"*. There is also a 106-page nutrition booklet that includes assorted recipes for you to sample.

You can find this item either through Amazon.com or at any of the 14 Linda Evans Fitness Center locations.

The *Linda Evans Beauty & Exercise Book* was released in July 1983. Published by Simon & Schuster, the book features 125 pages of Linda's tips for inner beauty and her personal workout routines. It's packed with photos and fabulous tips on how to create a new you!

Although currently out-of-print you can purchase this item through assorted retailers on Amazon.com and other online sources.

Unlike traditional skin care products that will only cleanse, moisturize, and pamper the skin, the Rejuvenique system has been specially designed to help reduce the appearance of wrinkles and achieve a smooth, toned, radiant look without harsh chemicals or any of the other time-consuming and expensive measures women will try to look younger.

The Rejuvenique system is available at assorted retail stores throughout the world and can be frequently be found on eBay.

This innovative program is divided into sections which can be done separately or in combinations to work out only those areas that need it. Routines can be customized to fit individual levels and lifestyles.

The first section is called "Energy." This second section is called "Power" and third part of the video is called "Grace". The video was produced by MCA Universal in coordination with Bally Fitness Centers and has a 60-minute run time.

Although no longer in print, this tape can be found on Amazon.com and for auction on eBay.

Diahann Carroll offers readers a chance to closely examine an interesting life as well as reap the insights gained by an author during the writing process. She shows how her *Dynasty* success is based on a lifetime of hard work and achievement. Although she does discuss the important men in her life, she does not "kiss and tell." Diahann is frank about her romantic failures, most often laying blame on her own insecurities and shortcomings.

Diahann's autobiography is available through various retailers and Amazon.com.

This incredible new CD features Diahann performing some of the great jazz standards with the soul of Dinah Washington and Ella Fitzgerald. Released on January 25, 2005, *The Magic of Diahann Carroll* has 22 tracks.

You can find *The Magic of Diahann Carroll* at most music stores or at variety of assorted online music dealers.

TRACK SELECTIONS

1. The Party's Over
2. Spring Is Here
3. But Not For Me
4. Glad To Be Unhappy
5. Change Of Heart
6. It's All Right With Me
7. I Should Care
8. Nobody's Heart
9. Why Can't You Behave?
10. Where Are You?
11. In Love, In Vain
12. Gingerbread Joy
13. Everything's Coming Up Roses
14. Misty
15. Shopping Around
16. Goody Goody
17. I Wish I Were In Love Again
18. All or Nothing At All
19. Am I Blue / Taking A Chance On Love / Happiness Is A Thing Called Joe
20. Dinah / After You've Gone / Stormy Weather
21. Heat Wave
22. Happiness Is A Thing Called Joe (Reprise)

Few women have lived such an exciting and dramatic life; fewer still have written about it with such candor, wit and headline-making honesty.

From her screen debut as a teenaged sex symbol to the behind-the-scenes drama of Dynasty - which has made her one of the most famous and instantly recognizable women in the world - Joan Collins recounts the painful horror of her youthful marriage to Maxwell Reed; fascinating anecdotes and stories of her Hollywood years, filled with such names as Marilyn Monroe, James Dean, Paul Newman, Harry Belafonte, Marlon Brando, Richard Burton, Ryan O'Neal, and Gregory Peck; her long romance with Warren Beatty; and her marriages to Anthony Newley and Ron Kass. Here, with its good moments, its sad moments, is the glittering life of an extraordinary, courageous and beautiful woman

Past Imperfect was released with three different covers for the hardback editions. Although you can purchase the U.S. edition through retailers such as Amazon.com and eBay, you can try ordering them from her official fan club. More information can be found on Joan's website at www.joancollins.net.

This title is also available in paperback.

With a generous variety of inspiring and step-by-step instructions, Joan advises on body care and exercise, pregnancy, skin care, make-up and hair care. She suggests the basic wardrobe for all seasons at a reasonable cost. She helps you lay the foundations of beauty and health for your children. Joan Collins' ideas and tips are helpful, encouraging and intelligent without being obsessive, and they all have the aim of allowing every woman, inner and outer, reach her full potential of vitality and attractiveness.

The Joan Collins Beauty Book is out of print and can occasionally be found on eBay.

On August 3, 1980, Joan Collins and Ron Kass heard the nightmare news that their eight year old daughter Katy had been hit by a car. When they reached the hospital they discovered that Katy had serious brain injuries and was in a deep coma. For six weeks Joan and Ron lived in a caravan in the parking lot beside the hospital's Intensive Care Unit. Two weeks after the accident Joan began to write a diary to record Katy's daily progress. Throughout the ordeal she was comforted by many letters she received telling her of parents who had suffered similar experiences.

Joan published her diary in the hope that it will give others the kind of help and support she herself received.

This book has been out of print for several years but a copy shows up every once in a while on eBay. You may also try ordering a copy through Joan's website at www.joancollins.net.

The lives and loves of five women - friends and foes - are played out against the glittering world of money, sex, power and glamour that is television - and Hollywood - today. Its fatal allure drives them. It has all the power to give them success beyond their wildest dreams, but it also has the power to destroy them...

Only one will become a superstar, attracting the envy and adoration of every woman, and many men, her past illuminated by the merciless glare of fame, her happiness at risk, her very life at stake - as one man, with madness and violence in his heart, watches from the shadows, determined that the woman of his tormented fantasies will become Miranda...

Prime Time was produced in both hardcover and paperback. This book can be ordered through Joan's website, various used book stores or assorted online retailers.

Love & Desire & Hate begins during World War II when people are trying to survive the atrocities heaped upon them by the Germans and Italians. One Italian general, in particular, does not need the excuse of war to satisfy his insatiable appetite for sadistic cruelty and perverted sex. For his victims, he is a nightmare waiting to happen...

Ambition, greed and lust are only at the surface of the churning emotions shared by the cast and crew of Cortez. It is love and desire and hate that drives one of them to commit an act of murder; that drives one of them to purge the past to make way for a future that can never be.

Love & Desire & Hate is available in hardcover, paperback and cassette through Joan's website or online retailers.

In the number one bestseller, *My Secrets*, Joan Collins reveals how she gets the maximum out of life. She shares her health, diet and beauty secrets, from her personal exercise and eating regimes to body and skin care, make-up and fashion. She explains the skills and positive attitudes every woman needs to make a success of her life: the ability to work hard and control stress, to cherish friends, family and lovers and to build up confidence through self-esteem.

With the help of Joan Collins' experience *My Secrets* will help women of every age to look and feel their absolute best.

My Secrets and *Health, Youth & Happiness* were both produced as hardcover, paperback and cassette. You can order a copy through Joan's website or at Amazon.com.

Katherine Bennet, a Hollywood icon has never been more satisfied with her dazzling successful television career. But stardom has a price - and although she has one of the most famous faces in the world, her heart is one of the loneliest. But soon, the very handsome Jean-Claude Valmer enters her life, sweeping her off her feet and into his bed. What begins as a storybook romance, bursting with passion, soon turns dark and sinister. For lurking underneath his innocent veneer is a Jean-Claude no one would recognize - especially the woman who has grown to trust him implicitly... *Too Damn Famous* is a look at what really happens behind the scenes of a Prime-Time soap opera.

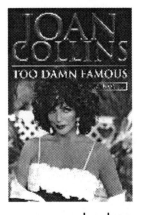

This book is available through Joan's website or Amazon.com.

Joan Collins is a legendary beauty whose glittering stage, film, and television careers have made her name synonymous with fame. Out of the spotlight, the drama and excitement of her personal life rivals the plot of the most compelling Hollywood blockbuster. Joan has worked and played with the most celebrated producers, directors and actors, and her career has been crucially intertwined with her marriages and personal life.

Second Act chronicles in candid detail and wonderful anecdotes the times, people and places she has known and has worked with - a wide-screen cast of characters that includes Brando and Branagh, Monroe and Madonna.

Joan Collins has written a captivating, hilarious, and very revealing insider's life story.

Second Act is available in both hardcover and paperback versions. Copies in either preference are available through Joan's website and a variety of online retailers such as Amazon.com and occasionally eBay.

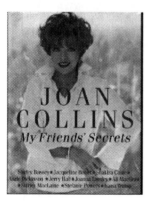

Candid, fascinating, practical and funny, Joan Collins' sequel to the best-selling *My Secrets*, on staying fit, youthful and beautiful, is a revelation. Through the course of over twenty interviews, with women between the ages of 40 and 70, Joan and her friends offer truly inspirational, yet down to earth advice on how to make the most of the "Generation Zest" years. *My Friends' Secrets* is available through Joan's website or through various online retailers.

When gusty flame-haired Millie McClancy defies her humble beginnings in famine-ravished Ireland to pursue a life on the stage, she becomes the first of four generations of beautiful and inspiring actresses who take the glamorous, yet precarious world of show business by storm. With turbulent love lives and a determination to succeed in common, Millie, her daughter Vickie, and eventually Vickie's daughter Lulu find themselves caught up in a series of dramatic and sinister events, which test their courage and resolve to the hilt.

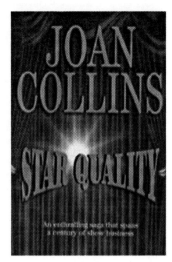

Star Quality is available through Joan's website, Amazon.com and other assorted retailers.

In *Joan's Way*, Joan reveals the secrets of how to look amazing, whatever your age. Joan shares many of her life experiences and the methods she has learned about such as how to deal with the bad and the good things in life. She will show you how to feel better about yourself inside and consequently you will look better. Included in this book are tips on how to achieve glamour, exercise programs, make-up secrets, dietary tips, relationships, skincare, assertiveness, entertaining, dressing for yourself and your lifestyle and happiness.

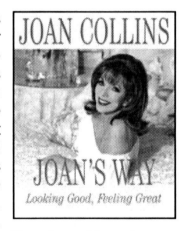

Joan's Way is available in hardcover and paperback. You can order a copy through her website or via nearly any online retailer.

Misfortune's Daughters chronicles the gripping, multigenerational saga of the wealthy Stephanopolis family. Beginning in the Golden Era of Hollywood, the beautiful and talented actress Laura Marlowe meets the young, dashing, and rich shipping magnate Nicholas Stephanopolis. After a whirlwind courtship, the two marry and move to the private Stephanopolis Island in the south of Greece. Yet heartache and tragedy soon find them and extend into the lives of their two very different but willful and ambitious daughters, Venetia and Atlanta. One is a beautiful and favored daughter who's bent on self-destruction; the other is a wallflower who buries herself in books and shies away from her privileged world. But both must confront the legacy and tragedy of the lives of their parents.

Sweeping across almost 60 years and jetting from New York to Paris, Los Angeles, and Greece, *Misfortune's Daughters* is an irresistible, page-turning tale that reveals the glittering life of show business and the grittiness of the journalistic profession. Drawing on her own knowledge and experience, Collins takes the reader deep inside the exclusive gates of wealth and luxury, exposing dark secrets and forbidden desires as two young women vie to break free from their family's shadow and become independent women in their own right.

Misfortune's Daughters is available in hardcover and paperback. It is available for purchase through Joan's website, retail outlets around the world and a variety of online retailers.

Chapter Sixteen

Tell Me More…

For those of you who just can't get enough of Dynasty, The Colbys and their stars, just visit these websites! We've gone through as many as we could find and these are the best of the best!

DYNASTY SERIES

Ultimate Dynasty – www.ultimatedynasty.net

Created and run by Goran Markovic, Ultimate Dynasty is exactly that! This site is filled with photos, facts, interactive material, forum boards and so much more! From the moment you enter the site until the very last page, you are guaranteed to be completely entranced with all things Dynasty.

Der Denver Clan – www.der-denver-clan.de

German fans, feast your eyes on this! Helge Ebsen has created one of the most fabulous Dynasty sites out there. Completely done in German, this site features some of the most creatively beautiful banner art you would ever want to see. In fact, you've been seeing it all the way through this book. She's constantly changing photos and other items around. While you're there, don't forget to check out the forum. It's to-die-for!

OFFICIAL CAST SITES

The Official Joan Collins Website
www.joancollins.net

The Official Pamela Sue Martin Website
www.pamelasuemartin.com

The Official Stephanie Beacham Website
http://simplystephaniebeacham.com

The Official Catherine Oxenberg Website
www.catherineoxenberg.com

The Official Tracy Scoggins Website
www.tracyscoggins.com

The Official Bo Hopkins Website
www.bohopkins.com

The Official Peter Mark Richman Website
www.petermarkrichman.com

The Official J. Eddie Peck Website
www.jeddiepeck.com

UNOFFICIAL CAST SITES

Tribute to John Forsythe
http://johnforsythe.tripod.com

Diahann!
www.diahanncarroll.com

Michael Nader – The Loyalists
www.angelfire.com/celeb2/nader

Emma Samms
www.emmasamms.net

Gordon Thomson
http://gtthomson.tripod.com

Heather Locklear
www.heatherdeenlocklear.net

Kathleen Beller
www.janvalk.nl/kathleenbeller

APPENDIX ONE

THEME FROM DYNASTY

Oscar and three-time Emmy Award winner Bill Conti is one of Hollywood's most sought-after composers and conductors for both film and television. His compositions have sold in excess of eight million albums. He is in great demand as a conductor of symphony orchestras throughout the United States. On November 10, 1989, his rich contributions to the entertainment industry were recognized when a star bearing his name was placed on the Hollywood Walk of Fame. In 1995, the American Society of Composers, Authors and Publishers (ASCAP) awarded Conti the Golden Soundtrack Award for lifetime achievement in film and television.

For the silver screen, Bill Conti has composed the musical scores for many box office giants including *Broadcast News, Baby Boom, The Karate Kid,* Goldie Hawn's military romp *Private Benjamin*, and most recently, *Spy Hard.* He won an Oscar for Best Original Score for *The Right Stuff* in 1983 and received two Oscar nominations for Best Original Song - one for the Sheena Easton hit record *"For Your Eyes Only"* from the James Bond picture of the same title. The other was for *"Gonna Fly Now"* from *Rocky.*

The soundtrack for the Sylvester Stallone blockbuster Rocky also garnered a host of other honors including a Golden Globe nomination, a Billboard Award nomination, a RIAA Certified Platinum Award, a Rock Award nomination, and a Grammy nomination for Best Original Score. *"Gonna Fly Now"* not only occupied the number one position on the Billboard magazine charts for the week of July 2, 1977, but also received an RIAA Certified Gold Record and two Grammy nominations for Best Instrumental Composition and Performance.

Bill Conti's work for the small screen has been equally as critically acclaimed, receiving a total of ten Emmy nominations throughout his career. He won two Emmy Awards in 1990 for developing the creative concept and composing the score for the running of the New York City Marathon, which was telecast on ABC. Bill conducted the Julliard Symphony Orchestra during the course of the marathon live from Lincoln Center - a first in television sports coverage. He won his third Emmy in 1992 for his musical direction during the telecast of the Academy Award Ceremonies, marking the first time an Emmy was awarded for a participant in the Oscar ceremonies.

Conti's relationship with the Academy of Motion Picture Arts and Sciences spans two decades, as he has been the musical director for twelve of the internationally-televised annual Academy Award ceremonies, most recently in 1997. For six consecutive years (1990-1995) he was nominated for an Emmy Award for Outstanding Individual Achievement in Music Direction for his impressive work on several of the Academy Award shows.

Although the public may not be aware of it, Bill Conti has composed some of the most recognizable themes for television broadcasts, including those for the 1984 *Good Morning America, Turning Point, World News Tonight, Prime Time Live, Nightline, ABC Sports, Inside Edition* and *American Gladiators*. He has also composed music for numerous television commercials advertising products for Honda, Pizza Hut, Sprite and Coca Cola. *"For Your Eyes Only"* was featured in a commercial for Merrill Lynch.

During the 1983-84 television season, Bill Conti set an all-time industry record for having composed the themes for five television series' playing concurrently in prime time. However, he broke his own record in 1986-87 when that number was increased to nine; *Dynasty, Falcon Crest, Cagney and Lacey, Lifestyles of the Rich and Famous, O'Hara, The Colbys* and many others.

In addition to composing, Conti spends considerable time traveling around the world as a guest conductor for many prestigious orchestras, including the Boston Pops, the London Symphony Orchestra, the Cleveland Orchestra at the Blossom Music Festival, the National Symphony at Wolf Trap, the Houston Symphony Orchestra, the Baltimore Symphony, the Florida Pops Orchestra, the Dallas Symphony, the Calgary Philharmonic, the RAI Orchestra of Rome, and the Graunke Orchestra of Munich. He has also been among the principal pops conductor for the Nashville Symphony in Tennessee.

Born in Providence, Rhode Island on April 13, 1942, Bill Conti began studying piano at age seven under the tutelage of his father, an accomplished pianist, sculptor and painter. At the age of 15, he organized a band and began to play for high school dances in Miami, Florida. He was a member of his high school band and symphony orchestra and won the *"Silver Knight Award"* from the Miami Herald for high achievement in the field of music. Conti received a bassoon scholarship from Louisiana State University, where he majored in composition and played jazz piano at many of the local night spots to help defray the costs of his education.

After Bill received his Bachelor of Music degree from LSU, he auditioned and was accepted at the Julliard School of Music in New York, where he studied with such musical greats as Hugo Weisgall, Vincent Persichetti, Roger Sessions, Luciano Berio and Jorge Mester. In 1965, Conti won the Marion Feschl Prize for having composed the best song of the year. He received a Bachelor of Music degree from Julliard, followed by a Master's Degree.

The *Dynasty* Theme music is included on the following eight pages in two different versions. The first is the original arrangement for piano and the second is the Easy Play version for beginners.

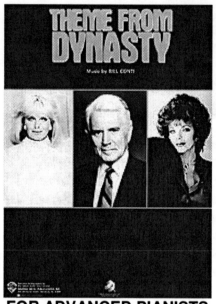

FOR ADVANCED PIANISTS

EASY PLAY FOR BEGINNERS

THEME FROM DYNASTY

Music by BILL CONTI

Theme From Dynasty - 4 - 1

Theme From Dynasty - 4 - 4

THEME FROM "DYNASTY"

CLARINET
FULL 'N' MELLOW
Medium ROCK

Music by
BILL CONTI

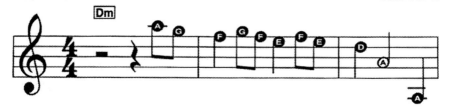

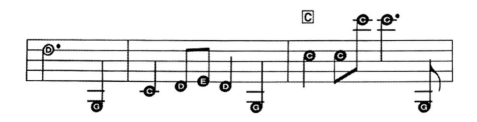

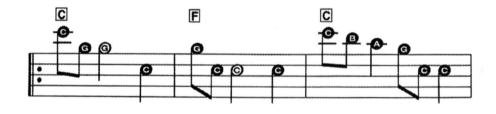

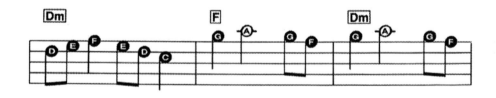

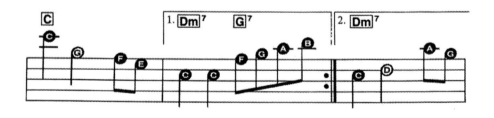

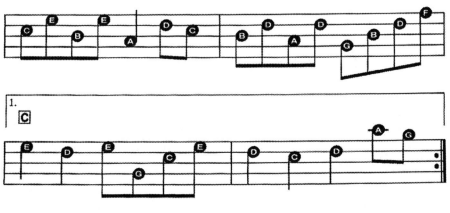

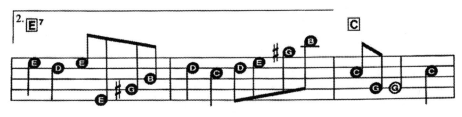

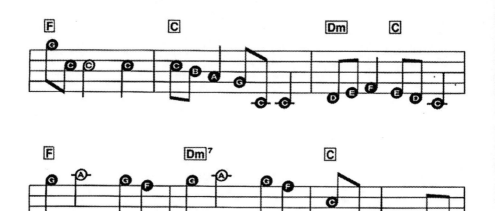

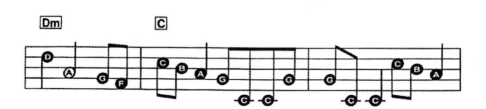

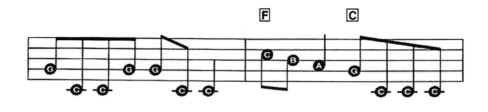

APPENDIX TWO

THE FILOLI MANSION

Located thirty miles south of San Francisco on the eastern slope of the Coast Range, the 654-acre Filoli estate contains a historic house and sixteen acres of formal gardens. The house was occupied from 1917 to 1936 as a private residence for its original owners, William Bowers Bourn II and his wife, Agnes Moody Bourn. In 1937 the property was sold to Mr. and Mrs. William P. Roth, who continued to maintain and enrich the estate. Mrs. Roth donated Filoli to the National Trust for Historic Preservation in 1975.

Filoli was built for Mr. and Mrs. Bourn, prominent San Franciscans whose chief source of wealth was the Empire Mine, a hard-rock gold mine in Grass Valley, California. Mr. Bourn was also owner and president of the Spring Valley Water Company comprising of Crystal Springs Lake and surrounding lands, which are now part of the San Francisco Water Department. Mr. Bourn selected the southern end of Crystal Springs Lake as the site for his estate. He arrived at the unusual name Filoli by combining the first two letters from the key words of his credo: "Fight for a just cause; Love your fellow man; Live a good life."

Mr. Bourn chose his longtime friend, the prominent San Francisco architect Willis Polk, as the principal designer for the house. Polk had previously designed the Bourns' cottage in Grass Valley, as well as their home on Webster Street in San Francisco. An inventive architect, Polk frequently combined several styles in the design of a single building, an eclecticism clearly evident in Filoli's design.

Construction of Filoli began in 1915 and the Bourns moved into the house in 1917. Bruce Porter was enlisted to help the Bourns plan the layout of the extensive formal garden, which was built between 1917 and 1921. Both Mr. and Mrs. Bourn died in 1936. The estate was then purchased in 1937 by Mr. and Mrs. William P. Roth, who owned the Matson Navigation Company. Under the Roths' supervision, the property was maintained and the formal garden gained worldwide recognition. Mrs. Roth made this her home until 1975 when she donated 125 acres, which included the house and formal garden, to the National Trust for Historic Preservation for the enjoyment and inspiration of future generations. The remaining acreage was given to Filoli Center.

A prime example of the California eclectic style, Filoli provides an inspiring vision of a new Eden, with bountiful land, plentiful resources and an emphasis on self-sufficiency. Built more than sixty years after the California Gold Rush that inspired massive migration to Northern California, and ten years after the devastating 1906 earthquake and fire in San Francisco, Filoli represented a desire to create a magnificent and enduring country estate.

Now operated by Filoli Center, the estate represents an excellent example of architecture and garden design from the first part of the twentieth century. The house is furnished with some of the Bourns' and Roths' original furnishings, the Martin collection and other pieces. During the blooming season, exquisite specimens of Mrs. Roth's collection of orchids are displayed in the rooms. The beautiful flower arrangements throughout the house are created with flowers from the Lurline B. Roth Garden by the Friends of Filoli Flower Arranging Committee.

Although the house is predominantly modified Georgian in style, other major architectural traditions are also represented in its design. The arched window heads of the first floor, the French doors, the exterior brick laid in Flemish bond, and the details of the trim are from the Stuart period, while the tiled roof is in the Spanish tradition. This eclecticism reflects a Golden Age in California's history, free from the conventional rules of design and exuding a pride in creativity and expression.

The floor plan is U-shaped, with the servant's wing on one side of the front courtyard and the ballroom on the other. The long Transverse Hallway runs north to south, parallel to the valley in which the house is set. Both the rooms of the house and the formal garden are organized along this axis. The residence, which connects to the garden wall, was sited to one side, preserving the valley floor and the grand vista to the north towards Crystal Springs Lake.

The house contains 36,000 square feet of interior floor space on two floors and a mezzanine. The spacious major rooms have ceiling heights of seventeen feet, while the ballroom ceiling is twenty-two-and-a-half feet high. There are forty-three rooms and seventeen fireplaces.

Since Filoli opened for public view in 1975, furnishing the house has been an ongoing process. Mrs. Roth donated many of the furnishings that she had used in the house when it was her home. Welcome donations were made by friends of Mrs. Roth, and by other generous donors. The goal of furnishing the house has been to furnish it as it might have been when the house was occupied. The major gift of eighteenth-century English furnishings in 1998 by Melville Martin has allowed us to present the house looking much like the home that it was. Various plants from the greenhouses, along with the flower arrangements, enhance that look.

The extensive sixteen-acre formal garden was planned and planted as construction of the house neared completion. The lawns and shrubs around the house were planted by the fall of 1917. The woodlands and the undeveloped Crystal Springs Watershed lands surrounding the estate provide a magnificent backdrop for the formal garden. The garden survives today as one of America's finest historic gardens.

Historical Marker for Filoli

It reads: This country estate was begun in 1915 for Mr. and Mrs. William B. Bourn, II. Architect Willis J. Polk designed a modified Georgian style country house; subsequently the carriage house and garden pavilion were executed by Arthur Brown. The formal gardens were created by Bruce Porter. In 1937 the estate was acquired by Mr. and Mrs. William P. Roth.

California registered Historical Landmark No. 907. Plaque placed by the State Department of Parks and Recreation in cooperation with the National Trust for Historic Preservation and with the Filoli Center, July 30, 1980.

This property was given by Mrs. William P. Roth and Family to the National Trust for Historic Preservation in October 1975.

ACKNOWLEGEMENTS

There are several people that I would like to thank for their contributions to the construction of this book.

I'd like to start with Goran Markovic for the beautiful cover photo. Five years ago he had designed a wallpaper for his *Ultimate Dynasty* website featuring John Forsythe and Linda Evans with the Carrington mansion in the background. It was beautiful and I asked him if he could move Blake and Krystle over and add Alexis to the picture. A few days later, he sent me the design and it was everything I had imagined it could be. At that time I asked if I could use it as the cover of a book on *Dynasty*. He graciously agreed. It took five years to get to this point and I just want to say thank you Goran for your kindness and creativity. I can't wait to see the newly revamped *Ultimate Dynasty*. If it's anything like the original, it's going to be fabulous!

Helge Ebsen is an absolute sweetheart. From the moment I saw the banners on her *Der-Denver-Clan* website, I knew they had to be included in this book so I asked if I could use them. She not only said I could use the banners but anything else I needed as well. At the time I had no idea of the magnitude of her site. It is phenomenal and contains the most beautiful photos you could imagine. It is part of those photos that you see in the episode guide for both *Dynasty* and *The Colbys*. So for those of you who are reading this book and enjoying some of the photos scattered through these pages, then please join me in thanking Helge for creating something so amazingly wonderful. You have my eternal thanks and I wish you nothing but continued success with your incredible endeavors.

Robin Wildschut has been the biggest supporter of this book since the day I announced it was being done. He remembered when I started it five years ago and contacted me earlier this year to touch base and offer his support. Throughout the process of writing this book I had more than one moment of frustration and just when I felt like throwing my hands in the air and saying forget it, there would be an e-mail from Robin waiting in my Inbox with even more words of encouragement. So Robin, thank you for your time, your notes and generous support. It meant more than I can say...

Thanks also goes to Jennifer Ellis for her wonderful story. When I originally asked for someone's creative assistance while planning the chapters of this book, she immediately stepped up to the plate and gave me not one but three different stories to choose from. *The Courtship of Blake and Krystle* was the perfect beginning to the series and an excellent compliment to the ending that I had written ten years ago. I'm pleased to have gotten the chance to know her and to now call her a friend.

Thanks to Robert Mycroft for sharing stories over drinks at Starbucks and for showing me the funniest damned out-takes from the series anyone would ever want to see. He has a *Dynasty* collection to kill for folks...

Industry thanks go to *Twentieth Century Fox* and *Bender/Helper Impact* for the use of their press materials, *Aaron Spelling Productions* for supplying information and assorted photos and to *Walt Disney Studios (Buena Vista Television Division)* for the use of part of the episode guide from *SoapNet, TV Guide, Daily Variety* and *VNU Media* for the *Hollywood Reporter* anniversary issue and the *Hollywood Foreign Press Association* for photos and art from the *Golden Globes,* and *The Filioli Center.*

To my sister-in-law Gloria, because without her coming over on weekends to help me type or to arrange photos, this book still wouldn't be finished. It's always nice to know that there's someone there who's always willing to roll up their sleeves when I need them. I don't think she'll ever know just how much I appreciate that.

For those of you who waited so patiently for this book to be completed and released, you have our undying gratitude. We just hope that it will have been worth waiting for.

Esther, Richard, Aaron, Duke, Elaine and Doug - You are responsible for shaping the lives of an entire generation of people. Thank you for sharing your creative genius with the television viewing audience.

Finally to John Forsythe, Joan Collins, Linda Evans, John James, Pamela Sue Martin, Gordon Thomson, Al Corley, Jack Coleman, Emma Samms, Catherine Oxenberg, Heather Locklear, Diahann Carroll, Michael Nader, Stephanie Beacham, Barbara Stanwyck, Charlton Heston, Tracy Scoggins, Claire Yarlett, Ricardo Montalban, George Hamilton, Ali MacGraw, Rock Hudson, Pamela Bellwood, Bo Hopkins, Dale Robertson, Maxwell Caulfield, Kim Morgan Greene and all of the other cast and crew members of Dynasty and The Colbys. This book would not be here if it weren't for the time and effort you put in to each episode. You are masters at your craft and we salute you...

THE END CREDITS...

The following items were utilized for the construction of this book and permission was granted by all parties.

Joan Collins – Past Imperfect

Joan Collins – Second Act

Joan Collins – My Friends' Secrets

Joan Collins – Joan's Way

Aaron Spelling – Aaron Spelling: A Prime Time Life

VNU Media – The Hollywood Reporter

Spelling Entertainment – Original Dynasty Material

ABC Television – Dynasty Press Photos & Movie Release

Twentieth Century Fox – Dynasty DVD Press Release

TV Guide – Artwork, Covers, Ratings, Video Footage

Walt Disney Studios / Buena Vista Television – SoapNet Synopsis

E! Entertainment Television – Video Footage

Helge Ebsen – Der Denver Clan – Assorted Photos & Banners

Goran Markovic – Ultimate Dynasty – Assorted Photos, Fan Memories & Book Cover Photo

Jennifer Ellis – The Courtship of Blake & Krystle

ANSWERS TO I REMEMBER IT WELL

1. Blake and Alexis were married in 1954 and Alexis was 17-years-old.

2. Cecil Colby's secretary during the first season was Jennifer and Katherine during the third.

3. Roger Grimes died three times. First a few months before Blake's murder trial, then shortly after Alexis left Denver and then 25 years earlier when Fallon shot him in the head.

4. The first song Blake and Alexis danced to was Bewitched, Bothered and Bewildered.

5. Dex's real name is Farnsworth Dexter.

6. Krystina was originally going to be named Emma.

7. Alexis was exiled in 1965.

8. Dominique's real name is Millie Cox.

9. Caress's book was titled Sister Dearest: The True Story of Alexis Morrell Carrington Colby As Told By Her Sister Caress Morrell.

10. Sammy Jo's parents were Iris Grant and Daniel Reece.

11. Alexis worked in Brussels as an artist's model.

12. Alexis' cousin Rosalind and her husband Hugh Bedford raised Amanda.

13. Mrs. Gunnerson's first name is Hilda.

14. Fallon's car was a Clinette.

15. Sable's company was named Pavilion Resorts.

16. Krystle's horse was named Allegree.

17. Alexis sang the Marlene Dietrich song See What the Boys in the Back Room Will Have.

18. Alexis was paid $250,000 per year to stay out of Denver.

19. The original name of Fallon's hotel was La Mirada.

20. Peter's lawyer was Dirk Maurier and he would go on to attempt a hostile takeover of Trouville Industries with Alexis as his partner.

21. Adam's son lives with his surrogate mother Karen and her husband Jesse Atkinson.

22. Blake and Alexis spent their honeymoon in Corfu.

23. Claudia was a patient in the High Meadow sanitarium.

24. Alexis made Blake Shepherd's Pie while they were in Singapore together.

25. Blake's father is Thomas Fitzsimmons Carrington and Alexis' father was Alexander Steven Morrell.

26. Gerard takes Joseph's place after his death.

27. Steven kills Matthew Blaisdel after Matthew takes the family hostage.

28. Congressman Neil McVane pushed Howard Mark Jennings to his death.

29. He gives Alexis a rattle with the initials AAC engraved in it.

30. Alexis offers Sammy Jo $20,000.00 to leave less $1,000.00 for every word she says before she takes the offer. She ended up with $15,000.00

31. Steven is married to Sammy Jo and Claudia.

32. Joseph committed suicide to keep Alexis from telling Kirby that her mother is a killer locked away in an insane asylum.

33. A psychic tells Blake about a person wrapped in a cloth that can't speak. Sammy Jo arrives the same day with baby Danny.

34. Krystle fights with Rita and then is escorted from Delta Rho by Sammy Jo.

35. Steven and Sammy Jo were involved with Bart and Clay Fallmont.

36. Adam and Fallon nearly start an affair before Alexis tells them that they are brother and sister.

37. Lancelot is Claudia's nickname for Matthew.

38. Adam has Jeff's office painted with the mind-altering compound Mercuric Oxide.

39. Fallon was "killed" in a plane crash with Peter and then resurfaced with amnesia, different colored eyes and a British accent that no one seemed to notice.

40. Nicole was Peter's wife before she tricked Jeff into thinking they were married.

41. Luke Fuller was a PR representative at ColbyCo who became involved with Steven. He was one of the casualties of the Moldavia Massacre.

42. Fallon married Jeff as a way of paying back Cecil for a loan given to Blake.

43. Krystle lost her baby after being dragged by a horse across a field.

44. Joseph set the fire at Steven's cabin trapping Alexis and Krystle inside.

45. Alexis' father – Adam inherited Alexander and Steven was her father's middle name.

46. Blake ends up raping Krystle in a drunken rage.

47. The master plan was to let the children take care of them while Blake and Alexis ran away to live on a deserted island.

48. Reveal

49. Burt McCann

50. The jewelry store was Jensen's.

51. Frederick Stahl was the German painter of the countryside painting.

52. Her Private Buccaneer

53. Adam went to Yale, Fallon graduated from Miss Drew's; Steven went to Princeton and Amanda went to the Sorbonne

54. Morgan's jacket was a beige and brown plaid design.

55. Charlie Braddock

56. Monica's nickname for Dex was "Uncle Dex".

57. Fallon got Randall from a street sign in Los Angeles.

58. The nun who came to Alexis was Sister Theresa

59. Fallon always "hid" in her thinking tree on the Carrington grounds.

60. Twenty-four children were invited to Krystina's party that never took place.

SCORING SYSTEM

Less than 20 – Did you just sleep through the entire decade?

20-39 – Not bad but you could use a little refresher course. Don't forget to buy the box sets as Fox releases them!

40-49 – Well you're not too bad after all… Pat yourself on the back for a job well done!

50-59 – Obviously you are a person with excellent taste in television!

All 60 – So you managed to be perfect huh? Are you sure you're not a Carrington or Colby already?

ABOUT THE AUTHORS

Judith A. Moose holds degrees in Broadcast Communications, Advertising and Marketing as well as an F.C.C. license. In 1995, she founded an Entertainment Publicity firm, which is now the JM *Media Group*. As well as handling the PR for several celebrities, Judith has assisted in the production of the *A&E Network's Biography* episode on Joan Collins, the *NBC 75th Anniversary Special*, seven *VH1 Specials*, and is currently serving as the Director of Media Relations for three feature films. In December 2003, she published her first book, *Together: A Sitcom Lover's Guide To Silver Spoons* and her second, *Another Time, Another Place: Quantum Leap* in November 2004. JM Media Group has been expanded and has launched a publishing division called Signing Stars. Next up on her list of things to do is her fourth book, tentatively titled *Their Hobby is Murder*, a guide book for the hit series *Hart To Hart* starring Robert Wagner and Stefanie Powers. *Their Hobby is Murder* is slated for a Spring 2006 release.

Paul D. Keylock is a gifted writer who is in the process of forming a PR service for celebrities in the United Kingdom. He has worked with Paramount Pictures U.K. as well as on several television and film productions. Paul is the personal assistant to Dynasty's Joan Collins. He makes his writing debut with Glamour, Greed and Glory.

Printed in the United Kingdom by
Lightning Source UK Ltd., Milton Keynes
138305UK00001B/248/A